Moreton Morrell Site

Terri C. Albert

University of Hartford

William B. Sanders

University of Hartford

WARWICKSHIRE
COLLEGE
LIBRARY

Prentice
Hall

Up| Warwickshire College   07458

Library of Congress Cataloging-in-Publication. Information is available

Senior Editor: Bruce Kaplan
Editor-in-Chief: Jeff Shelstad
Assistant Editor: Melissa Pellerano
Editorial Assistant: Danielle Rose Serra
Media Project Manager: Michele Faranda
Marketing Manager: Michelle O'Brien
Marketing Assistant: Christine Genneken
Managing Editor (Production): John Roberts
Production Editor: Renata Butera
Permissions Coordinator: Suzanne Grappi
Associate Director, Manufacturing: Vincent Scelta
Production Manager: Arnold Vila
Manufacturing Buyer: Michelle Klein
Cover Design: Kiwi Design
Composition: Carlisle Communications
Full-Service Project Management: Carlisle Communications
Printer/Binder: Von Hoffmann

Pearson Education LTD.
Pearson Education Australia PTY, Limited
Pearson Education Singapore, Pte. Ltd
Pearson Education North Asia Ltd
Pearson Education, Canada, Ltd
Pearson Educación de México, S.A. de C.V.
Pearson Education–Japan
Pearson Education Malaysia, Pte. Ltd

10 9 8 7 6 5 4 3 2 1
ISBN 0-13-035291-8

Dedication

...y from the monitor screens and to much-needed exercise.

Contents

Preface

...ronment. The Internet, the most pervasive electronic environment yet, is the catalyst for this area of study. It has been only since 1994 that the Internet has been a commercially available marketplace. During its infancy, the concept of a new economy fueled by soaring, unparalleled financial markets available over the Internet created uncertainty. How would it become an integral part of a firm's competitive arsenal, and specifically how could it be integrated into marketing science and practice? Although still in its "early days," we now know the Internet brings unprecedented opportunities; yet, the reality of its financial returns has settled in with the "dot.com bust" in the early spring 2000.

The Internet's commercialization generated considerable debate about whether the marketing discipline needed new conceptual frameworks to study this new phenomenon. The rapidly changing, new environment was a challenge to study empirically, since by the time any data were gathered the environment had changed. Students were provided with timely examples and practices about e-business marketing, yet because those practices and examples "aged" prematurely in this environment, their education was not timeless. Understanding the Internet's role in marketing requires both *timely* (situation-relevant) and *timeless* (part of a larger general concept) information.

With almost a decade of the Internet's commercialization behind us, meaningful research and its translation into a firm's marketing practices have begun to emerge. The slowdown of the financial markets and the compression in this electronic environment has facilitated such research. Thus, the debate on the creation of new models also have settled considerably. The primary focus is to examine a rich body of knowledge within marketing science and to test it in the electronic environment. Often, the existing models are not directly applicable but, through rigorous thought and study, they are adaptable. The ability to scientifically study the Internet, plus the need to provide a timely yet timeless approach to our students in the area of e-business marketing, led to this textbook.

The timeless element of our approach is to adapt marketing models to the Internet environment. We are timely in our approach with eight real companies as examples and practices of their online marketing experiences. Each company has a unique e-business marketing opportunity presented within the context of a marketing model. An Internet-based marketing process is applied to each company's opportunity.

E-business marketing requires an understanding of technological solutions. This does not mean students become programmers; rather, they need to understand how to leverage technology to maximize their marketing efforts. The need for this understanding is addressed by our text as well. Each chapter demonstrates the technological approaches and solutions within the marketing frameworks presented, as well as the case studies. We believe this combined marketing and technology philosophy further enhances the students' education by giving them a cross-discipline foundation that is timely yet timeless.

WHO SHOULD READ THIS BOOK?

We wrote this book for a variety of audiences:

- Upper-division undergraduate and graduate marketing courses in the electronic or Internet environment
- Executive education programs
- E-business marketing managers
- Information technology managers
- Executives seeking e-business direction and strategy for their companies

PEDAGOGICAL ORGANIZATION

Our book has 14 chapters, organized into three sections. The first section (Chapters 1 through 4) examines the conceptual frameworks of e-business marketing. Chapter 1 provides an overview of e-business in general and translates that into existing marketing concepts and models at an introductory level. This enables the students to transition from a general marketing to an electronic marketing orientation. Chapter 2 furthers this translation with the focus on the marketing mix and how it is used as leverage in the Internet environment. Chapter 3 introduces the value bubble Internet marketing process. This is a pivotal chapter as the value bubble is applied to each case study as an analytical and solutions-based tool. Chapter 4 concludes the first section by presenting an adapted communication model for the electronic environment.

The second section (Chapters 5 through 12) presents eight case studies of real companies' e-business challenges and opportunities. The companies, in these cases, have worked in university-based partnerships in excess of two years. Thus, benefit students from the opportunity to study the e-business decision-making process over time and to initially measure the companies' successes and failures. All of the companies have a brick and mortar presence; they represent the types of companies that struggle with the extent to which their business practices should transition into the Internet. Students and practitioners will be able to identify with the e-business marketing challenges and opportunities in the areas of integrated marketing communications, brand management, competitive strategies, pricing, services marketing, channel management (redefinition), and new product development.

The third section (Chapters 13 and 14) examines the future of e-business marketing and suggests extensions for the existing value bubble analytical tool. Chapter 13 examines the concept of customerization and the possibilities for this marketing approach. Chapter 14 gives students a research methodology for conducting online research. It also introduces an extension of the value bubble model.

SPECIAL FEATURES

- *End-of-Chapter Features.* There are four end-of-chapter features (each described below). They are presented for students to reflect upon the chapter's main points. Instructors may use these for written assignments.
  - *Collecting Your Knowledge: A Review.* Key concepts and terms are presented

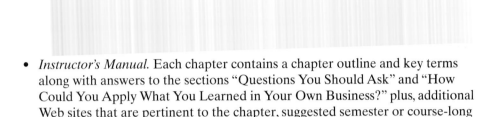

- *Instructor's Manual.* Each chapter contains a chapter outline and key terms along with answers to the sections "Questions You Should Ask" and "How Could You Apply What You Learned in Your Own Business?" plus, additional Web sites that are pertinent to the chapter, suggested semester or course-long projects, additional assignments, and other companies to research.
- *Companion Web site.* Here you can find PowerPoint slides available for downloading teaching suggestions, links to Web sites referenced in the textbook, and case studies. The site also features updates on marketing and e-business, keeping students and instructors apprised of the latest news and information related to their course.

ACKNOWLEDGMENTS

There are many contributors to every book—not just the authors. First, we acknowledge our students who inspired us to write this book. We saw, through them, an opportunity to contribute a unique textbook that would enhance their education with the timely yet timeless approach to e-business marketing. Further, their encouragement led to a cross-discipline approach that we believe is critical for our students to learn and apply as they develop throughout their chosen careers.

We would also like to acknowledge valuable colleagues and organizations that have been an inspiration to us not only for this textbook but also within the broader context of the marketing and information technology disciplines:

- Paulo Goes, Ph.D., a valued University of Connecticut colleague and collaborator who shares his philosophy from an information systems perspective and who embraces the cross-discipline perspective in the electronic marketplace. He is a pivotal player in the university partnerships with the companies presented in the case studies.
- The Marketing Department of the University of Hartford, for the department staff's enthusiasm and dedication to advancing the e-business marketing area.
- Jim Marsden, Ph.D., another University of Connecticut colleague whose ongoing support, guidance, and direction are greatly appreciated and acknowledged.

- GE Capital's Edgelab, for its staff's innovation and "out of the box" thinking and practices.
- The University of Hartford Interactive Information Technology program, which serves as a resource for human-needs-based technology savvy.

In addition, we would like to thank our friends who provided support and additional inspiration for this book:

- Karen File, one of the first educators to teach marketing on the Internet, whose bold and untiring dedication to this field remains a driving force in its advancement.
- Susannah Shickman, for her guidance and suggestions.

We would also like to thank and acknowledge the staff of Prentice Hall—Bruce Kaplan, Senior Editor; Danielle Rose Serra, Editorial Assistant; Melissa Pellerano, Assistant Editor; Renata Butera, Production Editor; Michelle Klein, Manufacturing Buyer; Ann Imhof, Project Editor at Carlisle Publishers Services—and the helpful suggestions by the reviewers:

- James Zemanek, East Carolina University
- Mohan K. Menon, University of South Alabama
- John Bennett, Stephens College
- Ken Williamson, James Madison University
- Angela D'Auria Stanton, James Madison University
- Catherine Campbell Griffioen, University of Maryland–University College
- Monica Perry, California State University, Fullerton
- Hope Jensen Schau, Temple University–Fox School of Business

Finally, the authors gratefully acknowledge the eight companies presented in the case studies. Although their identities are not revealed, they are great pioneers and innovators in the e-business marketing area. They have shared their goals, frustrations, and accomplishments openly. In addition, each company has been receptive and enthusiastic to experiment with the e-business marketing models suggested to them. Their partnerships are invaluable to the education our students deserve.

Hartford. Prior to joining the University of Hartford in 2000, Dr. Albert was an Assistant Professor at the University of Connecticut for three years. Prior to beginning her academic career, she spent several years in financial services marketing, particularly focused on leveraging technology for the delivery of services. She received her undergraduate education from the University of Maryland, and her masters degree and Ph.D. from the University of Southern California.

Dr. Albert's teaching portfolio encompasses digital marketing, services marketing, marketing research, and integrated marketing communications (graduate and undergraduate courses). In addition, she co-developed an e-business certificate program. She is a faculty fellow at the GE Capital Edgelab in Stamford, Connecticut, where she works on student and business teams developing digitized practices and processes.

Dr. Albert's research interests are in the areas of technology adoption across diverse groups (comparisons across sub-populations of the industrial and consumer markets). Her research has been published in both academic and industry publications.

William B. Sanders, Ph.D., is a Professor in the Interactive Information Technology program at the University of Hartford. He has been involved in several business enterprises, including Microbotics (creating software and interfaces for robots), Briefcase Software (producing digital interrogatories for attorneys), and Sandlight Productions (book and software marketing and production) where technology and marketing were never a separate entity. He is best known for more than 35 books in computer-related areas and is actively involved in software testing and development for major software firms. His undergraduate and doctoral degrees are from the University of California, Santa Barbara, and his masters degree is from San Francisco State University.

He is currently involved in teaching courses where human–computer interactions are examined as a social-psychological entity enabled through Internet technology at speeds never before available to the consumer. His research interests currently lie in finding how humans maximize social interaction over the Internet and how to use this knowledge to create improved interfaces between computers and humans.

CHAPTER

1

OVERVIEW OF
E-BUSINESS

technology strategies critical to successful **e-business marketing.** E-business is a
dynamic, rapidly changing, and thus an exciting business environment. To operate successfully in such a fluid, fast-paced environment, it is critical to apply the conceptual frameworks that are auspicious within successful practices and examples. This
book provides the key e-business marketing frameworks in Chapters 1 through 4. They
are **marketing** concepts, the marketing mix, the value bubble (an application of the
marketing concepts), and the communication models. Chapters 5 through 12 present
eight case studies that adopt the various marketing concepts or frameworks and the
accompanying technology strategies. Examining these companies' e-business marketing strategies will provide the combination of conceptual frameworks, practices, and
examples needed. Chapters 13 and 14 explore additional e-business opportunities in
the areas of services marketing and marketing research. For marketing majors, some of
the concepts and frameworks will be an excellent review; for nonmajors, a solid marketing foundation will be built.

The science and practice of marketing has, perhaps more than any other area of
business, benefited from technology. Technology facilitates or enables all components
of marketing: creating, promoting, and delivering goods and services to both the consumer and business marketplaces. This fact is best illustrated by the marketing opportunities available through the technology of the Internet.

This textbook identifies and dissects these opportunities for eight traditional, brick
and mortar businesses. The instability of the technology financial markets has caused
many to speculate on the demise of the dot-coms (virtual-only businesses), with traditional businesses capitalizing on Internet technologies to create another channel for
conducting business.

Technology as the enabler is not a new scenario. For instance, a parallel can be
drawn between the 1980s database marketing evolution and the impact of the Internet.
The database marketing evolution occurred because of the great advances in information systems technology. This period was characterized by users gathering considerable
amounts of information from multiple sources and organizing it into an effective database for communicating with customers and tracking purchasing behaviors.

In both the database marketing and Internet evolutions, technology as the enabler
contributes to more effective and efficient marketing. Yet this enabler is not a conduit
for destroying existing marketing models with the end goal of creating new ones for

the new channel. Rather, the existing models require degrees of modification to be successful in the electronic environment. The cases in this textbook illustrate modified, conceptual frameworks or models for eight real companies. This book's intention is to provide students with modified marketing models for the Internet channel that real companies utilize.

The Internet's business environment is referred to as e-business to differentiate this channel from others. An examination of the e-business components is necessary to build the analytical foundation for reading, comprehending, and synthesizing the case studies. You will notice that each component is directly tied to the existing marketing mix and associated conceptual models. In Chapter 2, we discuss these relationships in greater depth.

COMPONENTS OF E-BUSINESS

IBM originated the concept of e-business in October 1997. Its definition was further refined by the Gartner Group (1999). Gartner's e-business definition is "the optimization of a firm's business activities through digital technology." Strauss and Frost (2001) have expanded the definition to include five major components that will be used throughout this textbook. They are:

1. **e-commerce,**
2. **business intelligence,**
3. **customer relationship management,**
4. **supply chain management, and**
5. **enterprise resource planning.**

Each of these components is briefly described here, and then a more thorough explanation of their contribution to e-business marketing will be illustrated within the case studies (Chapters 5 through 12).

E-commerce, although frequently confused with e-business, refers directly to the transaction or the sale. It encompasses certain security and privacy processes that give online customers protection and safety from intrusion. The degree to which online customers acknowledge and experience this sense of security from a site will determine the possibility of initial and repeat purchases. As the selling component of e-business, it is important to recognize that the e-commerce or purchasing experience can be evaluated based on the recently identified e-service quality dimensions of the marketing process (Zeithaml, Parasuraman, and Malhotra 2000). In examining proven conceptual models and how they translate into the electronic environment, note that many of these e-service quality attributes have a strong, positive correlation with the traditional service quality measures introduced by Parasuraman, Zeithaml, and Berry (1985).

Business intelligence (BI), conducted online, is quick and efficient. It is the equivalent of competitive benchmarking, defined as "the art of learning from companies that perform certain tasks better than other companies. . . . The aim is to copy or improve upon 'best practices'" (Kotler 2000). In addition, business intelligence involves online marketing research and is frequently used for concept testing, surveys, focus groups, and observational studies (observing online behaviors). Chapter 14 will examine the marketing research or BI model within the electronic environment. The perspective will be one of current and future opportunities.

Customer relationship management (CRM) is an excellent example of a core marketing principle translated into the online world. Leveraging the technologies of online visitors and customers, CRM's traditional world counterpart is relationship

(Weitz 2001).

Supply chain management (SCM) focuses on the delivery of goods. SCM operates on the unified operations of all suppliers necessary for moving goods from the manufacturer to the ultimate customer. Successful SCM relies on integration and uniformity through "information sharing, joint planning, shared technology, joint problem solving and shared benefits" (Monczka and Morgan 1996). SCM is similar to a vertical marketing system (VMS), particularly when a manufacturer leads an administered VMS; that is, each member of the supply chain is a valued member or partner in the distribution of goods.

Enterprise resource planning (ERP) relies on technology to streamline a company's backroom operations. These operations may go unnoticed by the customer but are critical to maintaining or reducing the firm's cost of the sale. ERP is often referred to as the firm's "digital nervous system" (Kalakota and Robinson 1999). Within the services marketing literature, the blueprint shows a methodology for initiating effective planning. ERP uses the company's extranet and intranet sites that typically define the firm's behind-the-scenes business processes. Several software providers have developed systems for ERP.[1]

The first three e-business components have obvious marketing implications. E-commerce, BI, and CRM represent the front end of a business and its interactions with customers—that which is visible to the customer. For example, e-commerce addresses the transaction, which is highly visible to the customer. Business intelligence mirrors marketing research focused on identifying and implementing best practices to improve how a firm markets its goods or services within its competitive marketplace ("marketspace"). Customer relationship management is critical to any firm's success with long-term relationships that avoid customer replacement costs for the firm.

However, SCM and ERP have less obvious marketing implications. Both are quite powerful in their contributions to a firm's marketing efforts, although their back-end or backroom orientation is typically invisible to the customer. When SCM is ineffective or slow, and thus timely delivery and availability of goods to the customer are affected, customer dissatisfaction and frustration often lead to customer loss. ERP

---

[1]ERP software providers specialize by industry, company size, and application portfolio. In general, SAP is the front-runner for large manufacturing companies. Peoplesoft focuses on HR-related applications. Oracle Financials works well for accounting and financial applications. JD Edwards has a niche with midsize manufacturing companies, as well as Baan (Goes 2001).

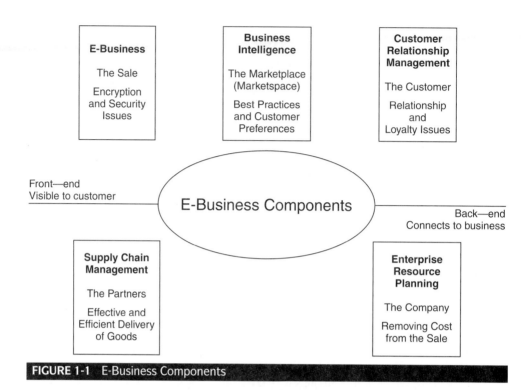

FIGURE 1-1 E-Business Components

affects a firm's pricing strategy. The ability to leverage technology for streamlined, internal processes reduces the cost of each sale. Companies may pass the savings on to the customer or create value-laden benefits to reinforce customer loyalty. In the traditional service marketing models, this is defined by the role blueprinting has in service design. Figure 1-1 provides an overview of the e-business conceptual model.

This textbook provides students with e-business marketing models that evolved from marketing concepts as applied to the electronic world of the Internet. Each case (summarized in Table 1-1) illustrates how a real company translated or adopted its

TABLE 1-1 Introduction of Case Studies

Industry	Marketing Mix Component	Marketing Model Employed
Specialized manufacturer	Promotion	Integrated marketing
Steel manufacturer	Price	communications
Distributor	Place and promotion	Pricing strategy
Utility company	Product	Strategic change
Not-for-Profit trade association	Promotion	Customer loyalty
	Product and promotion	Brand building
CPG supplier	Product	Services marketing
Insurance	Place	Channel management
Financial services	Product	New product development

marketing strategies utilizing Internet technology. An important learning outcome from each case is the translation of existing marketing models into this new, dynamic, and relatively misunderstood medium. A brief conceptual overview of the components of the marketing concept explored by these companies is provided in this chapter. Chapter 2 then provides in-depth coverage of how the marketing mix, specifically,

Consider the following definitions of marketing by renowned educators in the industry:

> Marketing is a societal process by which individuals and groups obtain what they need and want through creating, offering, and freely exchanging products and services of value with others.

> (KOTLER 2000)

> Marketing (management) is the process of planning and executing the conception, pricing, promotion, and distribution of ideas, goods, services to create exchanges that satisfy individual and organizational goals.

> (AMERICAN MARKETING ASSOCIATION 1995)

> According to the marketing concept (philosophy), the purpose of marketing is to understand the needs and wants of the customers and to create customer value through satisfaction and quality more effectively and efficiently than competitors.

> (HARRELL AND FRAZIER 1999)

These definitions have common themes and unique components that will help build a definition of e-business marketing. The first common theme of marketing is a process for creating and delivering goods, services, and ideas to customers. A second theme of marketing is based on exchanges that are valuable to both the customer and the company. The final common theme is many different groups are involved in the marketing concept. These groups, referred to as stakeholders, include **customers,** prospects, **employees, investors,** suppliers, and partners. Each has an important contribution to fully realize a successful marketing effort.

Table 1-2 shows each theme within the applicable components of e-business. It contains the themes, the associated case studies, and the primary e-business component(s) focused upon by the companies presented (although the cases present even more e-business components). This reference also provides a foundation for building the definition of e-business marketing.

TABLE 1-2 Quick Reference

Common Theme	Case Study	E-Business Component
Process to create and deliver goods, services, and ideas	• Financial services (Chapter 12) • Insurance (Chapter 11)	• E-commerce and business intelligence • Supply chain management
Valuable exchange process	• Steel industry (Chapter 6) • Utilities (Chapter 8) • Not-for-profit (Chapter 9) • CPG supplier (Chapter 10)	• Enterprise resource planning • Business intelligence • Customer relationship management • Customer relationship management
Many groups involved	• Specialty manufacturer (Chapter 5) • Hardware distributor (Chapter 7)	• Customer relationship management • Supply chain management

PROCESS TO CREATE AND DELIVER GOODS, SERVICES, AND IDEAS

In the first common theme, marketing has been defined both broadly (societal impact) and specifically (management) as a process for the creation and delivery of goods, services, and ideas. The traditional marketing models for achieving these processes are the new product development (NPD) process and the distribution channel process.

Certain components of e-business facilitate the product development process from both the societal and management perspectives. They are addressed within two e-business components—business intelligence and e-commerce. Business intelligence facilitates two major steps within the NPD process: idea generation (asking the customer to describe problems for which they need solutions) and concept testing. Technology enables such rapid turnaround time for the results that the NPD cycle can be compressed considerably. For competitive advantages, it is imperative to utilize this shortened time frame. For technology-specific products, product development and market testing also may leverage the Internet environment. The e-commerce component fulfills this common theme through the availability of product customization. Various Web sites allow online customers to customize the product before placing the order (e.g., www.dell.com, www.reflect.com, www.wsj.com). A case study from the financial services industry examines the development of an online product. It was chosen based on the company's need for more business intelligence than it was willing to invest in from both time and financial resources perspectives.

The second traditional model for addressing the first common theme is the delivery of goods, services, and ideas (place). The e-business component that primarily addresses distribution is supply chain management. SCM has become an important area of focus enabled by Internet technologies. Improvements in the distribution of goods help the firm also improve its **customer service** (e.g., quicker and more accurate delivery) and lower its costs as the coordination of distribution shifts from traditional to electronic based. This is also an area that many firms choose to outsource to a third-party provider. United Parcel Service (www.ups.com) has a successful line of business providing SCM for its **customers.** Marshall (www.marshall.com) has included an SCM consulting arm within its organization. These business offerings further indicate the growing attention for effective SCM. Note also that efficient and effective delivery of

---

The second common theme of marketing examines the **exchange process** is often viewed as only the transaction or sale. As competition has become more intensified due to less product differentiation and fragmented markets, successful companies now focus on the value of the exchange. Thus, the definition of exchange has been broadened to include the firm's relationship with its customers and other stakeholders (investors, employees, and suppliers). It has been argued by prominent marketing educators that the real competition is now among marketing networks, based upon who can provide the most meaningful exchanges or value-laden relationships with all stakeholders.

Several e-business components leverage the Internet technologies in the area of value-laden exchanges for both the customer and the company. The online capability for gathering and using data on customers' purchasing and information needs is unprecedented. Companies are using these Internet technologies as a means for developing and maintaining positive and powerful relationships across all stakeholders. The components of e-business that address these issues are CRM and BI.

Complex commodity industries (e.g., paper, chemical, and steel) are exploring the ability to build cost-effective online relationships while reducing their internal costs. With some relief from the pricing pressures, these companies are also finding internal financial resources to further nurture off-line relationships. In these instances, companies are using the ERP e-business component in conjunction with the CRM portion.

Consider the textbook case about a steel manufacturer. Faced with serious pricing pressures (further accentuated by online auctions), the company sought online technologies to reduce its transaction costs (thus maintaining its projected profit goals). By accomplishing this goal, the company's primary marketing goal was to differentiate itself in a small, customized steel product market through value-laden exchanges.

An exchange between a customer and an organization is not always financial. In not-for-profit organizations, this exchange is defined by a customer receiving goods, services, or ideas often without a specific transaction or sale; the financial exchange may be membership fees or government subsidies. These organizations are often challenged by the inability to differentiate themselves based upon their valued exchanges while being hindered by minimal financial resources to do otherwise. The Internet has provided an inexpensive avenue for creating valued exchanges between not-for-profit organizations and their customers (members). These exchanges can lead to differentiation in the marketplace and help them to develop a brand that identifies them as superior in their exchanges. The superior exchanges define positive CRM within the e-business equation.

A case from a trade association provides the not-for-profit capabilities of marketing enabled by Internet technologies. A small, 20-member organization was unable to differentiate itself among a few, large well-entrenched competing organizations. Its Web site and promotion were chosen as its competitive edge. Its goal was to emerge as having the best relationship network at a low cost (to the sponsoring members).

Customer service also has defined the value-laden exchange. Research has shown that satisfied customers are less likely to switch to a competitor; they are more profitable due to repeat and often increased levels of sales. The area of customer service is considerably underutilized in the online world. Many companies offer online customer service, but the data demonstrate that the technology and internal support are currently mismatched. Superior online customer service may well be the relationship network that differentiates the winners from the losers. Many e-business components contribute to customer service. Business intelligence identifies the best practices not necessarily of direct competitors, but rather those for which a company has fully realized and embraced the Internet technologies to effectively accomplish. Customer relationship management benefits from superior service, because such service supports the overall CRM goal of retaining relationships. CRM also can assist in building new relationships by establishing a reputation for superior service as part of its strategies. For companies with multichannel distribution systems, effective SCM is also a critical e-business component used to support the firm's service goals.

A case from the utilities industry examines customer service needs and wants. The company, facing stiff competition in the deregulation process, identified the Web as a potential competitive edge for its retail customers. In addition to providing convenient service to its customer base, the company was exploring ways to reduce costs.

A second case examines a different type of online service strategy as a competitive, value-laden exchange. A supplier in the consumer product goods industry sought to provide its customers with online communication and support that exceeded the competition.

MULTIPLE GROUP INVOLVEMENT

The three previous definitions of marketing indicate that more than one group are actively involved in the marketing concept ("organizations," "competitors," and "groups"). As mentioned, the different groups involved in the marketing concept are referred to as stakeholders. Prior to the emphasis on value-laden relationships and exchanges, the only important stakeholders were the company and the customer (and often in that order!).

With the shift to relationships and **value exchanges,** the definition of stakeholders was expanded to include every group who impacted how a firm conducted its business. As stated, this included customers, potential customers, employees, investors, and suppliers, because for a firm to differentiate itself as superior to the competition, everyone involved in its operation must be accounted for and contribute to its success.

Important stakeholders are customers and potential customers, whose needs and wants drive product creation and offerings that maintain vitality in the company. Their financial exchanges fuel the company's continuing growth.

Naturally, investors are important. Not only are their financial investments in the company essential for survival, but also their confidence in the company's performance is validation to the outside world that the company is continually strong.

Employees have always been known as critical elements to a firm's success. In addition to the importance of their being acknowledged as an individual stakeholder

of these five diverse groups to be informed and aware of the functions and activities of the firm that are most important to each, that is, customized or personalized to specific needs. These communication avenues are essential to cooperation and consistency. Although communication within the marketing concept is often thought of in relation to the customer, rapid advances in technology allow real-time communication between all stakeholders, which is especially critical for suppliers, investors, and employees. Customer communications are also enhanced by the Internet through customization and personalization. All groups need communication that is consistent in terms of the firm's brand or image and appropriate to their information needs. Technology has permitted "smart" or intelligent communications through sophisticated databases that marketers mine to ensure consistent and appropriate messages (the right audience receives the right message at the right time). Because communication opportunities define one of the most powerful marketing outcomes derived from the electronic environment, a brief overview of **integrated marketing communications (IMC)** is presented next.

Schultz, Tannenbaum, and Lauterborn (1995) addressed the concept and process of IMC. They examined the changes in marketing communications based on the technological improvements in database and analytical techniques (referred to as datamining). Initially, these techniques were used for customers and potential customers and were designed to generate sales, create synergy across all promotion, build customer relationships, and maintain a consistent brand message. The database provided the "intelligence" so that the communications were specific and targeted toward each recipient's needs and wants.

These communication objectives are equally important and easily translated to the other stakeholders. For example, IMC is a process that also facilitates the company's internal marketing efforts to its employees. The primary communication goal, with this stakeholder group, is to inform and empower employees, generally leading to increased productivity and employee retention. IMC also plays a role in managing the relationship with a firm's suppliers. Communication with the upstream and downstream suppliers, based upon the needs and wants of each group, reinforces the pursuit of the common goal to deliver goods and services more effectively than the competition. Targeted communication with the firm's shareholders and the investment community, in general, is critical. The goal is to present the company in such a way that investors continue to provide capital and thus increase the shareholder base.

Another aspect of IMC is the two-dialogue process that it creates. These targeted and specific communication messages directed toward the stakeholders' needs and wants are also invitations for the recipient to respond. The feedback or response creates a dialogue between the firm and important participants in its operation. The response will vary based upon the group; however, it ranges from a sale to delivery (fulfillment) to expressed confidence in the firm.

Two cases in the textbook examine how companies are leveraging Internet technology to communicate and manage their marketing efforts using the IMC concept and process. One company is a specialized paper manufacturer that is looking to the Internet to assist in consistent marketing communications across all stakeholders. The second company is a hardware distributor that is using the Internet for communicating change across its operations. These communications contain specific messages for each stakeholder. By using Web sites and multiple databases (collected online and off-line), precise and cost-effective communications result.

DEFINITION OF E-BUSINESS MARKETING

An analysis of the e-business components and widely accepted marketing concepts has been presented. This analysis has led to the following definition of e-business marketing.

> E-business marketing is a concept and process of adapting the relevant and current technologies to the philosophy of marketing and its management. Focused attention on the areas of e-commerce, business intelligence, customer relationship management, supply chain management, and enterprise resource planning provide a framework for effective adaptation. Although the electronic environment experiences rapid changes, the reliance on proven marketing models, in these areas, ensures continuity of the marketing process both online and off-line.

The opportunity for e-business marketing has been difficult to measure. Discussing its importance to advancing the science and practice of marketing is the goal of this book; however, we lack the consistent statistics to reinforce the vast opportunity that awaits the e-marketing concept and process.

The worldwide growth rate of online users continues to expand. As of July 2001, there were 510 million online users worldwide (www.nua.net) which is a 50 percent increase in the number from July 2000 (360 million). These online users have an equally impressive number of Web sites to visit. At the beginning of 2000, there were 4.6 million, in 2001, there were 8.4 million sites (www.OCLC.com).

The e-business marketing opportunity is most obvious in that 80 percent of the online traffic goes to 0.4 percent of the sites available (Lake 2000). This low percentage results from poorly designed sites that were unclear about online marketing strategies.

During the first few years of the Internet's commercialization, companies sought new marketing models to embrace. Most of these models focused on the sale or marketing efforts that ignored the effective delivery of goods, business intelligence (best practices), and customer service. It was the erosion of the technology financial markets that forced firms to rethink their online marketing efforts by identifying the breakdown. The breakdown was the lack of translating existing, proven marketing concepts and processes into the electronic environment. It became imperative to examine Internet technologies and the ways to successfully integrate them into the firm's marketing efforts. Thus, the opportunities available for successful e-business marketing efforts are extensive—perhaps even endless.

Yet, all of these positive statistics and direction contain a warning within a para-

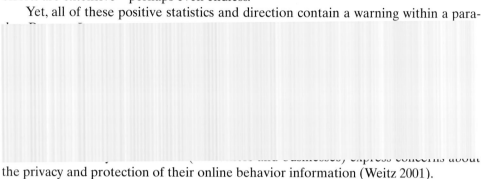

the privacy and protection of their online behavior information (Weitz 2001).

IS HISTORY REPEATING ITSELF?

As noted in the previous section, sizing the e-business marketing opportunity is difficult. Its commercialization is unprecedented, and the recent dot-bomb or demise of the dot-coms has created great uncertainties. New technologically based innovations often face these opposing forces of opportunity and uncertainty. One way to gauge how a new innovation may evolve is to look for a historical parallel. In this case, we seek a technology-enabled communication vehicle that had great impact on the science and practice of marketing. An examination of the various possibilities yields a parallel between the evolution of the radio and that of the Internet, particularly in the early days of radio. A brief, historical perspective is provided on the worldwide wireless (the previous WWW) in an effort to understand the possibilities for the Internet while reducing some of the uncertainties.

In 1899, radio was the result of technology capable of transmitting messages among a select group of individuals. It took 18 years for its evolution into a wide-reaching communication vehicle, providing information, entertainment, and advertising (sponsored content). For society, this invention had tremendous impact. The concept of distance and time for communicating information was forever changed. Information and entertainment were now transmitted simultaneously and no longer bound by geographical proximity. If people owned or had access to the appliance or equipment, their lives were changed. People scheduled their days around radio programs.

The radio and its communication opportunities also influenced business practices. Many have said that the marketing of goods and services was impacted the most. Although radio's early origins were in the one-to-one communication between several radio operators, it was credited as leading the mass-marketing evolution with its extensive reach. Companies saw the radio as a perfect medium to reach millions of households to promote their products and services (8 million households as of January 1925) (Jome 1924).

This technology-based communication vehicle afforded promotional opportunities leading to the first national, brand-name and image-driven marketing campaigns.

In addition, retailers discovered that their in-store promotions could be enhanced through radio promotion.

For their financial survival, radio developers "discovered" the concept of national networks and syndication (packaging and selling advertising with content) as the answer. Further refinement with radio broadcasting technology led to channel development: AM and FM channels allowed stations to specialize their content based on the types of listeners each station targeted.

Television capitalized on the continued technological enhancements while maintaining the practice of syndication, networks, and brand marketing. Programming was also specialized or targeted based on the viewing audience.

The Internet also resides in the category of an innovative communication medium enabled by technological advances. Although the Internet began in 1969 with military and educational funding, it was not until 1994 that it was publicly accessible through the World Wide Web, browsers, and servers. Many recognize the year as the "public Internet explosion" (Hanson 2000).

As with the radio, companies seized the ability to communicate with customers using the new Internet-enabled technologies. Marketing messages and materials were developed for global reach at a low cost and were electronically disseminated through the company's Web site. Interactive communication (one-to-one marketing) was available through the technology of tracking site visitors' behaviors.

The unprecedented commercial growth of the Internet has been measured in many ways. One of the most dramatic is its adoption rate compared with other technology-based communication devices. Figure 1-2 compares the adoption rate of the radio, television, personal computer, and Internet (Meeker 1997).

New Technologies Have Fast Adaptation Rates

The radio provides a historical examination of a technology-based communication medium (Yadav 2000). The parallels between the commercialization of the radio and the

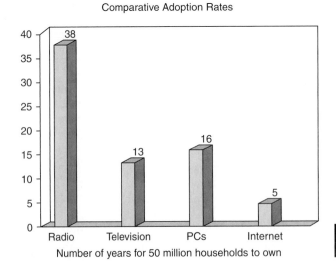

FIGURE 1-2 Comparitive Adoption Rates

Internet are numerous. Thus, the radio's evolution is often studied to provide an indication of how the Internet will evolve over time. This is not to imply that radio is now stagnant, however. Its longevity and contribution to the marketing discipline substantiate it as a viable source for guidance and direction for successful e-business marketing.

adopt new technologies to maximize their companies' effectiveness and efficiency. The trend continues today because the technology continues to grow and change rapidly.

For the most part, understanding and using the technology is not a matter of having to write code and debug systems. Rather, it involves knowing what technology can do, being aware of the different types of technology that are available, and working to incorporate the technology into a successful marketing plan.

IT Departmental Orientation and Goals

In their book on using a suite of tools to utilize shared resources across a network, Eckstein, Collier-Brown, and Kelly (2000) describe the ideal situation for a **systems administrator** in an IT department: All desktops on all computers all run on the same operating system, an autoconfiguration system ensures that all desktops are identical, and any personalized adjustments by users have been reconfigured to conform to the standard. The systems administrator has little to do but sit in the office and drink coffee. Eckstein et al. (2000) describe the reality of systems administration as one in which different platforms running different operating systems are not getting along, the networked printers are not printing, and phone lines are inundated with service complaints.

Eckstein et al. (2000) shed light on the ideal that too often plagues IT departments and represents the antithesis of progress in a company. IT departments seek a state of homeostasis (stability). Such stability is a good thing for the organization in that the necessary connections between computers can be made, work groups can share files, and databases can be accessed. However, to the extent that homeostasis becomes the goal for the IT department, it can be a potent force against change.

The difficulty in making changes is that those who want the change usually fail to understand the technology behind the change. For example, an employee in one IT department made a request for an upgrade in the browser installed on the system. The employee was told that the computers could not handle the upgrade. Knowing both the capacity of the computers and the requirements of the browser, the employee knew this to be untrue. When the employee further confronted top management about the request, the network administrator admitted that on the CD-ROM used to reconfigure the computers on the network to a standard state, the company had the older version of the browser. In other words, because the administrator did not want to change the CD-ROM, which was simply a matter of making changes on the hard drive and burning a new CD-ROM, the computers still had an older and inferior browser. In the development of software for the Web, it is important to have Web pages that will work on the old browsers, but a company must also take advantage of the features of the new browsers. For example, Netscape Navigator Version 6 and Microsoft Internet Explorer Version 6 adhere closely to the World Wide Web (W3C) Document Object Model (DOM) standard. The W3C sets the standards for browsers and the DOM for HTML and other Web-related languages. Keeping an old browser on the system for the convenience of the systems administrator meant keeping the available technology for marketing behind what users were currently using to view Web sites.

In a competitive business environment such **displacement of goals** can be fatal. Essentially, a department comes to see its own stability as the goal and not the dynamic goals of the company. If a company is attempting to keep abreast of the competition, reacting quickly to change is an essential part of survival. When any part of the company is entrenched in a system and is unwilling to change, whether it is IT, marketing, sales, or another key component, the company is in jeopardy.

By the same token that marketing managers must know about technology to avoid being controlled by arbitrary decisions in an IT department, they also must understand the limits of the company's technology. If a marketing strategy is designed around an unrealistic technology, either in terms of the technology's limits or costs, marketing managers will have developed a strategy doomed to failure. For example, if a marketing manager and the planning team devised a campaign centered around streaming video without understanding the limits of the bandwidth of their target market, the result could be a marketing campaign unavailable to the target market.

In part, the failure of marketing and IT to integrate effectively is caused by the antiquated models used in technology organization. Marketing and IT have been kept in separate departments, often with contradictory goals. The primary goal of IT has been to keep all systems up and running. To best achieve the systems administrator's goal, IT tries to standardize all systems and minimize any differences within the system. When new, better, or favored technologies surface to meet marketing goals, they are often thwarted by the IT department's resistance to modifying the existing system to integrate the new technologies. Perhaps the best example of this kind of resistance is between the general use of Microsoft Windows-based desktop PCs in most company departments and the art department's strong inclination toward using Macintosh computers. IT personnel have attempted to tell artists that they would be better off using one of the favored Windows PCs and also have recommended software. (Such recommendations are the equivalent of artists telling IT directors which networking system to use.) When the artists prevail in their demands, their systems can be integrated into the larger system. The process takes time and resources from what IT sees as its primary function—keeping a system running smoothly, even if other goals in the organization cannot be met.

Rather than maintain a system in which IT and marketing goals sometimes contradict, organizations must integrate elements of marketing and IT. Both sides must come to understand each other's needs. Complex systems that integrate different elements required to achieve a goal, such as marketing a product, reflect the real world. The real world requires a new type of communication between people who understand marketing, technology, and the other elements of business necessary to carry out successful strategies.

The concept of utilizing a task force of personnel from different departments is not new. Moreover, some organizations, most notably the military, have developed over the last 50 years the concept of combined arms. In the context of contemporary business where use of the Internet is a key marketing tool, organizational forms require flexible departments of personnel who can respond to the marketplace with the complex of skills required to compete successfully. The task force concept is in of

The concepts and point of view used in this book reflect practical necessity in a wired global economy. In subsequent chapters, the conceptual frameworks presented reflect the reality of quickly changing, diversified, and developing markets, brought about in large measure by the Internet and World Wide Web. Like the telephone, radio, and television, the Internet is a technology that has changed forever the nature of the marketplace.

COLLECTING YOUR KNOWLEDGE: A REVIEW

Key Terms
- business intelligence (BI)
- customer relationship management (CRM)
- customers
- customer service
- displacement of goals
- e-business
- e-business marketing
- e-commerce
- employees
- enterprise resources planning (ERP)
- exchange process
- information technology (IT)
- integrated marketing communications (IMC)
- Internet
- investors
- marketing
- marketing management
- stakeholders
- supply chain management (SCM)
- systems administrator
- technology-based communication
- value exchange
- World Wide Web

Questions to Ask
1. Who are the different shareholders in a business and what role does each play?
2. What are the basic components of an e-business?
3. What conflicts exist between IT and marketing departments? Why do these conflicts exist? How could they be resolved?
4. What different types of technology-based communications have existed in marketing? What is the business–consumer relationship between adaptation of a technology and using that technology effectively in marketing?
5. What role does technology play in supply chain management, and how does it relate to marketing?
6. How could a company use e-business to lower expenses and increase market share?

Application to Business

Create a department in which you have the personnel necessary to carry out a marketing plan. Do these personnel exist now in your business? What would happen organizationally if they were moved? What costs would be involved? How could tasks be accomplished if personnel who work on these tasks are moved?

If no e-business component is now in your business, develop a plan that would incorporate some aspect of e-business. What existing resources and personnel could be used? Which one would have to be recruited?

Web Sites to Visit

www.hillmancurtis.com This site belongs to a Web design firm. Find out what they have to say about making people look at your service or product. Hillman Curtis is a prime mover behind motion graphics on the Web.

www.mastercardintl.com/rpps/ If you plan to start your own online business, you also will be paid online. (Forget about the adage "The check's in the mail." Now it is "The credit card is in the e-mail.") This is MasterCard's site for RPPS. (If you do not know what RPPS is, go to this site to find out.)

www.useit.com/ This is the site of Jakob Nielsen, the granddaddy of Web usability. Almost everyone believes at least half of what he says. How can you not like a guy who says, "Don't listen to users." After reading why Mr. Nielsen makes that claim, you will probably agree with him.

2

THE MARKETING MIX

ing, and gave a brief introduction for the cases presented in Chapters 5 through 12. This chapter specifically examines the marketing mix and the Internet-enabled transformation it has experienced. We begin with a brief review of the marketing mix to facilitate understanding the impact on the mix into the online environment.

MARKETING MIX REVIEW

In 1960 Jerome McCarthy first introduced the concept of the marketing mix. It was composed of the four Ps that every marketing major can name quickly. These controllable, tactical marketing tools are used by firms to proportionally allocate their marketing resources based on their goals and objectives within their targeted marketplace.

A quick review of the four Ps is presented in Table 2-1 (McCarthy 1960; Waterschoot and Van den Bulte 1992; and Harvey, Lusch, and Cavarkapo 1996).

These four elements are evaluated by each firm and an appropriate mix is developed for the firm. It is considered the tool kit for each firm's competitive differentiation within their targeted markets.

It is critical to note that the four Ps and their implementation evolved from the selling point of view. For example, **products** may be created based upon a manufacturer's existing machinery and not necessarily based upon customers' needs and

TABLE 2-1 Definition of the Marketing Mix Components	
Marketing Mix Element (P)	*Definition*
Product	Variety, quality, design, feature, brand name, packaging, sizes, services, warranties, and returns
Price	List price, discounts, allowances, payment period, and credit terms
Promotion	Advertising, personal selling, sales promotion, public relations, direct marketing
Place	Channels, coverage, assortments, locations, inventory, transportation, and logistics

wants.[1] The **place** or distribution element may leverage existing channel relationships rather than focus on the customer's preferences for particular goods to be available at certain locations.

This selling orientation of the marketing mix was widely accepted and referred to as the "inside looking out" philosophy. While this was occurring in the practice of marketing, the science of marketing was building a body of knowledge based on segmentation (macro and micro) and customer behaviors (consumer and direct customers and businesses). The adaptation of this science into the marketing practice led to the philosophy of "outside looking in."

THE TRANSFORMATION OF THE MARKETING MIX

The four Ps marketing mix that focused on the company's selling perspective remains an important part of marketing science and practice. However, the influence of technology and the universal access to computers (both in the business and consumer marketplaces) drove the need for an increased customer awareness within the marketing mix—one that was customer-oriented (also known as customer-centric) and it reoriented a firm's marketing toolbox. The four Ps (selling orientation) have now been enhanced into the four Cs (customer orientation).

The four Cs are defined as:

1. **Customer solution (enhancing the Product "P").** The focus is to develop goods, services, and ideas that the firm's customer base wants to buy.

2. **Cost (enhancing the Price "P").** The focus is now on the relationship between value and cost. **Price,** as Schultz, Tannenbaum and Lauterborn (1995) state, is essentially irrelevant. Premium pricing is readily accepted if the customer's preferences are met or exceeded. This translates into the customer's evaluation of their needs and wants and the associated costs.

3. **Convenience (enhancing the Place "P").** The Internet has furthered customers' avenues for obtaining goods and services. Successful companies are now focusing on multidistribution channels based upon each customer's preferred way of obtaining goods.

4. **Communication (enhancing the Promotion "P").** "The motto of the age of the manufacturer—*caveat emptor,* let the buyer beware, is replaced by *cave emptorum,* beware of the buyer" (Schultz, Tannenbaum, and Lauterborn 1995, p.13). This transformation was introduced in Chapter 1, which highlighted the e-business marketing communication opportunities. With the financial markets' uncertainty with technology, many of the gains for technology-based marketing are now in the area of communication. Technology not only lowers the cost of communicating with a firm's stakeholders (customers, potential customers, employees, investors, and suppliers), but also has the capability to personalize communication with them in "real time." Although privacy con-

---

[1] This occurred based on the manufacturing overcapacity that was a result of World War II. The selling emphasis was necessary to effectively manage inventory levels.

cerns continue at high rates with online customers, ongoing research explores the microsegmentation opportunities that may mitigate these concerns.

THE INTERNET'S IMPACT ON THE MARKETING MIX

not the self-reported behaviors that many of the database marketing systems had to rely upon. The objectivity of the data provides even greater confidence in the marketing mix strategies and tactics developed.

This information has several marketing mix outcomes that are enabled by Internet technologies. The first marketing mix outcome is in the creation of a specific and targeted **promotion** or communication. By analyzing the online visitors' "footprints" (cookies, log files, site registration, etc.), the communication can be personalized specific to an individual's needs and wants.

The concept of **personalization** or one-to-one marketing was initially introduced by Peppers and Rogers in 1993. The Internet has facilitated the goals of one-to-one marketing by providing an objective, customer-behavior profile (as defined by the e-business components of business intelligence (BI) and customer relationship management (CRM). This leads to individualized messages and, through the interactive technology, two-way dialogue or messages. The customer or prospective customer profile used for customized communication becomes a springboard for many other marketing mix elements to be enabled by the Internet technology.

The customer solution or product element is enhanced by the Internet through customized offerings. For example, a firm's Web site (or electronic storefront) permits customers to design their own jeans or configure their computer hardware and software. This capability creates customer value and builds relationships with customers that would be very difficult to achieve in the traditional, bricks and mortar, environment. The customer relationship leads to retention that generally leads to a higher customer lifetime value. This also relates to the e-business component of CRM.

Another component of the marketing mix enhanced by the Internet is **distribution** (place or convenience). The online environment is more convenient than any other distribution channel for certain products and services. Customers value the ability to log-on, search for product information, make a selection, order it, and track its status until it reaches its final destination (e-commerce, supply chain management, and customer relationship management components of e-business).

The price or customer's cost component has evolved through the commercialization of the Internet (1994 and forward). Initially, the theory of perfect competition was being supported—that is, the lowest price would always win. This was particularly evident in the business-to-business online auction environment. Over time, this skepticism was reduced (although not erased) by the measured value placed on the convenience and customization available through the Internet. Lowest price is not always the winner; price or customer cost is a value placed on the product quality, support services (including customer service), ease of obtaining, and the relationship. This has even been noted in the commodities' industry (Chapters 6, 9, and 10).

In the area of services marketing, the Internet provides many opportunities for improving the delivery and marketing of services. One of the opportunities is the Internet's capacity to minimize the four characteristics of services that defined the additional complexities surrounding their marketing. These characteristics are:

1. **Intangibility.**   Services cannot be seen or touched as a physical product can be (for example, an education).
2. **Simultaneity.**   A service is produced at the same time it is consumed (for example, visiting a doctor).
3. **Heterogeneity.**   The delivery and quality of the service depends upon the provider of the service (for example, an abrupt and rude server in a restaurant can negatively impact one's service experience; whereas an exceptional server, at the same restaurant, can provide a very positive experience).
4. **Perishability.**   Because services are produced and consumed simultaneously, they cannot be stored or inventoried as physical goods (for example, an unsold airline seat cannot be placed in inventory for a future purchase).

These characteristics generated the need for additional marketing mix "P" components (the **four extra Ps of people,** processes, physical image, and productivity) in order for firms to allocate the appropriate marketing resources. Services marketing and the impact of Internet technologies are explored in greater depth in Chapter 13. An article by Berthon, Pitt, Katsikeas, and Berthon (1999) provided further details on services marketing opportunities within the international markets enabled by the Internet.

The above marketing mix components are applied to the customers and potential customers of a firm. In the electronic or Internet environment, three primary marketplaces have been identified: business to consumer **(B2C)**; business-to-business **(B2B)**; and consumer to consumer **(C2C).**[2] These marketplaces define the various customer opportunities on the Internet. Their examination has been relatively static, meaning that there is not a conceptual framework that permits a more adaptive or dynamic model for evaluating these markets as their technological sophistication increases over time. Such a model—**ranged marketing**—is presented in this text.

First, the B2C marketplace is examined within the marketing mix and the profile of this marketplace. Second, the B2B marketplace is examined. Ranged marketing is introduced and explained as the more dynamic marketing model because it measures and adapts to changes over time.

BUSINESS-TO-CONSUMER MARKETPLACE

The definition of the B2C marketplace is a company that sells directly to the final customer or end user. This is in contrast to a more traditional approach of a distribution channel. Figure 2-1 illustrates the differences.

---

[2] Online C2C marketplaces are defined by the auction sites such as e-Bay. These marketplaces are not addressed in this text.

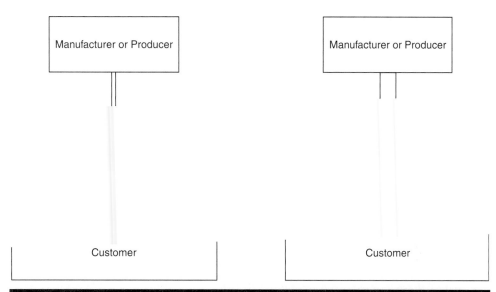

FIGURE 2-1 Comparison of Distribution Channels

B2C and Traditional Distribution

Within the Internet world, a well-known example of a B2C company is Dell Computer. Dell was one of the first companies to sell online direct to consumers and bypass retailers, distributors, and resellers. Amazon is another example of an Internet-based company with direct sales. This direct selling capability became quickly available to any company with the online storefront and operational support to accurately fulfill the order. The forecasted financial rewards remain impressive. Research, Inc. has projected that $185 billion of e-commerce sales will occur by 2004. This reflects 56 million new Internet shoppers.

However, the direct selling approach faces challenges. Although it created serious concerns within the existing supply chains or distribution channels that they would be eliminated, it soon became evident that both direct (B2C) and traditional distribution channels would continue operating. However, there was increased pressure on the intermediaries to add value to the transaction. Figure 2-2 illustrates this relationship.

For the end user or final customer, Internet technologies in the B2C marketplace are responsible for customer empowerment. This means that the customer or potential customer controls the interaction with the company and, in some cases, chooses to interact directly with the producer, manufacturer, or intermediaries. Prior to the Internet, many firms moved toward customer empowerment; however, the Internet has transferred this power directly to the customer. Firms participating with an electronic storefront must be customer-centric or lose out to a firm that is. Customers may now leave the electronic storefront or Web site with a click of the mouse.

In the pre–Internet-technology years, companies often relied on high switching costs to prevent customer loss to their competition. Switching costs were defined as negative consequences for changing from one company to another. Two types of switching

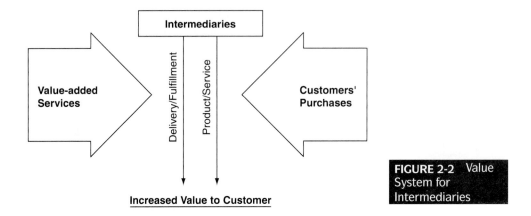

FIGURE 2-2 Value System for Intermediaries

costs were typically used in the business to consumer marketplace: high search costs, and loss of loyalty programs. The Internet-enabled marketplace has diminished, if not eliminated, these. For example, the search costs for purchasing goods and services have been lowered by the Internet for all participating firms. The comparison shopping sites (powered by shopbots—shopping robots) and sophisticated search engines or directories have reduced consumer search costs to almost nothing. There is no longer a switching cost associated with it. Loyalty programs have not been as popular online as off-line. Loyalty programs are the cornerstone of the financial benefits offered as part of relationship marketing. This lower use of online loyalty programs indicates that the relationship-building (CRM) characteristics have been modified for the online environment. The case studies presented in Chapters 5 through 12 will highlight the relationship-building opportunities afforded by Internet technologies.

Businesses facing the empowered online consumer have options for how to most effectively compete, and are able to address each "P" or "C" as detailed below. The most successful firms will be those that have seamless integration of all their customer databases (yielding efficient, effective, and customized communication or promotion).

• **Customer solution or product.** The ability to customize a particular good or service online is important, but it must address or be the solution for the customer's needs or wants. Effective Web site construction that capitalizes on the usability theory can enhance the customized online experience. In addition, many online customers cite the product's peripheral services as the differentiating feature—for example, the ability to buy an item online and return it to the physical store (even when the physical store may not carry that particular merchandise).

• **Cost or price.** It is common knowledge among online customers that the cost of an online sale is lower than in a physical or traditional store. Early in the Internet's evolution people thought that online prices should be lower than the same product in a brick and mortar store. This led to considerable conflict between the managements of physical and online stores. A compromise has been reached, among some companies, in which the accompanying information services and support (available online) justify paying the same cost. One industry where this has not been adopted is the airline industry.

- **Convenience or place.** Online firms can differentiate themselves through solid customer service once a sale or information request is completed. Timely and accurate fulfillment is critical (Strauss and Hill 2001) and may be achieved through Internet-based supply chain management.

- **Communication or promotion.** This can be the major gain for companies. The com-

or her next visit to the web site.

The **marketing mix** is a toolbox for implementing a firm's overall marketing strategies. Therefore, it is important to review the strategic model for marketing in a technology-enabled marketplace. Whether the products are technology-based or sold via the electronic storefront, there are four major shifts in the consumer marketplace. These shifts were recently identified by Parasuraman and Colby (2001) within the techno-ready marketing conceptual framework.

1. Consumers adopt technology at a different and a more highly individualized rate than for nontechnology-oriented products and services.

2. These individualized adoption rates and attributes that define them must be translated into the firm's marketing strategies and, ultimately, the marketing mix.

3. There is greater focus on customer service within the technological environment (whether the product is technology-based or secured via the technology-enabled environment of the Internet).

4. A single company can dominate a particular technology-enabled product, service, or sale. This company generally loses when another company introduces a new or better technology.

Each of these strategies has implications for the development of the marketing mix in a technology-enabled marketplace. The customer solution or product component is affected by the more individualized adoption rates. This supports a new **product development (NPD) process** that capitalizes on the speed of Internet technology for collecting data in the idea generation and concept-testing phases. Companies need to focus on the product life cycle in a new way. Rather than evolving through the traditional introduction, growth, maturity, and decline phases, the decline phase is replaced with the rejuvenation or reinvention phase for technology-based products and services (Sheth 2001). This continues to capture the innovators and early adopters as customers while capitalizing on the time required to acquire the late adopters and laggards to the product or service. The firm is then positioned to be the leader (winner take all) of the specific product or service being offered. Figure 2-3 illustrates the refocus on the product life cycle.

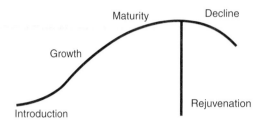

FIGURE 2-3 Product Life Cycle for Technology-based Products and Services

The focus on customer service marketing strategies has multiple-mix components that are affected. Within customer solutions or products, firms will need to develop certain warranties or guarantees for replacement of defective goods. Technical support customized to varying levels of technological sophistication is critical. The promotion or communication element is affected through the public relations component. It has become increasingly obvious to firms that dissatisfied customers now have an instantaneous mechanism for spreading negative public relations—it is called "word of mouse." Customer service also impacts the place and distribution or convenience marketing mix component. The disastrous December 1999 holiday shopping season for e-toys and Toys-R-Us clearly indicates the need for available inventory and as-promised fulfillment or delivery of goods.

The B2B marketplace will present a somewhat different perspective of the marketing mix and the impact of the Internet technologies in the implementation of these components.

BUSINESS-TO-BUSINESS MARKETPLACE

The B2B marketplace focuses on a company, its direct customers (other businesses), and its various suppliers. There may be several players with multiple levels of interaction or there may be a few players with only one level of interaction. Supply chain management contributes greatly to the efficient management of a company and its suppliers. This is one of the main components of e-business. This section will define how the Internet has impacted the marketing mix in the B2B marketplace and its supply chain management.

Most of the large financial opportunities or gains are predicted to come from the B2B marketplace enabled by the Internet technologies. Sources that forecast the B2B growth vary greatly. For example, the Boston Consulting Group (BCG) estimates $4.8 trillion of e-business–related revenues in 2004; Goldman Sachs estimates a more modest $1.5 trillion; and Jupiter is reporting $2.7 trillion for 2004. BCG also estimates that by 2004 40 percent of the B2B transactions will be Internet-based. One of the reasons the BCG's forecasts are considerably higher than others is their inclusion of cost savings in their revenue projections. Lowering the cost of the sale has become the "hook" for many companies. This is achieved through two e-business components—enterprise resource planning and supply chain management. A very noteworthy example of each is presented below:

1. Carrier Corporation (United Technology) saved $100 million in one year (2000–2001) by effective supply chain management. The company focused on its suppliers first and transitioned their transactions from the off-line to the online environ

its own methodology ranging from university partnerships to dedicated internal departments to external consulting relationships. GE's CIO said that "every process we have is going to be a pretty simple Web application supported by e-mail" (Murray 2001).

Numerous other B2B companies have reduced their internal costs, leveraged their supply chain relationships, and improved their inventory management enabled by Internet technologies. As presented in Chapter 1, the e-business component of supply chain management (SCM) was very similar to the vertical marketing system (VMS). VMS is the relationship between the manufacturer, wholesalers, and retailers. The purpose of the VMS is to develop a cooperative partnership among all the members of the distribution channel. SCM operates on the same philosophy. If the delivery of the product is inefficient (slow) and of low quality (damaged goods, difficult to receive replacements), the entire SCM will fail. Internet technologies have provided the ability to manage these multiple layers with communication efficiencies that benefit all involved parties—from the manufacturer to the end customer.

Another B2B Internet-enabled e-business opportunity had been projected within the manufacturing arena—the "leveling of the playing field" between the small to medium-size manufacturers and their large competitors. Although this manufacturing segment continues to be reluctant about e-business, this textbook contains three small-to medium-sized manufacturers who are innovators in their industries (Chapters 5, 6, and 10). They have graciously allowed us to present their e-business marketing strategies (enabled by Internet technologies). Remaining anonymous protects their competitive strategies.

RANGED MARKETING

The latter part of the twentieth century spawned **complexity theory** (originally called "**chaos theory**" and "fuzzy logic"). Complexity theory grew out of the observations made by scientists ranging from the apparently random offshoots of particles in cloud chambers to the mutations that lead differentiation in species. Fractals in mathematics and computer programming are further areas where complexity

theory found an audience that welcomed an explanation that would account for scientists' observations. Both of these theories recognize the hard facts of the world:
Things change and the change is almost never wholly predictable.

Complexity Theory

As applied to the business world, Lewin and Regine (2000) noted that businesses have
always faced uncertainty, as have participants in other areas of interest and endeavor.
In looking at the execution of almost any marketing plan, the exception rather than the
rule is that things happen as planned. The September 11, 2001 terrorist attacks on the
World Trade Center and Pentagon wrought havoc not only on the lives of those
directly involved in the assaults, but also on worldwide markets. Airlines suffered huge
losses, as did hotels, theme parks, and other businesses dependent on air travel.
Marketing plans for releasing films portraying violent assaults had to be shelved as
audiences turned to family-centered entertainment. The ripple effects included layoffs,
higher unemployment, and the resulting downturn in purchasing. No marketing plan
could have predicted the nature and ferocity of the attack, but any marketing plan can
predict that something unexpected is likely to occur and can be prepared with a range
of contingency plans.

Fuzzy Logic

Associated with complexity theory[3] is the concept of fuzzy logic. Proposed in 1965 by
Lotfi Zadeh (1968), the concept states that in computer modeling we need to consider
the unknown elements that make 100 percent predictions unlikely. The most common
example of fuzzy logic can be seen in weather forecasts. A report might forecast an 80
percent chance of rain on Saturday. It means that according to the weather model
being used, when the current conditions are present, 80 percent of the time it rains. As
more data become available, and the model improves, better predictions can be made.
However, if an 80 percent chance of rain is predicted while the model is being used,
and it does rain 80 percent in accordance with the prediction, the model is accurate.
Such a prediction is far better than a model that predicts a 100 percent change of rain
with only 80 percent accuracy. Neither model provides 100 percent predictive certainty,
but by leaving room for unaccounted variance, the model that predicts an 80 percent
chance of rain is more accurate.

In the same way that weather forecasts are based on models from historical data of
recorded weather, marketing forecasts need to base their predictions on historical market records. The number of relevant factors in both weather and marketing make them
comparable. Both are based on changing patterns about which only partial and often
contradictory information is available, both have to deal with unexpected factors that
were not introduced in the predictive model, and both must deal with elements over
which they have absolutely no control.

---

[3]"Complexity theory" is another name for "chaos theory." Chaos theory's core concept is that the complexity of the world is such that we cannot predict with full certainty what will happen next. Rather than focusing on the nihilistic notion that everything is out of control as is implied by the word *chaos,* the term *complexity* focuses on the need to be prepared to accept the unexpected.

Elements of Ranged Marketing

Taking complexity theory and fuzzy logic into consideration, the concept of ***ranged marketing*** looks at marketing as a process in which the unexpected occurs, change is certain, and the market is heterogeneous. The term "ranged" refers to change over time in a process and the heterogeneity in markets, services, and products.

processes, products, ideas, and inventions that might take years or even decades to transmit in the past. The overall result is that information exchange has never been greater, and with this exchange comes rapid change in all segments of life.

Planning and Change

In times of rapid change, planning is more important than ever. One erroneous conclusion to draw from the fact that change is constant and rapid is that planning is futile. Because one cannot predict with any certainty what will happen, any plan is doomed to failure because all contingencies cannot be accounted for.

Quite the opposite is true. Because we know that change will occur in unknown ways, a ranged marketing plan is essential. Only in times of stability is planning less important because markets are more predictable. However, in times of change, the marketer must take into consideration more elements, processes, and segments. A plan needs flexibility, but the flexibility is built into the plan rather than being patched on once the marketing plan has been put into motion.

The Role of Ranged Marketing

Ranged marketing is not introduced as yet another revolutionary idea in marketing. Ranged marketing is a conceptual framework to deal effectively with change. It gets away from the idea that if a marketing strategy is well organized and well planned, and everyone does their job, the world in which they execute the plan will be orderly as well. Ranged marketing forces a marketing plan to take into account what every marketing manager has known from planning to marketing the first widget—the world of business and commerce is complex and fluid. A marketing plan will not change either the complexity or the fluidity in the world, but it must consider both complexity and change to successfully deal with the real world.

Ranged marketing takes full advantage of Internet technology and other communicative technologies that are emerging and may eventually replace the Internet. Internet and Web marketing are not synonymous with ranged marketing. However, the World Wide Web and the Internet technology that makes the Web possible have brought about global changes that emphasize the need for ranged marketing. Because change and complexity have always been features of marketing in the business world, the need for ranged marketing is not new. In one example of ranged marketing, Gerry

Sweeney, e-Visa VP, said about Internet ads, "[they] are trackable and . . . have a certain amount of flexibility, so we can change creative messages on the fly. As we look at optimizing our advertising, we can see what is working for us—and what's not—and then modify our ad buys and the creative messaging on an ongoing basis throughout a campaign to maximize spending." (Saliba 2001) The flexibility in the advertising campaign stems from a ranged marketing approach that has built-in feedback for making changes as they occur or encountering unanticipated features in the market.

Ranged marketing does not imply that all past marketing wisdom is obsolete. Rather, ranged marketing is cumulative with other marketing concepts. Nothing about ranged marketing conflicts with the concepts of the great majority of marketing precepts. Obviously, ranged marketing directly contradicts marketing theories that assume a static market and marketing strategy. However, the concepts in the **Four Cs (customer solution, cost, convenience,** and **communication),** the need for planning, and other proven marketing precepts are consistent with ranged marketing.

Range of Change

The **range of change** refers to how much a product or service along with a marketing plan will change over time. Roger Lewin, an advocate of complexity theory, points out, "With the Internet and networks, the extent of business ecosystems is growing, and the pace at which the landscape within an ecosystem changes—thereby forcing changes throughout—is increasing." (Santosus 1998) At the very heart of ranged marketing lies the same argument. With increased rates of change, marketing is required to range its approach to consider how products and services will change, and how, when, and how much the market will change. The technology that drives the change is constantly changing, and the markets are impacted by such change. Marketing managers ignore change at their own peril, not because it's a new fad, but rather because it's an old problem that has been overlooked. Static models of marketing will work to the extent that they randomly hit the right place at the right time. However, by the same token, a broken clock is right twice a day. Dynamic models of marketing, including ranged marketing, treat change for what it is: a normal feature of the real markets to be addressed. The same technology that drives change can be used in marketing to keep up with the change—not as a nuisance but as an opportunity to perfect what marketing is meant to achieve.

COLLECTING YOUR KNOWLEDGE: A REVIEW

Key Terms

- B2B
- B2C
- chaos theory (see also complexity theory)
- communication
- complexity theory (see also chaos theory)
- convenience
- cost
- customer solution
- customized offerings
- Four Cs
- Four extra Ps of service
- Four Ps
- fuzzy logic
- heterogeneity
- intangibility
- marketing mix
- new product development (NPD)
- perishability
- personalization
- place
- price
- product
- promotion
- range of change
- ranged marketing
- simultaneity

Questions to Ask

1. What is the difference between the four Ps and the four Cs? How has e-business impacted the trend moving from one to the other?
2. What savings in marketing have been realized by using the Internet for marketing? What is a good example cited in this chapter of a company saving substantial amounts?
3. How have marketing services been affected by the Internet? What would

What components of the four Cs are now operable in your organization? Which ones are missing, and what would have to be done to add any of those missing?

If your company is marketing services, how could the four "extra Ps" (people, processes, physical image, and productivity) be incorporated into the marketing plan and enhanced by use of the Internet? Could the service itself be marketed over the Internet?

If your company uses a static marketing plan model, how could the plan be transformed into a ranged model? What features of the static model would have to be changed and which could be left as they are? What elements of ranged marketing could be introduced initially with the least disruption? How would you measure the difference between marketing using a static marketing model and a ranged model?

Web Sites to Visit

www.ecommercetimes.com Here's a site that will help you keep up with e-commerce and e-business. In addition to looking at the successes, it looks at where companies have failed. Also, you will find interviews with the people in charge of marketing on the Internet and they provide innovations and insights into e-business marketing.

www.cia.gov That's right, it's the Central Intelligence Agency's home page. However, if you're even thinking of doing international business over the Internet, you better know what's what in the country you're doing business with. Also, it's a good place to start looking for good places to do business. The CIA's *World Factbook* (available online) will give you the background on a country's economy—from Armenia to Zimbabwe.

www.visa.com Here's a Web site to keep an eye on for their use of ranged marketing over the Internet. Visa uses the Internet to market a wide range of branded financial products and to provide the resources to let others create online marketing. Versions of Visa's home page are provided in both English and Spanish—which shows how simple it is to use the Internet to reach out to a very big market indeed.

CHAPTER

3

THE VALUE BUBBLE

In Chapter 1 the e-business marketing conceptual framework was developed by examining the components of e-business and the marketing concepts and processes. Understanding the concept of e-business marketing led to a discussion of translating the marketer's primary set of marketing tools into the electronic world. Chapter 2 presented this technology-enabled transformation of the marketing mix. Now that a conceptual framework has been built for e-business marketing, the next step is to apply this science of marketing into the practice of marketing. This chapter makes that step in preparation for the case studies.

The Internet has provided companies with an additional channel for communicating with its various stakeholders and distributing its products and services. Trade and popular press publications suggest these outcomes are below expectations and, therefore, a disappointment. However, the marketing opportunities cannot be underestimated or ignored because of a lower than expected financial return of the dot-com or virtual companies. To fully realize the e-business marketing opportunities, it is imperative to develop strategies that are specific to this environment. To date, this has not been done effectively. Numerous studies find that firms are unclear about their Internet strategies and uncertain about how to translate their marketing messages into this new communication channel. (Chapter 4 will focus on the storyboarding concept for developing and communicating the appropriate messages for this channel.)

The most frequent misconception about e-business marketing and a firm's electronic storefront or Web site is that the marketing mix can be directly translated from one channel to another channel. For example, a company uses the same marketing message strategy on its Web site as it uses in its television or magazine advertisements. Although essential to maintain a consistent brand identity across channels, the message and how it is communicated may need to vary by channel. Often, customers and other stakeholders respond differently to the same message presented in different environments. This may seem obvious, but, within the e-business marketing of most firms, the term **brochure-ware**[1] substantiates this point. Appropriate message communication within the online environment is one of the most untapped potentials for e-business marketing. Other elements of the marketing mix (product and customer solu-

---

[1]Brochure-ware means a Web site or e-storefront that replicates a company's existing printed marketing materials or collateral. In the early days of Web site development (1995), this was often the first step into the electronic environment.

tion, price and customer cost, and place and convenience) have faced similar issues about direct translation from the off-line into the online marketplaces.

Some suggestions for marketing approaches specific to the online environment have been put forth, but unfortunately they have not been adopted or implemented to fully leverage the Internet technologies. One of the most comprehensive models is the

1. The lower cost of information delivery would lead to superior information delivery providing greater value to the online visitor.
2. Relationship building would be facilitated through the interactive nature of the medium.
3. The e-store or online presence would lead to a new definition of channel **(dis)intermediation.**

Our research finds that companies continue to use their existing marketing-mix toolbox and ignore the fact that this electronic environment is different and, therefore, do not take advantage of the above three opportunities. For instance, although information delivery costs are lower, very few companies leverage the technology to accomplish this in a meaningful and differentiating manner (Strauss and Hill 2001). Relationship building within very few online storefronts has been successful. Companies are not failing in maintaining relationships, they are failing to fully capitalize on the Internet technologies to increase the number of relationships while deepening the existing ones. The Internet is not going to disintermediate or eliminate distribution channels. Rather, it will enhance the delivery of goods and services. Thus, manufacturers or producers are avoiding channel conflict by not going directly to their end user or final customer. They are continuing to focus on their core competency (production of goods) and on the supply chain management element of e-business to reduce their overall costs through productivity improvements. Successful supply chain management should lead to increased customer satisfaction that drives loyalty and deepens the relationship. An article in the *Silicon Valley/San Jose Business Journal* (May 2001) discussed the poor online customer service between manufacturers and suppliers in the business-to-business (B2B) environment. It suggested that a continuation of this would negatively impact the growth of online, B2B e-commerce activity.

In this chapter we will examine the five steps of the value bubble. We have built upon this model in several ways. Each step is updated based upon the definition of e-business marketing as presented in Chapter 1. This will connect the model to the traditional marketing concepts and provide a platform for transition. Second, we will provide the Internet technology application to facilitate this transition. Third, the value

---

[2]This is supported by the 0.4 percent of sites that are visited (see Chapter 1).

bubble is a consumer-based model (B2C) that we adapt to the B2B marketplace. In Chapters 5 through 12 we will use the value bubble as an analytical tool for addressing companies' e-business challenges and opportunities.

FIVE ELEMENTS OF THE VALUE BUBBLE

The value bubble concept forces the inspection of five elements in an e-business Web site. They are the following:

- **Attracting**
- **Engaging**
- **Retaining**
- **Learning**
- **Relating**

The most successful e-business sites had features of all five of the value bubble elements. By no means did the five elements guarantee the success of an e-business, but those that were successful tended to pay attention to all five. So many e-businesses (or dot-coms) failed with the dot-com shakeout beginning in March 2000 that identifying all the factors leading to failure is far more difficult than pinpointing the factors commonly shared by the successful e-business Web sites. Because the value bubble was developed as a conceptual framework in 1996, clearly borrowing from other marketing precepts, the success of the e-businesses using elements in the value bubble may appear to be prescient. However, because standard concepts of a good marketing plan make up the bulk of the value bubble, few who understand marketing were surprised at the success of e-businesses that implemented those concepts.

APPLYING THE VALUE BUBBLE

Throughout the rest of this book, we examine a variety of cases in which the different elements of the value bubble have or have not been applied. In addition, we look at the different forms of application, their effectiveness, what the goal was and how the goal was attained or failed to be attained. This section provides an overview of the elements contained in the value bubble and some examples of how they were implemented and the technologies that were employed. However, the focus is on the concepts in the value bubble and the technologies are merely mechanisms to implement the strategies in the value bubble.

Attracting (Building Traffic)

The **attracting** phase of the firm's Web site is also known as building traffic for the electronic storefront. Within the traditional marketing concepts and models, attracting customers relies on communicating the firm's offerings and how these offerings create valuable exchanges. It relies on understanding the customer or potential customer's needs and wants. The communication must be effective and appropriate to the medium. The attracting phase is presented in Figure 3-1.

Similar to a brick and mortar or traditional store, the attracting phase for a Web site is the most critical. During the early commercialization phase of the World Wide

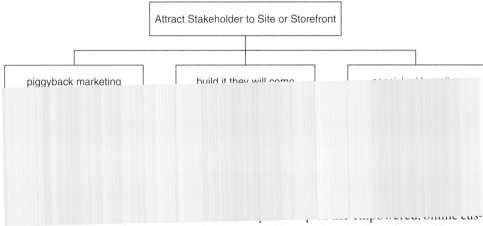

tomer (see Chapter 2) create new challenges while opening the door for significant e-business opportunities.

The first challenge in the attraction phase is to differentiate the Web site or e-storefront from the competition. This requires competitive benchmarking or the business intelligence (BI) component of e-business. A process of identifying and analyzing the firms with the best and most successful online attraction practices is necessary. These practices assist in building a Web site that will attract customers or potential customers.

The Web site must also be developed with the specific needs and wants of the customer. Through market research, the buyer's buying motives (underlying buyer motivations) and demographics must be understood. This need-based or **microsegmentation** process was introduced in the industrial marketing literature in the 1970s (Wind and Cardoza 1974) and an applied model was presented in the consumer marketing literature in 1997 (Peltier and Schribrowsky). The translation of the microsegmentation results into a Web site that attracts customers can be achieved through various Internet technologies. This results in a personalized interaction that encourages repeat visits and nurtures the online relationship (thus deepening the overall relationship).

Other tactics that facilitate successful attraction of the targeted customer are branding and advertising. The company's brand should be consistently displayed on the Web site—color, logo, and overall appearance. The Web site address or uniform resource locator (URL) needs to reflect both the company name and, to the extent necessary, a brief description of the site's objectives. For example, a detergent's Web site that is designed to provide washing instructions and helpful household hints should include the detergent's name and the site's purpose—www.allhelpinfo.com. The use of the brand's name plus the site's purpose further differentiates it from the competition and will build traffic in this first phase of attracting visitors.

Advertising the Web site does not only mean banner ad placement. The more cost-effective method is to use the firm's existing advertising mediums (television, radio, outdoor, direct marketing, print). These mediums display the Web site address prominently with a reason for visiting it (this is the greatest missed opportunity in the attraction phase). This type of promotion or communication is referred to as "piggybacking".

Product packaging provides another cost-effective advertising vehicle. Although most products display the Web site address, the same missed opportunity occurs. The potential online visitor is not given a reason or motivator to visit the site. By incorporating the reason into the product packaging containing the Web site's address, this opportunity is only partially addressed—it must be included in the promotional message across all advertising vehicles.

The technology for such attraction lies in animated eye-catching graphics and sound. Many sites still use banners made of animated graphics interchange format (GIF) files that are often more annoying than attracting; however, motion graphics on the Web are an important source of design in modern Web site development (Hillman Curtis 1999, 2001). Far from being the "dancing baloney" that was the hallmark of earlier Web sites, the more recent animated sites use the technology of shockwave files (SWF), especially Macromedia's Flash. The following are some general approaches used to attract viewers using different degrees of sound and motion—or neither! (Sanders and Windstanley 2001, 378–381):

THE BIG SHOW
Some sites provide dramatic and very exciting graphics and sound that, when first viewed, have a strong attraction to the viewer. Probably the most important feature of the big show strategy is that the word of mouth or "buzz" created by the site leads others to come view it for the show itself. However, the big show can detract from products and services, and after being viewed once or twice, it becomes more of a hindrance than attraction. Successful sites using a big show attraction provide a "skip intro" option or a "cookie" after the viewer has seen it once so that he doesn't have to see it again. (A "cookie" is a file attached to the viewer's hard drive after accessing a site. It can contain information that tells the computer to skip the introduction.) Also, precautions have to be taken so that the viewer does not keep running back into a "home page" made up of the show.

One of the more innovative uses of the big show strategy was a campaign launched by BMW. Using television ads that promised adventure movies at www.bmwfilms.com, the viewer could select the most recent movie or one of several others available, all featuring a BMW cast in a central role and online. The "ticket" to the movies was the e-mail address, name, and zip code of the viewer. The site provided different bandwidth speeds for the movies from the slower phone line speeds to Digital Subscriber Lines (DSL) and Cable modem speeds. In addition, the site let the viewer choose from three different online video viewers—RealPlayer, Windows Media, and Quick Time. All of these video players are available free and two can be used on the major viewer platforms, Windows and Macintosh. In addition, the site provided BMW movie players that automatically would load the BMW site and play enhanced movies. After watching each movie, the viewer was provided links to the cars in the movies where Flash-enhanced views of the cars were provided.

The cost of producing movies and highly animated big show productions is dropping dramatically with the introduction of low-cost digital cameras, Flash animation, and digital-editing movie programs such as Adobe Premier and Apple's First Cut Pro. Because BMW used well-known directors and elaborate sets and filming in international locations, its costs were substantial.

However, using low-cost alternatives puts such productions well within the means of small to medium-size businesses.

LITTLE ANIMATIONS AND SURPRISES

A more subtle approach can attract viewers with little animations th

mations are small, fully integrated into the functionality of the site, and never a separate entity from the site.

David Siegel (1997), in developing his concept of "Third-Generation Web Sites," argued that Web sites must include pages that act as lures to entice the viewer further into a site. By having little surprises and functional yet whimsical animations, the viewer is lured to see what else lies in store. Very small Flash files integrated into HTML pages can seamlessly add the kinds of attractive lures Siegel proposed.

NEW AGE FLOAT

For some products or services, a less dramatic but very effective way to use movement to get the viewer's attention is to use slow fade-ins and fade-outs to float different images on the screen. Accompanied by soothing music associated with New Age sounds, such pages promise peace of mind with a product or service.

FACTS UP FRONT

An alternative view to having the attraction from the "sizzle" is to show the "steak." A major influence on **Web usability** is found in the works of Jakob Nielsen (2000). His major concerns have been ways to keep bandwidth low and tell the viewer right away that a site has what the viewer seeks. The emphasis is on product focus because, as Nielsen correctly points out, most people who visit a Web site are hoping it will have a product or service they want. By presenting clear facts within an eyespan, viewers are more likely to be attracted and keep looking through a site until they find what they want and make a purchase decision. Any distractions in a Web page, such as gratuitous animation, are anathema to Nielsen's approach. A Web page should appear quickly and immediately show the viewers what they want to find— or at least a path to what they're seeking. Contrary to Marshall McLuhan who argued that the "message is in the medium," for Nielsen, the message is in the product or service.

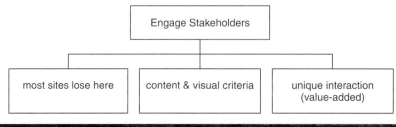

FIGURE 3-2   The Engaging (Building Loyalty) Phase

Engaging (Building Loyalty)

Once the e-storefront or Web site has attracted an online visitor, the challenges become more complex. It has already been established that the competitive arena is huge and, with the speed with which a visitor can move from one site to the next, the engaging phase becomes critical. The engaging phase is illustrated in Figure 3-2.

To be successful with engaging the online visitor, a Web site must be clear and precise with its marketing messages (refer to Chapter 4 on storyboarding). This communication has two components—form and substance.

Substance is addressed by using the marketing research or business intelligence (benchmarking and segmentation results) discussed in the attracting phase. This information is incorporated into the content of the Web site so it is designed to communicate the specific needs and wants of the customer. Internet technologies allow the site content to dynamically change based upon the entering visitor's preferences. This places even greater value on knowing about the online visitor's needs and wants. It will also increase the online loyalty of the customer as even greater value is placed on providing the "right product at the right time with the right message to the right audience" in the online environment. This becomes the cornerstone of a firm building its online customer relationship management (CRM) component of e-business marketing. The higher the value of the firm's interaction with its online customer, the higher the customer's satisfaction with the relationship. Research has shown that higher customer satisfaction leads to higher retention, less focus on price, and greater profitability to the firm due to this increased customer lifetime value (CLV). It is important to combine the online customer-relationship building with the off-line efforts. This further reinforces the need for seamless integration of all customer-contact databases and systems so that the firm has "one voice" to the customer regardless of the communication channel employed.

The e-commerce, or selling, component of e-business is also in the engage phase. In addition to interacting with the site (that is, the firm in an electronic form), the site's goal is to create a transaction or exchange that is valued by the customer and the firm. The site may or may not execute the transaction. For many firms, the completion of the transaction online is not an option. In these scenarios, the qualified sales lead is the desired outcome. Firms that complete the sale online must respect the privacy of the customer information provided and a secure processing environment. Online visitors express privacy as one of their primary obstacles for not transacting online. When the firm provides a clear privacy statement and abides by its commitments, this obstacle can be minimized. The use of secure servers and the protection software available will reduce fraud—also reducing privacy fears.

The technology behind user-engagement elements in a site stem from two sources. First, languages like JavaScript and Java and applications such as Macromedia Flash and Adobe LiveMotion all have **client-side** features that simulate engaging interaction. In its simplest form electron

interactive moment in a Web site lies in the fact that the code in the page that loads into the viewer's browser contains all the information necessary to carry on the interaction. Little quizzes, puzzles, or other elements that give the user something to do are further instances of client-side engagements.

The second kind of technology behind engaging the viewer can be found in **server-side** scripts. Scripts written in Common Gateway Interface (CGI), Active Server Pages (ASP), or Hypertext Preprocessor (PHP) pages and launched from the server consist of **middleware.** For example, an online form may send data to a server-side script written in PHP. The PHP interprets the data sent and then queries a database stored on yet another server. The database information is sent back to the PHP script, which then sends it to the browser so that the viewer can see the results. In this case the PHP is the middleware between the Web browser and the database. Because databases stored on servers can be very large, the range of information used as feedback to the viewer can be far more engaging than what can be loaded into the browser as part of a Web page.[3]

A quickly developing source of database information on the Web can be found in eXtensible Markup Language (XML) files. Using client-side scripts, XML data files can be read into an HTML page using standard JavaScript in an HTML page or Web applications like Flash as a front end. (**Front end** and **user interface** are used interchangeably. A **back end** generally refers to the server-side elements.) The ability of XML to be directly accessed by client-side scripts makes it a useful tool for setting up engaging features in a Web site.

Retaining (Strengthening the Relationship)

The elements or phases of the value bubble are sequential. With successful attracting and engaging phases, the firm's Web site or e-store has driven traffic or visitors to its site and then created a value-laden interaction within the World Wide Web using e-business marketing strategies enabled by Internet technologies. The key to the retention phase is to continue online visits and interactions. It is illustrated in Figure 3-3.

---

[3]In a very convincing argument, Nakhimovsky and Myers show how to develop client-side databases using JavaScript; although databases are generally stored separately on servers, they can be integrated into HTML pages and processed using JavaScript. (Nakhimovsky, Alexander, and Myers, *JavaScript Objects*. Birmingham, England: Wrox Press, Ltd.), 1998.

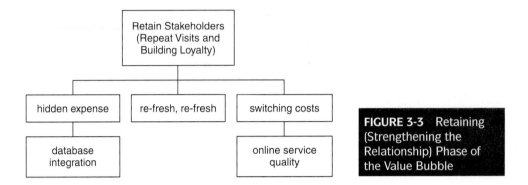

FIGURE 3-3 Retaining (Strengthening the Relationship) Phase of the Value Bubble

The business intelligence component is used to continue and enhance the online customer relationship. The interactive ability of the electronic medium creates a dialogue between the firm and its customer. In this environment, the empowered customer seeks information, services, and products that are specific to their needs and wants. The firm's goal is to address these needs and wants, which creates value for the customer and value for the firm.

There are two ways for a firm to strengthen the relationship with its online customers. The first way incorporates the customer's preferences for certain Web site features. It is defined by the quality of the electronic service provided to the online customer. The second is a broader relationship-building model incorporating the online and off-line interactions. This can be accomplished only through the customer information database integration. Firms that achieve the broader relationship with their customers are also able to assign a more precise CLV because they are examining the total relationship. Internet technologies facilitate the ease of accomplishing this; the challenge is total systems integration. However, once achieved, the database provides the firm with defined customer profiles that more precisely measure CLV potential. Firms are able to target the most valuable customer segments based on these profiles. This further solidifies the holistic approach to e-business marketing.

Online service quality often defines the customer's experience and is a factor in relationship building. These relationships have been observed and reported in the off-line (traditional) environment as well. Because this step of the value bubble focuses on strengthening the relationship, it is important to examine the online service quality research through the work of Zeithaml, Parasuraman, and Malhotra (2000). Their research provides a framework of perceptual attributes translated into dimensions of Web site features reported by consumers as ways they perceive quality of service delivered by the site. This work extended the traditional service quality body of knowledge into the Web-enabled environment. Service quality, as it has been defined, is the "expected and perceived quality of all the services" a firm provides (Harrell and Frazier 1999, p. 49). It is important to reemphasize that Web site interactions are another contact point between a firm and its customers. That is, the customer's perception is that the Web site is *the* firm. Three customer or visitor behaviors are measured within the e-service quality model: purchase, loyalty, and word of mouth. The firm's ability to create a positive customer experience through its Web site for each of these behaviors is critical. The e-service quality dimensions identified by the first phase of

TABLE 3-1 E-Service Qualities and Their Attributes[4]	
E-Service Quality Dimension	*Attributes*
Access	Site is quick to load; easy to find; other methods to contact company
Ease of navigation	Site functions like ...
Assurance and trust	Site's reputation
Price knowledge	Ability to compare prices for similar products and services; shipping costs disclosed early
Site aesthetics	Site has a balance of text and graphics (that don't affect loading time)
Reliability	Site consistently available; truthful about inventories
Flexibility	Site provides choices (payment type, shipping, returns, and searching capabilities)

Zeithaml, Parasuraman, and Malhotra's research are presented with their associated attributes in Table 3-1.

Zeithaml, Parasuraman, and Malhotra (2000) have begun the second phase of their research. Early empirical results indicate that there are two main factors or underlying dimensions of e-service quality dimensions: core service and recovery. The core factors are basic requirements to meet and exceed the online visitor's perception of service quality. Recovery focuses on problem resolution and the expected levels of customer service and follow-up. Both dimensions contribute to the overall customer experience.

The second component in the retention phase is the long-term relationship between a firm and its customer base. This is nurtured over time and over transactions. It is contingent upon successful database construction (all customer data from all channels in an integrated system) and database mining. The richness of the data analyses yields more accurate financial models that are used to calculate CLV. Every firm, to maximize profits, needs to develop the customer segmentation strategies that allow accurate targeting. This targeting should be based on customer buying behaviors (needs–wants), demographics, and psychographics. A firm evaluates each segment's profitability levels and develops the appropriate mix for its profitability goals. The Internet provides data on the customer's online behaviors, demographics (through registration), and psychographics.

[4]Zeithaml, V., Parasuraman, A., and Malhotra, A. *A Conceptual Framework for Understanding e-Service Quality: Implications for Future Research and Managerial Practices.* (Marketing Science Institute, Report No. 00-115, 2000).

Because the Internet-based data do not rely on self-reported behaviors or projected behaviors, the firm has more objective data to analyze.

Relationship marketing models are appropriate for this second component of retention. They are built between a firm and a customer based on satisfactory exchanges as defined by meeting or exceeding a customer's expectations of the inter-action (transaction, information request, etc.). In the traditional or off-line world, three value enhancing options are contained in the relationship model: financial, social, and structural (Berry and Parasuraman 1991). Rethinking this model and applying it into the online world, Web site features (as defined by content and form) drive the relationship. It can be argued that using the e-service quality dimensions from the first component are the important levers to the online relationship builder. The measurement of successful retention is the return visit rate from previous online visitors or customers.

The technology behind retention is found primarily in Web design rather than hardware or software. Several elements go into the Web site design that aid in retention:

- Auto-bookmark option so that it is easy for the viewer to find her way back to the site.
- Easy to navigate so that the user does not have a frustrating experience.
- Quickly shows viewer information that tells about the site. Even a preloader should have information that the site is loading, how much has been loaded and remains to be loaded, and some information about what will be seen when site is loaded.
- Options for both fast and slow Internet connections to take advantage of higher bandwidth pages for those with faster connections.
- A clear exit should show the user to the home page so that he does not feel trapped in a site and will return without fear of getting tangled up in a maze of pages.
- Some way of connecting to the viewer.

In many ways one cannot separate retention from relating (see Relate section below), and the technology involved for one is typically used in the other. The concept of retention is the first step in a relationship, which relies on learning (see the following section) about the parties who will eventually be part of the relationship. However, if retention fails, there is no opportunity for learning about customers or partners and developing the relationship.

A simple Web technology for using an initial visit for a connection for future visits is called a **cookie.** As mentioned earlier, a cookie is a file that a script in the Web page being viewed places on the viewer's hard drive in the form of a text file. The information from the initial visit can include virtually any combination of categories based on codes the developer puts into the cookie. A cookie is limited and can be updated only by return visits to the site. Unlike a database that can be fully controlled by the Web site owner, cookies are more limited types of files. However, by placing certain types of information in the cookies, when the viewer returns to the site "he or she can be automatically greeted" by name and even sent to a page with details about products or services in which he or she showed an initial interest. The purpose of a cookie for retention is to set the stage for ease of use and making a connection that will develop into a long-term relationship.

Learning (Building the Database)

Jackson and Wang (1994) described data-driven marketing as an evolution and a revolution. Although their database marketing models were developed for the traditional or off-line direct marketing environment, the concepts and applications are relevant in the online environment. Consistent with the underlying framework of this textbook, the online environment does not

reported data (gathered from site registrations, online surveys, and community or user groups). This information is combined with the firm's other customer databases to develop a composite profile of its customers online and off-line needs and wants. This phase is presented in Figure 3-4.

In both the off-line and online environments, the critical process is defining the key customer data. This requires marketers to evaluate the necessary data needed for their marketing decisions. These decisions focus on **customer lifetime value,** the marketing mix, and targeted marketing campaigns.

The technologies involved in learning are the same for two very different types of data. The clickstream data show which pages of a site were visited and in what order and how long the visitor remained on each page. The software used for gathering clickstream data records the URL of the current page and starts a timer. As soon as the visitor leaves the page, the timer is stopped and the name of the page and the amount of time spent is sent to a database or put into a cookie on the viewer's hard drive. All of this can be done with simple scripting languages like JavaScript. Storing the data in a database requires middleware like Common Gateway Interface (CGI), ASP, ASP.NET, or PHP and then some kind of database software. However, the freely available MySQL or Microsoft's popular Access can serve adequately as databases for clickstream data.

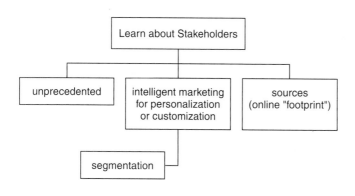

FIGURE 3-4 Learning (Building the Database) Phase

Having access to more information from the user supplied by the user can be extremely helpful in establishing a relationship; information actively delivered by the user contains the added advantage of information not available through clickstream data. For example, purchasing plans, income, location, and general demographics can be obtained through online surveys targeted at traditional marketing information.

Relating (Data-Driven Interactions)

The relating phase of the bubble applies the learning from the previous phase. Online customer communication is interactive and can be personalized at the individual level based on the data collected. To maximize the value of the relating phase, the online and off-line customer databases are integrated, leading to a holistic communication approach (see Figure 3-5).

The data-driven customer information (generated from the learning phase and off-line customer databases) provides input into the **attract, engage,** and **retain** phases. For example, Web site pages that are not frequently visited or have very quick click-through rates would be evaluated for message content and relevancy (Chapter 4 will discuss this in further detail). Online visitor behaviors also indicate the degree to which navigation flow is understood. These design or form issues require modification to meet or exceed the online visitors' needs and wants.

The analyses of the customer data (from the learning phase and other data sources) are used to develop customer segments or profiles. In the off-line, direct marketing environment, segments range in the number of customers per segment. The online segments, in contrast, can be a segment of one where the dialogue between the site and customer is customized on a one-to-one basis. This capability continues to fuel online privacy concerns. Therefore, the data and learnings are collected individually but applied within small segments (microsegments). This will reduce privacy concerns and maximize the online marketing experience.

One of the online personalization dimensions available is the recommendation of a next product or service or site content based on a customer's previous behavioral patterns. Several statistical models have been used and evaluated for effectiveness of the recommendation. Levin and Zahavi (2001) conducted an empirical investigation of these predictive models using segmentation. The automatic tree classifiers outperformed the traditional database marketing, judgement-based models—recency, fre-

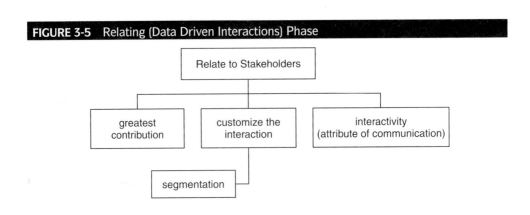

FIGURE 3-5 Relating (Data Driven Interactions) Phase

quency, and monetary (RFM). The tree classifiers do not require extensive statistical training to use or interpret the results.[5]

The underlying Web technology for retaining customers is found in e-mail technology and server-side auto-e-mailing capabilities. First and foremost, a customer who receives an e-mail addressing his interests uniquely, especially if it is written by

Other online retailers send more general announcements if the target audience is well-defined. For example, owners of Apple Macintosh computers make up a target market and retailers can send notices of sales to all Mac owners with whom they have made contact. For example ClubMac e-mails its customers graphic announcements about new products and sales. The e-mail also includes the URL for the enhanced version of its message in case the user's e-mail does not display graphics. The targeted e-mail helps establish a relationship between customer and retailer.

The e-mail technology is simple enough to grasp, but the real power technology behind targeted e-mail is the database setup containing current records of a customer's interest based on both purchases and interest expressed in feedback instruments. Data from the customer goes to smart middleware (e.g., PHP, ASP, CGI) that puts it into the right "slot" (record and fields) in the database. The e-business has information about products and services along with marketing schedules that go into another database. Marketing managers add the scheduling data to the business database. The smart middleware checks the business database to see what products or services are scheduled for marketing and sends e-mails to the targeted customers. Figure 3-6 shows the path beginning with the information provided by the customer and ending with the customer receiving feedback from the business. The retention is forged by reconnection between the business and customer based on information from the initial encounter generated by the customer when he first visited a site and provided information about his interests.

The process of building customer relationshps requires contact. The marketing goal to keep in mind is to entice the viewer to return to the site.

BUSINESS-TO-BUSINESS VALUE BUBBLE ADAPTATIONS

The value bubble has been examined primarily from the business-to-consumer online marketplace. However, the model is flexible and only requires minor modifications or adaptations for the business-to-business online environment.

---

[5]For additional reading, see N. Levin, and J. Zahavi, "Predictive Modeling Using Segmentation." *Journal of Interactive Marketing, 15*(2) (Spring 2001): 2–22.

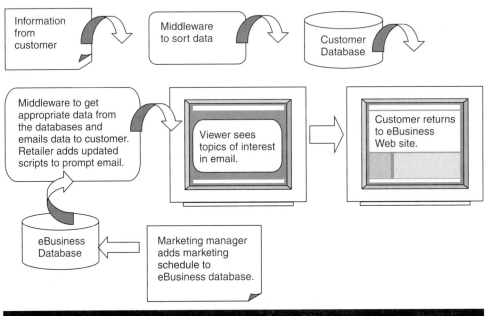

FIGURE 3-6   Customer's Path

These modifications are relevant for the pure business-to-business context. It focuses primarily on companies managing their supply chain and enterprise resource planning to leverage Internet technologies. However, firms recognize that their suppliers are also their direct customers. They must successfully communicate with their direct customers and suppliers (distributors, intermediaries) as well as their end customers using the online environment and avoiding channel conflict. In their communication with both the direct and the end customers, the previous discussion of the value bubble elements focusing on relationship building strategies still applies. Listed below are the model adaptations for the B2B environment focusing on supply chain management and enterprise resource planning.

• **Attracting.** The difference between the B2C and B2B groups in the attraction phase is the motivation for selecting and visiting a site. Within a supply chain, suppliers will visit a site to conduct various business activities with the other suppliers in the chain. The site must perform at satisfactory levels; however, the highly competitive environment of the World Wide Web has lessened because many of the business processes or activities have moved online. Within a firm, certain internal support functions (for example, human resources) may also be online in an effort to lower costs.

• **Engaging.** While visiting the site, the hosting firm must demonstrate cost savings through productivity enhancements to the supplier. If this does not occur, the supplier is apt to return to the previous traditional or off-line business practices.[6] For employee-

---

[6]This is mitigated by very large producers (leaders in their category) that require certain functions of the business relationship to be conducted online (for example, the Big Three auto manufacturers).

based services (companies using Internet technologies to perform internal functions), a poorly performing site can lead to employee dissatisfaction and perhaps long-term employee turnover.

- **Retaining.** By achieving cost savings through productivity enhancements in the engaging phase, a firm builds loyalty and repeat visits through continued enhancement

g ... ... B2B context, the exchange of inventory-level data leads to an online replenishment system that further enhances just-in-time (JIT) inventory practices. For a company providing employee services online, a personalized interaction is very important. This reduces the stigma that the company is only interested in cost reduction at the expense of personalized interactions with its employees.

Chapter 4 discusses the storyboarding concept. Storyboarding originated as a preliminary form of testing television commercials. In the online marketplace, storyboarding is expanded into a methodology for message research. It uses Internet technologies to facilitate data collection. In addition, the usability model is integrated into the traditional research methods.

COLLECTING YOUR KNOWLEDGE: A REVIEW

Key Terms

- attract
- auto-bookmark
- back end
- big show
- brochure-ware
- building traffic
- clickstream
- client-side

- cookie
- customer lifetime value
- disintermediation
- engage
- front end
- learn
- microsegmentation
- middleware

- new age float
- relate
- retain
- server-side
- user interface
- value bubble
- Web usability

Questions to Ask

1. Why are the steps in the value bubble important? Is there any real difference between using the value bubble in an e-business and in a bricks and mortar business?
2. Setting up relationships is always difficult even under the best of circumstances. How can a relationship be set up over the Internet? What is the nature of the business–customer relationship?
3. What role does learning about a client or potential client play in the value bubble? What technologies are available to help learn about customers?

4. What are the key strategies in attracting and retaining customers to a Web site? What role does product or service interest play? What Web technologies have been identified that will help in attracting and retaining customers?

Application to Business

Examine your own business and determine whether the five elements of the value bubble exist. Attraction is the most likely to be present, but what about the rest?

For your business what could be done online to process the five steps in the value bubble? What engagement and learning technologies are available that you could install online, and how would a marketing follow-up be created with both the engagement and learning technologies?

Web Sites to Visit

www.infiniti.com This is a site that's learning about visitors while you're visiting. It uses a clickstream method. (Remember that *learn* is one of the steps in the value bubble.) If you're interested, click on View > Source in your browser's menu bar. Then search the code for the word "Clickstream" and you'll find it in the JavaScript code. See how many other aspects of the value bubble you can find here.

www.symantec.com Here's a site you can establish a relationship with. Symantec is the maker of the Norton antivirus software that you may now have on your computer. The site is well-organized and easy to navigate (the kind Jakob Nielsen would approve of), but it's not too exciting. However, to have its target market resubscribe, it is trying to establish a relationship (relate) with its customers. It does that by providing a product feedback form where customers can state what they think is good or bad about the software, and by downloads that ask former customers to return and present clients to remain.

www.atomfilms.com and **www.shockwave.com** Attraction is paramount at these sites because they have a collection of small movies made for the Web. This may represent a marketing portal in the future, but the sites do offer more than attraction. They contain sign-up pages to view the films in an attempt to establish some kind of connection with the viewer.

CHAPTER

4

A COMMUNICATION MODEL FOR THE ONLINE ~~ENVIRONMENT~~

🛈 tional, off-line communication process is presented and adapted or modified for the online marketplace. The well-known contemporary research methodology used for testing commercial messages, storyboarding, is introduced for testing online message effectiveness as part of the feedback component. Usability theory is incorporated into this modified concept of storyboarding research.

THE COMMUNICATION PROCESS MODEL

The word *communication* is derived from the Latin word *communis* that means common. It is critical for the concept of "common" to be incorporated into how marketers communicate with the firm's stakeholders. The commonality indicates something is shared or understood between the communicating parties. This further advances the concept into one that helps deepen or further a relationship. To study and understand the communication process, it is necessary to take this commonality and separate it into its important components. The traditional communication process model has nine elements originally created for one-way communication (from the firm to the customer). The components are:

1. Sender
2. Encoding
3. Message
4. Medium
5. Receiver
6. Decoding
7. Response
8. Noise
9. Feedback

As technology enabled more two-way communication processes (firm to customer; customer to firm), this model was revised. The definition for each component reflects the two-way communication process.

47

- **Sender.** The sender is the creator or originator of the message to be communicated. Marketers are responsible for creating the communications between the firm, its customers, and potential customers. Other communications may be developed by public relations (media releases, governmental liaisons), internal departments (employee and supplier stakeholder groups), and investor relations (investor stakeholder group). The sender represents the firm and must be credible to the target audience for whom the communication was designed.

- **Encoding.** It is critical for the sender to identify and understand the needs, wants, and preferences of the target audience receiving the message. This leads to a more effective translation of the message through the appropriate words, sentences, and symbols that the target audience understands and values.

- **Message.** Messages may be constructed in a variety of forms and contexts. The message combines the sender's communication objective with the mechanics of its translation into an expression that is appropriate for the target audience.

- **Medium.** The medium is the channel through which the message will be communicated. Companies use personal, nonpersonal, and hybrid communication mediums (see Table 4-1, Harrell and Frazier, 1999 and Shimp, 2000).

- **Receiver.** The receiver is a member of the target audience and is the second player in this process (a sender is the other). In marketing communications, receivers are generally customers or prospective customers but may be from any other stakeholder group.

- **Decoding.** A receiver decodes or interprets the message. If the sender does not accurately understand the target audience or does not accurately encode the message using the appropriate medium or channel, the communication objective will not be achieved. Successful decoding occurs when the receiver derives value from the message.

- **Response.** In the development of the message, the sender (marketer) has certain expected outcomes from the receiver (from the designated target audience or stake-

TABLE 4-1 Personal and Nonpersonal Communication Mediums	
Type of Medium/Definition	*Medium Types*
Personal medium—direct communication between firm and stakeholder; high interactivity	Face-to-face (personal contact) Telephone
Nonpersonal medium—indirect or impersonal communication; little to no interactivity	Broadcast • Television • Radio • Outdoor Print • Magazines • Newspapers • Marketing collateral
Hybrid—receiver controls level of interactivity (requires a certain level of technology adoption)	Internet

holder group). The response is the same as this expected outcome. (It may be a transaction, exchange of information, etc.)

• *Noise.* Noise is anything that disrupts the flow of the entire communication process. It can occur at any stage of this process (**sender, encoding, message, channel, receiver, decoding, response,** and **feedback**).

.... that define the response or outcome can be cognitive (thinking), affective (feeling or attitudes), or behavioral (action such as a purchase). The sequence of thought for customers based upon their level of involvement with a product or service has great impact on their responses and has been studied extensively.[1] Four well-known response hierarchy models emerged from this body of research. To effectively design and communicate a message, the involvement of the target audience (or receivers) is critical.

The Adapted Communication Model for E-Business Marketing

By rethinking the traditional communication process and applying its concepts to the online or Internet environment, a marketer can create an effective communication strategy for its electronic presence. It is critical that the online communication is integrated with all other forms of stakeholder communication or misinterpretation and brand confusion will occur. This will be explored in greater depth in the case study presented in Chapter 5.

Each of the communication model's components are described with an adaptation or transformation into the Internet environment.

• **Sender.** In the online environment, the sender or source of the message is more collaborative than in the off-line environment. The sender group has representation from the marketing and technology departments of the firm. This must be collaborative to ensure that the total communication process achieves two goals: the desired outcome or response based upon the message delivered; and the appropriate implementation of the technology to communicate and deliver the message.

• **Encoding.** It is a marketing decision to select the appropriate words, sentences, and symbols necessary to achieve the communication goals. As stated in the sender component, the management information technology (MIS) department collaborates with the marketer on the availability and feasibility of technology to encode the message correctly.

---

[1]E. K. Strong, *The Psychology of Selling* (New York: McGraw Hill, 1925); Lavidge, R. and G. Steiner, "A Model for Predictive Measures of Advertising", *Journal of Marketing* (October 1961); E. Rogers, *Diffusion of Innovation,* 3rd ed. (New York: Free Press, 1985); and Michael Ray, *Advertising and Communications Management* (Upper Saddle, NJ: Prentice Hall, 1982).

- **Message.** A firm's Web site (enabled by Internet technologies) has greater flexibility in the form and content (substance) options. The messages can be customized to an individual visitor's preferences and dynamically changed to adapt to each visitor. Promotional offers can be varied based upon the customer lifetime value (CLV) of the online customer as well. Although these decisions are generally made by marketing departments, the MIS support is critical to provide the right message to the right customer at the right time.

- **Medium.** The Internet has been referred to as a mixed medium (personal and non-personal). One of its dimensions is interactivity within a computer-mediated communication model (Yadav 2001). Everett Rogers (1985) has defined this level of interactivity as "the degree to which participants in a communication process can exchange roles and have control over their mutual discourse." Without the Internet technologies available, the exchange and control would not be available. As a medium, the Internet expands the definition and capability of communicating.

- **Receiver.** In the electronic or computer-mediated environment, the receiver is an electronic visitor. Internet technologies provide the structure for collecting substantially relevant behavioral data (through the observation of the online visit). The data are critical to monitoring the success of the communication process. The electronic environment also creates an empowered customer who has more control and choices than in the off-line environment.

- **Decoding.** In the dynamic, electronic environment, an online visitor's reaction to successful message translation or decoding will be immediate. Firms may establish certain paths within their sites to adjust or alter the message if it was not decoded appropriately. This immediate correction will facilitate ongoing communication and build relationships.

- **Response.** The ability to track a customer's response to an online message is immediate and accurate. By observing customers' Web site behaviors, firms can objectively measure successful responses. Unsuccessful responses are equally important because the analysis of these failures leads to Web site revisions that improve the communication process.

- **Noise.** In addition to factors experienced in the off-line environment, the Internet has more complex noise possibilities. The differences between online visitors in their technological capabilities and connections create many possible distractions or interpretations of the message delivery. Sites can accommodate these differences through careful collaboration between the marketing and MIS departments.

- **Feedback.** The immediacy of the feedback through the Internet-enabled environment provides marketers with timely, accurate data to guide adjustments to their communication process. To fully realize this potential, marketers develop a feedback model that captures the appropriate data points. This may be accomplished through collaboration with the MIS department.

The response hierarchy models described for the traditional or off-line environment are currently being researched for adaptation into the Internet environment. The goal is to build an empirical model that reflects how to address the level of involve-

TABLE 4-2	Online Think, Feel, and Do Dimensions
Dimension	**Operational Definition**
Think	Site awareness generated by advertising (online and off-line), public relations, site visits, and bricks and mortar presence
Feel	Brand equity influenced by advertising (online and off-line), awareness, quality

High Involvement: Think → Feel → Do
Low Involvement: Think → Do → Feel
No Involvement: Do → Think → Feel

The online **think, feel,** and **do** dimensions examined empirically are defined in Table 4-2 (Ilfed and Winer 2001).

The hierarchical model that emerged from the research as most often observed in the online environment was the low-involvement model. Using the definitions above with the empirical models tested, the online (low-involvement) model is defined by the following sequence of online behaviors and consequences:

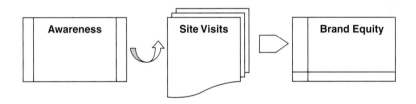

Marketers can incorporate this involvement model into the development of their communication objectives that rely on appropriate sequencing. Online visitors respond to Web sites in a low-involvement-response hierarchy. Therefore, building awareness is the first step (think) followed by the site visit (do) and finally building brand equity (feel). These empirical results indicate that a communication budget should initially focus on building traffic to the site and the brand equity will follow after the site visit(s). It also suggests that the switching costs of leaving one site for another are very low, indicating that the level of trial behavior online is high.

Given the minimal research available in the online environment regarding the communication process and response hierarchy models, it becomes dramatically more important to test the online communication process prior to implementation. This testing minimizes the failure of meeting communication objectives as well as reducing exposure to competitors of the firm's initial plans that may not succeed. The next section discusses a methodology for testing the communication effectiveness of the Web site prior to its implementation. It utilizes the message research testing from the advertising literature and storyboarding.

MESSAGE RESEARCH MODEL

In the traditional advertising literature, message-based research is often referred to as copy testing. The message being researched is typically an advertisement and most often television commercials. A study of advertising executives found that over 80 percent of the agencies surveyed conduct some pretesting for television commercial effectiveness. The rationale for focusing on the commercial is the substantial investment a firm makes in its creative development, production, and media time. It is imperative to research the target audience's response to the commercial before it is publicly played (King, Pehrson, and Reid 1993).

To minimize the cost of the commercial investment, firms work with their advertising agency on a preliminary viewing of the commercial. At this stage, it can be tested with effectiveness and revisions made before final completion. There are four types of prefinished commercial formats tested:

1. *Storyboards*—a series of frames or cells that depict the commercial's sequence of dialogue. Audio of the dialogue may be provided.
2. *Animatics*—a film of the frames or cells that provides movement to the presentation.
3. *Photomatics*—a film of photographs depicting the commercial's message.
4. *Ripamatics*—existing commercials are edited to represent the new commercial's message.
5. *Liveamatics*—a live action film of the proposed commercial. It is not completed and represents a rough cut of the final version.

Over the years, the advertising industry has been criticized for employing research, design, and methods that were substandard. In 1982 the industry confronted this issue and developed nine principles to guide its future research with more rigorous methodology. These principles—**Positioning Advertising Copytesting (PACT)**—were introduced into the advertising academic literature in 1982.

A firm's electronic communications with its existing and potential customers are broader than advertising (which is only one element with the marketing mix component of promotion/communication). However, the medium that delivers the communication is similar to a television screen with the additional characteristics of interactivity and additional control. Therefore, these principles are a relevant conceptual framework or foundation to adapt for online message research.

Each of the PACT principles is briefly defined below. Their adaptation to the online environment is included in this definition.

PACT Principle 1

The measurements employed by the message research study must be appropriate and actually measure the objectives of the message. Based upon the overall goal of the advertising (of which the commercial may only be a small portion), the attributes measured must reflect the goal and objective.

The application of Principle 1 to the online environment would be broader. Rather than measuring the advertising goals and objectives, the Web site or electronic storefront often has broader communication goals (transactions, relationship building, and branding). Each of these goals must be operationally defined and a measurement device selected. Using Internet technologies, online behaviors can often provide initial feedback about the effectiveness of the communication (length of stay, pages visited, content of e-mails sent to the firm, etc.). Online surveys, focus groups, and panel discus-

extracted, analyzed, and presented to the business analyst either on the Web or directly from the database software itself. For example, if a business used Microsoft Access as an online database, the file where all of the information from users has been stored could be extracted using a desktop version of Access or over the Web.

The most powerful use of the technology is an ongoing analysis of data as they are entered. As soon as the data are entered by the user, they can be passed to the middleware (e.g., CGI, PHP) and placed into a database. As soon as a new analysis inquiry is made, all of the latest data from the database are fed into the analysis so that any feedback to the business is current. In fact, if so desired, a manager could get an automatic update over the Internet. Figure 4-1 shows the data-gathering and analysis process.

PACT Principle 2

Many players are involved in the development of a commercial. They include several advertising agency professionals, the firm or advertiser, and the **research firm** conducting the study. Principle 2 focuses on the involved parties agreeing on how the research results will be used. In addition, this principle suggests defining the minimal acceptance levels for the advertising effectiveness before the study begins.

FIGURE 4-1 Data from Entry to Feedback

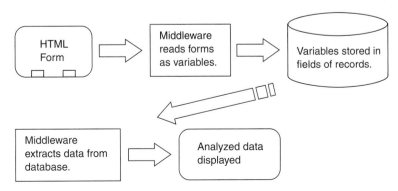

Data from entry to feedback:

In the online world, multiple parties will be interested in the research results. They are different than they would be in the pure advertising context—the marketing and MIS departments will use the results differently but in a collaborative manner. The Web site designer will also be involved as will a research firm (if online surveys, focus groups, and panels are employed). However, the process of agreement on the use of the results is as important in the online world as the off-line one.

The technology that gathers, stores, and analyzes data online is perfectly adapted for multiple interests in both design and use. Each role collaboratively carries out a finite but interdependent task as shown in the following:

- **Marketing Team.** Specifies the information required for a successful marketing plan.
- **Research Firm.** Creates questionnaires and other data-gathering tools based on information required by the marketing team.
- **MIS (or IT).** Creates the database and the analytical software. They can also establish **structured query language (SQL)** modules for different elements in the marketing plan and other relevant parties who may need the data (e.g., executive management, research firm, advertising). SQL is a standard method for communicating with databases. It allows users at remote sites to send instructions to databases on servers and receives information back. The middleware acts as the interpreter between the database and HTML page in the browser.
- **Web Design Firm.** Puts together a Web site that provides forms to fill in based on the data requirements. In addition, it will build the middleware to manage the data between the database and customers and business. (For smaller companies, the firm may also be the MIS department where the database will be designed.) The design firm will also create the necessary aesthetic elements so that the form best fits in with the overall look and feel of the corporate image and larger Web site.

PACT Principle 3

The message research will incorporate multiple measurements. Because the advertising objective is often multidimensional, the research measurements must reflect that.

Principle 3 is directly applicable to the online environment. Consistent with the online adaptations for Principle 1, the Web site has broader communication goals and objectives. This principle is even more critical on the Web.

The technology for multiple measurement on the Web can accommodate both the traditional modes of data gathering, such as questionnaires, and newer forms, such as clickstream data. As noted above, HTML pages can accept form input from users for traditional questionnaires. Likewise, clickstream data can unobtrusively follow the pages customers view, how long they view the pages, and even the sequence they follow. All of the clickstream data can be stored in online databases and even in the same records as the individuals who fill out questionnaires.

Online focus groups can be conducted using chat software. (Chat software provides real-time online communication.) The importance of using online focus groups lies in both the wide range of regions that can be brought together and the low cost in doing so. With increased bandwidth, online focus groups can be done with Internet video conferencing.

PACT Principle 4

Message research must be based on a model of human response to communica-

page designs, including all of the interactive elements on a page can be measured. In part the involvement of a Web page user depends on what interactive elements the page contains. A good deal of research in education has found that Web and pedagogy designs can increase involvement by providing learners with something to do (Sanders 2001; Sanders 2002). The technologies of dynamic interaction include such languages as JavaScript, Java, and DHTML, a host of server-side languages, and applications like Flash. So the technology behind involved communication is available now and can be done using very little bandwidth.

PACT Principle 5

This principle evaluates the need for the number of times an individual should be exposed to the advertising message. For television commercials, this information provides data that are used in the decision for the amount of **media** time to purchase.

Principle 5 is important to the firm's decision for how much investment is necessary to drive or build traffic to its site. An empirical study by Ilfeld and Winer (2001) found that **traffic-building** led to brand awareness and recommended that firms not lose site of Web site traffic-building campaigns. It is important for the marketer to understand how many (and for how long) traffic-building marketing activities are necessary to achieve the communication goals and objectives. The marketing activities include online and off-line ones.

The technology behind traffic building has two components. First, traditional advertising campaigns in print, on the radio, or on television can include the company's URL to alert the public to its existence. Second, Web technology can offer free *downloads*. A download is any computer-based digital file that can be received by a client computer. For example, a real estate firm could offer a free download of a mortgage calculator. The calculator itself could be nothing more than an HTML page with a JavaScript program generating the calculations and output. To drive the user back to the site, the download could include an automatic link to the company's site. For example, Sun Computer, Microsoft, and Apple Computer all include downloads at their sites for updates and upgrades of their products. Users are motivated to return to the sites to see the latest upgrades available. No other technology can provide the immediate gratification of a download.

PACT Principle 6

The research should use an effective test form of the advertisement (**storyboards, animatics, photomatics, ripamatics,** and **liveamatics**). Regardless of which prefinished form is used, it must be as complete and finished as possible. Otherwise, the respondents will be distracted by the lack of clear visuals and message from an incomplete or unfinished form.

Principle 6 is directly applicable to the online environment. The presentation of the Web site, in a message research study, should be clear and understandable. The complexity with a Web site (in contrast to a commercial) is the navigation and ease-of-use measurement (Davis 1989) that involves multiple pages being evaluated. This requires the research design to include how a visitor will move through a site and what the visitor reports as the communication message received. The various types of prefinished commercial testing forms must be modified in order to effectively capture these responses. A brief section on the mechanics of storyboarding as a form is presented at the end of this chapter.

Web technology not only offers a modular test bench, but the simplest test page of a Web site has the same worldwide applicability of a fully configured site. Given the digital nature of Web technology, testing different designs with different groups can be done globally. The tested Web pages can be incorporated into the final project without having to rebuild from the start.

By definition, Web sites are modular, and so the sequence of pages can be arranged and rearranged until the most effective mix has been achieved. A single design could be tested not only against other designs but also by itself. All of the data of user-response could be collected unobtrusively with different arrangements and compared to other designs. Middleware could orchestrate a series of different arrangements and comparative designs so that once the original design was ready, several different tests could be accomplished with self-monitoring software.

PACT Principle 7

The message research should be conducted in an environment that replicates the environment in which the commercial will be viewed. For example, a commercial message shown in isolation does not replicate the true, cluttered environment in which an individual will view it.

In the online environment, this principle is a critical component of the **message research model.** The vast number of Web sites and Web pages are not only a distraction but the empowered, online customer is a mere click away from switching to a competitive site. A research process that illustrates the incorporation of this is included in the last section of this chapter (A Sample Message Research Model).

As noted in Principle 6, Web pages are created and applied in the environment where they will eventually be launched. Unlike other technologies, such as television, where the viewer receives the sponsor's message as part of a program package, a Web site is more like an infomercial where the viewer is so interested in the product or service that she willingly watches. As part of a Web strategy to keep customers from "looking-and-leaving," some elements of a Web site should change regularly so that each time a viewer visits a site, something new is available. Therefore, testing should not only include an initial site but a range of materials that will be part of a dynamic site.

The hypertext environment of the Web is nonlinear and the ability to go from one place to any other place on the Web tempts the Web page designer to hold the viewer against his will. Whenever a viewer leaves a page, either by clicking on a link, back button, bookmarked page, or typing in a URL in a browser's address window, an *unload* event occurs with the current page. By trapping the unload event and sending *contra-dictory URLs, a Web page*

The sample in the research study must represent the target audience of the commercial. This principle is directly applicable to the online environment and message research.

The technology enables the marketer not only to test the Web site with representative target markets, but also in the same environment where the audience will view the finalized site. When considering microsegmentation and multiple target audiences, which is not only possible but preferable on the Web, the flexibility of the Web is such that it is cost-effective to have several different combinations of sites. Using a *single* back end (server-side scripts), any number of different front-ends (**client-side** HTML pages and scripts) can target different audiences. When considering microsegmentation, small and subtle differences can differentiate one audience from another, such as color combinations that may appeal to one group or another. Leslie Carbarga's work, *Designer's Guide to Global Color Combinations* (2001), provides formulas in cyan, magenta, yellow, and black (CMYK) and a red, green, and blue (RGB) color system for computer coding from different cultures. You can immediately see distinctive features in how different societies use color. Because a Japanese audience's color tastes are different from European and American tastes, simply by changing color combinations when testing for different cultures, you can see what impact color has on the target audience. Furthermore, because the Internet allows worldwide testing, reaching different audiences is not an issue at all.

Another consideration is the language of your target audience. Such a pronouncement may appear to be obvious, but Americans have been so accustomed to other people learning English that they fail to consider the importance of targeting worldwide markets in the language of the market. One of the more remarkable Web sites you will find is The Netherland's tourist site, www.holland.com. A dropdown menu inquires where the viewer is from. So if a viewer chooses Japan, a Japanese version of the site appears, whereas a person viewing from Germany sees the site in German (Figures 4-2 and 4-3).

PACT Principle 9

The study must demonstrate reliable and valid measures. This principle is critical for any research conducted. Reliability indicates a stability of measures, meaning that each time

FIGURE 4-2   A Dutch Site in Japanese

the same message is tested, consistent results will be found. Validity indicates that the results can be applied to the competitive environment with a degree of confidence.

Principle 9 is also directly applicable to the online environment and message research.

The research problems of reliability and validity are the same over the Web as they are in non-Internet applications. However, by taking multiple samples and using microsegmentation, you can have both. By exposing a Web design to two or more microsegments of the same target during the testing phase, you can help ensure reliability (the last section of this chapter and Figure 4-4, page 62, will provide a model for this research.) However, like all markets, a good deal of the validity can only be measured in the actual purchase of goods and services. With existing goods and services, validity can be tested by orders for purchases.

If the attention to the technology described in PACT Principle 8 is followed, most of the issues critical to validity and reliability will have been addressed as well.

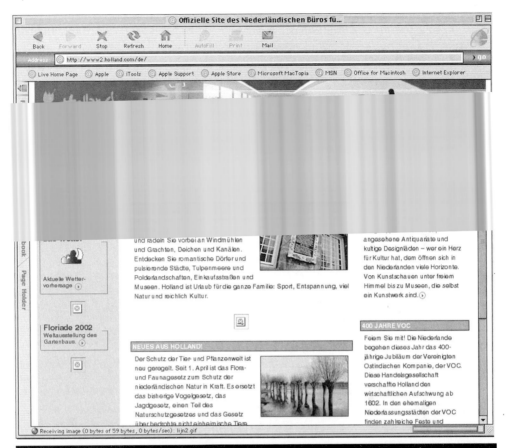

FIGURE 4-3 The Same Site in German

Although it is counterproductive and virtually impossible to isolate every variable or identify every microsegment in a market, identifying and defining the key microsegments is essential. Once they have been identified and defined by testing what the actual groups say they like or what they actually do using clickstream technology, the chances of creating a reliable and valid Web site are enhanced considerably.

A SAMPLE MESSAGE RESEARCH MODEL

This section provides suggestions for the use of storyboards, focus groups, and usability studies to effectively measure the communication goals and objectives of a Web site. It is important to first understand that a Web site has more than one communication objective that ultimately defines the site's communication goal or strategy. Each Web page needs its own communication objective—whether it supports other pages or functions as a stand-alone in terms of its message. The goal and supporting objectives

Storyboarding

This figure outlines how to storyboard a Web site. The storyboard concept is used to ensure that the site achieves its intended communication objectives (PACT 1). It is also used to test the effectiveness of the site with potential visitors (PACT 6 and 8), prior to development. Subsequent to design and development a usability study (PACT 7) is recommended.

Questions to answer prior to storyboard development:
1. Who are the intended audiences (visitors)?
2. What is the communication objective for each audience? The answers may fall in site typology: shopping (a sale or generating a lead), information, entertainment, and/or communication.
3. Each audience or segment will have a specific, and often unique, path in the Web site. Hence, it is important to identify the visitor's preferences upon entering the home page.

Home Page

> *The site is the firm. A Home page should represent the firm's brand and is analogous to entering a store—it should entice the visitor to enter and spend time. This is often achieved through a flash page that is visually compelling and captures immediate interest.*

Questions to ask about the home page:
1. What strategies were used in the attract phase of the value bubble? In other words, what possible expectations are created for the visitor?
2. Is the site's navigation structure presented so that each segment entering can easily identify its own "path" on the home page?

Main Pages

Page One: Message Strategy One	Page Two: Message Strategy Two	Page Three: Message Strategy Three	Page Four: Message Strategy Four	Page Five: Message Strategy Five

Visitors may view all main pages or select the most appropriate one(s) that address their needs from the site.

Questions for the Main Pages:
1. What combination of message strategies addresses each segment of audiences or visitors? The pages are customized to focus on specific communication or message strategies. A unique combination of pages yields a targeted message to appropriate audience or segment.
2. How can the firm increase the amount of time a visitor is engaged with the site (second step, engagement of the value bubble)? Many sites do this by configuring sites based on preferences known from previous visits) or selections/prompts on the home page.
3. What should the refresh content schedule be in order to maximize the return visit or retain phase of the value bubble? This becomes a cost consideration for the firm sponsoring the site. Based on an analysis of site visits/activity and communication objectives, companies determine the refresh schedule. To get the greatest benefit from the refreshing, notification (via e-mail or links) should be targeted toward previous visitors and potential visitors who match the segmentation strategy of the site.

Sub-Main Pages

Sub-main pages take the visitor deeper into the message strategy. For example, if message strategy two focuses on the purchase or a lead generation, there may be less content the visitor desires. Whereas, a potential investor for the company may be very interested in the company's background, financial performance, executive officers, and communication effectiveness. For this type of information, message strategy one may be more applicable.

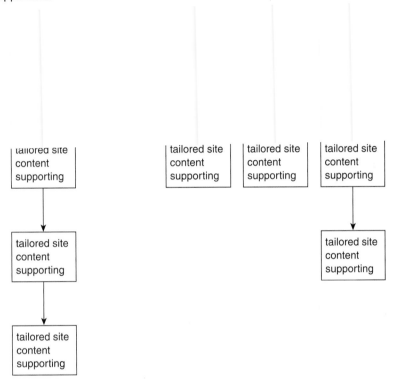

Questions for the Sub-Main Pages:
1. By going into greater depth with the site's content, a visitor is engaged longer (stickiness) and tends to return (retain phase of the value bubble). In message strategy two, the content depth is not as great as in the other strategies. How might a firm maximize the engaging and retaining phases? One approach would be to capture information about the visitor through a registration form. A firm would initiate further contact through e-mail to visitors and invite them back to explore other areas of the site, as applicable.
2. How in-depth should each message strategy be? This is addressed through the storyboarding research. Using focus groups or mall intercepts of the identified target audience(s), the storyboards are presented. As PACT 3 states, multiple measures are gathered. One of these measures is perceptions of amount of content covered and did it meet their needs. Based on the analysis, firms can determine content needed. After the site is launched, the analysis of clickstreams and log files will indicate the view time per page. This information also contributes to the content depth decision.

FIGURE 4-4 Storyboarding

are developed by the marketer working closely with product and service managers who provide details regarding the target audience(s). The site's communication goal must reflect (i.e., be consistent with) the firm's brand or image within the traditional and online environment.[2]

Following the development of the goal and objectives, the specific messages to achieve are designed. The marketer often develops a roadmap that connects the logic of navigating the site in order to achieve the overall goal. This road map translates into a storyboard type of prefinished site design.

Emerick and Round (2001) have developed a straightforward, visual tool for designing a Web site's storyboard. Figure 4-4 presents their process (adapted from page 132 to include the value bubble and PACT Principles models). The storyboards can be presented to a representative group of the target audience in focus groups (off-line or online)—mall intercepts, and one-on-one in-depth interviews are the most common setting (King, Pehrson, and Reid 1993). The following PACT principles are to be used:

- Relevant measurements
- Agreement with the use of the results
- Multiattribute measurements; model of **response hierarchy** is used
- Frequency of visits to achieve the communication goal and objectives
- A realistic prefinished visual replication of the site
- Testing in an environment that includes the competition
- Target audience representation and adherence to the measurement properties of validity and reliability

In addition, the online communication goal and objectives must be evaluated in a time-series design. Web sites must change regularly to increase repeat visits (the engage and retain elements of the value bubble—Chapter 3). The learn and relate phases can provide some of the data for ongoing evaluation of effectiveness, but the target audience input cannot be ignored.

As highlighted in the rethinking and adaptation to the PACT principles, the Internet environment has additional complexities. For example, the interactivity and control dimensions of the online environment must be accounted for in the message research studies. Nielsen has suggested that a group of four to five users, representing the target audience, actually use the site to perform real tasks. A usability lab is recommended for the setting.

The following eight chapters (Chapters 5 through 12) provide case studies from real organizations facing the ever-changing online environment as a new channel for each of the marketing mix components. Although the companies are protected in terms of their specific identity, each represents a major marketing challenge overcome by the Internet and its technologies. The adapted value bubble (Chapter 3) is the through-line connecting the cases, although the concepts and frameworks presented in Chapters 1, 2, and 4 are also incorporated.

---

[2]This text focuses on bricks and clicks (or traditional companies with a significant online presence). However, virtual companies can only succeed through communications that are presented in both the off-line and online environments.

COLLECTING YOUR KNOWLEDGE: A REVIEW

Key Terms

- animatics
- client-side

- media
- message

- response
- response hierarchy models

- marketing team

- research firm

Questions to Ask

1. What are the nine elements of communication and how can they be used effectively to create a business Web site?
2. What tools are available for planning an e-business Web site?
3. What parties should be involved in planning an e-business Web site? What type of communication should there be between the different individuals or groups involved in the planning?
4. What role does storyboarding play in creating a marketing Web site?
5. Why is PACT important in creating not only an advertisement but a Web site as well? Which of the nine elements of PACT most applies to Web site planning and design for marketing?
6. What Web and Internet technologies are available for meeting the principles outlined in PACT?

Application to Business

Which of the nine PACT recommendations went into building your company's Web presence? Which could be effectively added for an improved site?

When planning an addition to your current e-business site, who is involved and what role do they play? Are all of the right individuals or groups included and what role do the others play in relationship to a focused goal on marketing?

What technologies are used in your company's current Web site? What databases and middleware are employed? How were decisions reached on what technology to use? How much was based on the marketing goals and how much was based on IT (or MIS) preferences?

Web Sites to Visit

www.holland.com In case you missed this reference in the body of the text, this Dutch URL stands as a model for a truly global site. This tour site for The Netherlands defaults to English, but as soon as you select a country of origin from the drop-down menu, the language of the country of origin appears. Another interesting example of microsegmentation of target audiences can be found when selecting the United States or United Kingdom as country of origin. Both are in English, but the U.K. site appears with driving tours. Because the British are more likely to bring cars across the English Channel on a ferry or through the channel tunnel, driving tours are a more likely option than for visitors from the United States.

www.powerproduction.com To automate a storyboard, several different computer products are available. This site has a product, StoryBoard Quick, for the "artistically challenged." As long as you can imagine the sequence, this software will help you render it and it can use imported outlines from Microsoft Word and other text editors and word processors. For a complex Web site, a storyboard helps you create the sequence of events you want the viewer to see.

The book, *Film Directing Shot by Shot: Visualizing from Concept to Screen* by Steven D. Katz (1991) helps to take an idea and put the story into a movie. A marketing Web site is just as complex as a movie and understanding something about how movies begin with a concept and move to a reality will help you understand the process of Web site planning.

www.futurizenow.com This site demonstrates its understanding of business needs. Note that rather than a single business level, the site invites executives, managers, and change agents to select from a matrix of choices. The column headings of *Enter, Participate,* and *Engage Us Now* clearly show that this site involves the viewer as an active agent in the site rather than as a passive one. In fact, the founders consider their goal to be to help transform companies into "customer-led" enterprises. The cofounder of Futurize Now is David Siegel, author of *Creating Killer Web Sites* (1997).

CHAPTER

5

CASE STUDY 1

...g the first company

and its analyses, a brief overview of the organization for each case is important.

The eight companies were selected for many reasons. They represent a diverse group of mature industries. Each company has a traditional (i.e., bricks and mortar) presence, is entering into the electronic marketplace for competitive differentiation, and expects to realize financial gains from this effort. Every company has a particular marketing concept or model that is its primary goal and each uses the marketing toolbox enabled by Internet technologies to address these goals. Each case is presented and analyzed in-depth; however, to gain the most comprehensive knowledge from these cases, they must be examined collectively. That is, the reader should link all of the cases to fully experience the complexity and the richness of the e-business marketing environment.

Throughout the book we use a consistent format with the following set of components:

- **Company overview**[1]—description of products and services offered, markets served, competitive arena
- **Discussion of e-business marketing goal or strategy**—goal will be presented and discussed within the context of existing conceptual frameworks or models
- **Primary stakeholders** addressed by the e-business marketing goal—identification of the stakeholders that the designed Web site would be targeting
- **Value bubble** stages and Internet technologies selected—review of the value bubble stages that are critical to the achievement of the goal. Presentation of the Internet technologies employed to fulfill the goal

COMPANY 1 OVERVIEW

Company 1 is a manufacturer of specialty-engineered products that solve a range of insulation issues. These products serve automotive, biomedical, and various industrial clients. The company's clients use the products for conversion or incorporation into

---

[1] Companies are anonymous to protect their competitive advantage upon the implementation of their e-business marketing goal(s).

other finished products. Hence, Company 1 manufactures an **ingredient** rather than a completed product. The firm distributes its products through many distribution channels: distributors; **original equipment manufacturers (OEMs);** and resellers. Typical within a business-to-business environment, the majority of the sales are generated by the sales force and personal selling strategies. Some areas of Company 1 have automated purchasing among the customer base using electronic data exchange (EDI) and would consider expanding this self-service selling into an Internet-based process.

This company's corporate strategy is to be a solutions provider to its customers through continual advancement of product technology and creation of valuable relationships among all the firm's stakeholders. The firm stresses its global reach (with many of its locations being outside of the United States).

The company has financially struggled for several quarters. This is because of the decentralized nature of its organization—eight separate businesses each operating autonomously (Figure 5-1). In August 2000, a restructuring was announced that created two core businesses that focused on a market-driven structure of its two core product lines (Figure 5-2). The investment community's response has been positive and earnings are increasing. The company reported record stock price based on its restructuring and e-business strategies (May 2002).

Company 1 does not have any direct competition for all of its product lines from other manufacturers. Within each of the specialty products it manufactures (and holds a patent for the composites of material used), there are smaller, niche manufacturers that are competitors. These smaller manufacturers focus their corporate strategy or mission on technology, customer relationships, and a worldwide presence in a specific area of filtration and separation, or thermics and acoustics. The presence of these smaller niche manufacturers led Company 1 to pursue a differentiating strategy that their competition has yet to realize.

E-BUSINESS MARKETING GOAL OR STRATEGY

Company 1 examined a number of marketing opportunities in the electronic environment. It wanted to protect its powerful market share position for its products from the niche manufacturers. The company was justifiably concerned that its recent restructuring into two market-focused areas could give the niche competitors an opportunity not previously afforded. The company's former organizational structure was the same as that of several niche manufacturers and it retained the majority share across product lines. The restructuring may represent an opportunity for the niche manufacturers to erode some market share from Company 1.

To support its restructuring and protect its market share built over the years in a decentralized environment, Company 1 focused on an integrated marketing communications strategy for its electronic presence. Its primary goal was to communicate to various stakeholders that its brand not only remained superior to the competition but its restructuring would lead to an organization that provided a stronger family of brands. This would be accomplished through the consolidation of certain functions and operations for efficiency purposes.

Company 1, through its e-business marketing goal, would primarily address the e-components of customer relationship management. It should be noted that the CRM component will be supported by **enterprise resource planning (ERP)** within the internal

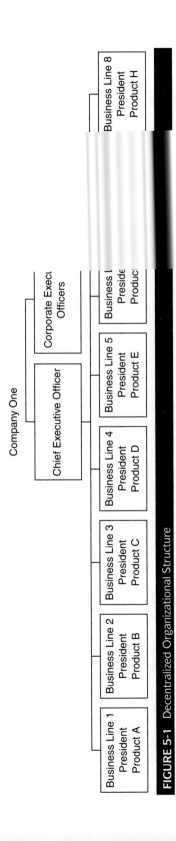

FIGURE 5-1 Decentralized Organizational Structure

The following labels appear in the figure:

- Company One
- Chief Executive Officer
- Corporate Executive Officers
- Business Line 1 / President / Product A
- Business Line 2 / President / Product B
- Business Line 3 / President / Product C
- Business Line 4 / President / Product D
- Business Line 5 / President / Product E
- Business Line (partial) / President / Product
- Business Line 8 / President / Product H

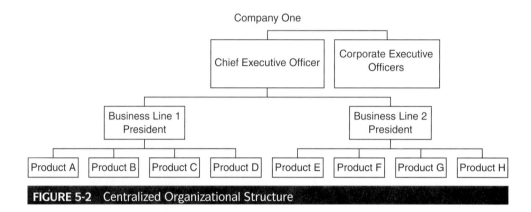

FIGURE 5-2   Centralized Organizational Structure

operations. The company's efforts demonstrate the common marketing theme (as defined in Chapter 1) that the marketing concept is designed to serve many different groups.

The company focused on integrated marketing communications (IMC) for its marketing. IMC was summarized by Shimp (2000, p. 18) as the "process [that] starts with the customer or prospect and then works back to determine and define the forms and methods through which persuasive communications should be developed." Company 1 adapted a marketing communications to specifically capture the electronic environment (Shimp). This adaptation is not only applicable for Company 1 but for any other companies pursuing an online IMC strategy. The following four primary modules are contained within this model:

Stage I. Reorganizing the company toward IMC strategy
Stage II. Understanding the competitive environment (measuring and evaluating in order to develop effective IMC strategies)
Stage III. Brand decision-making—strategic, tactical, and evaluative
Stage IV. Enhancing brand position within the marketplace

Each stage is now presented, in greater depth, to reflect its transformation into the Internet environment with specific illustrations provided by Company 1.

Stage I: Reorganizing the Company Toward IMC Strategy

In addition to the productivity enhancements realized through the company's restructuring, Company 1 had also identified marketing opportunities to pursue. Several members of the sales force had suggested greater levels of cross-selling or **up-selling** across the different business lines within the company. The completely decentralized structure had prevented this from occurring.

Company 1 addressed the **cross-selling** or up-selling opportunities by strategically repositioning its corporate identity as a total solutions provider across client and product categories. To be recognized and accepted in its competitive marketplace, Company 1 would have to communicate and demonstrate this capability. If successful, the niche competition would be less likely to capture any of the company's market share. The key to achieving these goals would be communication to various stakeholders with consistent branding messages.

The communication channels would be through the company's sales force, marketing brochures, and Web presence. The launch of the IMC campaign was the announcement of the new company logo that incorporated interlocking graphics representing a full service provider for its clients (the interlocking graphics also implied partnering with customers).

...mal assessment, Company 1 began to focus on its online presence. The benchmarking and customer interviews concluded that it was a communication channel that would be a differentiating factor for them. By understanding the environment and the buyers, Company 1 was in a position to influence the marketplace through an effective Web site.

Stage III: Brand Decision-Making

There are three subcategories within the **brand decision-making** stage. They are strategic, tactical, and evaluative. From this stage forward, Company 1 would focus on its electronic presence.

The strategic direction relied on identifying and targeting the communications to the various stakeholders. Internet technologies facilitate the accuracy and timeliness of the targeting. The objectives were to build sales through cross-selling and up-selling of products across industries; further enhance the customer's relationship with the firm; and counter any competitor's efforts to steal market share during the restructuring phase.

From the tactical perspective, the company's Web site would be designed to present its new organizational structure and provide electronic-based communications that reinforced its corporate strategy as a full-service, solutions provider. This message would be integrated across all the company's marketing communication channels to leverage the synergistic effect of the same message across multiple channels. The Web site would achieve the full service provider message by diagnostic, interactive tools that permit visitors to view a full array of the company's products to assist in fulfilling their needs.

The last subcategory, program evaluation, would be facilitated by the Internet. Through careful planning and identification of the communication outcomes, measures were identified and monitored online. This provided Company 1 with customer data for improvements or enhancements to the site.

Stage IV: Enhancing Brand Position Within the Marketplace

The above three stages, if successful, would enhance the company's brand position in the marketplace. Modifications are made based on information gathered by tracking and monitoring of online visitors' behaviors regarding the Web site's content and format.

Company 1 is in the early phases of implementation. Initial results are very promising. The new Web site was launched for one of the largest trade shows. Online behaviors have guided some site enhancements. The feedback from the sales force is very positive with constant requests for additional online features.

PRIMARY STAKEHOLDERS

Company 1 identified two primary stakeholder groups for its IMC strategy that would include the Web site as the integral channel: customers and investors.

Customers were selected because of the need to present the new brand image quickly. By promoting the site (primarily through the sales force and trade shows) to build traffic (visits), more customers would be able to experience the new Company 1 image. The online diagnostic tools are the first offered in the company's industries served. Other customer service functions will be added (order tracking, automatic inventory replacement) shortly to further solidify the full service provider brand or image.

Investors were considered an important online target audience as well. As it had for the customers, the company wanted to demonstrate its new image to investors through certain features on the site. The site contains an investment section that describes its financial performance. Investors are also able to monitor subsequent online strategies (for example, supply chain management) indicating productivity enhancements and lower cost of doing business.

Although not a primary stakeholder group initially, Company 1 has discovered its employees are another target audience. It is developing online resources for its employees. As expected, the restructuring from several independent businesses to two general market-driven product categories yielded some cultural transition issues. The Internet is a communication platform that will minimize many transition issues. This is because it is an objective communication channel that serves everyone in the same manner.

VALUE BUBBLE

The five stages of the value bubble (attracting, engaging, retaining, learning, and relating) have varying degrees of importance across the two primary stakeholders of the company's integrated marketing communications (Web-enabled) strategy.

Attracting

For the customers, the attraction to the Web site is primarily through the trade shows, marketing literature, and sales force. Company 1 will not have to invest to the extent many business-to-consumer sites do for traffic building or awareness. The site investment for the company's customers will be in the engaging, retaining, and learning phases of the value bubble. Once the customer visits the site and finds the full service provider brand or image, Company 1 must engage the customer (or potential customer) in specific, value-added interactions. The online design functions are the first phase for the site. Regular enhancements are necessary in order to retain customers' loyalty to the Web site, meaning they return frequently. Customer input is critical for deciding on the enhancements and the sequence in which they are introduced. The learning phase provides feedback on the engaging aspects of the site. Using metrics that track the time spent per Web site page, as well as the navigation flow, will allow Company 1 to revise its site as necessary to meet its communication goal. Through a registration, the company can gather other critical information on the online visitor. For example:

- Domestic or international location. The location assists in refining segmentation (as described above) and allows Company 1 to customize its site for the different preferences of domestic and international visitors.

The application of the value bubble phases is different for the investor stakeholder group. With this group, Company 1 will have to invest in building traffic to the site. Web site promotion (traditional and online), public relations coverage, bricks and mortar presence, and links from other, credible sites all contribute to someone being attracted to a site (Ilfeld and Winer 2001).

Attract Technologies

The technologies associated with attraction are those that catch the eye. A larger movement, even if the moving object is small, catches the eye over static objects (Tufte 1997). The site for Company 1 employed movement in two key areas. First, using Macromedia Flash, a very popular animation software, they created a "**logotoon.**" A logotoon is a form of animated cartoon where the company's logo animates to play a leading role. With the advent of improved Web animation, logotoons have come to be a method of morphing a company's logo into its strategic goals and mission. In this company's case, the logotoon had the following sequence. (Imagine a storyboard behind the planning.)

1. Two image outlines fade onto the screen.
2. The images rotate and then converge to show the company's logo.
3. An outline of the logo grows, and the solid logo shrinks and both fade.
4. The logo is replaced first by the animated phrase, "A World Leader in. . .," followed by list of products and services.
5. Next, four words—customized, creative, innovative, solutions—grow from the background forward to the screen and fade.
6. Finally, a succinct paragraph on the screen describes what the company does.

The entire logotoon takes no more than 15 seconds, but it draws the viewer's attention without creating a distraction by repeating itself. A very small Flash file—Shockwave Flash File Format (SWF)—does all the work using a minimum amount of bandwidth. **SWF files** are very small binary files compressed from Flash source code files (FLA). The logotoon is in the lower-left quadrant of the screen, taking up no

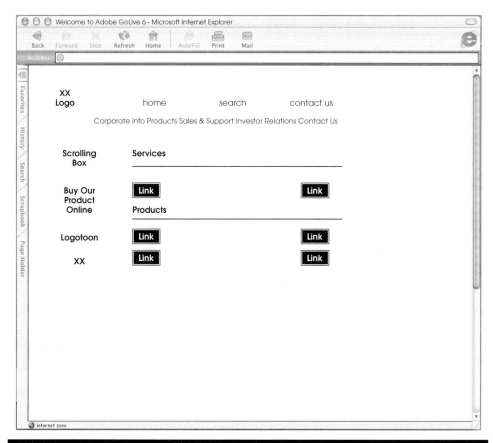

FIGURE 5-3   Company 1 General Home Page Layout

more than 15 percent of the Web page. Figure 5-3 shows the general outline of the page and where the key components are placed:

A second animated feature is situated immediately above the logotoon separated by a simple, static "buy our product online" message. The scroll box is reminiscent of a news ribbon using a vertical instead of a horizontal scroll. This area can be easily updated by changing the text to be associated with a **Java applet** that generated the ongoing scroll. A Java applet is a compiled program written in a language—Java—developed for the Internet. It can be embedded in an HTML page and executed from the user's browser. Like the SWF file, the Java applet is very small and can use text embedded in the HTML page. This arrangement makes it easy to put in changes to what will appear in the scroll box.

The scrolling text stops as each little company news item appears and then continues its scrolling after about three seconds—just enough time to read the little item. Java has the ability to make very fine and precise animated objects. The beauty of Java's use in this site is that it allows the Web designer, or even someone in marketing with a few instructions, to easily update what appears in the scroll window.

Both the logotoon and the scrolling text take up no more than a quarter of the page. However, their movement pulls the viewer's eye to the moving portion of the page. Larger movements on a Web page always pull the eye away from static objects or smaller movements (Tufte 1997), but they need to be used judiciously because they can be distractions. Company 1 avoids this dilemma in two ways. First, the logotoon is

... ... know that the site is loading.

Engaging

Once the visitor has entered the site, the engaging, retaining, and learning features of the bubble are important. To engage the customer stakeholder, Company 1 launched the first online design studio in its industry. The studio allowed the online customer to configure a customized product. This "blueprint" or plan was electronically sent to the Company's production staff, and a dialogue began between the customer and company for manufacturing the customized design.

The investor visiting this company's site can be an existing investor, potential investor, or a third party recommending investments. There are many successful investment sites that Company 1 can monitor for those effective interactive tools for engaging the visitor. Primarily, the investor wants easy-to-use navigation with current, accurate financial performance information. Financial calculators, expert commentary (text, audio, and video), press releases, and chat sessions have been identified (Albert) as interactive tools to achieve engagement.

Engage Technologies

Every Web page has generic characteristics to engage the user. The most common of these technologies is the link. Besides the double menu bars (see Figure 5-3), the Company 1 site has several link buttons. Beyond the home page, the viewer is engaged by some very interesting, but limited, selections from drop-down menus. Using **JavaScript,** a series of drop-down menus asks users, to specify what they want. JavaScript programs are written in an HTML page, and interpreted along with the HTML tags by the browser. JavaScript is not compiled and is easier to use with HTML than more sophisticated languages like Java. After going through a series of menus, the page "calculates" an outcome on a separate page. All of the data gathered by the selections in the pull-down menus and compiled using JavaScript and a new page appear with the results.

However, the way the script was written, it failed when used with Netscape Navigator. Although browser selection is a personal choice, we will not address issues of browser preferences. However, any e-business that fails to have **cross-browser compatibility** for a site might as well write off a major portion of a business. If JavaScript is used, the site should either have a browser-detection subroutine that will have a dual set of scripts so that both major browsers (Microsoft Internet Explorer and Netscape

Navigator) see essentially the same page or choose those elements of JavaScript that are cross-browser compatible. Fortunately, both browsers are coming around and adhering to the World Wide Web Consortium (W3C) and European Computer Manufacturers Association (ECMA) standards, and by version six, both browsers were very close to W3C standards and compatibility.

Different front-ends, such as Flash, can have far better cross-browser compatibility. Because Flash uses a plug-in that both major browsers include in their default configurations, the issue of using plug-ins is not the problem it once was. Most developers see Flash as essentially an animation tool and overlook the use of Flash as a cross-browser alternative to JavaScript. Flash's language, ActionScript, is very close in structure to JavaScript, and may find a larger role in serving as an engaging software front-end for an e-business site.

However, there is no excuse for having a key portion of an e-business Web site fail because it lacks either cross-browser or cross-platform compatibility. If an alternative is not available in developing an engaging site module, all involved in the Web site development should rethink what the nature of the engagement element of the site should be. When a portion of an e-business site fails, return visits are unlikely, and the work in attracting users to the site is undone.

Retaining

Retention or site return visits may be achieved by enhancements of the interactive tools as well as targeted e-mail messages linking both the customer and investor stakeholders to the company's site. To maximize site retention for the customers, the online design studio was frequently upgraded with new configuration tools. Company 1 would announce these through targeted e-mail messages and through their alliances with various trade associations. For the investors, Company 1 added new features and content specifically targeted to the investment community. They were announced through similar vehicles used for the customer stakeholder.

Retain Technologies

Retention, the "second date" between a potential customer and a business, is served in the structure and design of the site more than the technologies. Company 1 handles retention in several ways using the available technology.

The site is easily navigated and so the viewer does not come away with a frustrating experience of getting tangled up in a poorly organized site. The dual menu bars are extremely helpful. The top menu bar contains links for the following:

- home
- search
- contact us

No matter where the viewer goes in the site, the same home page with the company's logo stays at the top of the page. The home page is used as the entry and exit point. Wherever viewers find themselves, they can always click home to get back to the starting point.

The top menu bar contains a search engine to look in a database to find different products or services the company offers. An HTML form passes the search term to a back-end setup with a server called **ColdFusion.** Macromedia's ColdFusion works with a graphic interface to develop code very much like any other back-end such as the way PHP works with the Apache Server and ASP works with Microsoft NT Server. The difference is that the ColdFusion code is generated by a graphic interface rather than by hand coding as is typical with ASP and PHP. The ColdFusion middleware then accesses the database to see whether the search term matched.

... by the visitor. For the investor, this included the following:

- Existing or potential investor
- Third-party investor
- Specific information needs of the investor (aids in targeted e-mails announcing new features and content of the site)
- Characteristics of some of the company's investors (average investment dollars, length of time investment held, held singly or within a fund, and financial performance criteria for buying and selling the stock)

Company 1 focused on learning about its online customers through their use of the design studio. By examining which features of the studio the customer preferred and a pop-up survey that was presented at the end of that session, the company was provided with an evaluation of the studio. It would use this feedback for site upgrades and enhancements.

Internet technologies facilitate the data collection of the learning phase. It requires planning the type of data needed. Once collected, the communications can be targeted between the company and its stakeholders (in this instance, customers and investors). The increased level of knowledge allows the company to interact with these groups in the manner they prefer (i.e., meeting their needs and wants).

Learn Technology

The site uses several different forms, all run on a ColdFusion back-end, to learn about the customer. In the "Contact Us" link the site provides the following forms:

- Sales department
- Technical support
- General contact form
- Product information request form
- E-mail contact

The sales department shows a perfect example of microsegmentation. Each of the product and service areas is broken down into different links for both a toll-free number and a form on which the customer can fill in the particulars of her product or service needs. On the surface, each product information request form looks identical, but behind the scenes, the code identifies each request with a separate ID to the

ColdFusion server. In this way, the customer's product and service interests are sent to the correct sales representative. Included in the form are windows for the following:

- Products
- Name
- E-mail
- Job title
- Company
- Address
- City
- State and province
- Postal code
- Country
- Phone
- Comments

At the very bottom is a "Send Request" button that passes the information to the ColdFusion middleware and database.

The other forms—technical request, product information request, and general contact form—are all almost identical to the sales contact forms. The differences are found in the back-end software that makes microsegmentation categories for the records generated in the database. In fact, the only difference the viewer sees is that the contact form does not have a "Products" window where the viewer types in the products of interest. However, since the main purpose of the forms is to learn about the customer, very little need exists to have several different types of forms because the open-ended categories of both "Products" and "Comments" can be used to find out detailed interests of the customers.

Relating

The four preceding stages of the value bubble are critical for establishing the relationship with the online visitor. Unless the company is successful in relating back to the online stakeholder, the maximum effectiveness of this marketing model is lost. The relating stage acknowledges to stakeholders that the company understands their needs and how the company can assist in meeting those needs through its electronic storefront. In the relate phase, online visitors experience a more interactive exchange with the company.

For Company 1's online customers, the results of the survey and individual customer preferences for the features of the online design studio were used to upgrade the studio. By listening and acting upon this feedback, the company modified the studio and emailed its customers about the modifications. In one instance, Company 1 found some customers wanted to be able to archieve their designs and preferences rather than starting from "scratch" each time. The company developed a password-protected section of the studio for customers to store their designs.

The information gathered about the investors (in the learn phase) provided Company 1 with a valuable database. It designed customized electronic newsletters with the appropriate research for each investor. In addition, the executive suite of officers (CEO, COO, CFO) were available through discussion boards or chat sessions to discuss the financial health of the company with the investors.

Relate Technologies

The site's relate technologies are similar to those for the learn technologies. By having multiple types of contact technologies in the site and multiple points where contact can be made, viewers feel they can easily connect with the company. In the "Sales Contacts" section of the site, besides having the form, a toll-free number is provided

exactly who they need and can begin establishing the relationship between customer and company.

Probably the most ubiquitous of Internet technologies is the simple e-mail, and for relating to individual customers, it is still one of the best. Face-to-face and phone interaction are strong relationship-building blocks, but face-to-face encounters are expensive, hard to schedule, and often impossible, especially in a global market. Phone interaction is important, but the game of "telephone tag" exhausts both customer and business contact. On the other hand, an e-mail can contain all the information gathered by the learn technology. The delivered e-mail will wait until the client has time to read it, and both the business and its client have time to digest the information. The company's use of an e-mail option could be expanded a bit, and rather than using it as a last resort—using the online forms instead—it could be moved forward as a relate technology.

COLLECTING YOUR KNOWLEDGE: A REVIEW

Key Terms

- brand decision-making

- Cascading Style Sheet (CSS)
- ColdFusion
- cross selling
- cross-browser compatibility
- enterprise resource planning (ERP)
- ingredient manufacturing

- Java applet
- JavaScript
- logotoon
- original equipment manufacturer (OEM)
- SWF files

- SWOT analysis
- up-selling

Questions to Ask

1. What was the company's initial situation that led it to create an online presence? What was the nature of the company's structure and products before and after reorganization?
2. How was SWOT analysis used in developing a plan that led to a Web presence?

3. What elements of the value bubble did Company 1 use in its Internet strategy? What technologies were applied to that strategy?
4. What was the site's major shortcoming in using the technology for its site? What could have been done to remedy this problem?

Application to Business

What parallels exist between Company 1 and your company? Which of the Internet strategies used could your company use in those parallel areas?

With some exceptions, Company 1 made excellent use of Internet technologies. Which ones would be best suited for use in your company even if the products and services are different?

How could you improve on this company's Web site? What would you do to increase its market share?

Web Sites to Visit

www.godaddy.com Although this site has nothing but static images and text, it is well-organized and effectively attracts users with money-saving offers via e-mail. One strategy it uses is to offer domain names for $6.95 per year. (Domain names from registration companies go for between $20–$35 per year.) Using this lead-in, it offers web hosting for $9.95 per month, and then a trial Web site development tool for $14.95. Because small companies attempt to save money by creating their own Web sites, this service provides a low-cost Web entry into e-business. Other low-cost solutions are offered at this site as well.

In some respects this site looks like "brochureware," but its myriad of well-ordered and well-placed links provide the viewer with plenty of tempting spots to click in true HyperText fashion. The top menu bar contains all of the links that the richer compartmentalized offers below contain.

www.cysive.com Like the site described in this chapter, the Cysive site begins with a simple yet effective logotoon that brings the viewer's eye to the well-positioned logo in the upper-left corner of the screen. An ongoing Flash movie repeats its slogan, "solutions built without boundaries," showing different types of solutions associated with the company. Once off the home page, a clear set of link menus provide clear information to the user. It's a very clean business site and is enabled for both PDA and cell and digital phones with Wireless Application Protocol (WAP).

www.razorfish.com This is a very sophisticated site and an excellent example of microsegmentation. Its "Contact Us" link leads to five different forms, and provides contact information to 14 different cities where Razorfish has offices. Like the example company in this chapter, it too uses ColdFusion for its back-end. Its engaging design gives the user not only plenty to see but gizmos to click to find out more about the company.

6

ing and strategy development in a complex commodity industry. The company's executive officers identified the online world as an opportunity to address the continual pricing pressures for the steel it produced. The Company Overview presents a discussion about the pricing environment for steel.

COMPANY 2 OVERVIEW

Company 2 is a medium-size steel manufacturer. Its size places it in the category of a "minimill." The founder and original owner sold the company after its sixth year of operation to an international steel corporation. Four of the manufacturer's executives purchased the company in a leveraged buyout 9 years later. Their commitment was to focus on improving efficiencies, expanding the production of various customized steel products, and focusing on high-quality relationships and service. This management team was convinced that local ownership would permit those goals to be achieved.

Company 2 sells steel to **intermediaries** rather than the end user. Hence, its primary customer base is suppliers and distributors of the product. A secondary and smaller customer base is composed of companies that prefabricate some portion of the steel reinforcement for the end user (contractors, engineers, architects, etc.) (Figure 6-1). Company 2, as a **minimill,** limits its distribution to a relatively small trade area—that is, it will produce and ship its product within a predefined geographical radius of its plant. The shipment of goods outside of this predefined radius is cost-prohibitive.

Company 2 has a small number of minimill competitors. They are geographically within the company's trade area and are unable to maintain profitability if they ship outside of the area. For all of these companies, the greatest competition lies in the large steel manufacturers (domestic and international). Their size permits them the flexibility to ship to a significantly larger trade area—often intruding on the minimills. Minimills are forced to remain price-competitive and often differentiate themselves through enhanced service and relationship building.

Many complex commodity industries face similar pricing pressures. A brief overview of the steel industry and these pressures follows. It will facilitate an understanding of the decisions Company 2 made.

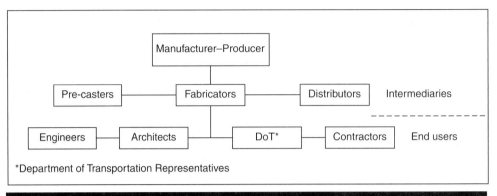

FIGURE 6-1   Company 2 Supply Chain

The last 11 years have been challenging for the steel industry as a whole. Although there was record product demand, prices (and profits) remained flat primarily due to an influx of supply from foreign markets. This record demand was attributed to the flat prices. Between 1995 and 1999, steel manufacturers' return on sales had been dramatically reduced.

In the commodity environment, the ability to raise prices is very limited. It can erode the manufacturers' customer base almost immediately. Thus, steel manufacturers had limited choices on how to improve their return on sales. Many of them invested in new technology that automated much of their production. This resulted in reduced overhead. Other manufacturers chose to consolidate with others—often international manufacturers.

In 1998 the pricing situation was further exasperated. This was primarily due to the Asian currency crisis. The demand for Asian steel reduced dramatically; however, inventories were at pre–currency-crisis levels. This led to a huge influx of Asian-produced, commodity steel into the United States and Europe. In the United States, prices plummeted to almost 34 percent lower than the previous year. After considerable lobbying efforts, legislation was passed that prohibited the "**dumping**" of excess, international inventory at depressed prices.

This legislation triggered a commission and ultimately a report on the global steel trade. Excerpts from the Chairman of the American Institute for International Steel (AIIS), Horst Buelte, are presented below. These comments were made approximately 6 months after the passage of the legislation and provide a perspective on the competitive environment within the steel industry.

In July 2000, AIIS issued the following statement regarding the U.S. Department of Commerce's "Report to the President on Global Steel Trade: Structural Problems and Future Solutions."

> While there are some positive points made in the U.S. Department of Commerce report, unfortunately this latest of government studies on the steel industry again missed the opportunity to look more deeply into the real causes of the problems experienced by the U.S. industry, and instead follows the standard refrain, that its problems are always someone else's fault, i.e., its foreign competitors.

The U.S. steel industry will finally have to accept that in the end, it will be free trade and competition that will prevail in international steel trade. Unfortunately, this study misses a chance to make that most important point. For over 30 years protection and subsidies have kept the weaker U.S. steel companies and facilities alive at the expense of the stronger companies. We believe that after 30 years in the protection racket, it is time for the

foreign steel company of any consequence that has not been sued for dumping in the U.S. market over the last two decades, even our NAFTA partners in Canada and Mexico. . . .

While the report is correct that the U.S. industry significantly improved its international competitiveness since the 1980s, the rest of the world has not been idle. Recent data provided by steel analysts suggest that the U.S. integrated steel industry still has the highest costs in the world. The challenge to the domestic steel industry to become internationally competitive, and not rely on protectionism, remains. . . .

The study is also correct in its analysis of the causes of the so-called steel crisis. The Asian financial crisis that brought increased imports of steel to the U.S. and reduced prices to steel customers spawned dozens of trade cases and ultimately, this study. What the study fails to point out in its analysis is that steel is not the only commodity that experienced lower prices, the prices of all metals and other internationally traded products declined during this period.

E-BUSINESS MARKETING GOAL OR STRATEGY

The company's executive officers (owners) elected to employ the Internet environment as a low-cost setting for selling its commodity products. The process would be to examine the key components of the industrial pricing model (Hutt & Speh 1998) and analyze the company's options. Some elements of the model would be less flexible for a **commodity-based product;** however, Company 2 thought it was imperative to strategize each of the steps. There would also be associated risk with being the pioneer rather than the follower for this e-commerce; yet, Company 2 felt the return outweighed the risk.

Company 2 is focusing on the e-commerce (the sale) aspect of the e-business components defined in Chapter 1. It is also focusing on the common marketing theme of providing valuable exchanges to its customers (this is defined within the customer relationship management [CRM] component of e-business). The value for the customers using the online ordering system is shortened delivery times and higher relationship pricing discounts.

The components of the **pricing decision process** are the following (Hutt and Speh 1998, p. 445):

1. Pricing objectives
2. Demand analysis
3. Cost analysis
4. Competitive analysis
5. Impact on firm's other products
6. Legal considerations

Company 2 recognized, as do most companies, that the pricing or cost component of the marketing mix is the only revenue-generating element. All other elements—product and customer solution, promotion and communication, and place and convenience—have their own associated costs.

The company's decisions within each of the pricing decision elements are presented below:

1. **Pricing objectives.** Company 2 evaluated the three possibilities: establishing and maintaining a predetermined net return on sales; increasing market share; or competing on price with its primary competitors. The company chose to increase market share because the cost of reaching new customers and retaining existing customers would be lower than traditional marketing efforts because of the Internet. It would then work towards maintaining its higher share levels.

2. **Demand analysis.** This is a multilevel process. It involves examining the marketplace and the company's product positioning within the context of pricing.

• Rather than focusing on the traditional pricing model of product cost plus desired markup, Company 2 took a different analytic approach to determining demand. It estimated potential demand, customers' price sensitivity, and what its potential profit might be across customer types or segments. For example, demand and sensitivity were higher among the large distributors than smaller suppliers who were more profitable on a per account basis; however, the large distributors' volume often compensated for their price sensitivity.

• Company 2 conducted a survey of its direct customers and end users to assess the product attributes that were perceived as most important. The survey indicated product quality, on-time delivery, and locally based service (Figure 6-2). These results provided objective data into their decision for how to communicate with existing and potential customers about their product's premiums and benefits. It also provided input into how to price the product as it entered the online environment.

3. **Cost analysis.** The determination of price for online sales was difficult. Company 2 would be a pioneer in this frontier—often, a risky role. The company could underprice all of its competitors because its cost per transaction would be reduced. Company 2 evaluated the cost determinants in terms of customer segments, quality needs, and product attributes (the survey data provided the analyses). The decision was to maintain the existing price for the online sales of their commodity product. However, additional premiums were available online. For example, Company 2 maintains a record of all sales (online and off-line) per customer. A rebate is provided once a company

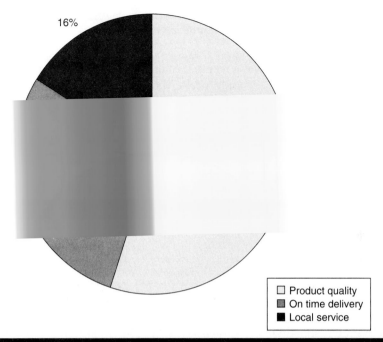

16%

☐ Product quality
☐ On time delivery
■ Local service

FIGURE 6-2   Customer Survey Results

achieves certain thresholds of purchases with Company 2. A company can visit their proprietary page to track their rebate status, order status, billing, and submit technical questions they may have to an assigned engineer (e-mail or phone—depending upon the customer's preference—answer is delivered on or before the next business day). Company 2 saw this as a long-term pricing strategy rather a short-term price war if it had merely lowered its prices online.

4. **Competitive analysis.** The company's competitive pricing strategy was to maintain existing prices with a financial loyalty program (rebates) and increased level of services (social and structural ties). This would disrupt the equilibrium of the commodity-based business at a greater level than a price reduction. Company 2 created a position of strength for itself because the premiums and benefits or services offered would take longer to replicate than matching a price reduction. Competitors would experience lag time in implementing the technology for production efficiencies and developing internal databases that would communicate with the Web site for e-commerce activities.

5. **Impact on other products.** The company's other product lines, similar to its competition's, were customized steel reinforcement goods. The steel products are manufactured on a per-order basis only, rather than produced for inventory and expected sales based on seasonal trends. For Company 2, the technological innovations employed for the e-commerce Web site assisted in production efficiencies for the customized business. Long-term, the company expects that customized sales will be generated from the Web site. At this point no consideration has been given to selling the customized

product, but future Web site enhancements will include technical libraries to inform customers about customized steel reinforcement products.

6. **Legal considerations.** The company's e-commerce efforts were led by an executive team. Corporate counsel was a member of the team. Legal implications were evaluated throughout the pricing decision process. The tracking, monitoring, and accessibility of customer information were protected through secured servers, user ids, and passwords. Company 2 instituted a regular checking system to ensure that this sensitive information was kept confidential. The financial, social, and structural programs for generating rebates and ultimately building customer loyalty (online and off-line) were within the legal requirements of the **Robinson-Patman Act** (Ritterskamp and Hancock 1993). The legislation requires well-documented policies and procedures that ensure price discrimination does not occur within commodity industries. The company's legal counsel developed and monitored those procedures.

PRIMARY STAKEHOLDERS

Company 2 carefully evaluated its e-business marketing goals and objectives. Because the company's focus is on the pricing component of the marketing mix and the e-commerce aspect of e-business, its primary focus will be on the customer stakeholder groups (current and potential). As a privately held company, the investor group is not as critical as if Company 2 were a publicly held company. Employees and suppliers are under consideration for future enhancements or different sites dedicated to their specific needs.

VALUE BUBBLE

In the business-to-business, commodity industrial environment, Company 2 is a pioneer with its site and the focus on pricing strategies enabled by the electronic environment. Thus, the company must evolve through each of the five value bubble stages (attracting, engaging, retaining, learning, and relating) to ensure it maximizes the e-business marketing opportunities.

Value Bubble Technologies
The company's Web site suffers from a poor use of code and graphics. The design exemplifies "**brochure-ware,**" and although it has good graphic design in the arrangement and proportions of materials on the page as well as colors, it suffers from a poor understanding of what graphics on the Web will look like. Figure 6-3 shows the general outline of the Web site.

Attracting
Company 2, similar to many other business-to-business settings, does not have a high volume of existing customers and its overall potential customer base is relatively known. This is because of the geographical trade area that it operates within and a known number of distributors and suppliers within that area. Therefore, the company's

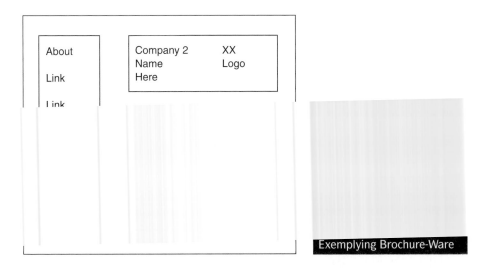

Exemplying Brochure-Ware

marketing budget was small and, as most steel manufacturers have traditionally operated, the marketing communication (promotion) is delegated to the sales force.[1]

The company will experience lower transaction costs as its e-commerce activities increase over time. These internal savings will fund the promotion of the Web site and future enhancements. Capitalizing on the research from Ilfeld and Weiner (2001), site visits are generated by online and off-line advertising; awareness as also defined by public relations' efforts, and bricks and mortar (traditional) setting; and links. Company 2 selected links and off-line advertising to focus on for the attracting phase of the bubble. The company has a strong bricks and mortar presence (manufacturing plant) although it was reluctant to conduct online advertising until the company could gauge the initial competitive response.

Off-line advertising included targeted, direct marketing programs to existing customers and targeted, trade journal advertising to reach potential customers (journals were selected based on their audience and ability to segment ads based upon geographical location of recipient). Links were established with well-known and highly credible trade organizations in the industry. Because Company 2 was a member of these organizations, a strategic alliance was developed between the two entities. Company 2 provided a link to the trade organization and the trade organization reciprocated. This relationship involved no cost between the two partners.

The Web site address was incorporated on all of the company's existing technical information materials. For example, technical documents that assist buyers in selecting certain gauges of commodity reinforcement include the site address. Every member of the sales force had company cards that included the site address. To reduce potential channel conflict between the sales force and the Web site e-commerce capabilities,

---

[1]For additional reading, see Schorsch, L. L., "You Can Market Steel," *The McKinsey Quarterly 1,* (1994): 111–120.

Company 2 expanded its relationship incentive plan to include existing customers' purchases on the site. New customers, first-time buyers generated by the site, were assigned to a salesperson based on their geographical location (consistent with existing policies).

Attract Technologies

In looking at the underlying technologies used in this site, the Web designer relied on standard graphic design and graphic design software used with paper, and the results show. On the home page, the site designer used graphics for the lettering of both the company name and "Quality" slogans. The logo is also done in standard graphics. Generally, designers attempt to avoid the problem of using an interesting display font as text in the Web site that is not typically found in a viewer's font set. For example, Copperplate is a popular designer font, but unlikely to be on most viewers' computers. Therefore, to make sure that the font appears the way the designer wants it to appear, especially if the font is part of the company's branding, a graphic display of the font is employed.

However, the designer did not use **antialiasing** in either the logo or other graphic text on the home page. Antialiasing is the process of reducing the "jagginess" on the edges by blurring them. When the antialiasing is not used, the result is that the viewer sees jagged edges. David Siegel (1997) said that this is one of the most basic errors in trying to create an attractive Web page. Most, if not all, graphic programs have antialiasing built into their software so that when graphic text is prepared for the Web, the fonts appear to be smooth and unremarkable to the viewer.

Likewise, the designer failed to incorporate antialiasing in the logo. A series of circles are used in the logo, and it is an attractive one that nicely associates with the company's product line. However, with all of the curves in the logo, the absence of antialiasing further detracts from the attractiveness of the site. Because the company's identity is tied into its logo, the jagged components of the logo make the company look shoddy and third-rate.

The final graphic component on the site that demonstrates the designer's lack of understanding of Web graphics is the set of graphic link buttons that make up the menu on the left side of the screen. Using white lettering on a red background for the menu buttons makes them appear to have "goose bumps." The bumpy appearance is usually a result of reducing a GIF file to a point where the colors are compromised, displaying further evidence of the designer's lack of knowledge of how graphics appear on a Web page. The designer could have used a table, given it a red background, and either used standard or antialiased font for the links. That would have used less bandwidth and removed the goose bumps from the main menu's background. Instead, the design makes the home page look less attractive.

The designer's lack of Web design knowledge does not imply that good design evolves from technology. Rather, good Web design is more than adding graphic design to a Web page. In paper-based designs, good designers must have some understanding of printing technology, how different papers show color, and how to mix colors. By the same token, Web page designers need to understand not only the fundamentals of design but also the design tools for the Web and how to create designs with a low bandwidth.

Engaging

Even though not evident in its current configuration, the plan for the site is to engage visitors through an easy to navigate and easy to use process. It will be designed to complete the sale in three clicks or less (this can be achieved once the registration form is on file—it contains the necessary billing information to conclude the sale).

Engage Technologies

An engaging site is easy to navigate, makes it easy for the customer to find what he wants, and gives the viewer an active role. Very little in this site's current state engages the viewer. Once the site has the planned "three-click" order form, it will be far more engaging.

The one technology used for engaging the viewer is a "library." A list of case histories is made available in **portable document format (PDF) files** for the viewer to either read online or download. PDF files contain fully formatted pages so that looking at a PDF file is like reading a magazine article. In some respects, PDF files are the ultimate **brochure-ware,** but used well, as Company 2 does in its site, they are excellent for engaging the reader in some activity. (Admittedly, reading a file that looks like a magazine article is somewhat of a passive activity, but the user can choose from several articles and find what she wants from the online library.)

Another engaging feature of the site is a set of conversion charts that let the potential customer view different product configurations. The customer can look at a set of figures providing different styles of steel reinforcement. It is a fairly passive engagement, but it gives the viewer some information. Had the site designer included a simple online calculator written in JavaScript, the viewer would be far more engaged in seeking and getting the information required.

Retaining

The retention or return customer is critical to maximizing the value of the company's e-commerce site. Upon reaching the Web site, a returning visitor is greeted by name and a review of recent purchases (this is allowed if the customer agreed when the registration form was filled out on a previous visit). Based on the customer's online purchasing activity and information provided at registration, the site can provide online technical documentation that is appropriate to the type of projects they are primarily engaged in (public transportation, commercial, residential, etc.). Company 2 has one advantage in the retention phase of the bubble. Because companies are placing orders

---

[2] Customer service initially was available during "normal" business hours (this is being monitored for requested activity levels during nonbusiness hours).

and can track the status and delivery of their orders online, they are motivated to return. Yet Company 2 did not want to stop there. The company saw value in implementing enhanced services (on a quarterly basis) to generate higher return visits. These services were announced through targeted e-mails and advertised on the company site. The services Company 2 offered were selected based upon customers' preferences noted on the survey conducted during the demand analysis step of the pricing process. By recognizing the needs and wants of its customer base, Company 2 developed a frequent schedule for enhancements. Most of the services were technical-information–based, in addition to case studies and opportunities for communication with other online users (building a community or network to discuss issues).

Retain Technologies

In its current state, the site does almost nothing to retain the potential customer. A poorly organized navigation system does little to encourage the customer to return. When the customer clicks on one of the products, he is given what appears to be randomly different outcomes. For example, when the viewer clicks on "Reinforcement Products" from the main menu, she is shown a jagged graphic of the product with a slow load time, and five further links. When she clicks on "Wire Rod," she sees a mill schedule. No intuitive navigation was to be found anywhere in the site.

Even the link names were confusing. To find a sales representative, the user either happens to find a product that has a submenu that leads to the name of a sales representative, including name, phone, and e-mail link, or happens to click on "Who's Who" in the main menu. No link has a "sales" label to give the viewer a better clue how to contact sales. The "Contact Us" link on the main menu has telephone numbers only and no further link to sales—not even a single e-mail address. The "Contact Us" page has a "get a map" link to www.mapquest.com so that if the viewer wants to drive to the company for more information, he can do so. Given the short range of the company's business, having an **online map** available to clients is an excellent use of Web technology not evident in the rest of the site.

Learning

Company 2 evaluated and decided on a pricing strategy, implemented through its Web site, based on customer input (traditional survey administered on the telephone). The Internet presence now extends the ability to learn about customers behaviors, attitudes, and preferences in a more time-efficient manner than a traditional survey by leveraging technology. The planned site will include a pop-up survey for gathering satisfaction from online users and requesting suggestions for future enhancements. Likewise, online behaviors will be tracked through clickstream patterns and log files. This will provide the company with feedback about the navigation and ease of use dimensions of the site.

The company also gathers internal data for its production cycles. Over time, the online orders (in conjunction with the off-line orders) provide data for developing manufacturing schedules that are seasonal or geographic in terms of their variations of product demand. Company 2 is also examining the online buyer compared to the off-line buyer to determine any characteristics that differ (geographical, types of projects, information needs, etc.). This will assist in its future marketing strategies.

Learn Technology

Like the rest of the current site, no forms or clickstream technology have been incorporated to learn about the customer. With its current configuration, the only hope of learning about the customer online relies on him finding an e-mail link and sending an e-mail to someone at the company who will use the information. However, the whole

...planned site. The collection and analysis of online survey data also will permit the company to address the ongoing needs and wants of its customers. By combining the off-line and the online customer databases, Company 2 will have a powerful tool for communicating with its customers in a personalized way. Personalized communication leads to stronger relationships between a company and its customer. This is particularly critical in the commodity industries where customer loyalty is typically low. Internet-based technologies are a powerful competitive asset for the companies that structure their online learning and relating to capitalize on this asset.

Relate Technologies

As noted above, about the only linking technology in the site is e-mail. A good sales representative who is contacted by e-mail may respond to the online customer in a positive and effective manner, but developing a relationship between a company and a customer should not rely on a haphazard connection between an individual in the company and the client. By having information about the customer in a database that could be accessed by the different departments in Company 2, no matter who contacted the customer, including a replacement sales representative, any company member would be able to make the connection. The planned questionnaire and clickstream technology to be added to the site need to be worked into a database so that a broader relationship with the client is possible.

COLLECTING YOUR KNOWLEDGE: A REVIEW

Key Terms

- antialiasing
- brochure-ware
- commodity-based product
- competitive analysis
- cost analysis
- demand analysis
- dumping
- intermediaries
- legal considerations
- minimill
- online map
- PDF file
- pricing decision process
- pricing objectives
- Robinson-Patman Act

Questions to Ask

1. What events led Company 2 to make the changes it did?
2. By minimizing the number of steps a client has to engage in to make a purchase, how is such a strategy engaging and retaining?

3. What elements of the value bubble did Company 2 fail to use in its Internet strategy? What technologies could have been applied? (Consider what Company 1 did with its Web site [Chapter 5] and compare it with what Company 2 did.)
4. With a limited geographical market range, what is the main purpose of setting up an e-business site?

Application to Business

Compare your company's Web site with the one described in this chapter. Is it merely brochure-ware or does it use dynamic features available on the Web to attract and keep a user's interest?

Is part of your company commodity-based? If so, what can be learned from the commodity-based plans of Company 2?

Suppose you have found a talented graphic artist who knows how to put together great-looking drawings on the Web. What and who else would you need to put together an effective Web site?

Web Sites to Visit

www.bethsteel.com The largest U.S. steel manufacturer's site uses all of the Web technology most effectively. The key element in this site is the focus on customers. At the very top of the main menu along the left side of the home page are nine customer links. (Ironically, the menu uses the white on red combination that Company 2 gummed up with goose-bump graphics.) It also makes excellent use of cascading style sheets (CSS) so that the designer did not have to use as many graphics with the associated load weight. In fact, the site exemplifies all of the steps in the value bubble.

www.usx.com/corp/ussteel/ecommerce/index.htm Getting to U.S. Steel's (USS) e-business portal is not exactly intuitive (and it should be), but once there, the viewer is treated to a history of e-commerce at USS and its "Steel Track" online program. In this largely B2B environment, a sophisticated tracking system allows customers to see where their orders are at any given time. However, you will notice that much of the page is about USS and not about its customers as is the case for Bethlehem Steel (see **www.bethsteel.com**).

www.foulds2000.freeserve.co.uk The meaning of "engagement" can be found at this experimental site. The site design engages the user at every step from the opening page to the last example the Web designer provides. It's one of those sites that has to be seen to be appreciated. This site is the exact opposite of brochure-ware and its material; although offbeat and demonstrative, it could add some very interesting and practical innovations for communicating with customers.

CASE STU

...large and diverse global corporation. Unlike the first two companies examined, Company 3 struggles with corporate missions that may not specifically represent its primary line of business. Second, Company 3 is currently below its expected market share levels and is, therefore, a potential divestment target for its corporation. Lastly, Company 3 elected to address its issues with a thoughtful, proactive, long-term planning perspective rather than a quick, short-term "fix-it" process. The company's e-business marketing goal is only one program formulated based upon this market-oriented strategic planning process. Summarization of the process and its outcomes are contained in this case as they apply to the company's e-business marketing decisions.

COMPANY OVERVIEW

Company 3 is a distributor for specialty hardware products. It has been in operation over 70 years. The company's distribution channel is composed of local outlets that are managed and staffed by local residents. This allows Company 3 to differentiate itself as a company interested in the communities it serves, which is in contrast to its competitors that have a less localized or neighborhood type of presence. Most of the Company's main competitors have shifted their sales channel to catalog and telephone sales with the first phases of their electronic storefronts (Internet-enabled) already operating. At this point in time, Company 3 continued to rely exclusively on personal, face-to-face selling. The cost of this sales distribution system continues to increase and impacts the firm's profitability. In addition, as competitors switched sales channels, Company 3 invested heavily in marketing campaigns to capture new customers. This campaign failed because the competitors promised ongoing quality service with dependable delivery of goods. It was unfortunate for Company 3 that its competitors delivered on their promises. In addition, one competitor began an aggressive referral program for its existing customers who referred new business. The positive word-of-mouth on this campaign not only increased the competitor's market share (from the two other large competitors), but Company 3 saw its market share decline.

The combination of the expensive physical distribution system (local stores staffed by local residents) and a competitor's successful new business marketing campaign sent warning signals to the company's corporate headquarters. The corporate management

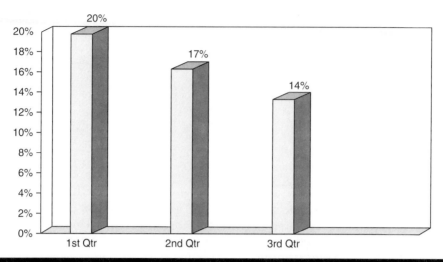

FIGURE 7-1   Company 3's Market Share

objective was to divest or sell strategic business units when their share was reduced by 10 percent during any fiscal year. The company's share (across product lines) had declined by 6 percent in the first three quarters (Figure 7-1). The company knew it had to rethink its current business practices without jeopardizing further share loss. Because Company 3 was very close to the target level for divestment, the president elected to meet with the chief executive officer (CEO) and chief financial officer (CFO) of the corporation. He wanted to present his plan for remaining a viable (profitable) SBU of the corporation.

The corporation had managed its strategic business units' objectives by using the General Electric market attractiveness **business strength matrix.** Company 3 had excelled over the years by carefully selecting the markets it entered with its hardware product array. It had been successful introducing new products based on customers' needs and wants. These products had continued to fuel profitability above expectations. The company's successful distribution strategy of local outlets managed and operated by local residents created customer loyalty that seemed unstoppable. Unfortunately for Company 3, one of its main competitors was quietly evolving a new distribution strategy. Short-term, the competitor's move toward catalog and telephone sales (after closing many of its local stores) seemed to help Company 3. Long-term, it became evident that the competitor had transitioned into a sales channel that met, and often exceeded, customers' expectations. By using the lower cost, direct sales channels (catalog and telephone), customers could order during nonbusiness hours. Company 3 could only service its customers during the local store hours. Company 3 strongly believed that its store employees provided more personalized service and technical support than a catalog or phone sale. However, the competition had addressed that through telephone customer support available 24 hours/7 days a week. The company's position on the General Electric model had shifted from strong business strength and high market attractiveness (protect position quadrant) to weak business strength and high market attractiveness (build selectively quadrant).

The president of Company 3 reviewed the unforeseen transition of his company through the GE Model during his meeting with the CEO and CFO. He was certain that a thorough market-oriented strategic planning process was needed immediately. They agreed and supported his recommendation.

The first step in the planning process was for Company 3 to quantify the gap

ment and commercialization cycle for new products was 24 months (following idea generation, screening, concept testing, strategy development, and business analysis). The most effective strategy for Company 3 was the intensive growth option. Company 3 chose to focus on selling more products to existing customers (increasing revenues), luring previous customers back, and up-selling to existing customers while developing new markets for existing products (increasing market share and revenues).

Company 3 began its business strategic planning process understanding its goal of intensive growth. It followed the steps for an SBU strategic planning process. A brief summary for each step follows.

BUSINESS MISSION

Company 3 will leverage its existing products further in current markets and identify new or untapped markets for the purpose of becoming an innovative leader in providing high-quality hardware and exceptional customer service to its customers. The first step in the company's strategic planning process was to conduct a strengths, weaknesses, opportunities, and threats (SWOT) analysis. It is composed of an internal level of analysis (strengths and weaknesses) and an external level (opportunities and threats). This analysis leads to identification of the key factors for the company to focus on.

I. SWOT analysis

1. Opportunities and threats (external)—the company's greatest opportunity was its existing physical sales and distribution systems. None of the competition had the same depth as Company 3. The main threat to Company 3 was the successful new way of doing business that its primary competitors had adopted. Company 3 could not be the pioneer in this area.

2. Strengths and weaknesses (internal)—the company's greatest strengths were its brand equity and company reputation. The corporation had invested heavily in all

---

[1]Many companies examine future desired sales and current projected sales in their strategic-planning gap. Because the company's performance is measured by market share, its president chose to focus on that performance measurement.

SBU's brand awareness and equity. Other strengths were customer satisfaction, employee dedication, and product quality. The company's weaknesses were declining market share, customer attrition, lack of timely innovation (sales channels), and financial vulnerability.

II. From the SWOT analysis, an objective was established with goals. The overall objective was to recapture share as positioned in the business mission statement. The goals were to determine the market-oriented actions to achieve it.

- Goal 1. Develop and implement sales distribution and customer service that is no longer based solely on physical store presence. In order to determine customers' preferences, Company 3 did an extensive market study of its existing customers and potential customers.
- Goal 2. Improve market share by 12 percent over 18 months (following redefining current business practices).
- Goal 3. Develop technological innovations for sales and service that exceed the competition.
- Goal 4. Leverage the strength of the brand to announce and implement these new practices.
- Goal 5. Develop alliances with current physical store management to facilitate the changes.
- Goal 6. Identify and enter new markets for existing products (increasing revenue and sales).
- Goal 7. Increase sales to existing customers through new sales and services channels.

III. The strategic formulation was focused on differentiation. Although Company 3 would not be the pioneer or market leader, it was going to learn from the pioneer's mistakes and take full advantage of technological innovations just announced.

IV. Specific programs were formulated to address each of the seven goals. Each goal was, however, contingent upon a leveraging technology to increase the sales channels. The specific e-business marketing goal to support this transformation is discussed in the next section.

V. The implementation phase was designed to follow McKinsey's 7-S framework (Peters and Waterman 1982). The technological capabilities (hardware) would be key to achieving the overall objective. Employees of the local stores were critical to the new sales channel success. This required training of and support from the company's corporate staff.

VI. Feedback and control. The goals provide a definition of the measures for success of Company 2. The company must develop the measurement structure so that the technology-enabled environment, in combination with the company's traditional reporting systems, captures the right data for each goal.

E-BUSINESS MARKETING GOAL OR STRATEGY

The overall objective for Company 3 is to increase its market share and recapture its previous leadership position. It has, obviously, missed marketplace opportunities.

However, the planning process has provided the focus and guidance for Company 3 to achieve its objective. The Internet-enabled environment will be key to the e-business marketing strategies that are part of the overall goals.

Company 3 carefully evaluated each component of e-business and identified goals within each:

tive benchmarking system to determine the best practices for its entry into the electronic environment. The results (such as encryption) drove the decisions. To avoid missing opportunities in the future, Company 3 developed a scorecard of its Web site (and its features and functionality) and instituted a monthly comparison of the competition's ratings with its own. Business intelligence was also designed into the site through log file analysis, click stream behaviors, and registration information. This feedback provides guidance to Company 3 on Web site design changes, as well as defining both the "who" and "why" of its online customers.

3. *Customer relationship management (CRM).* This would be the most challenging goal for the company's online storefront. The competition had invested heavily in transitioning customers online and providing superior service. However, the competition had neglected to continually collect online behaviors and customer feedback. Therefore, Company 3 could provide services that would create and deepen online relationships with customers' current and future preferences. Company 3 set up network desktops at all of its local stores and trained the staff on the Web site's usage. Employees were given incentives to demonstrate the site to customers. Customers were encouraged to come to the store to place their electronic orders.

4. *Supply chain management (SCM).* The company developed a specific, proprietary, password-protected Web site for its suppliers. Suppliers now had access to the company's inventory levels and were authorized to replace stock when certain levels were reached. This improved the delivery time for stocked items and reduced the company's inventory costs. For customized products, customers or employees of the store would provide a drawing (computer-assisted drawing software) that would be sent directly to the appropriate manufacturer. Order fulfillment time for customized products was accelerated by 60 percent, and this reduced the company's accounts receivable collection times.

5. *Enterprise resource management (ERP).* Company 3 carefully evaluated its internal business processes to identify those that could be brought online. Human resource manuals were placed online with appropriate links to certain sections (avoiding employees printing out the entire manual). In addition, online question and answer capability with a human resources staff person was established. Employees could adjust benefit levels online (as permitted by the benefits package). Office supplies were also ordered online through established relationships with suppliers.

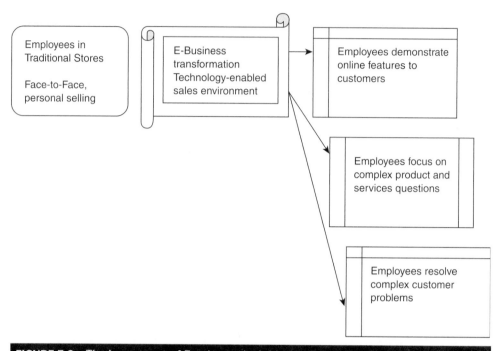

FIGURE 7-2   The Importance of Employees in Achieving E-Business Marketing Goals

This comprehensive, e-business marketing approach created an online strategy that Company 3 would carefully blend with its bricks and mortar sales channel.

PRIMARY STAKEHOLDERS

The targeted primary stakeholders for Company 3 were its customers (existing and potential) and employees. With customers, the company's goal was to create online transactions while building or deepening relationships. The employees were important conduits in achieving the e-business marketing goals. Figure 7-2 illustrates their role. Although suppliers were important to the company's overall e-business marketing success, initially they were not considered a primary target group.

VALUE BUBBLE

The value bubble stages selected to focus on were not exactly the same for the two targeted stakeholder groups. They differed only in the focus on the attraction phase for customers but not for employees.

Value Bubble Technologies

Company 3 made sophisticated use of the available Internet technology. Besides HTML, the company's page incorporated Cascading Style Sheets (CSS), JavaScript, **XML,** and **JavaServer Pages (JSP).** Extensible Markup Language (XML) is a language

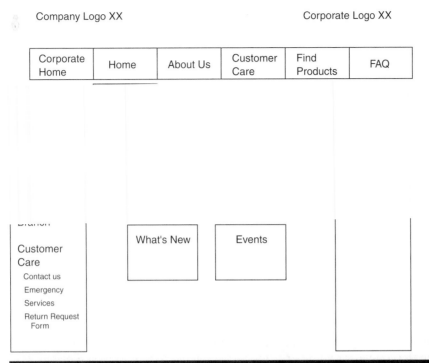

FIGURE 7-3 Company Home Page Design Showing Several Dynamic Components

for passing data between applications, and JSP is one alternative to Common Gateway Interface (CGI) and Microsoft's Active Server Pages (ASP). Sun Computer, a major competitor of Microsoft, developed Java, but many found that loading Java applets into a browser was somewhat time-consuming, and so developed **servlets.** Servlets are Java applets that run on servers, and JSP refers to the pages where they reside. However, JSP works in conjunction with HTML and can introduce new elements onto an HTML page. As an alternative to CGI and ASP programs, JSP servlets have the advantage of staying in memory once launched. For the customer, to whom all of this is invisible, it means that after the initial lag from a connection to a JSP servlet (a few seconds at most and certainly no more than a Perl file in a CGI page or an ASP page on a Microsoft NT Server), other connections to the same servlet are almost immediate.

Figure 7-3 shows the general outline of the home page.

Attracting

The attraction phase is important for customers because Company 3 is adding a new sales channel for their use. Company 3 chose to promote the site through four primary communication avenues. First, the company worked closely with the local stores. The in-store merchandising announced the site and suggested customers try their first online transactions in the store. A connected desktop PC was in close proximity to the merchandising. Employees were carefully trained to assist customers. Direct mail was the second approach. Company 3 had excellent customer information and developed a

TABLE 7-1	Company 3 Communication Avenues	
Communication Avenue	**Actions**
In-store	Merchandising and announcements of new online capabilities; in-store desktops and employees assisting customers (Figure 7-3)
Direct marketing	Direct mail to existing customers, prospects, and previous customers with customized promotions based on existing relationships and other purchasing characteristics
Trade journals	Advertisements and press releases about online capabilities; targeted journals based on geographical distribution and segmentation of subscribers
Sales promotions	Discounts provided to register with the Web site; used in direct mail, trade journals, and in-store

visually appealing announcement that was mailed to each customer. The company also bought targeted lists within its existing markets and the new markets that its analyses identified. Using customer profiles, the company selected potential customers in the new markets to receive its announcement. Third, all customers received a 15 percent discount on their next online order by registering on the site during their first purchase. Last, Company 3 advertised its site in trade journals covering its existing and new markets. Table 7-1 summarizes the communication avenues.

For the company's employees, the attraction phase was not as important. The types of employee services offered online were announced in a company newsletter. In order for employees to seek out certain information, they would have to use the employee Web site.

Attract Technologies

Initially, viewers are attracted to this site by elements external to the site itself. The home page has a number of attractions in the form of special offers and features. Moreover, the attractions to the site are random. On one visit, a graphic link with the promise of a free toy truck appeared and then on another visit a button with a virtual lighting center appeared but no toy truck. Other attractions are a "Hot Deals" button, the "Clearance Bin," and other tidbits to make the site more interesting than simply offering the same page objects with each visit. JavaScript generates the random appearances of different offers using a randomization function—a very simple built-in function.

For the most part the site does not attract with technology "sizzle," but rather with technology pushing information the customer is likely to need. Further, the site makes it very easy for the user to combine information about products, customer needs, and purchases. XML is a very efficient data organizing technology, and where client-side JavaScript cannot provide needed information, the scripts can quickly pluck the data from XML. Also, instead of having several pages appear and disappear, the same page stays on the screen, and the JSP technology replaces portions of the page with new information. However, the page does not use HTML frames. Instead, relying on JSP's ability to work with HTML, it replaces chunks of the same page, and so most of the "site" is actually a single page relying on the server-side technology and information bases to give the user what he wants without changing pages. The result is a very stable and appealing environment with a familiar menu of links always in front of the user, giving the viewer the maximum amount of information in a single eyespan (Tufte 1997).

Engaging

The engaging phase was a critical phase for the company's customers. A financial

~~~~~~~~~~~ ~~~~~~~~~~ phase was also important. If the site was not easy to navigate, it would cause employee morale problems and perhaps retention problems. The site was straightforward and simple to use. Company 3 built a prototype and conducted usability analysis with several groups of employees. Links were incorporated throughout the site (for easy navigation) and newsgroups and discussion boards were used for posting important shared documents.

Engage Technologies

The first engaging activity for the customer is to register. Whether or not filling out a form requiring minimal business information is much fun, the act of filling out a form is engaging. An HTML form and a verification script written in JavaScript go fairly quickly. A wide array of options is available for customers who register.

One of the most interesting and riveting components of the Web site is a virtual lighting center where the customer can design her own lighting in **virtual reality.** The viewer chooses one of the following options from a drop-down menu:

1. Retail Store
2. Office
3. Restaurant
4. Warehouse
5. Street Lighting
6. Classroom
7. Hotel Guest Room
8. Manufacturing Floor
9. Patient Area

The customer selects the type of room he wishes to light, and a photo of the room appears. Next, the customer selects from three columns representing different types of lighting—general, perimeter, and decorative. Under each of the three columns are four lighting styles. The customer then clicks a radio button for single or multiple choices of styles under one or more of the columns and clicks a "Light It" button. The selected room then lights up with the requested lighting. If the customer wants to compare different lighting combinations, all she needs to do is to click on a "Compare" button to bring up another room and lighting selections. Then the customer can see different lighting combinations side by side and see which one he likes the best. Just in

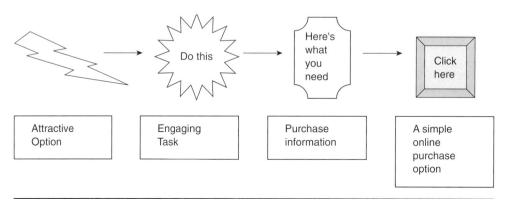

FIGURE 7-4   Ideal Use of Technology to Engage User

case the customer wants more information before making a purchase decision, the page has an option to create a 360-degree view of the room.

As soon as the selections are made, the products that make up the chosen lighting are presented in three rows with each row representing the different type of lighting categories. The product number and name provide the customer with a simple way of getting all of the information she needs to make an immediate purchase online. Not only has the engaging feature of the site involved the user, it leads the customer to the information needed for the purchase. The purchase decision is enhanced by letting the customer see what different lighting combinations look like in different business environments. All of this is done while engaging him in the site.

Perhaps the most interesting element of this particular engaging page is the simplicity of the technology. Other than the optional 360-degree view of the room, all of it was done with HTML and JavaScript. When a room is selected, the JavaScript simply creates a layer with the different images for the lit room. Once the lighting combination has been selected, JavaScript makes the image with the selected combination visible while the others remain invisible. To be sure, a very talented programmer did the code for the site, and the JavaScript for the page is extensive. However, the customer only sees what he should—a site that engages his interest and provides an interesting way to try out the product while the technology stays out of the way.

As an ideal use of technology to engage the viewer, the site accomplishes a seamless bridge between the user, the product, an engaging involvement in meeting customer needs, and a way to purchase the product online. Figure 7-4 illustrates this ideal condition.

Retaining

The retaining phase for customers was addressed by frequently adding new services and upgrading or enhancing existing ones. Company 3 carefully analyzed customer responses to the Web site's survey on satisfaction (a pop-up survey on the site). One question asked about future services and customer responses drove the company's selections. Company 3 sent out e-mail announcements promoting new services to existing online customers. This increased retention (return visits) as well. The in-store employees were also surveyed in order to gather face-to-face comments or suggestions to incorporate. To promote return visits from customers visiting the physical store, Company 3 continued its in-store merchandising to announce all of the site's enhancements.

For employees, a similar retaining strategy was used. In addition to an easy to use and navigate site, Company 3 solicited feedback from employees. The company added

a link on the home page explains how to use the site and the value in registering. Then a very thorough and clear set of explanations follows for logging on after registration (subsequent visits), finding products, and using all of the site's special features.

The registration process at the company's Web site is a bit troublesome, and it failed with the newest version of the major browsers. The registration itself is relatively short, and once registered, a new list of menus appears including these:

- My Catalog
- My Account

When the customer returns and logs on, her catalog and account, along with a welcome message naming the viewer and her company appears. However, because the company did not update the code for newer versions of the browser, occasional crashes occurred when the "My Catalog" account was accessed. Changing the software to accommodate newer versions of browsers must be planned in the Web site, not as an option but as an absolute necessity. No matter how well planned and executed an e-business site is, a plan must be in place for changes that inevitably occur—such as browser updates. In the same way that ranged marketing looks ahead to possible changes, the e-business needs to look ahead to changes in the technology and plan accordingly.

The other retain technologies used in the site included the randomized offers. Each time the user comes to the site, he can expect something new. A special offer, no matter how trivial, is always an important impetus to return to a site. Using the JavaScript's random selection of the "interest buttons" and a database regularly updated with clearance items, the site can remain fresh and interesting to regular customers who return to see what's new.

Another feature for retaining customers and helping them to locate products is what Company 3 named "iGuides." These interactive guides help the customer find what she was hoping to find and add to her shopping cart. With the items in the cart, the next step is to check out and purchase. To further retain the customer, an online credit line application is available using a PDF file so that it can be printed and mailed in. Alternatively, the program finds the nearest Company 3 outlet store based on the state and zip code entered during registration. If the customer does not care to go to the store or fill out a credit application, the site accepts credit cards. After determining the location of the company or individual making the purchase, the checkout process automatically determines whether tax should be applied to the total. In other words, the site makes it easy to purchase items and gives the customer several choices. It uses the technology available through HTML, JavaScript, XML, and the JavaServeet pages (JSP) to do the work for the customers so that the experience is informative and simple.

Learning

The learning phase for both targeted stakeholder groups was critical. Company 3 had developed measurement systems that were enabled by Internet technologies. Both online behaviors and demographic information were analyzed frequently. This provided a profile that Company 3 used for design modifications. The company also used it to customize the site's communication or promotional offerings for customers (based upon preferences and previous promotional behaviors). Since Company 3 had integrated its off-line and online customer information files, the customized communication reflected everything that was learned from the customer.

Learn Technology

The company used the log-on and account information from purchases to learn about customers. By entering information into the "My Catalog" module, the company was able to learn what most interested the customer. Likewise, when a purchase was made, the data from the purchase built up the information about the customer's needs. Unlike some of the other e-business sites that used clickstream technology, Company 3 used actual purchases and information supplied by the customer's actions in buying and not in what pages were viewed, as would be the case with clickstream technology. In addition, the customer provided account information that would be continually updated.

The advantage of the database storage of customer information on a company server over a cookie stored on the client's computer is that the database information is available only to the business and customer. With cookies, all the customer has to do to destroy any information the company has accumulated is to delete the cookie from her hard drive. All the information stored in the cookie file is lost when the cookie is deleted. An empty replacement cookie is automatically generated, but it is empty until the customer makes another visit. Finally, if the customer uses a log-in instead of automatic recognition by a cookie that is stored on the hard drive, the customer can log in from any computer and the same information that is used when logging in from the customer's primary computer is made available.

Relating

The relating phase for Company 3 provides an excellent example of how an integrated database can be an extremely helpful tool to provide exceptional communication with various stakeholders. This Company represents a very small percentage of companies fully maximizing these capabilities of technology. By combining all (off-line and online) customer contact information into one database, the company became "one voice" to the customer. Considering the strategic changes that the Company recently implemented, it was critical to its ongoing success to be unified. The return on the investment in integrating databases would easily outweigh its cost. This customer database allowed a store employee to monitor all the customer's purchases and, if the customer called the customer service number or sent an email inquiring about an issue, the store employee had a record of that interaction as well. This permitted store employees to speak with the customer as a representative of the Company as a

create a relationship between the company and customer. The ongoing updated account ("My Catalog") and welcome help forge a relationship between the company and customer. Purchasing lists make it easier to shop in future encounters because all of the items typically purchased are available for reorder.

Another technology the Web site can use represents a tie-in to the company's actual inventory and work flow. Company 3 has a handheld scanner that works with **personal digital assistant (PDA)** technology that can be used to create purchasing lists. The client company and its customers can use it to point to a bar code to enter and store a desired product. Then the scanned items in the PDA are placed in a special Company 3 cradle for uploading the scanned items and purchase quantity to the Web site for online purchasing.

Not only does Company 3 provide an inventory solution for its customers, it cements the relationship between the customer and company. Obviously the easily scanned products are not those of the competitor, and because the purchasing and inventory process are improved, the customer's operating costs are lowered and streamlined. Thus, the entire relationship between Company 3 and its customers makes the customer's business more profitable by reducing purchasing costs.

COLLECTING YOUR KNOWLEDGE: A REVIEW

Key Terms

- business strength matrix
- JavaServer Page (JSP)
- personal digital assistant (PDA)
- servlet
- strategic business unit (SBU)
- virtual reality
- XML

Questions to Ask

1. What set of circumstances led Company 3 to opt for an online solution to marketing?
2. How did the company's Web site use virtual reality to engage customers?
3. What elements of the value bubble did Company 2 fail to use in its Internet strategy? What technologies could have been applied? Compare the Company 1 and Company 2 Web sites.

4. How does the site created by Company 3 aid the customer from the outset? What does it do to help the customer find what he needs and make it easy to make an online purchase?
5. What are advantages of using customer-data stored on a company database instead of cookies located on the customer's computer?

Application to Business

Look at your company's Web site. Is any product or service available on your company's site that could be set up to give the customer a visual engagement with the product or service as Company 3 did with visual lighting?

If your company is an SBU or contains SBUs, what kind of relationship between the larger corporate enterprise could be integrated on a Web site? If your company has partnerships with other companies, which Web site elements could you use for mutual strengthening?

Go through your company's Web site with new and older browsers. See where the site fails and attempt to determine why. (If you cannot determine what caused the failure, ask someone in IT or MIS to explain why failure occurred.)

Web Sites to Visit

www.e-luminating.com This site is the online presence of a company that specializes in designing, hosting, promoting, and maintaining Web sites for lighting companies. It presents a customer-centered strategy for the viewer, and as a B2B site, the company has carved out the lighting industry as its niche market. The technology it employs in its site consists of JavaScript, CSS, and an interesting use of a *webbot*—a Web robot used for searching, checking, and verification. The site presents the company's online marketing strategy, and in it you will see several elements of the value bubble at work.

www.homedepot.com Home Depot's Web site provides a combination of online marketing and connecting the potential customer with nearby stores. One of the more engaging elements found on the site is a calculator to find out how much paint to buy for a project. The potential customer is asked to provide the dimensions of the room, and once that is done, the calculator tells the customer how much paint to purchase in gallons and pints for the ceilings, walls, molding, and doors. The site also contains several step-by-step how-to instructions for different projects to not only show site visitors how to carry out a project but also the different tools and other products required to complete the project—all sold at Home Depot. Most of the other components of the value bubble can be found here as well.

www.gm.com The General Motors Web site is interesting because it has so many SBUs. In addition to automobiles, it owns several nonautomotive SBUs, such as Direct TV. The organization of the site relative to its SBUs shows some connectivity, yet at the same time independence in design and function for the individual SBUs. Most of the sites have a link back to the main GM page, but once outside the more traditional offerings from GM (domestic autos), the sites are more independent in design and form. For example, the Saab, Vauxhall, and Direct TV sites have a different look and feel than the GM site.

CHAPTER

8

...ilities industry. The industry faces enormous challenges because of the transformation it faces. This transformation requires rethinking the industry's previous **monopolistic business model** and changing it based on three drivers of change:

Change Driver 1: Deregulation leads to competition and lower prices.
Change Driver 2: Technology leads to faster service and lower costs.
Change Driver 3: Globalization is necessary because companies need more customers to compete in the marketplace.

Company 4 is a case that addresses the second common theme within the marketing concept that extends into e-business (Chapter 1)—that is, marketing provides valuable exchanges between the stakeholders of a firm. This case will define these exchanges and the e-business marketing strategies for a transforming company.

COMPANY OVERVIEW

Company 4 is a 100-year-old utility company. Consistent with similar organization changes in the industry, it has become a **wholly-owned subsidiary** of a larger energy corporation serving a wider geographical area. Company 4 continues to operate under its own name within its local jurisdiction to maintain a local presence and its brand for customer retention purposes. The company has built and reinforced its brand based on its philosophy to leverage technological enhancements in the distribution of energy and increasing its operating productivity.

In keeping with the **technology-enabled philosophy**, the company's executive management was now evaluating its strategic options considering the three drivers of change and new competition that its industry faced. The company was particularly intrigued by a recent report that the chief marketing officer (CMO) brought to one of their strategic sessions. This report was from a comprehensive research study (including a **competitive benchmarking** and **best practices** analysis) conducted by Andersen Consulting on the utilities industry and its e-business strategies. At the end of 1999, the results had been released ("Most Utilities' Websites Lack Functionality Needed to Compete in the e-Economy").

The study initially warned utility companies that their e-business marketing was unimpressive. This was determined from an analysis of current utility companies' Web sites. The report noted that the majority of the sites lacked sophisticated features and functionality that would differentiate them. The CMO and chief information officer (CIO) at Company 4 agreed that the company's site was in this unsophisticated category. It was inconsistent with the branding that the company used in the traditional world. In addition, no services were offered to the online visitor—just company background and location. Company 4 knew that with deregulation now allowing customers to select their utility provider, companies were faced with numerous competitors and, perhaps, Company 4 could leverage its technology-focused philosophy to become more sophisticated online. Over time, the company may consider expanding into the global marketplace.

Company 4 was also interested in the savings that would result from expanding its online presence. The report said that the development of a sophisticated online presence would lower costs to the company. For example, online bill payment and its processing costs $0.60 per item while traditional payment processing (mailing a check, paying in person) costs $2.00 per item[1] (PriceWaterhouseCoopers 2000). These cost reductions also fulfilled the company's commitment to its customers that it leveraged technology to increase its productivity.

The report reminded the company that, as expected when a monopolistic industry faces competition for the first time, its response is to quickly focus on service and technology as its **competitive differentiation.** However, the Andersen report recommended a broader strategy. This included a focus on customer service to retain and build the customer base while reducing revenue loss. In addition, the utility companies needed to stop **brand erosion** and strengthen its brands (through exceptional service offerings). This would be the overall strategy of competitive differentiation.

Andersen's overall recommendation was that utility companies should develop Web-based models to build and insulate their brands from the competition. The lower cost associated with this strategy would offset some of the lower prices now necessary in order to compete. Company 4 embraced the overall recommendation.

The report provided a few successful Web-based models so that Company 4 could evaluate the best practices and develop its e-business marketing approaches based on what had been learned.

E-BUSINESS MARKETING GOAL OR STRATEGY

The company's executive committee made the general decision to pursue the overall recommendation from the Andersen report. Their next step was to identify the appropriate marketing model to implement in their online efforts.

The company's overall e-business marketing strategy was to become a solutions provider to its customers. It would use the technology-enabled Internet environment to provide premier customer service that was customized to the needs of each customer. The company would define its service strategy using the four-step model presented by Berry (1995). For Company 4 this strategy would lead to the goal of creating

---

[1]This does not include costs to print and mail the monthly statements.

a "branded customer experience"—meaning extraordinary customer service leading to customer loyalty (Stewart 1997). The company developed and implemented a plan to define its service strategy. The steps and results are presented below:

Step 1.   Determine the most important service attributes for meeting and exceeding

• Current and potential customers were surveyed. The survey questions asked about important customer service attributes for both the off-line and online environments. Company 4 knew that having consistent service offerings was critical to its branding efforts.

• Competitive benchmarking and best practices results were examined. The best practices online utility companies all had a traditional (physical, bricks and mortar) business, as well as an online business. Earlier research had indicated that online or virtual only upstarts would be the utility companies' greatest threat. However, those organizations did not survive (as observed in other industries with dot-com failures). For Company 4 this meant that its technology philosophy with a solutions provider branding strategy would compete with other traditional companies.

The results from both the employee focus groups and customer surveys were compared. There was considerable overlap or consistency. The most important service attributes were quick and efficient service for new or changing service (connect or disconnect); **electronic bill payment;** meter reading; setting up and tracking status of service appointments; and arranging monthly payments (fixed rate per month, budget billing, or flat fee billing; see Table 8-1). From the customer survey, one service recommendation appeared that was not mentioned by the employees. That was a **premium service category** for longtime customers (e.g., shorter wait time for service

TABLE 8-1   Comparison of Employee and Customer-Feedback Research Results

Electronic Service	*Employee Feedback (%)*	*Customer Feedback (%)*
New or changing service	37	40
Bill payment	20	17
Meter reading	18	15
Track service appointments	15	14
Monthly payment arrangements	10	14

appointments, longer payment cycle time—from 30 days to 32 days, etc.). This would be a reward program that would enhance the relationship between the company and the customer, further leading to loyalty (this is the e-business component of customer relationship management). By viewing the online best practices Web sites (business intelligence in the e-business definition), Company 4 was able to identify other opportunities not found in the employee or customer research (e.g., online sales or the e-commerce component of e-business). These results became the foundation for developing the online service offerings.

Step 2. Determine the important service attributes that make competitors the most vulnerable. Company 4 developed a scorecard of the attributes identified in Step 1. It created a list of competitors and began evaluating their online and off-line service offerings. Company 4 was particularly interested in identifying the gaps between the service promised and the service received. Whenever a gap was identified, Company 4 determined the source of the gap. In the traditional services marketing literature, gaps have been studied, and a conceptual model was presented by Parasuraman, Zeithaml, and Berry (1985) that focused on the design, marketing, and delivery of services. Recently, Zeithaml, Parasuraman, and Malhotra (2000) extended this model into the online world to include the design, marketing, and delivery of the Web site. The four gaps are these:

1. **Information gap:** service attributes that are company-centric and not customer-centric. This can be avoided with regular monitoring of the online customers' service preferences.

2. **Design gap:** Web site design that does not meet customer expectations. This is also minimized through monitoring of customer responses to Web site navigation and ease of use (downloading time, etc.).

3. **Communication gap:** the design of the Web site does not include or optimize the communication channel between the customer and the firm. This gap often occurs when the site design is the responsibility of the MIS department and the marketing department is either excluded or not fully involved.

4. **Fulfillment gap:** the Web site has operational deficiencies that prevent it from meeting the customer's online needs. This is observed more from the e-commerce sales activities; however, service-oriented companies must deliver the service promised.

The results from the scorecard analysis provided Company 4 with a clear set of opportunities based on its competitors' online service gaps. The company found that most sites had high gap values in information, design, and fulfillment. These gaps can be closed through a rigorous process of customer (existing and potential) monitoring. Company 4 had already begun this process in Step 1 of its service strategy development. Step 2 is the first step in designing an online sustainable competitive advantage (SCA). Steps 3 and 4 will complete the SCA development.

Step 3. Determine existing and potential service capabilities of the company. Assess service competencies and incompetencies, resource strengths and weaknesses, service reputation, belief systems, and "reason for being." Company 4 designed an internal assessment to measure its strengths and weaknesses, as well as its competencies and incompetencies. It captured its service reputation from both the customer-contact employees and customers (existing and potential). The company's belief systems and "reason for being" were clearly defined by its corporate tagline—"We are here to serve you." This portrayed the company's commitment to customer service, although it would now expand that commitment into the online environment.

The company's internal assessment found the following strengths and competen-

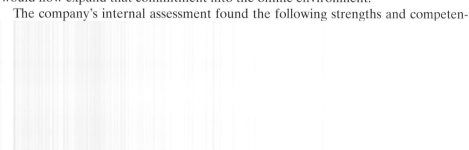

2. *Resource weaknesses*

- **Legacy computer system** (older mainframe computers running database management systems in which the organization has considerable time and money invested)
- Previous projects to migrate into more flexible database-driven architecture had failed
- IT department trained in legacy systems only

3. *Competencies*

- Ability to transition existing customer base into online service site (demographic, behavioral, and psychographic profiles indicate propensity to use technology)
- Full cooperation and support from customer-contact employees (as routine questions and requests migrated to the Web site, the employees would be able to spend more time with complex and difficult issues)

4. *Incompetencies*

- Inability to quickly reconcile the technological weaknesses in order to enter the online environment as soon as the company wanted

Step 4.   Develop a service strategy that addresses important, enduring customer needs; exploits competitor vulnerabilities; and fits the company's capabilities and potential.   Company 4 service strategy incorporated customers' (existing and potential) needs through solid market research and continuous monitoring to reduce service quality gaps. In addition to the research and monitoring, Company 4 would regularly conduct usability studies for the original site and subsequent upgrades or redesigns. This customer-centric (outside looking in), service-oriented approach will be a competitive advantage as other utility companies remained company-focused (inside looking out). Company 4 also has resources to promote the site and build traffic through its current marketing efforts. To address its technological weaknesses and incompetencies, Company 4 would outsource its customer interface to a well-established firm. This

TABLE 8-2   Company 4 Stakeholders and Web Benefits

Stakeholders	Strategy	Benefits
Customers	Online premium customer services	Convenience and efficiency
Suppliers	Online ordering and purchasing	Reduced paperwork and time efficiencies
Investors	Technologically enabled company	Confidence in company (willing to invest)
Employees	Online services and reduced internal costs	Convenience and efficiency

would allow the company to compete with other utilities' online presence without the delays that it would otherwise endure. However, Company 4 was only committed to outsourcing until it had the internal resources to operate its site.

Company 4 was now positioned to develop and announce its site. While the site was being designed, the company's executives strategized on how to maximize its potential.

PRIMARY STAKEHOLDERS

As noted from the case background and the service-oriented marketing strategy, the company's Web site was targeted toward the customer (existing and potential) stakeholder group. Company 4 has a long-term plan to increase the primary stakeholder groups. In the second phase of the site's plan, the suppliers will have their own section. This permits Company 4 to begin to convert its relationship with suppliers into an electronic environment. It will eliminate a tremendous amount of paperwork and support the company's increased productivity philosophy. Phase 3 of the site will have a section for investors only. Company 4 is evaluating the transformation of its routine internal processes into a Web-based environment. Pending the outcome of this evaluation, the company will decide when to address the employee stakeholder group. Table 8-2 summarizes the different stakeholders, the online strategies, and benefits.

VALUE BUBBLE

Deregulation has forced utility companies to recognize their customer base as an asset—to protect and leverage for additional sales and service opportunities. The most cost-effective and flexible environment to achieve this was the Internet-enabled, electronic storefront setting. The company's chief marketing and information officers worked closely with their staffs and the operations department to promote their new, service-oriented Web site. They focused on four of the five phases of the value bubble (Chapter 3): attraction, engaging, retaining, and learning. As Company 4 continued site upgrades and enhancements, the relating phase was increased.

Value Bubble Technologies
Company 4 used a wide array of technologies to solve specific problems. It did not appear to be married to any single back-end technology and used both JavaServer

pages and ColdFusion. In addition, it effectively used Cascading Style Sheets and JavaScript in the bulk of its pages. Flash technology was effectively employed in the introduction to the site, including animation and sound. Included in the site was marquee scripting to run a welcoming banner across the main page. The site also incorporated download links for both PDF and Microsoft Word files.

three links are included in the text— "Our Community", "I want Company 4's Product", and "Comments". Five links highlighted with colorful text and graphics run along the bottom portion of the main page. They include links to the following:

- About Company 4
- Customer Sales and Services
- Products, Technology, and Safety
- Marketer Services
- Architects and Engineers

On the right side of the main page is a detailed link menu. On the top of the menu are links to the following:

- Search
- Site Map
- Legal Notice
- Contact Us
- Important Links
- Shortcuts To Popular Pages

Below the top portion, which only takes up about 15 percent of the vertical menu bar, are the remaining links:

- Main Page
- About Company 4

    - History
    - Service Areas
    - Directions
    - Investor Information

- Community Center
- News Center
- Career Opportunities
- Local Weather
- Online Services
- My Account

Given the elaborate navigation menu, the site did not use available JSP technology or HTML frame sets to keep the menu on the screen while it loaded new pages into frames. Instead, each time a link is clicked in the menu or elsewhere on the page, an entire new page, including the menu, had to be fully reloaded. Thus, rather than having an unblinking menu and other standard page features appearing steadily on the screen, an entire new page replaces the current page. When the new page comes to the screen, the menu and other standard elements of the page appear exactly in the same location, but do so with a flicker or blink that gives the site a fractured and somewhat disconnected flow. The main menu on the right is context sensitive so that parts of it change depending where in the site it appears—requiring a new menu—but using a stable menu with drop-down selections would have allowed the same selection availability with less appearance of seeming instability.

Overall the use of and implementation of the technology in this site is uneven. It has excellent examples of implementing the value bubble in its use of the technology, but it also has technical breakdowns and unattended details in the site. In examining the specific features of the value bubble technology, both good and bad examples of site construction are evident. (Nothing about the relate technologies is included because they were not yet fully planned at the time of this writing.)

Figure 8-1 shows the general outline of the home page.

Attracting

For Company 4, this is critical for expanding its current customer base. As its existing customer base is technologically ready (reporting adoption of many current technology-based products and services), the company will utilize its existing communication

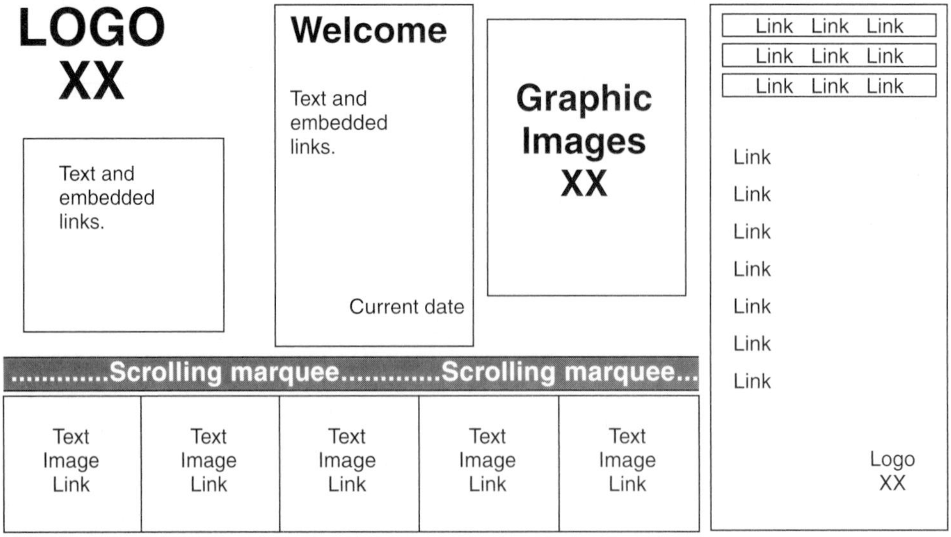

FIGURE 8-1   Company 4 Home Page Design Showing Graphic and Text Links in a Well-Organized, Redundant Navigation System

channels to promote the site. The monthly statement and any written form of communication will include an invitation to visit the site. All customers will receive a promotion code to enter upon an initial visit. This code will activate an e-mail response thanking them and asking for their feedback about the site.

Attracting potential customers (who likely are customers of other utility compa-

generating the "buzz" about a new site. Ilfeld and Weiner (2001) found that buzz generates traffic. In their research, buzz is defined by links, PR, and online and off-line advertising. This research result clearly supports the demise of the statement "Build it and they will come."

Attract Technologies

The attract technologies employed in the site itself are the introductory Flash movie, the generally good graphic design and photos, and consumer-related information. The opening Flash movie is a warm and welcoming one with the all-important "skip intro" link to give the viewer the option to forego seeing the intro movie. The skip intro cuts down on the time a viewer has to wait to get the main page loaded, and after viewing the Flash movie once or twice it is simply too long a wait until the information-rich site fully loads.

The Flash movie pumps the following sequence of animated messages accompanied by upbeat music and photos and graphics of "customer" and "employee" photos:

- A fresh look at what a utility should be
- Dynamic changes
- Improved services
- Better value
- Energy solutions

After the perky and upbeat introduction, the main page (home page) appears ready with a big "Welcome" graphic and a father and son playing on a teeter-totter. The first and main image is not at all related to the company's product or services but appears to be an ideal image of family fun and values. A set of links with images of the company's logo, services, and products ties in the family image of the "customer."

The viewer sees a repeat of the key messages in the Flash movie in the first paragraph of the welcoming text. Using Cascading Style Sheets, the links in the text are fairly subtle, highlighted in blue but not with the default underlined text of a link. As a result, the welcoming message does not have the chopped up and uneven appearance of sites that use the default parameters for links.

Engaging

For Company 4, it is necessary to monitor visitors' responses to the online services. The services were selected based on research results but, in the online world, people often change their minds when they initially use or navigate a site. Usability testing minimizes this but research indicates that self-reported preferences still change. To engage the online visitor and receive this feedback at the same time, the company will set up a visitor community section on the site. First-time visitors will be invited to join. The community section functions as an online focus group with announced, moderated session times. Participants who are the company's customers receive a discount on their utility bills. The community and focus groups will discuss the various services and functionality of the site. Results are compiled and reviewed daily with the CMO and CIO. Adjustments are made to the site. Other engaging strategies include the range of online services available, the site's ease of use, and the quick downloading times.

Engage Technologies

The technologies used to engage were in disarray when the site was examined. The site was not presented as an incomplete one or "**under construction**," but rather a fully operational one. As noted in discussing the company's strategy, Company 4 planned to set up a visitor community section. It did have two links to a community center that began as an HTML page, but the link failed repeatedly, and so the viewer never could get to either the engaging information or any technology. The one engaging link that was working, and a very good idea for engaging the viewer, was a link to the local weather. However, because the utility site did not use frames, as soon as the link to local weather is clicked, the viewer is out of the company site with nothing but the "back" key to reenter the company's site.

In looking at the code for the pages that were available, it was clear that Company 4 had not yet set up any clickstream technology to monitor the visitor's selections on the site. The search page was set up, but it did not work. Having a search page is a good engaging activity for any e-business site; however, having one that does not work properly is a bad reflection on the company.

Another very interesting and engaging page used simple GIF files with a set of instructions to explain how to read a meter and to conserve energy. In fact, looking at the site map, the company had listed several other links with everything from the history of the organization to a "Kid's" page. Different log-ins were available to marketers and customers, and each showed promising links to engaging information.

Retaining

Company 4 developed a plan to introduce new information sources or features on a monthly basis. It would announce the release of each via targeted e-mails (as provided by visitors), online and off-line advertising, and press releases (similar approach in the attraction phase). Visitors see a headline announcing the upcoming new feature or service. To be successful in the retaining phase, visitors must return to the site and conduct activities that fulfill the goals and objectives of the site and on-line visitor. A plan for ongoing enhancements is necessary to accomplish this, and Company 4 was well-prepared for this phase.

Retain Technologies

Because so many of the pages in the site failed, all of the retain technologies in the world could not make a viewer want to return to the site. Beginning with a warm animated welcome, and well-organized navigation system, the site totally falls apart because of the broken or inoperable links. Jakob Nielsen (1999) rightly notes that "under construction" pages should not be included in a site. As soon as the viewer sees the dead-end "under construction" page, that usually heralds the end of the visit to the site. Even worse than an "under construction" notice is an inoperable link, especially to a page in the site. If a page is not complete, no link should be made to it until it is complete. In this way, everything the viewer sees works as expected, and the site is

. . . . (CGI) that both sent the Webmaster an e-mail and immediately sent the customer an automated e-mail. The automated e-mail would inform her that the inquiry would be addressed and a follow-up response would be sent as soon as the e-mail had been read and the problem solved. As it is currently set up, the Webmaster link is buried at the bottom of the "Contact Us" page.

Having a company Webmaster may be fine for a very small company with a very talented Webmaster, but the whole concept of a Webmaster may not be a very good one for a sophisticated site. Any good design firm is going to have more than a single talent on the team. A developer will do the client-side programming; a graphic designer the artwork and design; a second back-end developer creates the middleware; there is a database designer; and a manager who understands how all of the parts fit into the company's strategy. The technical work of maintaining the server is done by an IT department or hosting service. Rather than a Webmaster, a corporate site needs a combination of a public relations expert, a technical expert, and a manager who can bring the different pieces of a site together to make repairs where needed. In fact, a company may be better served by a Web design firm that includes a maintenance and update service. Then, if something fails, it can be addressed by the right mix of expertise required rather than by a Webmaster whose talents are focused on a single aspect of the site.

Learning

By outsourcing the original processing of the Web site's database, Company 4 worked closely with the marketing, information technology, and operations staffs to design appropriate Web-data gathering tools. The company would receive feedback from visitors in various ways described above. Clickstream or log file analysis was the additional learning component added by the company in this phase. It would be an integral element of the overall plan for learning about the company's online visitors.

Learn Technology

All the learn technologies that gather and store the data were either not included in the site or failed. The planned registration process had been set up using ColdFusion, but it failed, so any idea that the information could be used to learn about the viewer failed along with it. From testing the site on different browsers, it became clear that the site needed updating for the changes in the newer browsers. During this update period, several alternatives were available. First, using JavaScript, the version of the browser viewing the site could be determined. If the browser was a newer one, the viewer could either be informed that the site was being updated or to try an older browser to view the working site. Second, the whole site could have been shut down and a simple "bulletproof" (i.e., one made entirely of minimal HTML , JavaScript, and GIF or JPEG graphics) site placed in its stead informing the viewer that the site was a temporary one but to look for the newer one in the future. Because the site had excellent design and graphics, this second alternative would have worked well. Even the learn technologies used, such as ColdFusion and databases using SQL, could have gathered data from users while the main site was under repair. However, the choice to simply let the site fail precluded any hope of learning anything about the visitors, and the site gave visitors a negative message about the company.

COLLECTING YOUR KNOWLEDGE: A REVIEW

Key Terms

- best practices
- brand erosion
- communication gap
- competitive benchmarking
- competitive differentiation
- design gap
- electronic bill payment
- fulfillment gap
- globalization
- information gap
- legacy computer system
- monopolistic business model
- premium service category
- technology-enabled philosophy
- under construction
- deregulation
- Webmaster
- wholly-owned subsidiary

Questions to Ask

1. What forced Company 4 to consider adopting a marketing strategy driven by the new technology?
2. What are the four types of gaps that Company 4 had to contend with and what role did technology play in each?
3. What were the key change drivers for Company 4 and how did it plan to implement them?
4. What elements of the technology plan were implemented in the company's site and which ones did they fail to implement or implement incompletely?
5. What were the major target groups that Company 4 planned to address separately in its site?

Application to Business

What is your company's plan to update its site? Who is involved? What role do they play? How are the different key roles integrated?

Look at your company's site and see if any of the elements either fail to work or have not yet been implemented. Are any of the pages labeled "Under Construction?" What type of feedback system is involved in your company's Web site? If corrective feedback came from customers, who would respond and how?

Could your company save money in the same way Company 4 planned to if it used a technology-enabled philosophy?

Web Sites to Visit

www.pge.com The Web site planned by Company 4 seems to have been achieved by Pacific Gas and Electric. Even though under Chapter 11 reorganization at the time it was

spikes in 2000–2001 led to the company's filing for protection under Chapter 11 of the bankruptcy laws.)

www.coned.com Another utility company that effectively implements the value bubble is Con Edison. Virtually all of the planned technology initiatives envisioned by Company 4 can be seen in action at the Con Edison site. It uses technologically savvy techniques combining Flash, JavaScript, HTML, and ASP on the back-end. Ironically, the graphic design of

other sites. The site itself, while making good use of JavaScript and Flash to drive the more dynamic elements in the site, did not appear to use very much back-end technology other than an effective use of ASP in its contact page. Instead, it outsourced features like bill payment to other companies that specialized in software to handle such processes.

CHAPTER

9 ‖ CASE STUDY 5

C ompany 5 is a not-for-profit trade association. It was selected for three reasons. First, the Internet is often credited with leveling the playing field between the very large and the very small organizations. Company 5 is a very small institution with one very large, main competitor. Second, any study of marketing cases must include a not-for-profit organization. It is important to understand the applicability of marketing models on organizations that are not profit motivated. Third, this case focuses on creating a brand for an organization that does not currently have one. It also does not create tangible goods. The mission of the organization is to create derived demand by providing member and industry services (to be described in the next section). The brand will be used for promotion in both the online and off-line efforts of the organization; however, the organization's focus is online. This case illustrates the marketing concept's common theme of valuable exchanges (Chapter 1).

COMPANY OVERVIEW

Company 5 is a global, not-for-profit trade association in the building industry. Its mission is to be the industry's leading source for credible information on the benefits and applications of specialized building materials. The organization achieves its mission through three main avenues of member support:

1. Educational and technical or engineering expertise
2. Ongoing liaison with appropriate governmental and regulatory agencies
3. Objective analysis of various building materials by different types of construction

Company 5 is funded through membership dues, sales of technical publications, and government grants. The organization has various membership levels that represent the supply chain within its industry: manufacturers or producers; distributors and wholesalers; and the end users (architects, general contractors, and engineers). Figure 9-1 has the distribution of the various members or constituents. The company's overall goal is to increase primary demand for customized building materials. This goal improves the profitability of producers, distributors, and wholesalers while providing the end users with a materials option that is also less expensive than the traditional alternatives coupled with improved performance levels.

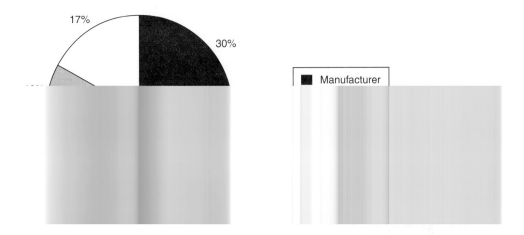

Company 5 has been in existence for 80 years, yet the market share for the specialized building materials product is less than 1 percent. It's attributed to the efforts of its main competitor. The competitive trade association has been in existence for 90 years and promotes traditional building materials use. Their ongoing lobbying and marketing efforts are effective and underwritten by millions of dollars in membership dues, although the company's budget is less than 10 percent of this competitor's. Twenty years ago, Company 5 was close to bankruptcy and its competitor attempted to incorporate its efforts into its organization. Desperate to keep a separate image and focus on the specialized building materials, the company's membership raised additional funds to avoid the merger.

Company 5 has three full-time technical employees. It is managed by an executive director and management committee composed of its producer and manufacturer members. The director and management committee (with extensive employee input) decided that it needed objective, quantitative input on ways to serve the marketplace more effectively. A two-pronged market research project was developed and executed. The first phase was to survey distributors, wholesalers, engineers, architects, and general contractors regarding their perceptions of the specialized building materials and the company's image. The second phase of the study was designed for manufacturers or producers to assess their level of awareness of Company 5 and the organization's reputation for the services it provides. Overall, the survey research results indicated that Company 5 needed to create an image with the various constituencies that it served[1]. A challenge existed in accomplishing this goal—the avoidance of channel conflict between the manufacturers and producers, the intermediaries (wholesalers and distributors who are the direct customers of the manufacturers), and the end users (the decision makers for the building materials selection).

With constrained financial resources, Company 5 had the formidable task of creating and marketing a brand in order to address the marketplace needs. The Internet

---

[1]Company 5 did not have a favorable or unfavorable image. Rather, it did not have any image.

was the most viable option from a financial perspective. The issue became the effectiveness and receptivity of the organization's membership and the industry. The executive director and management committee conducted a **segmentation analysis** on their target audiences. Careful and rigorous analysis indicated their audience was both accepting and embracing technology to satisfy their needs. Many of the company's target audiences were defined as technically trained (engineers, architects, as well as the engineers employed by the manufacturers and intermediaries). Therefore, it was determined that the Internet was the appropriate medium for the image or brand building campaign supplemented by the off-line or traditional environment.

E-BUSINESS MARKETING GOAL OR STRATEGY

Company 5 began developing its brand through further analysis of the survey research data. A **perceptual map** indicated that Company 5 did not correlate with any of the attributes that were important to the survey respondents. However, the company knew, from the map, which attributes were most important to existing and potential members (representing the industry). The attributes are presented in Table 9-1

For Company 5 these attributes were already being addressed by the existing organizational structure. It was executing its mission statement with numerous information sources and building project support programs (i.e., templates, financial analysis). Developing a strong Company 5 brand would involve communication and promotion about the existing programs and services. The company must continue to monitor its customers (existing and potential members as well as the industry at large) on their needs and wants from the organization (the business intelligence component of e-business).

Company 5 decided to adapt the **branding strategies** model originally presented by Mohr (2001). The model's emphasis on the high-tech environment supported the company's online branding focus. Each of the eight steps in the model were carefully planned and executed by the company. A summary of each is presented below:

1. Continually monitor the environment (members; employees; industry, governmental, and regulatory representatives) in order to identify and develop ongoing, **value-laden enhancements**.

TABLE 9-1 Key Attributes and Magnitude of Importance

Key Attribute	Percent Stating Very Important or Important
Providing current and timely technical assistance (electronically, by telephone, by fax in descending order of importance)	85
Visible, lobbying efforts with the government and regulatory agencies	50
Design templates for using various materials	35
Objective, comparative financial analysis of different materials used (across all materials available not restricted to the specialized ones the organization promoted)	30

• Company 5 was using the results from its initial survey to address the needs of members, employees, and industry representatives. It began a regular secondary research project to monitor the governmental and regulatory changes. This research was supplemented by in-depth interviews with appropriate representatives. The company's analysis of the secondary and interview data yielded a need from governmental

brand awareness and build strong brands (Mohr 2001; Ilfeld and Weiner 2001). Zeithaml, Parsasuraman, and Malhotra (2000) have defined these experiences as **e-service quality**. The definition of e-service quality being the "extent to which a Web site facilitates efficient and effective shopping, purchasing and [or the] delivery of products and services". Online customers defined certain Web site features that impacted the quality of their online experiences. An analysis of the features yielded two dimensions of e-service quality: **core** and **recovery** (Parsasuraman 2001). Company 5 incorporated the core dimensions into its Web site design:

> **Efficiency**—easy to navigate; well organized; loads quickly; easy to use
> **Fulfillment**—delivers on schedule (Company 5 would receive online orders for specific documentation or manuals that were mailed to the requestor); sends what was ordered; and is truthful about availability of offers
> **Reliability**—site availability; site does not crash or freeze the visitor's computer
> **Privacy**—visitor information is not shared

• The second component of **e-service quality** is recovery from a negative experience. Company 5 chose to address this through its toll-free telephone number. Three employees handle the calls regarding any questions, problems, or negative experiences associated with Company 5 (off-line or online).

2. Focus the brand communication through long-term–oriented advertising and public relations rather than short-term sales promotion.

• Company 5 developed a targeted communication strategy that used advertising and public relations as the vehicle to promote its brand. It also included personal selling through the members' sales forces. The advertising included specific trade journal publications that were targeted toward the building industry. Company 5 advertised its member services and new Web site offerings in these publications. In addition, the company had its on-staff technical experts publish articles on various building materials and the materials decision-making process. This added objective credibility to the organization's paid advertising. Both were designed to drive traffic to the Web site and clearly define the types of tasks that could be accomplished on the company's site. This approach would support the branding strategies by simplifying the decision-making process and minimizing the risk associated with building materials decisions. Company 5 did not develop any sales promotion associated with Web site usage.

3. Develop communication strategies to reach opinion leaders and generate positive "word of mouse" and mouth.

• Company 5 used the results of its in-depth interviews with government and regulatory agencies to develop ongoing communication with these agencies. In addition, current members identified the industry leaders whose endorsement of the trade association would be very important to positive word of mouse and mouth. Company 5 included these opinion leaders in its annual meetings (as keynote speakers) and participation in the various trade shows that its members and the industry identified as important. Company 5 was careful to emphasize its focus on the online environment through the opinion leaders. Because the company knew that its target audiences were technically oriented, the Internet or technology-enabled services would be consistent with the target audiences' needs and wants. The company also needed to target the decision makers and the users who influence them regarding building materials selection. Through the research study, Company 5 was able to determine the proportionality of each (See Figure 9-2).

4. Create an image or brand based on the company and not specific to the services or product(s) it endorses.

• The company's branding strategy must focus on the organization with its value-laden services seen as its product offering. To achieve long-term organizational branding, the company created a brand that defined the organization as a credible source for the building industry. Its brand image was one of comprehensive, current, and objective information on the variety of building options available to the industry. Although Company 5 possessed expertise in certain customized or specialized building materials, its brand image had to be a knowledgeable and credible source for numerous building material options.

5. Develop a visual image to support the branding strategies.

• Company 5 consulted with visual experts in the industry. Because the research indicated that it did not have a positive or negative image, it sought to visually demonstrate its mission and capabilities to serve its membership and the building industry at large. Company 5 needed to visually project itself as innovative, global, and a current

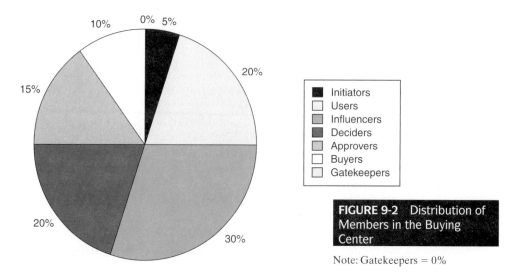

FIGURE 9-2 Distribution of Members in the Buying Center

Note: Gatekeepers = 0%

source of objective and credible information to reinforce its brand or image. The visual experts created several visual renderings for the executive director and managing committee to review. The visual decision was one that focused on the global perspective with a tagline that stated, "The only source for building materials selection." The combination of the visual globe with the uniqueness of the organization would convey

tion services from Company 5 based on each group's identified needs or wants. For example, the intermediaries prefer a more educational level of information services that they use to train their sales force. This customized information allows the intermediaries to have a more informed sales force that can provide better service to the end users. Company 5 customizes the intermediaries' Web site with training suggestions; this differs from an end user who receives a technical online library to address technical questions. Extensive follow-up noted that the end users used the company's site extensively but often asked for further details from the intermediary (the firm providing the building materials). The intermediary had, through Company 5, a well-trained, objective customer service and sales force staff. The combination of this off-line (face-to-face interaction) and the online services gave Company 5 the strong brand image that it desired through its Internet-enabled channel.

7. Establish strategic alliances.
   - Upon establishing its credibility with the government and regulatory agencies, Company 5 easily formed online **strategic alliances** with these organizations. Links and positive word of mouth and mouse was generated from these sources. Various trade publications also provided links to the company's site and additional endorsements. For Company 5, its greatest challenge was the opportunity to form a strategic alliance with its main competitor. Over the last two years, the competitor had begun to focus on standardized building materials. Its expertise, in this area, was confirmed in the research conducted by Company 5. The competitor wanted to create an alliance with Company 5 in order to collectively address a broader market. For Company 5, this created concern about the loss of membership fees (for example, could the competitor's members visit the company Web site without becoming members?). Although the competitor had similar concerns, its extensive membership and financial resources diluted the level of its concern. The two organizations decided on a mutually beneficial path. The Web sites for each would contain a link to the other organization; however, a visitor who was a nonmember to the site linked to would have to provide information and an intent to join.

8. Develop an Internet presence that is consistent with the branding strategy.
   - For Company 5, the branding focus would be online supplemented in the off-line environment. The company used the research from Zeithaml, Parsasuraman, and

Malthora (2000) that measured the online visitors' perceptions of their experiences with an organization's Web site. Mohr (2001) extended these perceptions into the successful or unsuccessful delivery of brand messages through the online environment. The company's Web site design focused on providing the services rated the highest by its target audience: members, industry, and governmental and regulatory groups. The company's online branding was rational in nature. This means that the Web site provided services to its target audience that were informational and analytical. The Web site will provide the most relevant services to its target audiences. This will affect a positive online customer experience that supports a positive image. Within the e-business components, the CRM aspect will be addressed through these positive experiences (that is, deepening the relationship).

PRIMARY STAKEHOLDERS

Company 5 has numerous stakeholders that its online strategies were designed to address. The stakeholder groups are somewhat different in this not-for-profit organization. For example, the company's customer stakeholder group is also the investor group because its membership dues fund the organization's operating expenses. The supplier stakeholder group in this not-for-profit organization is also a member of the customer group. Employees remain a critical stakeholder group for the organization.

Company 5's online branding strategy was focused on potential members, industry representatives, and the governmental or regulatory agencies. These groups are classified in the customer (existing or potential) stakeholder group. Therefore, the company's site was focused on its customers' needs and wants from their online experience. In order to achieve segmentation across the different groups of customers (manufacturer or producer, intermediary, end user, government or regulatory organization), Company 5 designed customized pages for each group. The home page provided easy to use navigation to locate the customized site for the visitor.

VALUE BUBBLE

Company 5 will launch its Web site employing all five stages of the value bubble (attracting, engaging, retaining, learning, and relating) for potential customers. For existing members, the company will focus on four of the stages. Company 5 will address existing and potential customers with the same value bubble strategies.

Value Bubble Technologies

In comparing the ambitious and seemingly effective strategy for its site, Company 5 failed to implement its stated goals in its site. Instead of having the dynamic site planned, it ended up with more brochure-ware of the same type seen in Chapter 6. The site elements are static, the graphics are not antialiased, resulting in jagged edges and blotched surfaces. Very little about the site is engaging and very few of the powerful tools available on the Web are employed. The pages are well designed in terms of layout, balance, color, and the standard design elements for paper or other static products. Navigation is clear, but the execution of the navigation leads to several dead-ends where the viewer is left with "page not on this server" messages.

The site is effective as a technology case study of how an Internet marketing plan can be sabotaged by limited Web design and development skills, knowledge, or effort. The case study also shows why marketing managers need to understand something about the technology behind the site. If nothing else, the ragged-edged graphics should have set off alarm bells to Company 5 that the Web designer was doing some-

design, they will produce ugly pages. Company 5 had a very talented graphic designer who simply did not understand very much about Web design technology. Finally, a Web design team needs a good developer who understands Web and Internet technology and software development. Usually, the personnel in an IT or MIS department know about developing and maintaining databases, and so they may not really understand all of the required technology necessary for an effective Web site (e.g., HTML, JavaScript, and Internet middle-ware.) The developer must be able to work effectively with the designer to meet the marketing requirements.

Figure 9-3 shows the general design of the home page and most of the rest of the pages in the site. It also shows the general navigation design.

Attracting

To attract new customers or members to the company's site, three promotion and communication elements of the marketing mix will be used. Online and off-line advertising, public releases, and personal selling will be employed. As Mohr (2001) and Ilfeld and Weiner (2001) have found, brand awareness occurs after the site visit and not before. Thus, the marketing challenge is to drive or build traffic to the site. Online advertising for Company 5 would include links on all existing members' sites to the

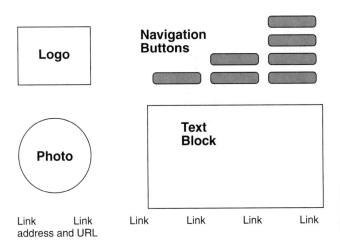

FIGURE 9-3 Company 5 Home Page Design, attractive in a static environment but not on the Web

organization's site. Off-line advertising would be in trade journals whose readership profile matches the company's member profile. Press releases would also be targeted for specific trade publications. The sales forces of the existing members would promote the organization and its site. Because one of the company's services is to provide its members with technical building material information, potential members (often an existing member's customer) are frequently exposed to the types of services available through membership. This supports the longer-term promotional approach recommended in the second and third steps of the branding strategy (advertising, PR, and word of mouth).

Attract Technologies

One of the lures to bring customers to the Web site was the promise of technical information. Once potential customers arrive at the site, though, the word "technical information" is nowhere to be found. Instead a button labeled "publications" goes to a page that has "tech facts" and "case study" tab headings. The term *publications* is far less attractive or informative than *tech facts,* and so the viewer sees nothing specific leading to technical information. The tech fact sheets and case studies are presented in PDF files that either can be viewed on the screen or printed out in a fully formatted style. The PDF files constitute more brochure-ware, but they still provide value for joining the organization.

Within the publications page is a small link to "Best Seller Publications." When clicked, a page appears with several publications listed and links to a second and third page of listed publications. The prices range from 50 cents to $30, and to order the material, the viewer clicks on an "order form" link. The order form is printed on the screen with instructions to print it out, fill it in, and either mail or fax it to Company 5. Residents outside the United States are advised to allow 1 to 2 weeks and that all orders are shipped within 7 days. Phone and fax numbers are provided, and no credit cards are accepted.

The technology is available for all of the publications to be put into PDF files that can be downloaded instantly. (Why some and not all were at this site is unknown.) The customer must wait 1 to 2 weeks for a shipment outside of the United States and a week for the company to ship it. Thus, the customer is forced to wait for half a month or more for a process that takes minutes over the Internet. The entire brochure-ware mindset not only affects the way the site is designed, it affects the way e-business is conducted, and information that could be had immediately is made far less attractive by not using the Internet technology.

Likewise, the lack of an online credit card account adds further to the antiquated method of mailing a check, waiting for it to be received, waiting for the order to be filled and then waiting again for the shipped information to be received by the customer. Online credit cards, used so effectively by Company 3 (among the other payment alternatives), adds to the effortless, quick, and efficient e-business mix. Some hosting services even offer to set up and maintain online credit cards, effectively providing an IT "substation" for the company.

Engaging

Existing and potential Company 5 members will be engaged in the site through various targeted services. As discussed in the previous section, the site will be customized for manufacturers, intermediaries, and end users. The information needs for each group are determined through continuous monitoring. Upon registration online users will receive the customized pages based on which group they select. Groups are not restricted from certain pages on the site. The intent is to present the preferred services

is sent to a page that is still under construction with no information about the members at all. However, if he happens to click the "Contact Us" button, he is provided with a very effective link to all of the members, along with URLs to the member company home pages and an e-mail address to the contact person. Likewise, all of the member companies have their addresses and phone and fax numbers listed as well. So although member information *is* available on the site, it is not easy to find.

As noted above, the information services are a mixed bag and, while engaging to the extent they can be found and are informative, some links generate a blank PDF file, and the "best sellers" can only be had by non-Internet alternatives. One information link is decorated with strike-though lines and does not operate. Instead, a small link leads the viewer to an updated paper-only option for the information for a quoted price. This has the effect not only of making the site look hopelessly amateurish, but also of suggesting to the viewer that the information was once free to download but now requires a paper version that must be purchased. A better alternative would have been to delete the old link and let the user find the publication with all of the other for-charge documents.

The registration process that could be handled with a simple HTML form and back-end to CGI, PHP, ASP, or JSP is not implemented as called for by the plan. Instead, the link to "join the organization" gives nothing more than a brochure-ware pep talk and then a P.O. box address, phone, fax, and e-mail contacts to get an application. Even an online application that could be printed out and mailed in is better than this implementation. As it now stands, the potential customer first has to mail, call, or e-mail for an application which is then mailed or faxed to the potential client. Then, after the user fills it out and mails back the application, she can join. So instead of taking the opportunity to engage the user with an online form, the user is divorced from the site by inexplicably dated alternatives.

The brand's image is presented not as technologically savvy but as hopelessly inept. The viewer is treated to a navigational maze. In some of the links in the site, when a button is pressed to return to the home page, the viewer gets a "page does not exist" message. If the viewer can find what she wants, it is almost by blind luck and not design. For example, one of the more useful online pieces of information is found under a "Did You Know That" link. The link is not news, but rather information about making conversions to a metric system. The viewer is given a formula to show how to make the conversion. Here is a perfect opportunity to provide the user with an online calculator that would make the conversions. A simple JavaScript routine and HTML form could be used to engage the viewer, but instead only the formula is provided.

On the same page a very useful table shows the member or potential member the spacing supports required for the materials the organization is based on. It then points out that the same information is available to download from the publications page. Since it is not news, it should not be with the news but someplace that better ties in with technical information.

Retaining

Company 5 will further deepen its brand by motivating repeat visits. To accomplish this goal, the site will frequently update its content and offer new services (as determined by the monitoring). Online visits must be a positive customer experience as defined by e-service quality attributes. To the extent that problems arise, Company 5 will resolve them through its internal customer service. As new content and services are added, promotion occurs. Online and off-line advertising, press releases, and personal selling highlight the new feature(s).

Retain Technologies

To motivate repeat visits, Company 5 planned to keep updating information about its activities and events in which it would be involved. In this one area, it seemed to have accomplished its goal. The link to "events" showed a series of seminars to be offered in different parts of the country with good advance notice about the date. Likewise, it had a graphic of its convention booth and the convention where it would be displaying its services along with the booth number. The technology behind this updated information was simply an updated page. More elaborate technology would have used a database with a complete list of events and activities scheduled into the future that would automatically update the page, but given the number and scheduling of events, it was probably easier and just as effective to have the Web monitor update the page itself. Also, given the fickle nature of scheduling, long-range planning can lead to announcing seminars or other events that are cancelled, and setting them up in a database is probably the wrong technology to use in any case.

Another retain technology that was to be implemented was some kind of online client-monitoring to update content and offer new services. As seen in previous chapters, anything from online questionnaires to clickstream monitoring is available to do this. However, few technologies were implemented in this site. The branding strategy that called for continual monitoring to adapt to a quickly changing environment was only implemented by providing e-mail addresses and fax and telephone numbers. However, these were provided on the "Contact Us" page, along with member contact information and links to related organizations, which do not suggest the main object was to monitor client feedback.

Learning

Company 5 will have a registration section on its site. This is necessary to ensure it supports its members while expanding its membership base. The registration provides a rich database of information about the visitors' preferences, demographics, and company affiliations. This data will be incorporated with the clickstream and log files tracking. By examining on-site and online behaviors overlaid with descriptive data (demographics and preferences), segmentation refinement can be accomplished. These data provide input into the future enhancements of the site.

The extensive database allows Company 5 to further solidify its brand. The information collected will be used to personalize the interaction with each return visit. It will use previous behaviors (such as technical information read or requested) to offer new services matching the profile of the visitors' information needs. Company 5 will monitor the frequency of technical information requested and, when the volume reaches a predetermined level, will offer to provide a seminar on the topic (it would simultaneously be offered via Web conferencing, video conferencing, and face-to-face). This would be provided to members as part of the company's services. Using the relating phase of the value bubble, the company can create deep, positive associations with existing members and attract new members with its innovative approaches.

Relate Technologies

The most labor-intensive form of relating over the Internet is by using e-mails written individually to clients. A good database of clients could generate informative e-mails that would automatically send technical or other information to its customers. However, the planned extensive database that would allow Company 5 to further solidify its brand and individualize customer response never materialized.

In the absence of a good database, telephone, fax, and e-mail can be used as long as the company is willing to allocate the required resources to staff the phones and respond to faxes and e-mail. Of these technologies, e-mail is the easiest to use because it does not rely on temporal coordination as do phones, hard copies, and faxes. In addition, e-mails provide cut-and-paste information that can be used in reports or other forms of communication so that the customers do not have to reenter data.

COLLECTING YOUR KNOWLEDGE: A REVIEW

Key Terms

- all customer-contact points
- branding strategies
- core (e-service related)
- efficiency (e-service related)
- e-service quality
- fulfillment (e-service related)
- perceptual map
- privacy (e-service related)
- recovery (e-service related)
- reliability (e-service related)
- segmentation analysis
- strategic alliance
- value-laden enhancements

Questions to Ask

1. What was the key strategy that Company 5 used to design its Web site?
2. How is e-service quality evaluated and measured?
3. What elements of the overall company Web site strategy were actually implemented when the site was built?
4. Which of the company's goals were not met and what Internet technologies could have been used to meet those goals?

Application to Business

Examine your own company's strategic plan for implementing a Web site. Does the actual site live up to the strategic plan? If not, what could be done so that it does meet the strategic goals of the company?

Looking at the service component of your company, which of those components are handled online?

What would you need to do to put together an effective Web site design team? What key personnel in your company could be effectively recruited and which ones would have to come from a Web design company? What advantages and disadvantages are there between using in-house personnel in your company and hiring a design firm? Who in your company would absolutely have to be involved in creating or redesigning your company's site.

Web Sites to Visit

www.aci-int.org The American Concrete Institute is an organization similar in type to Company 5. However, it actually implements what Company 5 planned to implement in its Web site. For example, the membership application is online and ready to be filled out and submitted and paid for online with a credit card. However, the application can also be printed out and mailed or faxed to the organization and payment can be made by check instead of credit card. It not only provides a simple way for the customer to join the organization online, but it gives him options as well.

www.crsi.org The Concrete Reinforcing Steel Institute is another service organization involved in concrete support. Its Web site has implemented most of the goals envisioned by Company 5. With dynamic menus and several different forms, attractions, and easy navigation, this site, while a bit boring designwise, is a good example of how a service organization can effectively use the Web.

www.womensconsortium.org A very different type of service organization is the Connecticut Women's Consortium. Beginning with a musical and animated opening, this site is a lively one attractive to women. With the goal of improving behavioral health care for women and their children, the site is an information resource for women. The site has several publications that can be downloaded and a resource library where online searches and orders can be made.

It makes very good use of Flash for an attractive opening. Flash is able to create both low-bandwidth sound and animation to invite viewers into the site. ColdFusion is employed for entering publication requests and contact information in its database. Excellent graphic design gives the site further attractive features.

...consumer packaged goods industry and, therefore, provides some insights into the e-business marketing approaches being used within the industry. Second, Company 6 operates in an extremely competitive environment that is classified as pure competition (many competitors offering the same product or service without differentiation). Lastly, Company 6 evaluated several marketing alternatives that could differentiate it from the competition. Its executive committee used customer (potential and existing) research results as a competitive tool to guide its decision to enter the online environment. Although its product line would be the same, **customized online services** would allow Company 6 to differentiate itself (moving from pure competition to monopolistic competition). Within the common marketing themes identified in Chapter 1, this case illustrates that "marketing is based on exchanges that are valuable to both the customer and the company."

COMPANY OVERVIEW

Company 6 is a supplier in the consumer packaged goods industry (CPG). The company designs and manufacturers packaging for any type of product container. There are three groups involved in designing the package—the CPG company's advertising agency, its **internal marketing** department, and its designers. Although these three groups do not vary, the specific individuals involved change based on the brand that is being packaged. This collaborative process ends with the package design that Company 6 then manufactures.

Company 6 has a strong, positive reputation with its customer base. It is quick to produce (manufacture) and provide on-time delivery of the finished product. The company invests heavily in technology to support efficient manufacturing and the most sophisticated, collaborative designing software. This has maintained a loyal base of customers over the last two decades. However, the company's two main competitors recently completed massive upgrades to their design and manufacturing technologies in order to compete. The company was concerned that its loyal customers might try the competition's new technology and, potentially, switch.

The company's CEO led a 2-day planning session with the executive officers (finance, marketing, operations, and information systems) to discuss the company's competitive strategies. The overall strategy was for Company 6 to provide an array of customized design services that would be superior to its competitors'. Through ongoing monitoring, Company 6 would enhance and add services based on its customers' needs and wants (this would address the customer relationship management component of e-business). To be able to quickly address these needs, the company identified the Internet as the channel to deliver these services.

The first step for Company 6 was to determine the needs and wants of its customers (existing and potential) and their readiness to accept services delivered online. Company 6 contacted its local university and commissioned a research study led by marketing faculty and their MBA marketing research class. Company 6 met with the faculty and students to determine the study's objectives. A telephone-administered survey was designed and administered to a random sample of advertising agencies and consumer packaged goods designers. This survey assessed the respondents' satisfaction levels with their current providers of packaging design and manufacturing. A loyalty question was also posed. The survey also measured perceived value of certain design services. Six questions from the technology readiness index were used to measure the respondents' willingness to embrace and use technology to accomplish their work (Parasuraman 2000). Company 6 was not disclosed as the survey sponsor (administered blind). However, the company was able to identify its own customers' data. This allowed it to compare satisfaction levels between its customers and an aggregate of their competitors' customers (this is the business intelligence component of e-business). Company 6 also surveyed its employees who worked with the advertising agencies and CPG designers. Their input was critical to the development of the design services. Company 6 was also evaluating the option of collaborative online design in which the employees would be using the Internet-enabled services. Therefore, the technology readiness of the employees was important to measure. The customer satisfaction survey results are displayed in Figure 10-1.

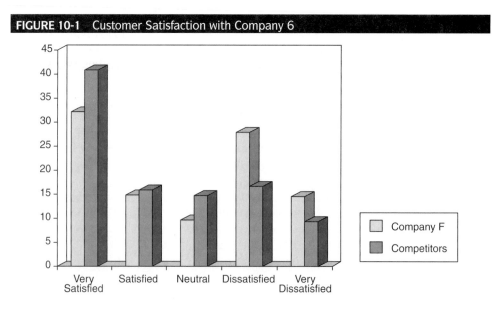

FIGURE 10-1   Customer Satisfaction with Company 6

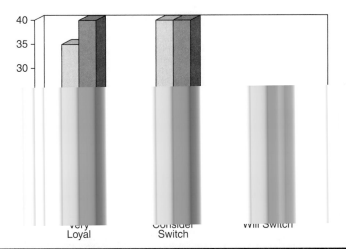

40 –
35 –
30 –

Very
Loyal

Consider
Switch

Will Switch

The company's customer base had higher levels of dissatisfaction than its competitors with accompanying lower levels of very satisfied customers. These results indicated the need for Company 6 to focus on offering services that would increase the satisfaction among its customers.

The company's **loyalty ratings** were also lower than the competition's. The results are presented in Figure 10-2.

The combined lower satisfaction and higher switching rates (Company 6 and its competitors had the same level of customers considering switching) further emphasized the need for the company's strategic change.

An analysis of the survey results yielded several services that Company 6 and its competitors' customers wanted. By developing services that would appeal to both groups, Company 6 would solidify its existing base while providing attractive services to the 40 percent of its competitors' customers who are considering switching to another company. Table 10-1 gives a list of services rated as either very desirable or desirable by 50 percent or more of the respondents[1]:

Employees were asked to provide the most frequently requested services and support from their customers. A rank order list was developed and the preferred or desirable services indicated by the customers were in the top 10 of the list. Additionally, the employee list had invoicing, benchmarking or scorecard of the competing brands, and a costing system.

The technology readiness index (TRI) scores for the survey respondents were high. Their scores for optimism and innovation were significantly above the average, whereas their discomfort and insecurity with technology scores were very low. The TRI scores of the company's employees closely profiled those of the company's customers. Because of the high technology readiness of the company's customers and employees, it chose to develop its competitive services online.

---

[1]Services are in descending order of desirability.

TABLE 10-1 List of Services	
Service	*Percentage Saying Very Desirable and Desirable*
Online, real-time collaborative design tools (ad agency, CPG, and manufacturer's designers use interactivity)	68
Real-time project status (production or manufacturing) including delivery schedules	58
Online research applicable to its business (category management, marketplace trends, secondary and syndicated research results)	52

E-BUSINESS MARKETING GOAL OR STRATEGY

Company 6 would use the survey research results to develop an online customer portal. The portal's first release would contain the top three services preferred by the customer. The second release would incorporate the remaining seven services that the employees said were requested. Company 6 developed a services marketing plan that used the pyramid model (an extension of the triangle model).

The pyramid model was introduced by Parasuraman (1996) to account for the effect of technology on the triangle services marketing model. The pyramid model is presented in Figure 10-3.

The service marketing model extension accounted for the impact of technology-enabled service delivery. In the academic research literature, a body of knowledge called self-service technologies (SST) is evolving. However, the interactions between the company, employee, and customer remain with technology as another dimension.

Company 6 developed its services marketing plan focusing on sophisticated technology (that would be upgraded as available) supporting its internal, external, and **interactive marketing** strategies. The company's plan is presented below:

Internal Marketing ("enabling the promise") (Zeithaml and Bitner 1996) Company 6 used the survey research results to assist in its selection of the online services to be offered. This action sent a message to design employees that Company 6 valued their opinions. During the site construction, Company 6 asked employees to participate in usability testing and incorporated their suggestions into the navigation and logic flow of the site. A group of employees was selected to co-develop the training materials for both the employees and customers of Company 6. This inclusion in the process of developing and delivering the services motivated employees to perform above the average.

External Marketing ("setting the promise") (Zeithaml and Bitner 1996) External marketing is aimed directly at the customers. It focuses on the marketing mix components (product and customer solution, price and cost, promotion and communication, and place and convenience). In services marketing, there are three additional Ps: people, process, and physical evidence (Booms and Bitner 1981). (Some services

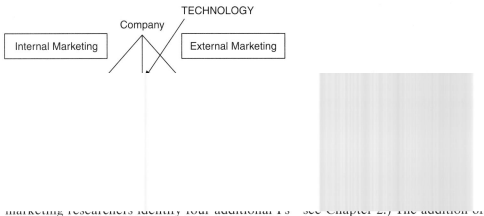

marketing researchers identify four additional Ps – see Chapter 2.) The addition of technology into the marketing mix provides greater flexibility and improved processes. (See Table 10-2, which focuses on how Company 6 addressed the seven marketing mix components for its new online services.)

Interactive Marketing ("delivering the promise")   (Zeithaml and Bitner 1996) Interactive marketing occurs between the employee and customer. Often, self-service technology omits the employee interactive component. This is due to cost savings and a desire to provide services in a consistent manner (reduce the heterogeneity of service delivery, see Chapter 2, 20). However, to Company 6, the employee linkage was critical. That is the reason why it stressed its online studio design center as **real-time collaboration** with all the designers involved: advertising agency, CPG designers, and Company 6 designers.

Within the interactive marketing component, there are two quality elements: technical and functional. The technical element is measured by customer satisfaction with the Web site features and its operation. Its content, navigation, ease of use, quick loading time, and delivering the service promised define the technical elements Company 6 monitored. The specific content provided by the Web site reflected the survey results: online studio supporting collaborative, real-time designing across several different individuals; project (including production) scheduling and status (including production and delivery); and competitive intelligence (category management, secondary and syndicated, and shifts in the consumer marketplace). The research component of the Web site would be housed in an online research library. It would include a sophisticated search function so both internal and external customers could quickly access current research findings that contribute to their business decision processes.

The **functional quality elements** centered on the value provided by the company's employees. Because the employees would interact with the other designers through Internet-enabled technologies, there would be functional quality elements within the online environment. Company 6 would continually monitor both quality elements through pop-up surveys on the customer's site. The employees would be surveyed on the **technical quality elements,** too. The company would compile the data and analyze it for technical and functional suggestions for improvements. To the extent the company implements the recommended changes, the company, the employees and the customers would benefit from increased value-laden services. For the company, this will deepen the relationship with its internal (employees) and external customers. More loyal customers and

TABLE 10-2   Marketing-Mix Components for Online Services

Component	Online Service
Customer Solution (product or service)	Company 6 designed an extensive array of customized services for its customers (internal and external). These services were selected based on the results of a customer and employee survey.
Customer Cost (price)	The online services would not have an associated cost with them. However, the site was password-secured for Company 6 employee and customer-use only.
Communication (promotion)	Company 6 chose to promote the site in a cautious manner. The company was concerned that it would lose competitive advantage by advertising the specific offerings. Company 6 advertised its new high-tech–high-touch studio in targeted trade journals and at trade shows; but it required the company-issued password for full access. To protect itself even more, the company created a separate site for potential customers to try before having complete access.
Convenience (place)	By offering the services online, customers could access the design studio at any time (24/7). Access was available from any computer because it was password protected.
People	In traditional services marketing, face-to-face or personal delivery is necessary. It also creates variability because each employee has a different style. Online, the delivery would be consistent. However, the personal contact was not lost since the company's designers would interactively collaborate with the ad agency and CPG designers.
Physical Evidence	Company 6 also developed a new logo to represent its reliance and trust in its technology. In addition, customers would find great benefit in the time savings provided by the online design studio. It would also reduce production time.
Process	Service delivery relies on backroom or operational support to effectively serve the customer. This support must be transparent to the customer. In the online world, the processes are enabled by technology. They can be efficient and consistent. Company 6 was committed to leveraging current technologies to achieve the efficiencies. It would tie the manufacturing, production, ordering, and scheduling to its online studio Web site.

employees are very profitable to a firm. In addition, the company's online offerings were less expensive to offer than the same services in the traditional or off-line environment.

PRIMARY STAKEHOLDERS

The company's services marketing strategy focused on its employees and customers. The company was following the **service–profit chain** introduced in 1994 (Heskett, Jones, Loveman, Sasser, and Schlesinger 1994). This profit chain quantifies the value of the typical qualitative measures found in service delivery (satisfaction and loyalty). It relies on the employees and customer interacting in a mutually beneficial relationship. Figure 10-4 presents the underlying logic of these relationships:

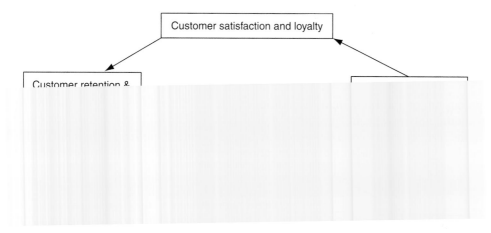

This underlying relationship has eight causal links[2] that contribute to the success of the services delivered. This relationship and the following linkages are the rationale for the company's focus on its employee and customer stakeholder groups as it enters the online environment with customized services to correct its sliding loyalty and satisfaction ratings.

1. Customer loyalty drives profit and growth.
2. Customer satisfaction drives customer loyalty.
3. Value drives customer satisfaction.
4. Employee productivity drives value.
5. Employee loyalty drives productivity.
6. Employee satisfaction drives employee loyalty.
7. Internal quality processes drive employee satisfaction.
8. Top management leadership underlies the chain's success.

Future releases of the company's Web site will include other stakeholder groups. Suppliers will have access to the company's inventory levels to maximize just-in-time replenishment of materials. As a publicly held company, Company 6 will create an investment opportunity section on its site. This section will discuss the online design studio and research center but, to protect itself from competitors' accessing the full site, only a small sampling of the site's capabilities will be shown.

VALUE BUBBLE

Four stages of the value bubble will be employed for the customer stakeholder group. They are engaging, retaining, learning, and relating. For the employee stakeholder group, three stages will be used—engaging, retaining, and learning. Although Company 6 will promote its site to attract customers, the advertising will be minimal to protect its proprietary design studio and research library. This is unlikely to diminish the company's opportunities because the network of individuals (ad agencies and CPG designers) is relatively small. Therefore, word of mouth and word of mouse will

---

[2]Adapted from Heskett J., T. Jones, G. Loveman, W. Sasser, and L. Schlesinger, "Putting the Service Profit Chain to Work," *Harvard Business Review* (March/April 1994).

help promote the site as well. Attraction for the customer stakeholder was more subtle, and it is discussed primarily in terms of the technical and not the aesthetic aspects.

Value Bubble Technologies

The company's site is minimalist as far as the underlying technology used. Many of the sites discussed in this book were created by designers using professional Web development tools like Adobe GoLive and Macromedia Dreamweaver. Usually the main designs are put together using the site development tools and then the developer hand codes the details. However, this company's designer used none of these powerful tools but instead relied on very simple technology resulting in a simple but generally effective site. The following technologies were detected:

- Animated GIFs
- HTML
- JavaScript
- Embedded e-mail
- Image mapping
- Frame sets in HTML

The company's logo is an **animated GIF** that slowly rotates in the upper left corner of the home page. Below the rotating logo are six rollover graphic links that make up the menu bar, one each for the following:

- Investor Relations
- Operating Divisions
- News
- Recycled Packaging Material
- Contact Us
- Help

To the right of the menu bar is a collage with the names of the company and three additional links hidden in the collage. The graphic appears as a single element but in fact is a table with rollovers that change colors when the mouse is moved over them. The rollovers in the collage have links to:

- Products
- Packaging
- 100 percent Recycled Paperboard

Centered beneath the collage with the links is a text graphic indicating the New York Stock Exchange code for the company.

At the bottom of the home page are two lines of text links. The top line replicates the links embedded in the collage in addition to a "Company Overview" line. The bottom line is a repeat of the vertical graphic menu bar along the left side. Figure 10-5 shows the general layout of the home page.

Attracting

Given the nature of the stakeholders and overall strategy of the company, attraction was not a major priority—or even a priority at all. However, in examining the site,

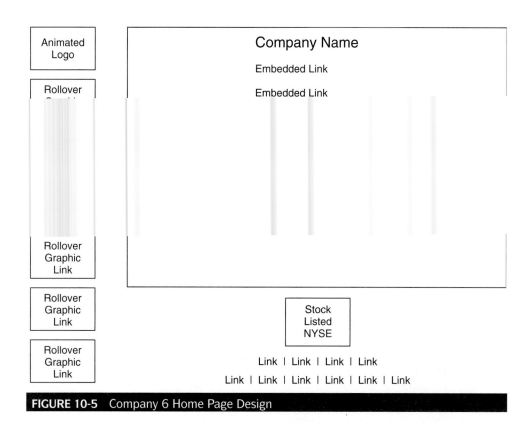

FIGURE 10-5   Company 6 Home Page Design

some subtle but important technological aspects of attraction were found and are included.

Attract Technologies

Although company 6 did not have a planned program focusing on attracting new viewers in the first phase, its site did have a fairly standard HTML tag for attracting viewers. This particular technology is shared by most of the other sites discussed elsewhere in this book. When search engines look key words in Web sites, they look for metatags. The metatags contain two primary types of information organized around *description* and *keywords.* The company's metatag contained the following metatag for description:

```
<META NAME = "description" CONTENT = "Company 6 produces packaging, 100%
recycled paperboard, laminated paperboard products, folding cartons, corru-
gated boxes, displays, plastic packaging, partitions, mailers, contract pack-
ing and recycling services.">
```

In planning to attract viewers, a good description is essential. When the search engine discovers the keywords used in the search, the viewer first sees the description. If the description clearly communicates what the viewer wants to see, he is more likely to click on the link and visit the site. During the planning phase, the marketing leader of the site development team should provide the Web developer with the exact description.

As can be seen from the company's description, key products are listed in a simple declarative statement. No marketing or sales message is used that might include terms like "highest quality," "best selection," "customer service," or any other adjective to say more than a list of products. The products need to be in front of the viewer, but motivating messages should also be part of the description.

The second metatag contains all of the keywords a potential customer might enter into a search engine. In this metatag, the designer should take into consideration different spellings a viewer might use. Company 6 used the following metatag for its key search words:

```
<META NAME = "keywords" CONTENT = "Packaging, folding cartons, mailers,
envelopes, boxes, corrugated, displays, contract packing, partitions,
dividers, ocme strips, agricultural supplies, tier sheets, pallet sheets, top
caps, pads, die-cut products, protective packaging, recycled paperboard,
chipboard, trim rolls, odd-lot board, boxboard, fiberboard, testing labora-
tory, graphic design, structural design, tubs, drums, coverboard, furniture
components, laminated paperboard, recycling services, recovery services">
```

The list of words provided for the search engine in the metatag clearly covers the spectrum of products offered by Company 6. However, words like "boxboard," "coverboard," and "paperboard" should be listed as "box board," "cover board," and "paper board" as well. Even if the word is misspelled in the metatag, the point is to include different possible ways a viewer might spell the search term.

Secondly, the keywords should include terms that, while not technically correct in the industry, are ones commonly used in the search keywords. For example, a common reference to a "corrugated box" might be "cardboard (or card board) box." Using the search word "cardboard box," the company's site was not listed using the Excite and Yahoo search engines. However, the company's competitors were listed.

Engaging

The site is designed based upon employee and customer feedback for desired online services and support. Thus, it is customized based on their expressed needs and wants and this will encourage initial engagement on the site. Company 6 must ensure that its technology operates efficiently to continue site engagement. This involves training both the employees and customers when enhancements to the design studio occur. As searching techniques are refined in the research library, an announcement and discussion of the changes must happen in advance of the implementation.

Engage Technologies

The plan for including engage technologies in Company 6's revised site is vague and general. Clearly, though, the site intends to include some type of feedback form for both customers and employees. Using middleware like ASP, PHP, or ColdFusion and an SQL database, setting feedback forms is most engaging.

One engaging online technology that could be included in the site using JavaScript or Java is an online carton calculator. To estimate the size of a carton requires room enough to encompass the product plus additional room for folds in the box materials and any protective materials that must be included in the box with the product. The potential customer has an interesting, practical, and, most importantly, engaging activity at the site.

As the site is currently displayed using the older Web technology, the engaging elements of the site are **inline links**. An inline link is a link within a body of text

... links provide nontinical choices for the reader, and although the blue underlined text does break up the flow of the text, linked text can be muted with a less obtrusive color and no underline by employing Cascading Style Sheets to restyle the text link format.

The negative aspect of inline links in this site is the lack of a "back" button in the targeted link to return to the linking page. Although inline links generally chop up the ideas in a paragraph, they should not leave the viewer in a corner of the site without some kind of "return to the text" button. The back button on the browser can be used, but a viewer is less confused if a back button is placed on the target page.

A final engage technology is provided in a dynamic facilities location map. The viewer can see all of the company locations in North America on the map, including Canada, the United States, and Mexico. Each type of facility is color-coded, and if the viewer passes the mouse over the facility-type beneath the map, dots appear on the map in the same color as the facility-type label at the bottom of the screen. For example, if the mouse is passed over "Uncoated Paperboard Division" (purple), purple dots appear showing where the facilities for that division are located. The information given is a general overview of the company's facilities, but more importantly, the activity engages the user. The technology employed image mapping and JavaScript to create the map and interactivity.

Retaining

Repeat visits to the company's site may be encouraged through the repeat business of its customer base. The online benefits (shortened production times and project management tools) will contribute to retention. Continual monitoring of the customer and employee visitors guides the company in its ongoing development of the site. As suggestions are implemented, Company 6 will promote them on its site and through targeted e-mails to its customers (the e-mails would come from the employee who works with the ad agency and CPG designers).

Retain Technologies

If the company's current site had anything to retain the visitor, it is its well-organized base of information. Using frame sets to control links, the site is fairly easy to get around and find information. However, the site is designed more to get the potential client together with a bricks and mortar reality than an online one. The different operating divisions are easy to find as are the different facilities belonging to the company. Employees can find different parts of the company easily on the site because it gives phone numbers and faxes for different components of the company, which are spread out nationwide, with offices in Canada, Mexico, and Chile.

An up-to-date news link is designed with the purpose of stimulating return visits for at least some of the target audience. New products are announced, but instead of having a link to a page that shows the new product and possible applications, the news release contains a phone number and e-mail address. The rush to stick with traditional information sources is a definite shortcoming of the site. All of the traditional links can and should be maintained, and the site does an admirable job to that end. However, it uses the Web more like an online phone directory than a truly new source of contact in its own right.

Learning

In addition to its continual monitoring of customers' needs and feedback about the site's performance, Company 6 will track online visitors (employees and customers) through their log files or clickstream behaviors. This provides observed data on the navigation of the site and frequency of usage for each designated section. It will also provide information on how well the logic flow of the site works for each stakeholder group. The company can overlay the customer profiles (based on customers' initial registration for a user ID and password) with the site behaviors to create a comprehensive database.

Learn Technology

The current site uses a single monitoring technology—embedded e-mails. None of the online monitoring has been installed (clickstream or logs), and no log-in form is in evidence. Currently, most of the e-mail links are to sales so that if an online communication is made, it will be to the best point of contact for a business transaction. If e-mail data are arranged in a company database for later retrieval and site adjustment, then some learn technology can be said to be in use. However, the reality of the current site is that no learn technology whatsoever has been installed.

Relating

Company 6 will initially use its database to personalize the interaction for its external customers. Based on the customers' most frequent path through the site, a specific configuration of pages will be assembled for that visitor upon her next visit. If the visitor wants to perform other tasks on the site, she will be able to navigate the site as well. Visitors will be given the option to opt-out of this personalized configuration of the Web site. Company 6 will provide its privacy statement on the home page to ensure customer confidentiality and protection of visitors' information.

Relate Technologies

Like most of the other technology for this site, other than e-mails, no relate technology is evident. The company's plan to use the learn technology to greet the return visitor with an array of tailored information is not yet installed. Each time a visitor returns to this site, he sees exactly the same set of pages available on the first visit and is treated like everyone else.

COLLECTING YOUR KNOWLEDGE: A REVIEW

Key Terms

- animated GIF
- customized online services
- interactive marketing
- internal marketing
- service–profit chain
- technical quality elements

plan was put in place to implement both quality components by Company 6?

4. What technologies will Company 6 have to incorporate to realize its goal to learn about customers and employees and respond accordingly?

Application to Business

How much company loyalty do your company's customers have?

Looking at the service component of your company, which of those components are handled online?

What would you need to do to put together an effective Web site design team? What key personnel in your company could be effectively recruited and which ones would have to come from a Web design company? What advantages and disadvantages are there between using in-house personnel in your company and hiring a design firm? Who in your company would absolutely have to be involved in creating or redesigning your company's site.

Web Sites to Visit

Exercise (in futility): The internet sites of companies in the corrugated container business omitted some of the largest container companies in the United States. The Internet search engines rely on the information in metatags and a company registering with a search engine. However, this segment of industry in the United States seems to be way behind other industries when it comes to using the Internet effectively. Those that were found were usually flawed in one way or another. For example, one site made use of frames with a menu of products along the left side of the window and the content in a much larger window to the right of the menu. However, the site developer had several scripting errors, and when moving from one screen to another, the entire frame set would appear in the right window with ever-decreasing screen space as the whole frame set kept crowding into the right window.

Assume you want to find and purchase packaging materials for your company's product. Using any words that come to mind, go to some different search engines (e.g., www.excite.com, www.yahoo.com) and see what you can find.

www.dydacomp.com The Dydacomp company has software packages to set up online selling for e-businesses. Although their technology using ASP as a back-end to some database is an excellent way to generate all of the technology needed to launch the elements of the value bubble, the site itself employs little of the value bubble. Nevertheless, Dydacomp's products would be invaluable for the corrugated packaging industry, and some of the better corrugated box companies were using them.

www.fibrebox.org One corrugated packaging association, Fibre Box Association, reveals a good deal about the attitude of its members toward Internet business. Click on the membership link at this site and look at the different companies that belong. The member companies that have Web pages have convenient links to them. About half the companies did not have links, and some that did were broken. One member company that had $1.9 billion in net sales in 2000 didn't even have metatags on its home page.

www.boxusa.com This is the site that Company 6 and the Fire Box Association should visit to see how to create a site that employs all of the elements of the value bubble. The site opens with a very attractive Flash movie and then uses a highly interactive navigation system to lead the viewer into the site. An interactive location map engages the viewer as she looks at the different plants and products in the United States. A "Customer Connectivity" link helps to retain customers and establish relationships. Overall, the site is a great one for achieving the goals sought after by Company 6. However, with all of the ingenious use of technology, the site does not have a simple metatag that helps search engines find it!

CHAPTER

11

study to demonstrate how the distribution (place or convenience) factor of the marketing mix is being impacted by Internet technologies. In 1995 as the commercial era of the World Wide Web exploded, many companies believed they could minimize, perhaps eliminate, the intermediaries between the customer and the producer or manufacturer. Companies saw the opportunity to increase their profitability and, in cases of pure competition, become the low-cost providers because their distribution costs would be considerably lower to their customers. The term **disintermediation** (eliminating intermediaries) became popular among companies with any number of channels between them and the end customer. Therefore, the intermediaries' reaction to the Web presence of the producers was very negative. This channel conflict and debate about disintermediation lasted for a few years.

During those transition years, some producers and manufacturers attempted to transition various product-line sales onto their Web sites. Other product lines remained with the existing intermediaries. Producers quickly discovered various unplanned issues with disintermediation. Those issues focused on fulfillment, customer service problem resolution, and other operational components that producers were not organized to handle. Although they were accustomed to shipping large volumes of goods into the members of their **distribution channel,** the producers were not equipped to handle the smaller orders, track individual lost items, or handle and credit individual returns. Most companies (for example Levi Strauss) began to rethink the concept of disintermediation. As a result a new distribution process evolved that capitalized on the Internet technologies in combination with the distribution channel members, the producers, and the end customer. The term for this process is **reintermediation.** Reintermediation is defined as creating new relationships among the producer, its distributors, and the end customer for more efficient delivery of goods and services. It has also been defined as the "reintroduction of an intermediary between consumers and a producer" (Word Spy 2001).

Therefore, this case illustrates the first common theme among the marketing concepts: "Marketing is a process for creating and delivering goods, services, and ideas to customers" (Chapter 1). This case looks at the supply chain management (SCM) and customer relationship management (CRM) aspects of e-business. As with most of the cases in this textbook, business intelligence (BI) is also important.

COMPANY OVERVIEW

Company 7 is a provider of homeowner insurance policies. It provides the most competitive insurance of this type. It elected to focus on one type of insurance to differentiate itself from the larger insurance firms that underwrite multiple coverage types. The home insurance product or service, similar to most insurance products, is mature. Thus, Company 7 wants to lower its distribution costs through a reduction in services and a broader market reach within its distribution channels. Its current distribution is a three-level channel design that is illustrated in Figure 11-1.

FIGURE 11-1
Three-Level
Channel Design

The company's executive management decided to meet with the intermediaries within its **three-level channel system.** The purpose of the meeting was to strategize alternatives for removing costs from the distribution system. An obvious direction would be the electronic environment with its Internet technologies that drive costs out of the transaction (Chircu and Kauffman 1999). Company 7 had heard of industries that had leveraged the World Wide Web in order to sell their products directly to customers—bypassing their traditional distribution system. The company was particularly interested in the automotive industry's use of online car sales.

From the perspective of the company's intermediaries (providing sales, delivery, and servicing of the homeowner policies), this meeting was of great concern. Staff felt that Company 7 might change its distribution strategies from using intermediaries to disintermediating its process. Disintermediation would mean direct insurance sales between the company and customer. (See Figure 11-2)

This distribution model would certainly lower the company's costs by eliminating the distribution channel. The intermediaries needed the company's homeowner insurance offering. It was a very competitive and **well-branded product,** that was frequently requested by the customer.

The meeting between the company's executive management team (CEO, COO, CFO, CMO, and CIO) and the intermediaries was difficult. Company 7 needed lower transaction costs and a three-level channel system seemed costly. The Internet enabled the company to lower these costs by streamlining the distribution system (eliminating some, and perhaps all, of the channels). It would also give a broader market reach at a lower cost. The intermediaries believed that their sales, delivery, and service channels provided the face-to-face sales that customers wanted for their insurance policies. They offered to conduct an extensive study of their operations to determine areas of possible redundancy and reduce costs in that fashion. The intermediaries would expand their market reach through direct marketing efforts. They would equally share the cost with Company 7 (previously, Company 7 had paid for all marketing programs). The conflict between Company 7 and its intermediaries would not be resolved during this

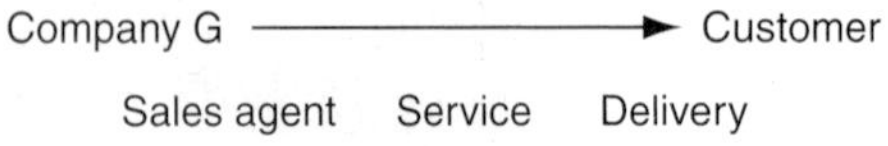

Company G ———————————————→ Customer

Sales agent   Service   Delivery

FIGURE 11-2   Distribution
After Disintermediation

strategy session. However, the two groups agreed to sponsor a survey of homeowner's insurance and determine what the customer's needs and wants were. The results of the survey would direct their efforts.

An independent marketing research company was hired to develop, administer, and analyze the survey. The telephone-administered survey contained a number of

(the choice was online and face-to-face) was perplexing. The marketing research company analyzed the open-ended comments for this question and noted a trend. More than half of the respondents in the choice category indicated that it depended upon the complexity of the coverage. If the coverage was straightforward, the online environment was preferred; with more complex decisions, a sales agent was preferred.

A similar trend was observed with the customer service preference. Policyholders preferred the online environment for routine basic questions (using a "**frequently asked questions**" (FAQ) Web page with an e-mail option for further explanation). The telephone was preferred for more complex service problems or issues. Open-ended comments supported the need for the customer to be provided the flexibility of choosing which channel to use.

There was a greater difference when asked about the delivery of the insurance policy. Figure 11-4 presents the survey results.

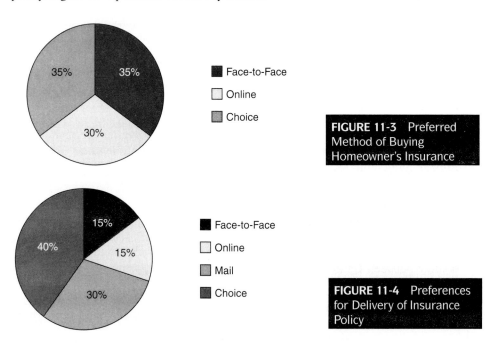

Face-to-Face
Online
Choice

FIGURE 11-3   Preferred Method of Buying Homeowner's Insurance

Face-to-Face
Online
Mail
Choice

FIGURE 11-4   Preferences for Delivery of Insurance Policy

The delivery channel currently mails 50 percent of the policies and delivers the other half in person. These intermediaries were unprepared for their customers' preferences. By analyzing the **open-ended comments (in research),** it was determined that customers would choose a delivery mode based on the flexibility to receive the documents face-to-face.

Company 7 and the intermediaries discussed the survey results at length. Customers did not prefer one channel over the other; rather, they wanted the flexibility to choose. Therefore, there was no support for disintermediation although the current intermediary services needed to be technology-enabled to meet the customer's needs and wants. This would increase customer loyalty to the intermediaries that would drive additional sales, profitability, and commissions.

E-BUSINESS MARKETING GOAL OR STRATEGY

The company and its intermediaries developed a distribution plan around reintermediation. It would be defined as:

> The combination of traditional and Internet-enabled technologies to deliver products and services based on customer preference. By combining the traditional and online business capabilities, the distribution channel members would be able to quickly identify and capitalize on future enhancements to improve their profitability through technological innovation.

Company 7 also identified this as an opportunity to improve its relationship with its distribution channel. Rather than treat the intermediaries as their customers, Company 7 reoriented its approach to become partners whose common goal is providing premium sales and service to the homeowners insurance market. Among the four groups (three intermediaries and Company 7), a channel decision was made. To accommodate the delivery flexibility, it would be necessary to combine the sales and delivery intermediaries. The company's distribution channel would be two-level as shown in Figure 11-5.

Reintermediation was redefining the company's channel structure by consolidating one intermediary into another. Additionally, the new distribution network would be able to communicate across all levels using the technology channels in combination with the traditional channels.

The company's CIO and CMO were assigned to develop the technologies and marketing strategies that would achieve the reintermediation. Their evolution into a fully integrated delivery system (online and off-line or traditional) provided Company 7 with some specific opportunities:

- Deepening the relationship with existing intermediaries
- Developing relationships with new intermediaries (moving from a selective to an intensive distribution system)

FIGURE 11-5   Distribution Channel After Reintermediation

- Providing the technology to improve productivity for the intermediaries, and ultimately, for Company 7.

Company 7 will deepen its relationship with its current intermediaries by providing the technological environment that customers prefer. Rather than the intermedi-

the intermediaries to provide customized service to the customers. More tactically, Company 7 would also include online marketing support for the intermediaries' use. This included collateral material that an intermediary could customize and print for its sales process. Company 7 also provided the delivery channel (now combined with sales) with a routing system for each type of delivery preferred by the customer. The delivery intermediary used this data as input into its production schedule. This efficiency helped the intermediary with its staffing and saved the channel level money through this enhancement. Other processes were migrated to the online environment: pricing, underwriting policies, billing, loss control, and claims. This gave the intermediaries ultimate convenience through the access of information necessary to conduct their business. It gave them the flexibility to reach into geographical markets that were previously difficult due to the restricted times that intermediaries had access to company support representatives. However, if the intermediaries wanted to speak with a Company 7 representative, they could do so during regular business hours.

Company 7 wanted to empower its newly organized intermediary structure. The company asked the groups for ways to help. Overwhelmingly, the intermediaries wanted research on the methodology to identify those individuals needing homeowner insurance. With this market intelligence (BI and the e-commerce components), Company 7 and the intermediaries would collaborate on the methods to identify these individuals. The company designed a Web site that discussed the features and benefits of its policy. The intermediaries would select targeted individuals to receive either an e-mail or a direct marketing piece (mail, telephone) that would direct them to the Web site. A toll-free number into the sales intermediary was included for those less likely to use the technology. Research results from the automobile industry indicated that the potential customer who researches the product online before approaching the sales channel is more informed and qualified. This leads to a shorter sales cycle time and reduces the transaction costs for the selling intermediary.

To develop relationships with new intermediaries (selling, delivery, and servicing), Company 7 was careful to select those with outstanding reputations (that is, they were similar to those already in the company's distribution channel). The online and off-line offerings would be the same for any new intermediary who signed a long-term contract with Company 7. For Company 7, the confidentiality of its new offerings (interactive off-line and online) was critical. The new intermediaries were, therefore, closely evaluated and scrutinized. Company 7 continually monitored its distribution channel members to identify conflicts quickly. The company had three full-time staff (in the operations department) who were responsible for the ongoing monitoring and conflict resolution. Positive word of mouth and mouse helped promote the company's progressive entry into the **integrated environment** (online and off-line).

The technology to improve productivity on behalf of the intermediaries and Company 7 was a critical step in the company's e-business marketing strategy. Many internal processes would be available to the appropriate intermediaries online (with off-line support as needed). The online continuous availability was an asset to the intermediaries. For Company 7, their employees could access the information electronically—a tremendous savings from the previous paper-based systems.

PRIMARY STAKEHOLDERS

Company 7 focused on two stakeholder groups: its suppliers (through its distribution channel) and its customers (existing or potential)—homeowners' insurance policyholders. Although the company did not have direct contact with the customers, it provided the marketing tools, enabled by technology, to provide premium service to them. The results of the customer survey indicated the need for flexibility in the purchase, delivery, and servicing of the policies. Company 7 recognized the value of investing in the reintermediation of its channel to address those needs. It carefully avoided direct customer contact while empowering its channels. Company 7 also changed its relationship orientation with its channel from being a customer to being a partner or a strategic alliance. Although Company 7 provided significant technological infrastructure to the intermediaries (at no cost), the company gained internal efficiencies and provided the flexible service that its customer base desired. This would benefit Company 7 as its product moved into the product life cycle's maturity phase.

VALUE BUBBLE

Company 7 would focus on three of the value bubble stages for its intermediaries—engaging, retaining, and learning. The company would rely on its partners to drive customer traffic to an information-based site on homeowner's insurance (developed and hosted by Company 7). Interested purchasers were routed to the sales and delivery intermediary. Although Company 7 planned to leave attraction to their site up to intermediaries, they did not ignore an attractive design. However, the metatags in their main home page provided little information, and when using the search word "insurance," the company's site did not appear in one of the major search engines. However, a number of the subsites connected with the company had extensively detailed metatags that helped customers find the company's subsites.

Value Bubble Technologies

Company 7 makes sophisticated use of JavaServer Pages (JSP), frames, PDF files, Cascading Style Sheets, and generated and unique JavaScript, and it uses its Web site to quickly respond to events. The day after the terrorist attacks on the World Trade Center in New York City, where one of its offices was located, Company 7 used the center of its home page for special messages about the attack. Viewers were informed that company employees in the building got out and away safely before it collapsed. In addition, the company provided two dedicated phone lines for employees and their families to call to check on their relatives who worked for the company and announced the creation and availability of employee assistance teams for counseling provided through an additional toll-free number.

the company was strong. It stated that even though it and other insurance companies would be hurt by the disaster, by no means were they on the economic brink. The statement pointed out that insurance companies existed to insure against catastrophic events, and while the costs were terrible, they were able to weather the current storm.

The importance of using the Web site in this manner for Company 7 was underscored by the lack of other communication available to the company on such an instant and widespread basis. With aircraft grounded and telephone communication jammed, the Web site served as the perfect communication medium to a wide audience. Telephone modems communicated with servers not affected by the incoming calls into New York City or Washington, D. C., and the Web pages could be sent on lines not as likely to be affected. Likewise, T1, cable modem, DSL, and other high-speed data transfer lines were not affected by the high volume of telephone traffic in and out of the targeted cities. Figure 11-6 shows the general outline of the company's home page.

Engaging

The engagement of the intermediaries was initially straightforward. Company 7 and its distribution channel members had met and jointly decided on the integrated reintermediation strategy. The sales channel would be able to present the policy based upon the customer's preferences: face-to-face, online, or a combination (based upon the complexity of decisions). The physical delivery of the policy would also be based upon the customer's preferences (mail, personal, online, or combination). The company's online scheduling process would engage the delivery side of the distribution channel. For customer servicing, Company 7 would develop a service-oriented site. It would contain frequently asked questions (routine questions identified by the customer service representatives and continuously updated). These features and functionality would engage the intermediaries on a short-term basis. For the long term, Company 7 planned continual monitoring of the customer's preferences (through techniques described in the learning phase) and developing enhancements and new offerings based on the customer's preferences and those articulated by the intermediaries.

Engage Technologies

The site effectively engaged the viewer in a number of ways. A policyholder, claimant, incident-reporter, or witness is able to provide information for a claim.

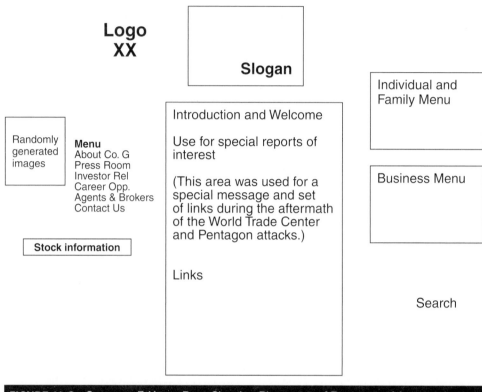

FIGURE 11-6   Company 7 Home Page Showing Placement of Emergency Messages and Links

Once the site user establishes a relationship with Company 7 using one form, the correct page with another form appears. Using CGI and scripts written in Perl, data are then sent to a database for processing. The nature of the engagement is more one of convenience than of an engaging interest, but it effectively involves the viewer.

Another engaging element of the site is a page to get an insurance quote online. However, instead of using CGI, the information is handled by JavaServer Pages. When the viewer accesses the page with the quote form, the window in the frameset is replaced by a JSP page where the potential customer enters information that can be placed into a database for processing. The quote page both engages the viewer and makes it easy for him to get an online quote.

A third engaging online feature Company 7 instituted is a number of different calculators. Included were the following categories:

1. Retirement

- Income after retirement
- How retirement affects expenses

2. Roth IRA

- Effects of tax rate changes on decision

- Converting IRA to Roth IRA
- What IRA can one contribute to?

3. Savings

As planned, the frequently asked questions (FAQs) section was included as part of an "Education Center." The calculators, a glossary, and a "Learn About Investing" page combined with the FAQs make up the education center. The pages that provide investment education are thorough and informative and filled with examples and cautionary tales about not investing for retirement early. The many topics are set up as links and engage the viewer through a series of selections. The added information provides the potential customer answers to questions that could reduce the transaction time with a sales representative.

Retaining
Repeat visits to the site would be addressed through ongoing upgrades and enhancements. As intermediaries adjust to the integrated environment, Company 7 projects increased online usage complimented by off-line support. Company 7 will also regularly update its customer Web site to feature stories regarding homeowner issues and the necessity of homeowner's protection (via insurance). It will be customized based on theft, flooding, fire, and catastrophic occurrences. The approach will be factual, not fear-based, and the intermediaries will provide input and feedback on the content.

Retain Technologies
One of the little elements in the site that brings a certain newness to the home page each time the site is visited is a random collection of photos. Each photo shows one or more people looking upward toward the viewer. Different gender, age, ethnicity, and styles are represented. For instance, an upscale black family of three, a businessman and businesswoman in suits, a young informally dressed Asian woman, an elderly couple, and an informal young man are all displayed. A simple JavaScript line of code provides the engine to generate the different JPG images.

Another of the retain elements on the site is a Spanish language link (Español). The link is below a link about work the company is doing with a major university to bring information to its clients about Alzheimer's disease and driving. Once at the page with the Alzheimer's article, all of the other links are in Spanish. However, when any of the links are clicked, everything reverts to English. For example, the link to "Productos comerciales" (commercial products) returns to the main home page in English. Why Company 7 elected to have a single article in Spanish and not a mirror site in Spanish is a mystery. Whatever attraction to Spanish-speaking audience may have been initiated is lost because of its limitation. The technology is no different from that of the English pages, just the language. All that the site designers and developers would have to do is to first develop the English language site, and then edit the site to create a mirror Spanish language site.

The feature story on Alzheimer's disease itself is part of the planned retain strategy. The article is interesting and set up to inform the viewer about the findings from a university study sponsored by Company 7.

Learning

It is critical for Company 7 to monitor the Web site usage of the intermediaries and the customers. Although the company is maintaining a somewhat anonymous position to the end customer, its brand name is well-known and supports the selling and delivery intermediary. To ensure the company continues to meet the preferences of its partners and customers, clickstream behaviors and log files will be analyzed by the company's marketing and information systems staff. They will identify trends by group on the navigation (logic and ease of use on the site), length of time on specific pages ("stickiness"), and frequency of visits. These behaviors will be incorporated with demographic information provided by the online visitor to develop a complete profile. Based on the results, Company 7 will collaborate with its intermediaries on the appropriate adjustments necessary to improve and enhance its online offerings.

Learn Technology

The learn technology is made up of clickstream and data that users provide in online forms. Because the clickstream technology is transparent to viewers (they cannot see its tracking their selections), knowing its location within a Web site is not important for the viewer. Moreover, the clickstream technology did not appear to be consistent throughout the site. Some pages had code that could have been used for tracking clicks and other pages did not. Apparently, some parts of the site system had been updated and others had not.

When a company attempts to learn about the viewers through online forms, those forms should not be difficult to locate in the site. However, Company 7 forms are difficult to find, and once found, they are difficult to find again. The problem is multiple sites with unclear connections. The company's site is actually a series of different sites, and it is clear that different designers and developers created the different subsites. When navigating the site, a link to "annuities," for example, results in going to a site (not just a page) that covers annuities. When the viewer clicks "home" instead of going to the main page of the main site, the viewer is taken to the home page of the annuities site. Each site has different domain names. For example, the site for "Institutional Liability Funding" (ILF) had a domain name of ilf.companyglife.com and the page for annuities was www.companyginvestor.com. The site guide for the two subsites did not include a link to www.companyg.com, the main home page that links all of the subsites. The result was that if the viewer wanted to fill in information forms for feedback from the company, she would find herself in a Byzantine maze of subsites with different styles and even navigation systems.

The registration form for investment uses JavaServer Pages to pass the information to a database. However, the form itself is found by a circuitous route. From the main home page, the viewer selects annuities or mutual funds from a menu for individuals and families. (A total of six selections are on the menu.) The viewer is then taken to a page in the "financial" site. If she selects "Home," she is not taken back to the company's main home page but is taken to the home page of the financial subsite. At

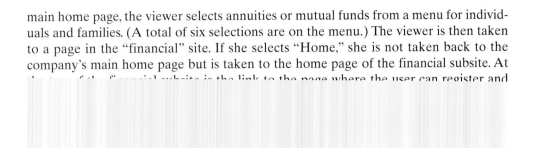

relate component of its site, Company 7 will need to create an improved and consistent navigation and information system.

COLLECTING YOUR KNOWLEDGE: A REVIEW

Key Terms

- disintermediation
- distribution channel
- frequently asked questions (FAQs)
- integrated environment
- open-ended comments (in research)
- reintermediation
- three-level channel system
- well-branded product

Questions to Ask

1. How did Company 7 plan to invoke disintermediation using the Web? Why did it want to engage in disintermediation as a company strategy?
2. What led Company 7 to invoke reintermediation after disintermediation? What role did the Web play in reintermediation?
3. How did Company 7 use the Web to respond to a catastrophic emergency? What was Company 7 able to do using the Web that could not be done with other modes of communication?
4. What will Company 7 have to do to affect its learning strategy on the Web? What kind of site structure does Company 7 have that may lead to problems with customers and what can it do to improve it?

Application to Business

Has your company been involved in disintermediation? If so, was the Web used to replace intermediaries and was it effective? If your company has had a bad experience with disintermediation, how might it revitalize its sales using reintermediation and the Web?

Does your company include an online strategy to reduce the transaction time in sales? How does it do that, and if not, what Web elements would need to be created and implemented?

How could your company's Web site be used to respond to an emergency? What possible expected emergencies occur in your area (e.g., tornadoes, hurricanes, power failures) and what process would have to be in place to make sure the information would be effectively disseminated?

Web Sites to Visit

www.prudential.com Prudential Financial is similar to Company 7, but its site, while less appealing designwise, provides a clearer navigation system. It uses a single domain name for the entire site even though its offerings are broader than those of Company 7. The design and menus are consistent throughout. Like Company 7, Prudential used its home page to provide special information after the World Trade Center terrorist attack and toll-free numbers to expedite claims. It also contained a detailed and clear explanation of its demutualization (the process of converting a mutual life insurance company into a stock life insurance company) to reassure customers.

www.redcross.org and http://**DisasterRelief.org** Sites that must deal with emergencies on an ongoing basis inform e-business sites how to design for rapid and constant change. The Red Cross site is quite simple, relying on links to separate pages using a design template for added news. A story can be quickly added by inserting text into a template page and providing a link to that page from the home page. The Red Cross also uses ASP technology for a search engine within its site.

www.travelers.com Travelers Insurance has a relatively simple site and does not take advantage of much Web technology, but it proved to be very effective. During the aftermath of the World Trade Center attack, it posted messages on its home page for both clients and employees. The employee and agent links to the catastrophic events were telling because of the many offices Travelers and Citibank had located in the financial district that was closed off during the aftermath of the attack. Using Web pages and PDF files, the site gave its agents and employees detailed information about how the company would operate with the loss of office space in lower Manhattan. The company ran special ads in the *New York Times, Daily News, Newsday, New York Post, Wall Street Journal,* and *Washington Post.* A PDF file shows what the ad looked like so that agents would know what to tell customers. Ironically, all of the material provided on the Web comprised phone or fax contacts and not e-mail or Web links that would have been far more efficient and available because the New York City phone lines were jammed.

focuses on a failed **new product development (NPD)** process. The failures are attributed to the shifts that occur in the existing marketing models and strategies because of rapidly changing technologies and competition (Ranged Marketing, Chapter 2). Company 8 closely followed the high-tech NPD process, but failed to acknowledge its core competencies and new entrants into the marketplace. This case will examine the company's new product development, its withdrawal from the marketplace, and how the company addressed its future online presence. The case addresses the common marketing theme of "marketing is a process for creating and delivering goods, services, and ideas to customers" (see Chapter 1). Company 8 focused on using the online environment for the e-commerce and customer relationship management (CRM) components of e-business to the consumer marketplace. It failed to monitor the environment by not gathering sufficient best practices and **competitive benchmarking** (the business intelligence component of e-business).

COMPANY OVERVIEW

Company 8 is a financial services firm providing consumer banking services in the United States. It has focused its retail banking business in 20 noncontiguous states throughout the country. Among the company's highlights are these:

- 2 million retail banking customers
- Third-largest home owner equity lender
- Tenth-largest private bank (only for individual clients)
- 200 retail locations
- 1,000 automated teller machines (ATMs)
- Third-largest provider of student loans
- Full retail bank checking and loan product array
- American Banking Association, three-time winner for most technologically sophisticated retail bank franchise (1999, 2000, 2001)

Company 8 has two other competitors within its geographical markets. The company is the predominant bank measured by **household market share statistics** (percentage of households that identify Company 8 as their primary bank). Company 8 has retained a consistent 30 percent market share as a primary bank, whereas its two competitors have 20 percent and 18 percent share as primary bank.

Company 8 does not, however, take its impressive highlights and dominating share for granted. It regularly measures customer satisfaction of its customers and its competitors' customers. The marketing department provides the executive management with a quarterly report that tracks the following:

- Primary bank market share
- Several satisfaction indicators
- Willingness to recommend
- Length of banking relationship
- Image attributes of the institution

Over the last three quarters, the company's technology image, overall satisfaction, and willingness to recommend were gradually declining (length of banking relationship remained constant). Figures 12-1, 12-2, and 12-3 present the results compared to competition.

The company's executive management evaluated the declining trends. It was concerned that although the company received the American Banking Association's technology award, its retail customer base did not perceive it as a technologically advanced institution. (The ABA award was for the company's sophisticated intranet and extranet that were invisible to its customers.) Therefore, Company 8 decided to develop a new high-tech retail banking product as the means to improve its image ratings. The company's internal analysis of its competitors indicated that this would overcome and improve the satisfaction and willingness ratings, too.

FIGURE 12-1   Bank's Image (Attribute: Technologically Advanced Services[1])

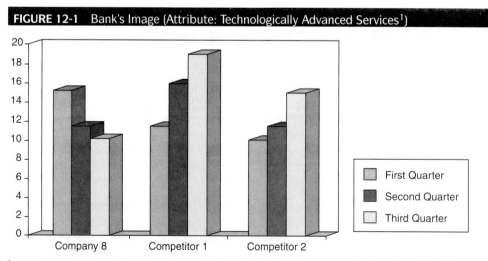

[1]Rated on a scale from 1 to 20 (1 = does not describe the bank; 20 = completely describes the bank).

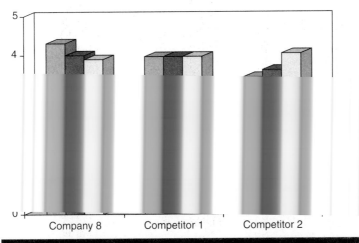

FIGURE 12-2　Overall Satisfaction[2]

[2]Based on a scale from 1 = very dissatisfied to 5 = very satisfied.

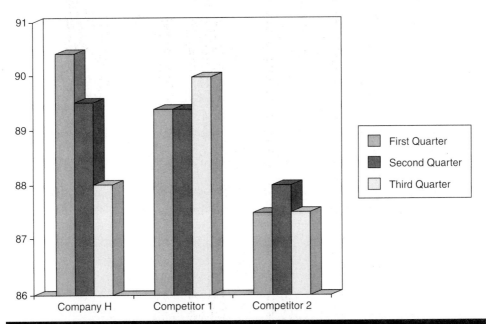

FIGURE 12-3　Willingness to Recommend (to a Friend, Family Member, or Associate)

E-BUSINESS MARKETING GOAL OR STRATEGY

The company's decision to develop and release a new, high-tech retail banking product meant using the new product development process. The first two steps of NPD are **idea generation** and **idea screening.** The marketing and information systems departments met with the company's advertising agency to conduct these initial steps in the process.

Idea generation relies on knowing customers' preferences. The company's ad agency had participated in a syndicated research study on consumers' interest in technologically based banking products. The results indicated high levels of interest in the market segments that Company 8 served. Company 8 also interviewed the employees in their retail locations for their input. Both the survey results and the employees noted that these consumer segments (30–45 years of age; high levels of education and income; and characterized as entrepreneurial) were very interested in an Internet-based product for starting their own business. Several potential products were voiced during a brainstorming session. They varied from proprietary software (offered through Active Server Pages—ASP) that guided a user through starting a business and leveraging technology to the development of an electronic store to online consulting services offered through Company 8 (at no charge if the customer's profitability was at the targeted level).

Idea screening looks within the company to determine if the idea is consistent with the company's overall objectives, strategies, and allocation of resources. Company 8 had invested heavily in technology for its intranet and extranet. It felt that extending these high-tech services to its retail customers was the right move. Idea screening also sorts all the ideas developed in the previous step based on a success and failure rate. This step in the process leads to the product development strategy.

The accepted idea (with the highest probability of succeeding) was an electronic store infrastructure for consumers wanting to develop their own businesses. This product allowed Company 8 to capitalize on the combination of the two new product development strategies in the high-tech environment: market-driven and technology-driven. In the market-driven strategy, Company 8 would fulfill an articulated need or preference in the consumer marketplace for assistance in developing their own businesses. The technology-driven strategy would be the extension of the company's current technological infrastructure into creating the electronic store (ideally, this product would be the first of a stream of high-tech products and services). The company did acknowledge risks within both strategies. In the market-driven strategy, it could be caught off guard by new technologies from an unexpected source of competition. In the technology-driven strategy, Company 8 risked the technology not performing or a lower product demand than expected. The company would now shift gears from the traditional NPD's discrete eight steps: idea generation; idea screening; concept testing; market strategy development; business analysis; product development; market testing; and commercialization. Company 8 began **organizational improvisation** (Moorman 2001)—meaning that the NPD planning occurs at the same time as the process is implemented. This improvisation has three criteria for success that Company 8 believed it met. Table 12-1 lists each criterion and the company's ratings on its performance for each.

Because Company 8 anticipated the electronic store to be the first of a stream of technology-driven products, it developed a **technology map** that would begin with this product. A technology map is defined as "the stream of new products both breakthroughs and derivatives (incremental improvements based on new technology) that the company is committed to developing over some future time period" (Mohr, 2001, pg. 10).

The technology map contains four steps as developed by Capou and Glazer (1987), adapted by Mohr (2001) and summarized below:

Step 1. Technology Resources Available   This step involves an internal audit of the company's technological resources and how they are currently deployed. The

TABLE 12-1 Company 8 Performance and Improvisation	
Improvisation Criterion for Success	*Company 8 Performance*
High levels of internal knowledge	The company's information technology department was well trained and had developed a state-of-
the electronic store product.

resources may be existing products, internal experts, and business processes. A major outcome is to identify the gaps between existing resources and need resources for new developments.

Step 2. Address Resource Gaps   The resource gaps identified in Step 1 are analyzed and alternatives for closing the gaps are determined. There are three alternatives available: internal production (make); external purchase (buy); or strategic alliance (co-develop).

Step 3. Determine "What to Sell"   In the high-tech environment, a company can license the technology (that is, it is the product or service) or the technology enables a new product. There are five options: license or sell the technology; sell a prototype; sell components to original equipment manufacturers; sell a final product ("out of the box"), or sell a complete solution.

Step 4. Evaluation of New Product   The ongoing management of the technology map involves the evaluation of a new product and whether to discontinue or not; as well as the protection of the intellectual property. (The company's technology map is presented in Table 12-2.)

In keeping with the organizational improvisation process, the company began developing its promotional strategies for the new product. This was led by the advertising agency and marketing department. They would target their current customers with a special offer of free hosting for the first 90 days (other fees included a monthly flat fee[3] for maintaining the site and handling the transaction volume). This offer was worth $150.00 per customer account. The agency wasted no time developing a direct marketing program to solicit sign-ups for the electronic store. In-branch merchandising was also designed, created, and shipped to the branches. Every employee was eligible for the product's lucrative incentive plan. To receive the incentive, customers had

---

[3]The monthly flat fee was $1,000.00.

TABLE 12-2 Technology Map Assessment	
Technology Map Step	*Company 8 Assessment*
Step 1: Resource inventory	The company's technological inventory was quite positive. Its intranet housed its human resources function (benefits, training, travel, and activities), new product teams, and online research. The extranet managed its procurement, suppliers (e.g., check orders), and partnerships. This infrastructure was current and efficient. The company also had a basic internet Web site. There was ample server capacity to house thousands of electronic stores. The major gap was in developing a standardized product that would become an individualized electronic store for its customers. Otherwise, the product would be cost-prohibitive.
Step 2: Address resource gaps	The company identified three areas to focus on developing its standardized electronic store: ability to develop a Web site structure and customers customizing it for their particular store-look[a]; ability to cash-enable the sites (accepting and processing payment); and ongoing maintenance (Web mastering). Company 8 would partner with one of the credit card associations to cash-enable the site and outsource the Web mastering. It asked the internal information technology department to design an architecture of a site that, with online instructions, could easily be customized.
Step 3: Determine "what to sell"	Company 8 was committed to providing a total electronic solution for its customers.
Step 4: Ongoing management	Although the company was confident that the product would be successful, it decided that 300 electronic stores had to be operating by the end of the second year. Otherwise, it would withdraw it from the market. The company's corporate counsel had filed with the Patents & Trademarks Office (PTO) to protect its proprietary store configuration.

[a]These issues were being dealt with prior to the major Internet Service Provider's (ISP) offering customized personal Web sites to its subscribers.

to maintain their electronic stores for 6 months. As soon as the information systems department had tested its standardized architecture with individual customization and was confident in its performance, the company was ready to communicate it to the marketplace. Finally, the product was tested and given the "green light." The next day, in-branch merchandising was installed and Company 8 was ready to accept sign-ups.

The initial sign-up rate was considerably lower than expected—considering the $150.00 savings for the first three months (with no further obligation to continue). Branch employees were asked to call their customers and encourage sign-ups. The incentive plan was enriched. Sales remained dismal for the first 10 months. Company 8 decided to conduct some online focus groups to identify the sales obstacles.

Four online focus groups were conducted in one evening. Two groups were composed of selected customers who had signed up for the electronic store. The other two

[text obscured]

individually. Conversely, the groups who had signed up for the product had higher absorptive capacity. Their feedback, however, was that customization was difficult and technical support was not readily available. Company 8 decided to incorporate these findings into a revised product offering. By the end of the product's first year, the customization of the electronic store could be done at one of their branches with a specialist. For customers more technologically savvy, online or telephone support was available. Company 8 saw a slight increase in sales during the first 90 days of the reintroduction. At the end of the second year, however, it had only 75 electronic stores in operation.

Because it was considerably below its target cutoff of 300 e-stores at the end of the product's second year, the company's electronic store was withdrawn from the market. The company held a meeting to determine why it had failed. It had closely followed the new product development process for the high-tech environment and believed it had been prudent with its organizational improvisation. The most likely reason for failure was that Company 8 had stepped too far out of its core competency—retail banking—without asking its customers. It had reacted too quickly to the lowering satisfaction, willingness to recommend, and technological image ratings. Even though the syndicated research and observational analyses from branch employees indicated this was a product its customers wanted, the product that was created still failed. In retrospect, the company determined it should have conducted concept tests among its customers. This would determine if its customers truly wanted their retail bank to provide this type of technology service. Company 8 also recognized the need to accommodate different levels of technology skills and readiness when releasing a technology-driven product. One avenue to achieve this would be a Web site that was created for all the e-store users. Through protected passwords issued only to the product owners, this online support center would have training available along with online customer service representatives. It would also create a sense of community among the e-store product owners and potentially overcome some of the variation in technological sophistication.

In the future the company would conduct more specific research when its ratings declined, rather than quickly attempting to resolve them. As it turned out, during the 2 years of the electronic store product release, the company's satisfaction, willingness to recommend, and technology image ratings had all improved.

PRIMARY STAKEHOLDERS

The main stakeholder group for the electronic store product was the customer (existing and potential). If the e-store had succeeded, Company 8 could consider this competitive advantage as a positive message for its shareholders. This would be the second group of stakeholders addressed.

VALUE BUBBLE

The advertising and marketing department did not initially include the value bubble in its promotion or communication strategies. This was another mistake in the release of this technology-driven product. Because the e-store was Web-based, online marketing would be consistent with the product type. The use of direct and other traditional marketing approaches may not have been the right source with the right message for the right audience. Technologically savvy customers may ignore the traditional marketing tools. For example, this type of customer (targeted for the e-store product) is less likely to visit a physical branch office to conduct their banking business. They more often choose self-service technologies to conduct their business (automated tellers and online banking).

If the value bubble had been used, each of the five phases would have contributed to the marketing of the e-store product. This next section explains how each of the value bubble steps would have benefited the company's plan.

Site Technology and Value Bubble Instances

Although Company 8 closed its e-store, it does maintain an online presence with most of the products from the e-store still available online. However, instead of a store metaphor, the company opted for a multiple-site model that more or less cobbles together different subsites much in the same way as shown in Chapter 11. The main bank page opens to an Active Server Page (ASP) suggesting an immediate link to a database.

The JavaScript in the site is used extremely efficiently. JavaScript can appear in the HTML page, be loaded from an external source, or both. By using an external source, several functions can be written once and then reused within each of the pages in the site—even from different domains. Company 8 uses JavaScript for controlling the several different windows from the different domains that appear and keeps track of where everything is and what to open and close. Generally, the JavaScript keeps the main home page window open and opens and closes the other. It is also used to show and hide different layers in a page, which is one way to keep additional material available on a page. A second external source of JavaScript is called up to display fee tables. Hence, any page on the site can call up only the external JavaScript needed, thereby saving on the time it would take to load unneeded script.

Another interesting use of technology in the Company 8 site is its use of external Cascading Style Sheets (CSS). The idea behind CSS is to give the Web page designer the ability to position and format text on a page. Company 8 created a CSS template to be used with all of its pages in all of its sites. Thus, when a new page is added, the external CSS can be called up to ensure uniform appearance in colors, fonts, and general layout. However, at the same time, CSS can be inserted into an HTML page to fine-tune the design for a special application within a single page, and that is exactly what Company 8 did.

The home page for the site is organized around three general menus and several drop-down menus. The three general menus are:

retains the overall corporate solor scheme

home page and not that of a subsite (as shown in Chapter 11).

This site also made use of Java applets for its calculators. One of the newer browsers would not load the applets, and because Java has been migrating steadily to JavaServer pages, it was not surprising to find that although newer browsers had no problems with the JSP pages used in the site, a seemingly simple feat like loading a Java applet was problematic. However, in creating the site, monitors in Company 8 should have checked the site thoroughly with new browsers to make sure their software worked correctly. Failure to do so has the consequence of pushing away potential clients.

Figure 12-4 shows the general home page design.

FIGURE 12-4   Company 8 Home Page Showing Where Emergency Messages and Links Were Placed

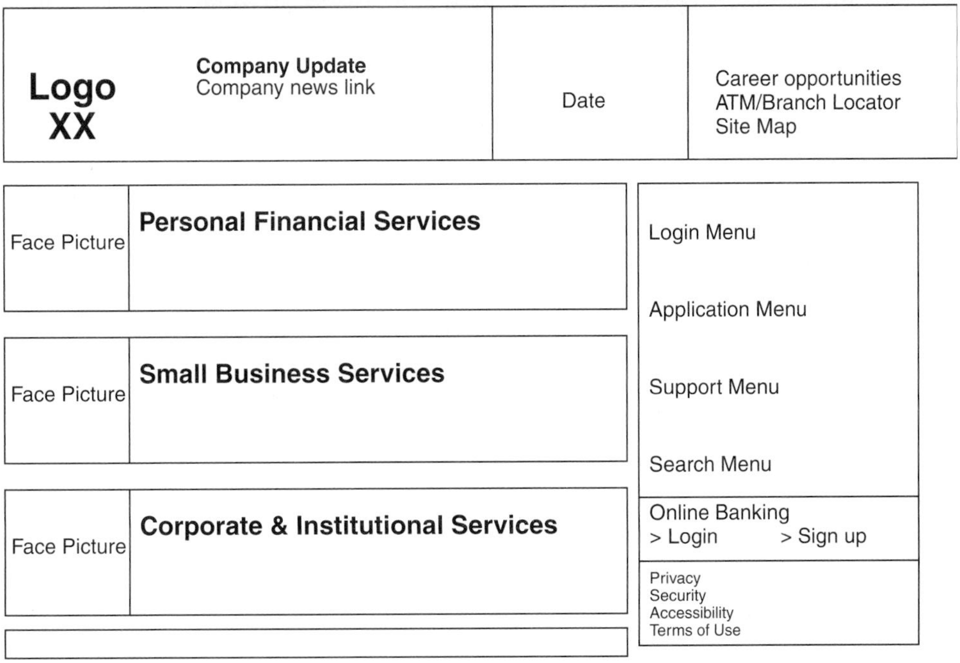

Logo XX	**Company Update** Company news link	Date	Career opportunities ATM/Branch Locator Site Map

Face Picture	**Personal Financial Services**	Login Menu
Face Picture	**Small Business Services**	Application Menu / Support Menu / Search Menu
Face Picture	**Corporate & Institutional Services**	Online Banking > Login > Sign up / Privacy Security Accessibility Terms of Use

Attracting

Company 8 could have used the online and off-line environment to build traffic to a demonstration site of the e-store—online links at appropriate sites (for example, the bank's Web site and the credit card partner's site). Targeted online advertising based on keywords used on a search engine would assist in driving traffic. Although protecting its state-of-the-art product, Company 8 could have staged a series of press releases to generate demo site visits. All of these factors would have been compatible for driving traffic to a Web site (Ilfeld and Weiner 2001). At the demonstration site, an option to sign up or receive additional information (via e-mail, phone call, or branch employee visit) would be readily available. The special offer of free hosting for the first 3 months would have been advertised as available to the first 100 online sign-ups.

Attract Technologies

Although the general design is modestly attractive, very little of the technology available to make a site more attractive was in evidence. A simple yet fundamental inclusion for any business site is the use of metatags to help search engines find the site by name or product. Both a description and content metatag provide search engines with the necessary information a potential customer is likely to seek. However, after entering several key terms, such as "Personal Financial Services," Company 8 never was found, but several of the company's competitors were.

A search using the branding name immediately located the Web site. Because Company 8 did not use a description metatag, however, only a simple and uninspiring "Welcome to Company 8" appeared in the search engine mentioning none of its services. Given the simplicity of adding metatags in a page's HTML and the needed information, the decision not to do so was extraordinary. Even Company 7, (discussed in Chapter 11), used very descriptive and content-laden metatags in its subsites even though it failed to do so for its home page.

Engaging

Once potential e-store customers signed up for the site, they would be issued a password for the e-store support center. This site would accommodate the diverse technology experience of the product owners through a basic questionnaire administered on their first visit. The site would present navigation and content based on the customer's level. A community section would have threaded discussions and online chat capabilities among customers. As needed, the company's technical support staff would be included for troubleshooting and problem solving. Illustrations of effective and ineffective Web design would be provided in one section of the site. That is, helpful hints on the number of graphics, downloading times, text layout, and so forth would be presented. Another section would provide Web graphics and drawing tools. More sophisticated e-store customers could design their site from a wide selection of software available and save the site through the support center. A Company 8 technician would then upload the site onto the company's server.

Engage Technologies

Several types of engaging activities were available in the Company 8 site. First, the site contains a whole set of information-gathering activities to engage the viewer. For example, the site contains links for such chores as managing daily finances, financing an education, and planning for retirement. Each of these pages has information about different options available using services provided by the company using simple HTML and some graphic files. Second, the site has a series of calculators written in

ciently encoded so that none of the information showed up in the source code. However, the comments in the source code indicated that the encoded materials were developed in 1997, which by Web standards is quite old and, if not updated, the site's pages cannot take advantage of the newer browser **document object models (DOMs).** As the DOMs change, newer features can be added to a site, and at the same time, some older browser elements are degraded. Nevertheless, it worked well enough, even though the site was relatively slow compared with other sites, and some of the Java did not work correctly with some newer browsers.

Retaining

It would be critical to have the e-store customers return to the support center frequently. All updates and enhancements to the technology supporting the stores would be announced well in advance. To ensure customers frequently returned to the support center, Company 8 would send e-mails every time an announcement was posted. An option to unsubscribe from the distribution list was available. The support center would also update its Web design helpful hints section monthly. Company 8 would promote these enhancements so the e-store customers could remain competitive in the online environment. By providing these tools, the company could reinforce frequent visits.

Retain Technologies

The retain technology was quite good, but the messages associated with technology were bland at best. On both major browsers in the newer versions (6.0 and newer), a customer is able to have the browser retain account numbers and log-in information. When the customer returns, all he needs to do to log in is to click a log-in button, making it simple for him to access his account. However, when the account comes up, no message greets the customer by name, company, or in any other way to indicate that the visitor is somehow special. One way Company 8 could do that is by using a cookie on the customer's computer; however, the company uses a log-in process, so the database containing the customer's financial records could easily contain that information. Then, when the customer logged in from any computer, she would be welcomed with some kind of greeting. Instead, a last log-in message like the following is presented to the customer:

You last logged in on September 18, 2002 at 07:57:02 AM

Such information may have some fleeting value to the customer, but it hardly constitutes a greeting.

Learning

Through the customer registration (on the initial support center visit) and online behavior tracking, Company 8 built a rich database of users. It permitted the company to profile the type of e-store customer. Using this information, the company would target prospects. It also monitored customer satisfaction with the site's content and functionality through pop-up survey methodology. During the visit, the survey would appear and the customer could bypass it for that visit or hold it until later in the visit. For customers who did not want to participate in any of the surveys, there was an opt-out button.

Learn Technologies

Most of the learn technology in the site was provided by either ASP or JSP linked to databases. When the customer fills in account information, all of the data are stored in a database. Likewise, in the "Forum" page, the data entered by the customers tell the company which of the major categories of information the customers are interested in or concerned about. Included were the following categories:

- Account Information
- Bill Payment
- Customer Service
- New Features
- Transfers
- Other/Miscellaneous

Such categories can help Company 8 see at a glance where the customers have the most interest. The details in the "suggestion box" provide added information that can be used to improve the site and the company's services.

It was difficult to discern whether the site used clickstream technology, but with the numerous ASP, it certainly had the capacity to do so easily. The fact that the site reported to the customer the time of his last visit indicates some kind of learning using the technology. A JavaScript time object easily could be placed into a variable and sent to a back-end where it is stored in a database. The technology itself is simple enough. Using it well is another matter, and if and how Company 8 incorporated the information is unclear. It was not in their plan.

Relating

To understand and relate in a personalized manner to the e-store customer, Company 8 would customize the site's navigation based on each visitor's profile of activity. When a customer visited the online technical support representative, they would be contacted within 36 hours to follow up on the issues. If the problem was recurring, the representative would offer a phone call or personal visit for resolution.

As stated previously, the actions within each of the value bubble phases are suggested or proposed for the e-store product. The failure of the product was not attributed to any single mistake or oversight; however, it is important to recognize the need to promote an Internet-enabled product (such as an e-store) through the channel in which it is delivered. This was a serious oversight by Company 8.

Relate Technologies

new separate window opened when the site was accessed through the home pages. It indicated that customers could make a donation through the company's physical offices, online through bill payment, or directly to the American Red Cross. However, although Company 8 indicated that its customers could make a donation, it made no mention of any assistance it provided itself. Thus, instead of a "Join us in helping . . ." message, it more or less made it easy for the customer to help on his or her own.

COLLECTING YOUR KNOWLEDGE: A REVIEW

Key Terms

- competitive benchmarking
- document object model (DOM)
- household market share statistics
- idea generation
- idea screening
- new product development (NPD)
- organizational improvisation
- technology map

Questions to Ask

1. What did Company 8 initially plan for its online store? What were the two types of risks the company faced when creating the product?
2. What were the four steps for the technology map Company 8 planned on taking?
3. How did Company 8 effectively use the technology to effectively engage customers?
4. Although Company 8 used very powerful Web technology well, how did it fail to relate to customers in its Web design?
5. What did Company 8 fail to do in relating to customers? What would have to be changed in its site for staff to effectively relate to potential and current customers?

Application to Business

Company 8 failed to take into account the value bubble when it launched its online store. However, it had the technology in its site to use the value bubble effectively and in fact did so in a number of places on the site. What aspects of your company's site intentionally or unintentionally used one or more aspects of the value bubble and how were the steps applied online?

Setting up technology to relate can be tricky at best. In view of the company's failure to instill any steps to relate to its customers, what aspects of your company's site could be changed to better set up a relationship with your company's customers?

In emergencies and catastrophes, the Web has proven to be an invaluable source for communication and generating community action. If a catastrophic event struck your business, how could the Web be used to both relate to customers and effect a useful service for the community?

Web Sites to Visit

www.citibank.com Citibank has multiple sites accessed through a welcome page. The user selects a country and chooses from a drop-down menu of the bank's several services, including online shopping at "CitiPlaza" in addition to more conventional banking services. By setting up external partnerships in its CitiPlaza (e.g, Lands End, Overstock.com), Citibank is able to make its site a "one-stop" shopping and banking site. After the World Trade Center and Pentagon attacks, Citibank used a separate window to inform viewers that it had made a $15 million contribution to the victims of the catastrophe. The company also indicated its concern over its employees missing at the World Trade Center. (Company 8 simply asked its customers to make a donation.)

www.citizensbank.com A relatively small bank and competitor of Company 8, Citizens Bank emphasizes personal service and customer attention. Among other elements on the bank's site that make that point are three commercials available to the viewer in both QuickTime and Windows Media player formats where kind and concerned representatives from Citizens Bank help customers. The ads, which run on television, are presented as examples of what the viewer can expect if she becomes a customer. Any bank would be well-served to note how Citizens Bank works to build relationships between itself and its customers on the Web.

www.bankamerica.com Very similar to Citibank in its expanded services, including online shopping, Bank of America uses its Web site to bring in customers from states where it does not have physical offices. For example, if a customer in Connecticut wants to open a Bank of America account, the interactive Web site responds that its closest physical bank is in Virginia and will open an account there for the customer. Thus, all of the banking can be done online without having to ever use a physical branch of the bank.

Like other large U.S. banks, the Bank of America had offices in the World Trade Center. The bank provided an online report to its employees (referred to as "associates") and customers, and announced both a $1 million donation and that it was making its banking centers available for donations to the victims of the terrorist attack. Instead of supporting the American Red Cross, the Bank of America had links to september11fund.org that was organized by the United Way and the New York Community Trust to provide financial support to the victims of the attack.

CHAPTER

17

CASE STUDY

Chapters 1 and 2 focused on presenting extension of existing marketing conceptual frameworks into the electronic environment. Chapter 3 presented a specific framework (the value bubble) for marketing a firm's electronic presence or Web site. In Chapter 4, communication research was presented within the electronic environment and the need to thoroughly understand individual stakeholder' specific preferences and needs from the electronic environment. The eight case studies (Chapters 5 through 12) presented various marketing challenges and obstacles that firms used the electronic environment to address. Each firm employed elements of the value bubble model to market its site.

The Internet technologies available to firms extend marketing options even further. However, many firms do not have the systems flexibility or marketing resources to take full advantage of the technology. It is important to understand some of the future possibilities. Therefore, in this chapter, a conceptual model that was introduced by Wind and Rangaswamy (2001) is presented. Their model is extended by the e-business components and the value bubble presented in this text thus far. The challenges for firms embracing this model are addressed through some of the existing services marketing frameworks presented later in this chapter. Although the eight firms examined in the case study chapters are not using the **customerization** model, future e-business marketing goals or strategies would lead to elements of customerization. A table is presented to demonstrate how the model may be appropriate for future consideration for these companies.

Wind and Rangaswamy's customerization model is enabled by Internet technologies. Customerization defines the exchange process of marketing in the context of complete customer control. Because the Internet empowers the online visitor or customer, customerization is a natural fit in the electronic environment. It addresses the company's challenge of low searching and switching costs (competitors are a mere "mouse click away") with marketing and business strategies that will entice customers to remain loyal to them (both online and off-line). This chapter will explain the concept of customerization and extend it within the e-business components and the value bubble elements that translate the science of marketing into the practice of marketing.

OVERVIEW OF CUSTOMERIZATION MODEL

Customerization is a buyer- or customer-centric marketing model. It develops a relationship between two dimensions: one-to-one marketing and mass customization. This means that a firm can move along a continuum of personalized marketing (one-to-one) at the same time it is customizing products and services (including information) for its online customers (existing or potential). For a firm to have high levels of one-to-one marketing *and* mass customization (i.e., customerization), its internal operations must have the capability to customize based on a customer's specific request ("build to order process"). This includes a comprehensive database that facilitates personalized or one-to-one marketing. The Internet technologies are able to combine the two dimensions, and when the internal processes are available, they provide a highly valued, customer-centric interaction with the firm. Customerization is based on furthering the relationship with the customer by having the firm and customer become co-producers.

A cornerstone of the model's foundation is the seamless integration of all **databases** within the firm. In the business-to-business marketplace, this includes linkages into the customer's databases that are relevant to the co-production philosophy of customerization (for example, inventory levels to automate replenishment). Effective customerization follows a straightforward, customer-centric path:

- Customers visit a Web site and design their own products or services, which are produced and delivered based on the customers' preferences.
- Subsequent visits are customized to the customer's previous visits (combining traditional or bricks and mortar stores with the electronic storefront interactions). This may be a personal greeting on the site, recommendations for the next purchase, or special tailored offers.
- Communication, outside of the Web site, is also tailored based on the data gathered on the customer. E-mails are targeted toward the individual customer's needs. For example, if an online visitor or customer asked about the material used to manufacture a pair of jeans, the company could provide additional information or education on fabric types and their origins. This allows the company to leverage its knowledge base for its customer's benefit.

A unique characteristic of the customerization model is its flexibility. It was not developed to substitute for other marketing models but rather as an additional tool for the practice of marketing. The internal requirements (e.g., database integration, operations, and production) must be available to adapt the model. However, the model relies on a combination of marketing approaches. This includes traditional, mass marketing, and targeted direct marketing techniques employed through the Internet and physical marketplaces. Firms can allocate a percentage of their marketing budgets to each of the three. The allocation can vary across product or service category based on the company's profitability goals.

At this point, we extend the model into the context of e-business and the value bubble's components. Customerization has eight enhanced marketing outcomes in this extension. Each is briefly defined as follows:

Outcome 1. Developing or Deepening Customer Relationship

Customerization capitalizes on a fundamental principle of relationship-building. That is the design of a two-way interactive communication between its customers and the firm. Customers becomes empowered by specifying their own designs of the firm's goods. Customers and firms learn from one another during this process and build levels of trust and respect. These elements of a relationship create high switching costs for the customer and protect the firm from customer attrition. By using the Internet technologies available, firms can gather and process information in "real time" that enable the dialogue to be accurate and timely.

The customer relationship outcome of this model is clearly seen in the customer

known and be visited (attracting). Several cases presented strategies for building site traffic. Upon arrival at the site, there must be an interaction that is relevant to the visitor (engaging). In the co-production of goods and services, engagement could be readily achieved; however, it must conform to the ease of use and other usability factors presented in the cases or the customer or visitor will exit quickly. The retention (or return visits) rely on the visitor's previous site experience (e-service quality dimensions) and continual updating of the features and content. Learning and relating are, perhaps, the most important for relationship development and deepening. The understanding and communication of the customer's specific preferences through a well-designed site will be a major determinant in building and maintaining a successful relationship (this drives profitability through customer lifetime value—CLV).

Outcome 2. Transitioning Experience-Based Decisions

A major online challenge is that search-based decisions are readily achieved while **experience-based decisions** are more difficult. The Internet environment allows customers to search for information, recommendations, testimonials, and price comparisons in order to evaluate product or service offerings across competitors. Experience-based decisions are complex because the ability to experience the goods (for example, clothes) is more difficult. Many online companies are using three-dimensional displays to overcome this (for example, the automobile manufacturers' Web sites), but the transition has been slow. Customerization has a "design and discover" process within its co-production philosophy. This process allows online users to design the product and then see it on the screen. The ability to observe the outcome of their specifications provides the experience that is necessary. This is particularly important to the company that doesn't want to produce a customized design only to find an unhappy customer ("it did not look or fit the way I thought it should") and a product that it cannot sell.

Outcome 2 is demonstrated in the CRM and supply chain management (SCM) e-business components. The ability to experience the product is critical to customer satisfaction that drives loyalty and retention. This is critical to successfully managing the customer relationship. A company must also have the support of its suppliers in order to present the visual experience of the product prior to its production. Manufacturers are necessary for retailers that want this feature on their site, but raw materials suppliers are critical to the manufacturer's ability to achieve an accurate look and description of materials used.

This outcome taps into two value bubble steps: engaging and retaining. The ability to view the customer's design prior to production will engage the visitor into the site—they will remain there for longer periods of time (stickiness) and are more apt to explore the site further (as long as they have a positive on-site experience). By transitioning the experience-based decisions to an online environment, customers would return to the firm's site for future designing and viewing of their customized design, recognizing that their risk of dissatisfaction is low.

Outcome 3. Customizing the Interaction

At the core of customerization is Outcome 3—customizing the interaction. This outcome relies on accurate databases that integrate all the customer information a firm possesses. The databases may be from the traditional environment merged with the online data (captured in two ways—behaviors through clickstream and log-file analyses and customer-provided information). To effectively customize the interaction, a firm must have accurate segmentation strategies. Segmentation for online customers may not be the same as in the off-line world. It is critical for the appropriate analyses to be conducted and segments identified. In the online world, many suggest that each individual is a segment and the technology can support individual customized communication. It appears to be more realistic to create microsegments and develop a site's interaction based on a very small microsegment with some personalization included. This approach addresses the curvilinear relationship found by Zeithaml, Parasuraman, and Malhotra (2000) between personalization, customization, and privacy concerns.

Customizing the interaction is also found in two e-business components: CRM and business intelligence (BI). To have effective customized interaction, the online segmentation strategies and the most effective interaction with each must first be established. This is the business intelligence component. It relies on prudent data gathering and rigorous ongoing analysis to be effective. Once this intelligence is identified and implemented, the customization of the dialogue can occur. It is this customized interaction that is critical to further the relationship (CRM).

The learning and relating steps of the value bubble are the most important for customizing the interaction. If these two steps are not well executed in the site's design, the development of the online segmentation strategies will suffer. The level of relating on an individual level poses concerns described above. It would be necessary for a site to communicate with its visitor or customer and determine the level of personalization desired.

Outcome 4. Co-Develop Products and Services

In addition to customers designing and customizing their products or services, the firm also collaborates with its customers on new products and services it should offer. These online collaborations are one of the firm's market research stages. The firm may also do test marketing of the new product or service online with its existing customers.

The firm participates in two e-business components: BI and CRM. The business intelligence is defined by the customer feedback on co-developed products and services. In addition, the firm would participate in a competitive benchmarking or best practices analysis to examine the competitive environment if it launches the new product. Customer participation within a firm's decision-making process leads to stronger bonds between both parties. These stronger associations build customer loyalty and increase retention. Both of these aspects are critical to effective CRM.

For the value bubble, the most important stage for Outcome 4 is the engaging stage. Online collaboration will increase the time and involvement a customer will ~~provide the site. It is important to have a sophisticated site, particularly during the~~

Customerization requires a firm to invest in technology to enable the online co-production and collaboration. This is consistent with the value chain developed by Porter (1985) that contains nine activities to create customer value—technology is one of these activities. By increasing value beyond the competition, customers are more satisfied, more loyal, and willing to pay a premium for exceptional value. The Internet environment allows firms to improve their value chains in a more cost-effective manner than in the physical bricks and mortar system. It also facilitates pricing on a per-customer basis.

The e-commerce or the transaction component of e-business is defined with Outcome 5. There is value derived from the transaction and, to the extent the exchange is positive along the e-service quality dimensions, premium pricing would be accepted.

Because the online environment provides an opportunity to charge a price based on the relationship with the customer, the contribution of the value bubble is in the learning and relating phases. The tracking of the customer's purchasing behaviors allows the firm to customize its pricing based upon the relationship and CLV. The online co-design and production feature (as long as it is more appealing than the competition's) supports premium pricing, but the Internet technologies allow the firm to have a range of pricing. This knowledge would be used to customize price.

Outcome 6. Interactive Information Exchange

The Interactive Information Exchange leverages one of a company's existing assets—information about the products and services it provides. Companies tend to underestimate the value of their information and their expertise in certain areas. With the ability to quickly search and retrieve information through the Internet, this asset may be packaged as a unique support service (via a search feature on the company's site). The company would not relinquish any competitive advantages because its proprietary and confidential information is not included.

Outcome 6 also capitalizes on the CRM e-business component. The ongoing customer contact and provision of unique services increases retention and switching costs for customers.

The ability to access a firm's expertise or knowledge fits well into the engaging and retaining steps of the value bubble. Customers can search for pertinent information that pulls them further into the site. They will return when additional information is needed or another type of information is needed that is offered by the company.

Outcome 7. Distribution Channel Choice

Outcome 7 provides customers with their choice of delivery options. They can have it shipped to a preferred location (home or office) or it can be delivered to a store for pickup (based on location convenience). This choice may create channel conflict for members of a distribution network that rely on physical store sales. However, as demonstrated in Chapter 7, company management can minimize this with careful planning. The online environment has also created an outsourcing opportunity for product distribution. Companies such as Federal Express, DHL, and United Parcel Services offer logistics and delivery outsourcing services. Through the real-time information processing available through the Internet, orders may be delivered in a shorter time period.

The e-business components reflected in Outcome 7 are supply chain management (SCM) and enterprise resource management (ERP). By giving customers a choice, the company must be prepared to deliver the product in various ways. Whether it is an outsourced function or not, the suppliers must operate cooperatively with the common goal of quick, efficient delivery at the preferred location. If an internal department is responsible for the delivery, the internal operations must be efficient and capitalize on the technology available (ERP).

Outcome 7 uses the retaining step of the value bubble. One of the frequently mentioned issues with online transactions is meeting the promised delivery time. When customers also have a preference for delivery location, it is critical to be accurate on both. If promises are kept, customers will return to the site and continue their relationships with the firm. If promises are not kept, they will not return and potentially will tell others about their negative experiences.

Outcome 8. Personal Brands

Personal brands transfers the brand from the company to the customer. It is consistent with the overall customerization model of total customer empowerment through the model's buyer-centric orientation. Thus, the product or service brand is replaced with the customer's own name or a name chosen by the customer. Companies with well-entrenched brand awareness and equity were originally concerned about this loss. However, the brand or company image does not vanish. The power of the brand is sufficiently strong with the customer, and the customer will continue to be brand-loyal. However, in the buyer-centric, co-production environment, the customer has the flexibility to control how the product or service is personalized through the mechanism of the branding. This has been successfully demonstrated by Reflect.com, the online-only firm that customizes beauty products for women.

The CRM e-business component is demonstrated through the personalized branding. It further empowers the customer and continues the relationship with the firm as a partner.

Within the value bubble the personalized branding facilitates the engaging and retaining steps. Through the creation of their own brand, online visitors or customers will be more engaged with the site. Their visits will be longer and more likely to be positive. The positive experience will increase the likelihood of return visits (retaining). Companies following the customerization model may also employ the learning and relating steps. By creating the customer's individual brand profile, the company learns more about the customer and uses the information to relate in a personalized style. Customers can use their profiles to recreate or reorder their personalized brands.

The original customerization model and the extensions provided above illustrate how companies of any size can participate in a buyer-centric model. That is, the size of

1. Managing the customer experience in the co-production environment
2. Pricing of products and services that are not eligible for premium pricing

These challenges are identical to those identified in the services marketing literature. From this body of research, several service marketing principles have evolved. By applying some of the traditional and electronic service principles, these challenges can be addressed.

In 1990 the original gap model of service quality was introduced by Zeithaml, Parasuraman, and Berry (1990). The model identified four sources of gaps between customers' expectations about the quality of services to be delivered and their perceptions about the quality of services delivered. The source of the gap is the firm that fails to measure what is important to the customer. By conducting solid market research and implementing accurate segmentation strategies, the firm designs and delivers its services based on the customer's expectation. This reduces the gap (ideally to zero). This model has been evaluated in the online environment by Zeithaml, Parasuraman, and Malhotra (2000). Four online gaps were also identified and, as in the original research, the source of the gap was the firm—except this time it was the firm's Web site falling below expected levels of service delivery. To effectively manage the online customer experience, firms using the customerization model must develop the site while focusing on the attributes that are most important to the customer. It is also critical to have ongoing evaluation or monitoring of the customer's evaluation of the site experience. (Various strategies regarding design and data capture will be presented in Chapter 14.)

The second challenge focuses on the inability to premium-price certain types of products or services. To remain competitive, a firm cannot charge more for the same product that is co-produced or co-designed with the customer on the site. The firm must, however, be able to maintain its revenue stream, and premium pricing was the avenue for offsetting the costs associated with customerization. In these situations, the services marketing literature suggests three models: Shostack's molecular model (1977); Eiglier and Langeard's core and peripheral model (1987); and Lovelock and Wright's flower of service (1999). All three models examined the core service provided and the additional services (analagous to the augmented product) that would enhance the core service's value. Shostack's model focused on the core benefit while Eiglier and Langeard's model centered on a core service with additional services supporting it. The flower of service has the core service surrounded by high-value supplementary services. In customerization, the flower of service model increases the value to the customer and justifies premium pricing (as long as the added services are considered valuable—this is determined through market research).

APPLYING CUSTOMERIZATION TO THE CASE STUDY COMPANIES

The eight companies presented earlier in this text do not currently have the system flexibility and marketing expertise to adapt the complete buyer-centric co-production model (Company 6 is the closest of the eight). However, customerization is a future consideration for each company. The eight main outcomes of the model and its extension were examined based on each company's strategy and goal. Table 13-1 indicates the applicable outcomes for each company and the conditions necessary to experience the customerization outcomes. Each company's e-business marketing goal or strategy can facilitate the first two outcomes: developing the relationship and customizing the interaction.

The next section presents an in-depth examination of the Internet technologies available for the companies' customerization possibilities.

TECHNICAL ANALYSIS

The technical analysis for e-business sites begins with the specific marketing goal and examines the Internet technology used to accomplish the goal. Depending on the goal and the implementation of the technological solution, the technology is either apparent or not. In the case studies for this book, the great bulk of the technology used could be examined by looking at the source code for the different pages. The source code refers to the various HTML tags, JavaScript coding, and any other code used to create the Web page (e.g, Cascading Style Sheets). Other technology had to be inferred by examining the references to other code and assumptions about what the technology did based on what could be seen in the pages. To begin the technical analysis, the different types of Internet and Web technologies were divided into the following five categories:

- HTML
- JavaScript and Cascading Style Sheets
- Middleware
- Compiled code
- Databases

To see how each of these technologies was analyzed, each will be examined separately.

HTML

All browsers have a menu selection to view the page code. Most Web pages are composed primarily of HTML. All HTML does by itself is to describe a page. Using tables, some quite complex, HTML can place graphics, text, and links virtually anywhere the designer wants on the page. (Weinman and Weinman 2001) Other tags set the fonts,

TABLE 13-1 Necessary Conditions to Experience Customerization Outcomes		
Chapter and Company Label	*Conditions Necessary*	*Customerization Outcomes (Outcome No.)*
Chapter 5—Company 1 Ingredient manufacturer	Online design of the insulation product; need to position company as knowledge	• Transitioning the experience-based decision (2) • Interactive information exchange (6) • Developing the relationship (1)
Chapter 7—Company 3 Hardware distributor	Company allows customer delivery to existing store-front or to another location; creates a private-label business for its customers to resell the hardware under the customer's brand name	• Personal brands (8) • Developing the relationship (1) • Customizing the interaction (3)
Chapter 8—Company 4 Utilities	Customers are willing to pay a premium for certain services; develop a knowledge exchange with retail customer base	• Premium pricing acceptance (5) • Interactive information exchange (6) • Developing the relationship (1) • Customizing the interaction (3)
Chapter 9—Company 5 Not-for-Profit trade association	Rigorous analysis of segmentation data; build an integrated communication process based on visitor profile; incorporate visitors' expertise in information exchange	• Interactive information exchange (6) • Developing the relationship (1) • Customizing the interaction (3)
Chapter 10—Company 6 CPG supplier	Online design studio can be expanded to co-production; premium pricing when requested services are available; develop client portfolio to deepen relationship	• Transitioning the experience-based decision (2) • Premium pricing acceptance (5) • Co-develop products and services (4) • Developing the relationship (1) • Customizing the interaction (3)
Chapter 11—Company 7 Insurance	Gradual transition to offer direct broker or agent channel to customers; continue to develop intermediary relationships; refine segmentation strategies for end customer	• Distribution channel choice (7) • Developing the relationship (1) • Customizing the interaction (3)
Chapter 12—Company 8 Financial services	Use online new product development process; ability to use personal brand for electronic storefront	• Co-develop products and services (4) • Personal brands (8) • Developing the relationship (1) • Customizing the interaction (3)

colors, links, forms, and other page elements. By examining the tags and their attributes, it is possible to see different features of the page and what technologies HTML calls upon to complete a given task. For example, a form tag might call for an action to a certain type of middleware:

```
<form method = "POST" action = "http://www.sandlight.com/cgi-bin/cust.pl">
```

The tag tells the viewer that the data placed into the form are being processed using Common Gateway Interface (CGI) and a Perl script. Even though HTML cannot perform the kinds of database functions that Perl can, it reveals the method the page developer used.

JavaScript and Cascading Style Sheets

JavaScript and Cascading Style Sheets (CSS) are embedded in HTML but are not themselves HTML technologies. CSS can be used with XML pages and most other Web-based languages to format output. JavaScript provides dynamic content and interactive elements in a Web site (Sanders 2002). With the exception of the two sites characterized as "brochure-ware," virtually all of the sites examined contained some JavaScript. Likewise, while not as ubiquitous as JavaScript, most of the sites took advantage of CSS to both format the sites and provide a simple template for keeping consistent colors, fonts, and formats throughout the site.

Both of these technologies take advantage of external code sets. External code sets cannot be viewed directly from an HTML page because they reside on separate pages, possibly even on separate servers and domains. Some can be viewed by following the path to the source and opening them like any other Web page. Where possible, they were followed to their source and examined to determine how a value bubble element was created.

Middleware

The type of middleware a site employed was evident by examining HTML form actions as noted above. However, most of the source code for the middleware was unavailable for examination. The most common middleware found was Microsoft's Active Server Pages (ASP) and CGI/Perl. ASP is typically written in a language called VBScript. However, ASP pages can also accept HTML, and although the VBScript disappears when viewed in a browser, it is not too difficult to discern the nature of the script behind the page by looking at the remaining HTML.

Evidence of change in the middleware was evident in a number of sites. Macromedia's ColdFusion was discovered, as were JavaServer Pages. Likewise, the move, led by IBM to Linux operating systems for their servers may encourage more companies to enlist PHP, a JavaScript-like open-source middleware that runs on Apache servers. Because Apache servers make up over 60 percent of the servers currently in use on the Web (Web Server Survey, September 1, 2001, by Security Space <www.securityspace.com>), and 43 percent of the Apache servers have PHP modules, we expect to see more PHP middleware in the future. Also, Microsoft's .NET middleware will replace ASP as its primarily supported middleware. Unfortunately, .NET is not backwardly compatible with Microsoft's ASP, and so its growth may be slower than was the case with ASP.

Compiled Code

was not difficult because other technologies ate the page elements that Flash can create.

The JSP pages were typically identified through the *action* attribute in a *form* tag in the same way that ASP, PHP, and CGI files are identified. However, JSP pages are Java servlets that compile and run on the servers instead of the client browsers, as is the case with Java applets. Moreover, they are far more powerful than scripted middleware such as ASP, PHP, and Perl. JSP can create and insert a page into a single HTML page that is not part of a frame set. At the same time, they can handle middleware chores of sending data between an HTML page and database. Like Flash pages, the identification of the JSP extension led to examining the working Web page to deduce what role JSP played.

Databases

The databases required the most inferential work and a good deal of assumptions. If HTML forms were found on the pages asking for information that required storage, databases were assumed to be in the background somewhere. The nature, scope, and size of a database was another matter. Whether an Oracle system backed up the Web pages or Microsoft Access was the main data storage system was unknown. One could infer that if PHP were used as middleware that MySQL would be a likely database, but such assumptions were untested. About the only likely assumption was that they were some kind of structured query language (SQL) database. This assumption is based on the fact that the middleware communicates with databases through structured query language.

In some cases, databases were used to pull up inventories of services or products. Rather than having a direct link to a product or service page, the link would be to middleware, and the only reason for connecting to middleware in these circumstances would be to get information from a database.

HOW SELECTED INTERNET TECHNOLOGY INTERFACES WITH ORGANIZATIONAL GOALS

A successful marketing manager can improve her record by getting to know a population's purchasing habits. Whether the knowledge is gathered over the Internet using clickstream technology or by examining purchasing studies based on sales and inventory records is moot. The issue is to get the marketing information. The only reason that a corporation should even consider using Internet technology is to meet organizational goals and not for the sake of the technology itself.

Some corporations do have goals of building Internet infrastructures. The goal may be as simple as wiring offices and establishing desktop connections to a local area network (LAN). More ambitious goals may be to set up intranets and extranets or launch an online "store." However, these goals need to be more than a vague hope that the Internet and Web reaches so many markets that something good must come of it. The collapse of the "dot-coms" beginning in 2000, that had grown at exponential rates in the 1990s, was based on the simple fact that the companies were not turning a profit. Infrastructure money that was sunk into expanding the company technologies, while necessary, never resulted in the astronomical profits predicted by the business models.

In a post-dot-com era of Internet technology applications, the analysis of organizational goals needs to examine exactly how the company will prosper with Internet technology. As noted at the outset of this chapter, the customerization model can be realized by the use of Internet and Web technology. The technology is not a goal in and of itself. The customerization model provides specific ways of addressing marketing issues that can be realized using the technology, but the question remains: Is the technology worth bothering with at all?

The value bubble provides steps for implementing some or all of the principles of customerization. We have examined how the technology applies to the steps in the value bubble and how the value bubble steps apply to different aspects of customerization. Now we discuss how different aspects of customerization tie into Internet technology.

Technology of Relationship-Building

The idea that technology can be part of **relationship-building** sounds like manufacturing the worst possible type of pseudo–gemeinschaft relationship (Goffman 1959). Sociologists characterize close personal relationships found among family and friends as **gemeinschaft** and those functional relationships needed for business and other impersonal interactions as **gesellschaft.** Those relationships that pretend to be affective and personal for a functional end are **pseudo–gemeinschaft**.

However, like technologically enhanced communication from the advent of the telegraph and telephone, **pseudo–gemeinschaft relationships** were not invented by technology, and they certainly are not enhanced or magnified by Internet technology. Rather, by coming to understand more and more about a customer's needs, the client relationship is based on understanding what a customer wants and needs and serving those needs. The technology used to get, store, and retrieve information about a customer is relatively simple as noted below:

- Customer-provided information entered in a form (**HTML** or Flash technology)
- Middleware to send information to and retrieve it from a database (ASP, PHP, CGI, ColdFusion, JSP)
- Database to hold and organize information
- Web page to display personalized information (JavaScript, Flash, JSP using information)
- E-mail to keep in touch with customer. This can be done by a service representative or through bulk e-mails customized for a client set. For example, PHP

script can loop through a MySQL database and generate e-mails tailored to different client profiles

Technology and Experience-Based Decisions

One of the more phenomenal examples of providing a sample experience with a service was America Online's (AOL) free sample of its Internet Service Provider (ISP). Several free hours of online services were delivered through the mail on 3.5-inch diskettes and later, CD-ROMs. The postal-delivered diskettes and CD-ROM then connected the potential customer to the online service. Once the customer had an experience with AOL's service, the expectation was for some percentage of samplers to become subscribers. By making deals with computer manufacturers, AOL, as well as Microsoft, also provided free sample services available in the computers customers purchase.

The software industry also allowed customers to experience their products prior to purchase using online technology. Many software programs have trial software that either has a limited time it can be used or disabled features. The customers are able to use the software, and if they like it, they can either purchase it from a retailer, online or brick and mortar, or download an unlocking key that enables all features and removes time limitations.

Technology for Customizing the Interaction

Microsegmentation requires precise database information about what a customer wants. As the customer's wants and needs change, the interactive modes must be flexible enough to change as well. The most flexible products available are digital. A digital product can be customized if it is built to allow adding and deleting features. For example, Microsoft Word can be customized by the user. The customer can change the toolbars, the content of the toolbars, and several other features that best fit his needs at any given point in time. In the same way, and using the same technology, business–client interactions can be customized.

The automated interaction that can be generated with cookies (digital ones), preformatted responses using artificial intelligence (AI), and customized Web pages is only part of the solution. Some customers may be more comfortable with e-mail interaction and eschew log-in procedures or the idea of cookies being planted on their hard drives. If that is the case, microsegmentation strategies can be used to personalize "handmade" e-mails and to design more precise e-mails to customers in any given microsegment.

Likewise, as part of a ranged marketing plan, user information culled from Internet technology can note the changes in customer behavior and market additional services and products. Clickstream or log technology discussed in the learning step of the value bubble is the same technology for customizing interactions with customers.

Technology in Co-Developing Products and Services

Many companies call their services "products" with the idea that a reference to a *product* will generate a value not found in services. It somehow gives the service a more tangible character to call it a product. For example, in the insurance industry, different plans of service and coverage are referenced as a range of products. However, for co-developing products, it may be prudent to examine a product as a service. Marketing has always had more flexibility with services than with products. Products are finite, but services are almost infinitely flexible and negotiable. Even ranged products such as automobiles, where a customer can purchase anything from the basic model to one described as "loaded," can have only so many features. A problem with treating services the same way as products is that services are created as modular units with prepackaged blocks rather than customized services made up of microprocesses to best meet customer needs. Pricing has become modular as well and eases the problem of showing customers what they get for their money.

However, using computers and microsegmentation, microprocesses become tailor-made packages of products and services. Today, even a simple desktop computer has more than enough power to price any combination of microprocesses into a tailor-made service and, in some cases, a product. In working with customers to develop products and service packages, the Internet plays a key role.

In the area of publishing, as an example, customized books have been profitably published for individual sections of college courses. Professors select from a collection of articles, chapters, or original work of their own making, the publisher binds and publishes the book, and the professors use them in their courses. The tailor-made books can be used as main or supplementary texts, and they provide exactly what the professors need. Over time, the product can be updated. Similar publications have been produced for corporations needing books for training or other specialized areas that would not warrant a general publication.

With the Internet, not only can producers and customers collaboratively create products and services, but the effort can be done collaboratively over the Internet. For instance, sample designs can be e-mailed in PDF files or placed on a Web page to be downloaded for approval by clients. Changes can be made along with adjustments until the customer gets exactly what she needs. Likewise, task forces made up of independent developers or partner companies can collaborate over the Internet for creating a wide range of services or products that a single company may not be able to make.

Technology and Premium Pricing Acceptance

Premium pricing has always been a complex issue because of profit margins. If a premium-priced product or service is purchased over a generic product or service, the profit margin may be so low as to negate the premium price. In large measure, the technology must reduce the cost of customerization so that premium-priced goods and services are profitable.

One organizational concept useful in this context is **independent interdependence.** The concept refers to coordinating independent specialists who are not a part of a single corporate entity, but who work together to create a customized service or product. As noted in the previous section, independent developers and partner companies can work together to use their combined resources without having to hire and

the information globally available. Those companies with information as part of a service or as a product can package information in several different customized configurations and make it available to their customers at very little cost to the business itself. Using anything from Web pages to PDF files, the Web and Internet are ideal information distributors.

Technology and Distribution Channel Choice

As noted in the previous section, the Internet is an ideal source for distribution of information as a product or service. Likewise, virtually any digital product, along with documentation, can be delivered over the Web and retrieved at multiple sites thereby providing distribution channel choice.

The Internet aids in nondigital products as well by providing online product tracking. The customer can tell at any time where his product is in the delivery pipeline and plan accordingly. Federal Express, UPS, and all of the other private delivery companies provide this service. Likewise, the United States Postal Service makes Internet tracking available to customers. Using this tracking system, customers can make informed decisions on which service best serves their goals.

Using a combination of global positioning satellites and the Internet, trucking companies can show customers precisely where their delivery is at any given point in time. Delays caused by weather, traffic conditions, or mechanical breakdowns can be immediately communicated to the customer over the Internet.

Technology and Personal Brands

The idea that a brand belongs to the customer and not the producer is important to customerization, and in some respects has been going on for some time. For example, Intel makes the processing chip for Dell, IBM, and Gateway computers, but the branding is with the companies that assemble the package and not the many companies that make the chips, drives, interfaces, and operating systems.

Personal brands, especially in B2B environments, are enhanced by computer technology in the creation and duplication of styles identified with branding. The kind of interactive development for a branded product or service is further enhanced and made possible by collaborative development over the Internet.

COLLECTING YOUR KNOWLEDGE: A REVIEW

Key Terms

- compiled code
- customerization
- databases
- distribution channel choice
- experienced-based decisions
- gemeinschaft relationships
- gesellschaft relationships
- HTML
- independent interdependence
- interactive information exchange
- personal brands
- psuedo-gemeinschaft relationships
- relationship building

Questions to Ask

1. What is the relationship between customerization and the value bubble?
2. What are the eight outcomes of customerization?
3. How is it possible for customers to have decision-making experiences over the Web or Internet?
4. What Internet technologies could be employed to enhance personal branding?
5. Compare digital and nondigital products in the customer choice of delivery channels. What alternative delivery channels exist for digital products that are not available for nondigital products?

Application to Business

Look at your company's Web site. What outcomes associated with customerization does it employ? Look at Table 13-1 and put your company in the matrix to help you see what if any customerization is in place now.

Even though it may be difficult, how could your company develop personalized branding for customers and how could it do this over the Web (See www.reflect.com below to get some ideas).

How does your company involve the customer in creating a product or a service. If it does not, how could an Internet solution involving a revised Web site and e-mail facilitate such customer involvement?

Web Sites to Visit

www.cdnow.com The CDNOW site illustrates how technology can provide consumer experience in decision making. It provides several different formats for listening to music excerpts. This helps the consumer make a more informed decision and attracts customers who want to "test drive" products prior to purchase.

www.reflect.com This site exemplifies customerization. The potential customer and return customer go through a process of "beauty consultation," "custom formulation," and "sensory matching." From the online process, individually-tailored skin creams, shampoos, and other beauty products are developed for the customer. The last step in the process—*sensory matching*—allows the customer to select a fragrance to go with the product, packaging for it, and a name for it. All of the information for the customer's individual set of beauty products is saved, and return customers can get their custom collections of various beauty aids via a reference to the information they have provided on a prior visit to the site.

www.excite.com Once logged in and signed up, the user is invited to personalize her site. Several different options are available—from a selected stock to a horoscope. The user can also change the color scheme to her liking and move the different elements around the page until it looks right to her. This customerized portal serves the customer by providing her with exactly the setup she wants and it serves the business by having a customer who uses the portal where links to online e-business and banner ads abound.

CHAPTER
14 | RESEARCHING E-BUSINESS

This textbook provides a conceptual framework for e-business marketing. The models presented are enabled by Internet technologies. In the case studies, the company's marketing goals and strategies were examined in the context of the Internet-enabled environment. This environment facilitates the marketing science and practice through its ability to collect information and interact with a company's stakeholders based on their specific needs and preferences. Although database marketing has similar advantages, the Internet technologies increase the speed of the collection, interpretation, and customized interactions (the application of data interpretation). The Internet also offers a wide variety of inexpensive and effective data collection techniques.

In this closing chapter, we examine the research process within e-business marketing. The e-business marketing research process is part of the business intelligence (BI) component of e-business. The application of the research results may address any (or a combination) of the other e-business components: e-commerce (EC); customer relationship management (CRM); supply chain management (SCM); and enterprise resource management (ERP). This chapter focuses on the applications of the e-business marketing research process and results through a company's Web site. We categorize the types of research applications as setup, maintenance, and evaluation. The traditional research process is presented, followed by specific steps and extended models for the three categories of e-business applications.

THE RESEARCH PROCESS

The traditional marketing research process is shown in Figure 14-1. It has five main steps with subcategories under each. Next, each step is defined within the context of traditional and e-business marketing (Burns and Bush, pp. 72–82).

Step 1. Defining the Business Opportunity, Problem, or Challenge
This step sets the stage for how helpful the research results will be. Ill-defined opportunities, problems, or challenges cannot be operationalized or measured effectively. Defining the issue leading to research is often difficult. Often a company "senses" something is going on in its competitive arena but does not have sufficient information to be certain. In this case, the first step would be to determine if there is an issue or

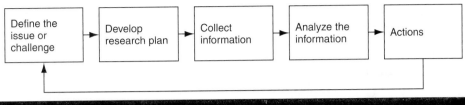

FIGURE 14-1   Marketing Research

problem occurring. Once the opportunity or challenge is defined, research objectives are developed. These objectives translate the defined challenge into measurable com-

3. Profits
4. Order reduction—from dealers
5. Increased complaints
6. Competitive actions—special offers, price reductions, etc.

Using "increased complaints" as an example, a company would first define the problem in more detail. This is typically achieved by evaluating the customer service complaints by product or service and type of complaint. A trend is identified, such as customers of a retail bank complaining about too many self-service options) (ATM, online banking, investment services) and the lack of more personal service. The bank wants to respond to its customers' issues. This would be translated into three research objectives:

1. How important is the convenience of the self-service banking options?
2. What is the profile of the customer complaining (demographics and product ownership)?
3. What is the overall customer satisfaction with the bank?

The potential e-business marketing problems or opportunities for a firm center around its Internet presence or Web site. Some of the problems or opportunities would be indicated by the following:

1. Fewer Web site "hits" or visits
2. Reduction in overall time spent by online visitors (lower stickiness)
3. Increased e-mail complaints about the site or other company issues (product or services offered, company brand or image)
4. Reduction in click-throughs from company banner ads
5. Lower online sales volume
6. Specific pages or sections visited less frequently

For illustrative purposes, we will examine "Fewer Web site 'hits' or visits." Properly built and designed Web sites have mechanisms for tracking visits (see Setup Strategies, below). Also, many large research companies, for example Nielsen, gather online hits for various sites across industries. On a daily, weekly, monthly, or quarterly basis, companies can compare themselves to competing sites. If the individual site-counting mechanism and this type of benchmark (despite some data collection issues) confirm a reduction in hits, a problem or challenge may be present. The company needs to understand why the visits are declining. Three research questions suggest themselves for this issue:

1. Why do people come to the site (information, purchases, research, etc.)?
2. What are their satisfaction ratings with the overall experience on the site?
3. Do gaps exist between expected site performance and the perceived site performance?

The results from this type of research contribute to the three areas of setup, maintenance, and **evaluation strategies.**

Step 2. Developing the Research Plan

Five actions comprise this general step:

1. Deciding on the research design
2. Determining the types of information needed and sources
3. Evaluating different data collection options
4. Developing the data capturing device
5. Deciding who and how many will participate

A range of research designs is available. Beginning with **exploratory research,** the researcher attempts to discern general patterns. When many of the issues and elements in a market are unknown, exploratory research attempts to define the parameters of the market and ferret out pertinent variables. The market researcher attempts to identify the different market segments and what they have in common with one another and how they differ. For example, on a Web site advertising hybrid automobiles (gasoline and electric cars), exploratory research may consider everything from the type of computer the page viewer has to socioeconomic status. Data on computer type can be determined by an unobtrusive script in JavaScript that passes the information to a database. The socioeconomic data would have to be found by the user entering data into a form. The pages viewed and the amount of time the user spends viewing a page using clickstream scripts provide exploratory data on viewer interests.

Once exploratory research is complete, researchers begin to look for connections between **independent** and **dependent variables** in an attempt to identify cause and effect. The process of identifying cause and effect spans the gamut of research design. A **questionnaire** with one set of questions representing the independent variable (cause) and another set of questions representing the dependent variable (effect) can be put into an online form to create a quasiexperiment. For example, a researcher might be looking for the differences between groups who follow through on making an online purchase of music and those who do not. If the groups have a single difference, other than making an online purchase (dependent variable), then that difference may prove to be the causal variable. The key independent variable could be anything from gender to age or some combination of variables. When looking at more than a single variable, which most researchers do, the analytical phase of the research is called **multivariate analysis**.

The most exacting type of research to isolate the causal variable is called *an experiment*. The classic experiment has two groups that are randomly placed into an **experimental group** and **control group.** Each group is measured in terms of a set of criteria. The researcher hypothesizes the cause for a certain behavior and introduces the cause **(experimental variable)** to the experimental group *only*. After the experimental group has been introduced to the experimental variable, it is again compared with the control group. If any differences are observed, the differences can be attributed to the introduction of the experimental variable. For example, test market studies are considered experimental in their design because they control the geographical location of a ... may use a new packaging or

tors is to examine the sites they ...
engines (for example www.google.com). The Internet technologies for tracking online behaviors facilitate using the descriptive research design for online research. In addition, the technology for online surveys (pop-up surveys on a Web site and e-mails with links to a survey questionnaire) are abundant (Greenfieldonline.com is an example). As in the traditional environment, causal or **experimental research** is not often conducted online. One example of a causal study would be to develop a Web site with a series of banner ads on it. Participants are invited to review the ads and select the one that is most appealing to them. By controlling where, how many, and which ads are reviewed, the research results can indicate which ad would perform better online. This could be conducted in a computer lab and, after making their choices, participants could be interviewed to discuss their ad selections. It could also be conducted online but some control is relinquished. The problem with conducting research on the World Wide Web is that it is indeed worldwide, and separating experimental and control conditions would be quite difficult.

There are two types of information sources: primary and secondary. Primary data are collected for the specific research problem or opportunity. Secondary data have already been collected but for a different reason. Access to secondary data has dramatically increased with the database technologies and, in particular, the searching capability of the Internet. Often companies find that secondary data are less expensive and easier to obtain, and may address their research issues. With the ease and lower cost of primary data collection provided by online surveying techniques, companies are finding the ideal scenario is a combination of both sources of information.

The varieties of data collection options for the online and offline research environments are very similar. Although the face-to-face option relies on wider acceptance of certain Internet technologies, surveys, focus groups, and panels are readily available online. A main limitation to online data collection is the skewed access—certain groups (e.g., younger, more affluent) may be more likely to have and use the Internet.

When conducting early telephone interviews, the same problem was confronted by researchers and had to be addressed by combination surveys that used telephones as well as nontelephone access. More recently the skewed **population** was also encountered with unlisted telephone numbers but was solved using random digit dialing technology. If the research issue focuses on the current online user population, this limitation is reduced.

There is little difference in the thought and design of the data-capturing device for the off-line versus online environments. The mechanism for their delivery will be different although the translation of the research objectives into research questions for data capture is one of the most critical steps in this process for both environments. Consideration must also be given for closed-ended versus open-ended questions and the issue of identifying the research sponsor or not (blind versus disclosed). Online research devices (for example, online surveys) have an advantage over off-line surveys. When a response to one survey question selects the next question to be posed, the skipping pattern is transparent in the online environment (as well as telephone-based surveys), whereas it is the respondent's responsibility in a self-administered survey.

The determination of the population (the entire universe of targeted audience) and **sample** size (a subset of the population) are contingent on the research issue and objectives. For many studies, certain segments of individuals are isolated. The number of participants varies based on the type of design: an exploratory study may include a smaller number than a descriptive **survey,** or casual design. However, the thought process to determine who and how many is the same in the off-line and online environments.[1]

Step 3. Collecting the Information

In the traditional research environment, a trained professional usually conducts the data collection (face-to-face, telephone, mall intercept). Online, the data collection is provided by the respondent or participant. The one exception is the online focus groups that are moderated by a trained facilitator. Internet technologies have dramatically reduced the turnaround time for receiving the data from a project. There is no data entry and the ability to reach the number and type of respondents necessary is also faster. The greatest problem lies in getting a representative sample of the population, even if that population is made up of online users.

Step 4. Analyzing the Data

An analysis plan begins with the research objectives developed during the first step of the research process. At that point in time certain measurements are established for the study. Then based on the type of research design and information source, a more detailed analysis plan can be formulated. It is during this phase of the process that the researcher begins to address the issue, opportunity, or challenge. The analysis leads to recommendations and actions that are supported by quantifiable evidence (the ultimate goal of the study). This step of the research process is the same for the online and off-line environments, but is often shortened because data are available so much faster online.

---

[1]See Burns and Bush, *Marketing Research,* 3rd ed. (Upper Saddle River, NJ: Prentice Hall, 2000) pp. 420–451 for an in-depth discussion.

Step 5. Actions

Most marketing research texts have the preparation of the final report as the last step. This often sends a message to researchers that once the report is presented, the project is over. The research results must be "converted" into actions that address the business issue or opportunity. Otherwise, the resources allocated to the study are wasted. In addition, it is critical that the actions selected are in a feedback loop to the first step of a research process—identifying opportunities and challenges. The process is an evolving one, not one that ends with the final report. This is certainly critical in the online research environment. With the insecurity brought on by the dot-com failures (beginning in 2000), the environment must be tested and evaluated for the most effective competitive strategies. Thus, the e-business marketing research process emphasizes the

three areas: setup, maintenance,

firm's offerings.

expanding the communication and distribution channels that a company employ. Visitors may also be potential customers, thus the Web site is expanding the company's reach (generally geographical extensions). The research issue is translated into research objectives. Some of the potential objectives are these:

1. What are the most important characteristics of the Web site to an existing or potential customer?
2. How does the firm's Web site perform on each characteristic?
3. How does the firm's Web site compare with its competitors' sites?

Previous research indicates that there are three essential components for the initial setup of the site: Web site quality, frequency of updates, and speed (Berthon, Pitt, Katsikeas, and Berthon, 1999).

Web site quality is defined by interface quality, ease of navigation, text content, graphics, motion, and sound. Interface quality and ease of navigation are elements that all good Web sites require. Text, whether static or moving, must be clear yet minimal. Unlike paper-based information, such as a brochure, the use of text requires a far more judicious use. Research has shown that a reader requires from two to three times the amount of time to read printed text as text on a Web page (Nielsen 1999).

Motion graphics and sound can be either a highly attractive and interesting part of a page or what has been characterized as "dancing baloney" (Sanders 2001, p. 35; Tufte 1997). Motion graphics and sound must be fully integrated into a page and give the viewer an opportunity to "skip intro" or turn off the sound. The quality of a Web page is not measured by the amount of technology the page shows by way of animated and audio additions but rather how those elements provide a comfortable addition for the viewer.

The frequency of content and functionality updates has been shown to attract customers, and more importantly, entice them to return. Frequency of updates is the characteristic that tells the customer that the firm "behind" the site cares enough to be actively involved in its enhancement and improvement based on the preferences of its visitors. This is analogous to in-store merchandising and the message it conveys to its shoppers.

The speed with which a page appears in the viewer's computer is analogous to service speed (in the services marketing literature). Just as customers will not wait in line for a long time (if there are other choices), online visitors will not wait for a slow Web site to load. The speed of a site is based on bandwidth and the speed of the server. Of these two, bandwidth is far more important because the speed at which a site loads in a client's computer is based on bandwidth. Unfortunately, the Web site designer must design with the lowest common denominator in mind. Most new modems at this writing have a speed of 56.6 KBs or 56,600 bits per second. A Web page should take no longer than 10 seconds to load lest the viewer leave the site, and so under perfect conditions a 500K Web page would be the largest page in a site. However, because ideal conditions rarely exist, most experts suggest pages no larger than about 60K to 80K (Nielsen, 1999). A fast server helps get the page off the Web server and into the packets sent across the Internet; however, the fastest server in the world will not help a big page load faster than the speed of the client's Internet interface hardware. There is a low switching cost associated with clicking to another, faster loading site.

These three characteristics or site attributes are critical to the setup strategies. They support the first three steps of the value bubble—attraction, engagement, and retention—with the emphasis on attracting visitors. In the online environment, it is very important to create the site recognizing that the site is the firm to visitors. This is necessary whether there are physical stores serving the customer or if the customer is being served only by the site. Companies will have other specific challenges or opportunities for their sites that must be researched. However, these three general site attributes should be the foundation of the setup strategies.

Maintenance Strategies

Maintenance strategies are necessary to create site loyalty and facilitate sales. The challenges and opportunities for firms center around knowledge–knowing and understanding the online visitors' preferences and ensuring their interactions capture those preferences. The types of research issues within the maintenance strategies are these:

1. Who are the site's visitors (demographics)?
2. What types of online activities or behaviors do they display?
3. Where else on the Web do the visitors go?

The ability to capture primary research data in a time- and cost-effective manner facilitates companies' conducting research and monitoring continuously. Firms are able to collect sufficient data to define their visitors within like clusters or segments and continually reevaluate the segments for any changes. The research design would be a combination of two descriptive methodologies: observation and self-report. Observation data would be collected from the clickstream behaviors and log files. The self-reported data will come from online visitors filling out registration forms. Although the Internet technologies enable segments of 1 (only one member is in the segment) and the associated, one-to-one interactive dialogue with them, the privacy and security concerns necessitate reconsideration of this option.

A research study (utilizing the four steps presented in Figure 14-1) was conducted focusing on maintenance strategies. The objective was to develop a data collection and

TABLE 14-1 GIST Model	
GIST Stage	**Definition**
Gather	Explore Internet technologies and tools to obtain information about visitors' attributes and behaviors.
Infer	Utilize data mining technologies and statistical analyses to build a profile based on who the visitors are, where they come from, and understanding clickstream behaviors.
Segment	Match like-users to create segments (nanosegments). Use nanosegments as input into the maintenance strategies focusing on redesign and repositioning of the site.
Track	Create a continuous feedback loop into "Gather," etc.

the online visitor based on customer's preferences. ~~increased~~ increased loyalty and stronger relationships between the firm and its customers (CRM e-business component).

Maintenance strategies address the online selling process as well. Companies need to measure how important online sales are to their visitors. The percentage of online shoppers has not grown as dramatically as initially predicted (fear of stolen credit card numbers, return policy issues, and broken promises—an item is not in-stock although the site indicates it is). Therefore, a site may not have to complete the transaction online; however, the site must take the sale to the point where it can easily be completed via the telephone, mail, or e-mail. Some firms are concerned that online sales will cannibalize their existing physical store sales. This is another research issue for the firm to explore. Our research indicates that most online sales are incremental to the traditional sales channel; however, each firm should quantify this for its particular competitive environment.

Evaluation Strategies

One of the leading e-business researchers has identified the customer's online experience as one of the "hottest" topics in e-business marketing research (Hoffman 2001). Two information sources measure online experience: site-centric and customer-centric.

The site-centric measures site activity, including the following:

1. Daily, weekly, and monthly Web site visits ("hits")
2. Length of time spent on the site ("stickiness")
3. Frequency of visits for each page or separate section on the site

Customer-centric sources are self-reported and combined with data captured on the visitors' actions prior to entering the site, while they are on the site, and which site they go to next (this is available through the clickstream or logfiles). Only a few conceptual models exist for identifying and measuring the customer experience. The models that have been developed are from the service quality frameworks. As the site is the firm, the customer's interaction and experience are similar to the service quality models established. Throughout this book, there are references to the work by Zeithaml, Parasuraman, and Malhotra (2000) on measuring the online customer experience. Their research measures the gap between expected and perceived levels of service provided by the site. In general, they found that online visitors are not as clear about their site expectations and rely on their experiences with other sites. The research has also identified two main dimensions of online service quality: core and recovery. Core services are the basic expected site performance issues (load times, site availability, delivery as promised, etc.), whereas the recovery issues focus on how quickly mistakes are resolved and the manner in which the company resolves them.

Companies and their customers can benefit from rigorous and ongoing site-centric and customer-centric research. The research results guide companies in their site redesigns based on objective data analysis. The combination of the maintenance and evaluation strategies leads to the most effective Web site a company can offer its customers.

COLLECTING YOUR KNOWLEDGE: A REVIEW

Key Terms

- control group
- dependent variable
- evaluation strategies
- experimental group
- experimental research
- experimental variable
- exploratory research
- GIST
- independent variable
- maintenance strategies
- multivariate analysis
- population
- questionnaire
- sample
- survey

Questions to Ask

1. What are indicators that a Web-based business needs some kind of redesign?
2. Under what conditions would a company most want to use exploratory research methods?
3. What does a company have to know in order to conduct experimental research?
4. What are the components of experimental research?
5. What online tools can help in the conduct of survey research? Exploratory research?
6. What are the different foci of maintenance, setup, and evaluation strategies?
7. How is the GIST segmentation model used in maintenance strategies?

Application to Business

What stage of research knowledge does your company's Web site use? Is the knowledge at the level where exploratory research is necessary to learn about your customers, or is it at a stage where online experiments could be conducted to maximize its functionality?

What indicators are now in place with your company's Web site that serve as indicators for success or failure other than the amount of business it generates? What percent of your company's business is generated by the Web site?

In looking at the criteria of page appearance, site updating, and loading speed, what type of research would be necessary to measure how well your company's site is faring using these criteria?

Web Sites to Visit

www.barchart.com Here's a site that will warm the heart of any technical data aficionado. Once data is gathered for market research, it needs to be understood clearly, and Barchart.com does exactly that using (what else?) bar charts. Actually, Barchart.com has two different types of entries into its site. Subscribers have a log-in that gives them access to a greater and more customerized set of data and a visitor entry. The latter provides a wide array of data from different businesses.

geographics; the latter has categories for different specific markets such as B2B, retailing, small business, and advertising. A nice feature for students at the site is a glossary for different online terms you will need to know for engaging in e-business.

www.researchinfo.com This is another great site for e-business students. It includes links to an online discussion forum on market research, an employment board, market research calculators you can use online, and–best of all–a

Bibliography

Albert, T. 2000. "Internet Marketing Provides a Competitive Advantage in a Global paper.

American Marketing Association. 1995. *Dictionary of Marketing Terms,* 2d edition, Peter D. Bennett (ed.), Chicago: American Marketing Association.

Andersen Consulting. October 1999. "Most Utilities' Web sites Lack Functionality Needed to Compete in the E-Economy." *Andersen Consulting Report.* Summary available online: www.ac.com/news/newsarchive/10.99/ newsarchive_101399.html.

Berry, L. 1995. *On Great Service.* New York: Free Press.

Berry, L., and A. Parasuraman. 1991. *Marketing Services: Competing Through Quality.* New York: Free Press.

Berthon, P., L. Pitt, C. Katsikeas, and J.-P. Berthon. 1999. "Virtual Services Go International: International Services in the Marketplace." *Journal of International Marketing,* 7, no. 3, 84–105.

Booms, B., and M. J. Bitner. 1981. "Marketing Strategies and Organizational Structures for Service Firms." In J. H. Donnelly, and W. R. George (Eds.), *Marketing Services.* Chicago: American Marketing Association, 47–51.

Buelte, Horst. "Positive Proposals Drowned Out by Same Old Protectionists' Song." Speech delivered on July 27, 2000. Press release (complete speech) available online: www.aiis.org/

Chircu, A., and R. Kauffman. 1999. "Analyzing Firm-Level Strategy for Internet-Focused Reintermediation." *Proceedings of the 32d Hawaii International Conference on System Sciences.*

Curtis, Hillman. 2000. *The Art of Motion Graphics.* Indianapolis, IN: New Riders.

Davis, F. September 1989. "Perceived Usefulness, Perceived Ease of Use, and User Acceptance of Information Technology." *MIS Quarterly,* 319–339.

Eckstein, R., D. Collier-Brown, and P. Kelly. 2000. *Using Samba.* Sebastopol, CA: O'Reilly.

Eiglier, P., and E. Langeard. 1987. *Servuction: le Marketing des Services.* Paris: McGraw Hill.

Gartner Group (GG). November 1999. *Monthly Research.*

Goes, P. December 12, 2001. Interview.

Goffman, Erving. 1959. *Presentation of Self in Everyday Life.* New York: Doubleday.

Hanson, W. 2000. *Principles of Internet Marketing.* Cincinnati, OH: South-Western College Publishing/Thomson Learning.

Harrell, G., D., and G. L. Frazier. 1999. *Marketing: Connecting with Customers.* Upper Saddle River, NJ: Prentice Hall.

Harvey, M., R. Lusch, and B. Cavarkapo. Fall 1996. "A Marketing Mix for the 21st Century." *Journal of Marketing Theory and Practice,* 1–15.

Heskett, J., T. Jones, G. Loveman, W. Sasser, and L. Schlesinger. March/April 1994. "Putting the Service Profit Chain to Work." *Harvard Business Review.* 164–174.

Hoffman, D. July 2001. "The Tools, Tips, and Traps of Doing E-commerce Research." Presentation at the AMA Faculty Consortium on E-Commerce. College Station, TX.

Hutt, M. D., and T. W. Speh. 1998. *Business Marketing Management,* 6th ed. Fort Worth, Texas: Dryden Press.

Ilfeld, J., and R. Weiner. July 2001. "Generating Web Traffic: An Empirical Analysis of Web Site Visitation Behavior." Presentation at the AMA Faculty Consortium on E-Commerce. College Station, TX.

Jackson, R., and P. Wang. 1994. *Strategic Database Marketing.* Lincolnwood (Chicago), IL: NTC Business Books (NTC Publishing Company).

Jome, H. 1924. *Economics of the Radio Industry.* New York: A. W. Shaw.

Judge, P., February 2001. "How I Saved $100 Million on the Web." *Fast Company,* 174–181.

Kalakota, R., and M. Robinson. 1999. *E-Business: Roadmap for Success.* Reading, MA: Addison-Wesley Publishing.

Katz, Steven, D. 1991. *Film Directing Shot by Shot: Visualizing from Concept to Screen.* Studio City, CA: Michael Wiese Productions.

Kierzkowski, A., S. McQuade, R. Waitman, and M. Zeisser. 1996. "Marketing to the Digital Consumer." *McKinsey Quarterly,* 2, 180–83.

King, K., J. Pehrson, and L. Reid. September 1993. "Pretesting TV Commercials: Methods, Measures, and Changing Agency Roles." *Journal of Advertising,* 22, no. 3.

Kotler, P. 2000. *Marketing Management,* Millennium Edition. Upper Saddle River, NJ: Prentice Hall.

Lake, D. February 2000. *The Web: Growing Two Million Pages A Day.* Available online: www.thestandard.com/research/metrics/display/0,2799,12329,00.html

Lavidge, R., and G. Steiner. October 1961. "A Model for Predictive Measures of Advertising." *Journal of Marketing,* 61.

Levin, N., and J. Zahavi. Spring 2001. "Predictive Modeling Using Segmentation." *Journal of Interactive Marketing,* 15, no. 2, 2–22.

Lewin, R., and B. Regine. 2000. *The Soul at Work: Listen ... Respond ... Let Go: Embracing Complexity Science for Business Success.* New York: Simon & Schuster.

Lovelock, C., and L. Wright. 1999. *Principles of Service Marketing and Management.* Upper Saddle River, NJ: Prentice Hall.

McCarthy, J. 1960. *Basic Marketing: A Managerial Approach.* Homewood, IL: Irwin.

Meeker, M. 1997. *The Internet Advertising Report.* New York: Harper Collins.

Mohr, J. 2001. *Marketing of High-Technology Products and Innovations.* Upper Saddle River, NJ: Prentice Hall.

Monczka, R., and J. P. Morgan. January 1996. "Supplier Integration: A New Level of Supply Chain Management." *Purchasing,* 120: 110.

Moorman, C. 2001. "Market Learning Process." In J. Mohr, *Marketing of High-Technology Products and Innovations.* Upper Saddle River, NJ: Prentice Hall, 56–57.

Murray, Matt, and Jathon Sapsford. "GE Reshuffles Its Dot-Com Strategy to Focus on Internal 'Digitizing'." Bland B4.

Nakhimovsky, Alexander, and Tom Myers. 1998. *JavaScript Objects.* Birmingham, England: Wrox Press, Ltd.

Nielsen, Jakob. 1999. *Web Usability.* Indianapolis, IN: New Riders.

PACT Agencies. 1982. "PACT." *Journal of Advertising,* 11, no. 4, 4–29.

Parasuraman, A. July 2001. "E-Service Quality: Conceptualization and Measurement." Paper presented at the AMA Faculty Consortium on Electronic Commerce. College Station, TX.

Parasuraman, A. May 2000. "Technology Readiness Index (TRI): A Multiple-Item Scale to Measure Readiness to Embrace New Technologies." *Journal of Service Research,* 2, no. 4, 307–320.

Parasuraman, A. 1996. "Understanding and Leveraging the Role of Customer Service in

External, Interactive, and Internal Marketing." Paper presented at Frontiers in Services Conference. Nashville, TN.

Parasuraman, A., and C. Colby. 2001. *Techno-Ready Marketing: How and Why Your Customers Adopt Technology.* New York: The Free Press.

Parsons, A., M. Zeisser, and R. Waitman. Winter 1998. "Organizing Today for the Digital Marketing of Tomorrow." *Journal of Interactive Marketing,* 12, no. 1, 31–46.

Parasuraman, A., V. Zeithaml, and L. Berry. Fall 1985. "A Conceptual Model of SQ and Its

of Excellence: Lessons from America's Best Run Companies.* New York: HarperCollins.

Porter, M. 1985. *Competitive Advantage: Creating and Sustaining Superior Performance.* New York: Free Press.

PriceWaterhouseCoopers. June 2000. "The Business of E-Business—The Strategies to Exploit the Changing Marketplace."

Ray, M. 1982. *Advertising and Communications Management.* Upper Saddle River, NJ: Prentice Hall.

Ritterskamp, J. Jr., and W. Hancock. 1993. "Legal Aspects in Purchasing." In H. Fearon, D. Dobler, and K. Killen (Eds.), *The Purchasing Handbook.* New York: McGraw Hill, 529–544.

Rogers, E. 1985. *Diffusion of Innovation,* 3d ed. New York: Free Press.

Saliba, C. August 3, 2001. "I-Marketing Interview: Visa." E-Commerce Times. www.ecommercetimes.com/perl/story/ 12314.html.

Sanders, W. B. 2001. *Creating Learning-Centered Courses for the World Wide Web.* New York: Allyn and Bacon.

Sanders, W. B., and M. Windstanley. 2001. *Server-side Flash: Scripts, Databases, and Dynamic

Development.* New York, NY: Hungry Minds, Inc.

Sanders, William B. 2002a. *JavaScript Design.* Indianapolis, IN: New Riders.

Sanders, W. B. 2002b. "Third Generation Web Sites and Learning." In *New Strategies in College Teaching: Succeeding in Today's Academic World.* New York: Allyn and Bacon, 209–228.

Santosus, M. April 15, 1998. "Simple, Yet Complex." *CIO Enterprise Magazine.* Online at www.cio.com/archive/enterprise/ 041598_tec.html.

Sheth, J. N. February 2001. "e-Merging Theories in Marketing." *e-Merging Theories in Marketing: Learning from the Past—Looking to the Future.* Plenary Session, winter Educators Conference, American Marketing Association.

Sheth, J. N., and R. S. Sisodia. 2001. "Feeling the Heat—Part 1". In J. Sheth, A. Eshghi, and B. C. Krishnan (Eds.), *Internet Marketing.* Fort Worth, TX: Harcourt.

Shimp, T. 2000. *Advertising and Promotion: Supplemental Aspects of Integrated Marketing Communications,* 5th ed. Fort Worth, TX: Dryden Press.

Shostack, L. April 1997. "Breaking Free from Product Marketing." *Journal of Marketing,* 34–43.

Siegel, D. 1997. *Creating Killer Web Sites.* Indianapolis, IN: Hayden Publisher.

Silicon Valley/San Jose Business Journal. "Poor Service Stifles B2B Growth," May 16, 2001, sanjose.bizjournals.com/sanjose/stories/ 2001/05/14/daily34.html.

Strauss, J., and R. Frost. 2001. *E-Marketing* (2d ed.) Upper Saddle River, NJ: Prentice Hall.

Strauss, J., and D. Hill. Winter 2001. "Consumer Complaints by E-Mail: An Exploratory Investigation of Corporate Responses and

Customer Reactions." *Journal of Interactive Marketing,* 15, no. 1, 63–73.

Strong, E. K. 1925. *The Psychology of Selling.* New York: McGraw Hill.

Tufte, Edward, R. 1997. *Visual Explanations.* Cheshire, CT: Graphics Press.

Van Waterschoot, W., and C. Van den Bulte. October 1992. "The 4P Classification of the Marketing Mix Revisited." *Journal of Marketing,* 82–93.

Weinman, Lynda, and William Weinman. 2001. *Creative HTML Design 2: A Hands-on Web Design Tutorial.* Indianapolis, IN: New Riders.

Weitz, B. 2001. "Critical e-tailing Research Issues Pertaining to Technology Readiness and e-Service Quality." Paper session at the *American Marketing Association's Winter Educators Conference.*

Wind, Y., and R. Cardoza. 1974. "Industrial Market Segmentation." *Industrial Marketing Management,* 3, 153–166.

Wind, J., and A. Rangaswamy. 2001. "Customerization: The Next Revolution in Mass Customization." *Journal of Interactive Marketing,* 15, no. 1, 13–32.

www.nua.net/surveys/how_many_online/ world.html.

www.logophilia.com/WordSpy/reintermediation. asp (Word Spy 2001).

Yadav, M. July 2001. "Computer-Mediated Interactivity: The Construct and Implications for Product Migration and Marketing Strategy." Paper presented at the 2001 AMA Faculty Consortium on Electronic Commerce. College Station, TX.

Yadav, M. S. 2000. "Thinking Strategically in the Electronic Marketplace." *Retailing Issues Letter,* 12, no. 2.

Zadeh, L. A. 1968. "Probability Measures of Fuzzy Events." *Journal of Mathematical Analysis and Applications,* 23, 421–27 (based on a 1965 paper).

Zeithaml, V., and M. J. Bitner. 1996. *Services Marketing.* New York: McGraw-Hill.

Zeithaml, V., A. Parasuraman, and L. Berry. 1990. *Delivering Quality Service: Balancing Customer Perceptions and Expectations.* New York: Free Press.

Zeithaml, V., A. Parasuraman, and A. Malhotra. 2000. *A Conceptual Framework for Understanding e-Service Quality: Implications for Future Research and Managerial Practices.* Marketing Science Institute (MSI), Report no. 00–115.

Index

Plumbing and Mechanical Services:
Book 3

Plumbing and Mechanical

A. H. Masterman and R. M. Boyce

Stanley Thornes (Publishers) Ltd

First published in 1990 by:
Stanley Thornes (Publishers) Ltd
Delta Place
27 Bath Road
CHELTENHAM
GL53 7TH
United Kingdom

04 05 06 / 13 12 11 10 9 8

A catalogue record for this book is available from the British Library

ISBN 0 7487 0233 4

Page make-up by Acorn Bookwork

Printed in Croatia by Zrinski

Contents

Preface

The text closely follows the requirements of the syllabus in craft technology, working processes and associated subjects, the primary aim being to assist the student towards that qualification.

Although mainly written for those commencing a career in the mechanical industry. In addition to those mentioned above, this book should prove invaluable for technician students and for students attending Links, Foundation, Youth Training Scheme or Employment Training programmes.

Acknowledgements

The authors and publishers are grateful to the following for permission to reproduce textual material and illustrations:

Armitage Shanks Ltd; Burn Bros (London) Ltd; British Oxygen Company; Copper Development Association; Lead Development Association; British Gas plc; CORGI; Electrical Electronic Telecommunication and Plumbing Union; Glynwed Foundries; Hepworth Building Products; Institute of Plumbing; Ideal Standard Ltd; IMI Yorkshire Fittings Ltd; Joint Industry Board for Plumbing Mechanical Engineering Services in England and Wales; Marley Extrusions Ltd; City and Guilds of London Institute; Osma Plastics Ltd; Key Terrain Ltd; The Worshipful Company of Plumbers.

They would also like to thank Polypipe plc for supplying the front cover photograph, which shows blue and black MDPE pipe and fittings.

Every effort has been made to reach copyright holders, but the publishers would be grateful to hear from any source whose copyright they may unwittingly have infringed.

1 Gas supply and services

... and apply the emergency procedure for escapes of gas.

4 Select suitable materials for gas supplies and services.

5 Recognise and name the components of a domestic gas installation.

6 State the purpose and function of components used in domestic gas installations.

7 Demonstrate knowledge of the working principles of common components.

8 Recognise and identify domestic gas appliances.

9 Have knowledge of the construction of flues for gas appliances.

10 Demonstrate knowledge of soundness testing procedures for new and existing gas installations.

Domestic gas supply

Gas supply

About 90 per cent of the gas used for domestic purposes in Great Britain is natural gas from beneath the North Sea. The other 10 per cent, in the form of liquid natural gas at a temperature of $-160\,°C$, is imported from North Africa in special tanker ships and stored in underground tanks. This liquid is converted into a gas which is then used to provide bulk supplies to many of the area gas boards.

Composition and characteristics of natural gas

Characteristics

Contains no carbon monoxide and is therefore non-poisonous.

Contains no sulphur and therefore hardly corrodes appliances.

Contains no moisture so condensation boxes may be omitted.

Requires approximately $9.5\,m^3$ of air per $1\,m^3$ of gas for complete combustion.

Table 1.1 *Composition of natural gas*

Constituents	%
Methane	94.70
Carbon dioxide	0.05
Butane	0.04
Ethane	3.00
Propane	0.51
Hydrocarbons	0.27
Helium	0.03
Nitrogen	1.30

1

May contain dust; if so, filters will be required.

Gross calorific value 37 MJ/m³.

Flame velocity of 350 mm/s.

Relative density 0.55 (air = 1.00).

The Gas Safety Regulations

The Gas Safety (Installation and Use) Regulations 1984 make the codes of practice for gas installations enforceable by law where they relate to the safety of the gas user.

Installers of gas equipment and appliances need to be conversant with these codes of practice and must ensure that all their work conforms with them.

Users of gas appliances are required to observe the Gas Safety Regulations in that they will not use, or cause to be used, any appliance they either know, or suspect to have:

1 An escape of gas,
2 Insufficient ventilation for safe usage,
3 A flue not working properly.

A faulty appliance must be disconnected from its supply and the supply capped or plugged. In the event of an escape of gas, the supply must be turned off, the apartment ventilated and the Gas Corporation notified immediately. No attempt must be made to use the installation again until it has been made sound.

Installation of pipework

All pipes and fittings used for a gas supply must be of approved materials. Gas supply pipes must not be fitted inside a cavity wall. They may pass through a cavity wall but only when passed through a correctly fitted sleeve. A sleeve is recommended (Figure 1.1) whenever a pipe is passed through a wall.

Pipes must not be run through the base of a load-bearing wall or under the foundation of a building. All modern buildings have the gas, electricity and water supplies electrically

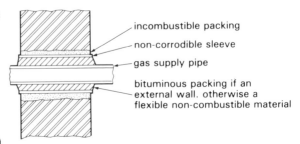

Figure 1.1 *Detail for solid wall, which also applies to cavity wall*

bonded together and this bonding should not be disturbed. When it is necessary to break into a bonded installation, a temporary continuity bond must be fitted as shown in Figure 1.2.

When a new installation has been completed, or an extension to an existing installation, the new pipework must be sound in terms of a correctly applied pressure test. Existing installations must be tested to ensure that they conform to the recommended soundness tests, and when any new pipework is connected to an existing installation, the whole of the installation must be tested again to ensure that it is sound within the regulations laid down.

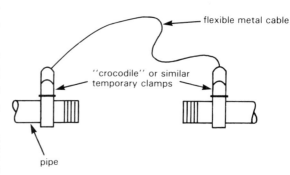

Figure 1.2 *Temporary bonding wire*

Fitting gas appliances

It is most important that the correct ventilation requirements are available in the room or compartment where the appliance is fitted.

Any flue to which an appliance is to be fitted ███ ███ ███

███ ███ ███ ███ ███ ███ be fireproof. The gas rate to an appliance burner is set by adjusting the appliance governor to the correct pressure setting, and checking the gas rate at the meter test dial (Figure 1.3). It is very important that the correct gas rate to the burner is obtained, otherwise the appliance will be inefficient, and dangerous products of incorrect combustion may occur. Prior to any appliance being left for a customer to use, it is necessary that all safety controls and flame failure devices are tested and left in full working order.

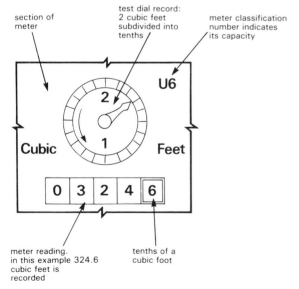

Figure 1.3 *Gas meter dial*

Gas meters

To conform with the Gas Safety Regulations, meters are now made from pressed sheet steel. Previously tinplate with soldered joints was used, but these materials and method are now redundant. In the ███ ███ ███

███ in buildings above two storeys in height. Such placements are only allowed in single or two-storey premises if there is no other practicable site, in which case the meter and its connections must be either:

1 Of fire-resistant construction, or
2 Housed in a compartment which has a fire resistance of not less than 30 minutes, or
3 Connected to a service pipe which has a thermal cut-off device incorporated on the inlet side of the meter control cock.

Every new meter, meter control, meter governor and meter by-pass must be installed in an accessible position for inspection and maintenance and the meter control must be capable of being easily operated by the customer. Generally the installation of meters is the responsibility of the Gas Corporations, or their authorised contractors. Most modern meter installations must be fireproofed for at least 30 minutes. Figures 1.4, 1.5 and 1.6 (overleaf) show typical installations.

If a meter is removed for the purpose of making a connection close to the outlet, care should be taken that the inlet and outlet connections are sealed to prevent the possibility of an explosion or fire. Upon refitting, the connections must be tested for soundness and the meter purged of air before relighting any appliance.

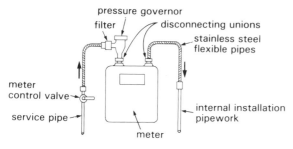

Figure 1.4   *Gas meter connections for domestic buildings*

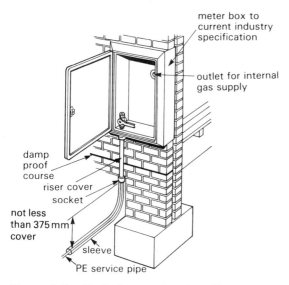

Figure 1.5   *Typical meter box installation*

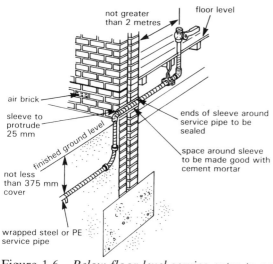

Figure 1.6   *Below floor level service entry to gas meter position*

Emergency procedure for escapes of gas

1   Turn off the gas supply.
2   Ventilate the room or compartment by opening doors, windows, etc.
3   Eliminate all sources of possible ignition, including electrical equipment which may cause a spark, such as plugs and switches.
4   Check that no person has been affected by the escape of gas.
5   Warn all persons in the vicinity who may be affected.
6   The source of leakage must be traced and located by the correct testing methods, and repaired as quickly as possible.
7   If the fault or fracture cannot be repaired for any reason, then the Gas Corporation regional office must be notified at once.

It is illegal for any person to ignore a leakage of gas to the danger of some other person.

If a leak occurs do something about it at once.

Domestic installations (Figure 1.7)

The service pipe should be laid at least 375 mm below ground level and with a fall towards the main of 1 in 120 if possible. Where the service pipe enters the building, it must pass through a sleeve. The pipe should be centralized in the sleeve by means of a non-setting or bituminous compound, and the sleeve itself secured throughout the thickness of the wall.

The service pipe should be joined to the main by a connector or union coupling to facilitate connection or subsequent disconnection. Service pipes are usually run in either unplasticised PVC or low carbon steel to BS 1387. Fire risks generally preclude the use of PVC internally, and a steel pipe is usually connected to the PVC at the point of entry into the building and run into the building up to the meter control. Steel pipes being buried underground, laid into concrete, or recessed into walls should be painted and wrapped against corrosive

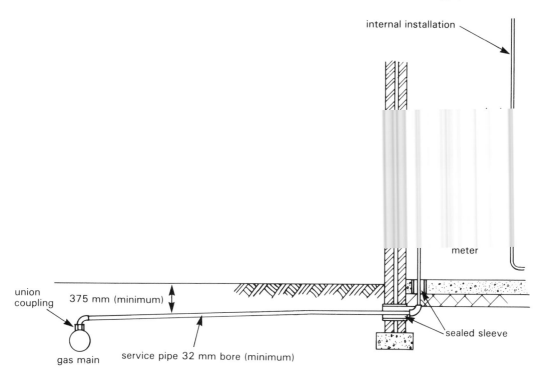

Figure 1.7 *Service pipe installation to a domestic dwelling*

attack. Pipes that run along external walls must be fitted into 'stand-off' clips or brackets and wrapped in plastic tape.

Internal installation gas supply pipes are similar to those used for hot and cold water systems. Steel, copper and lead are suitable for natural gas.

All pipework must follow the recommended codes of practice both for the quality of the material and the standard of any fittings used.

Pipes must be installed in accordance with the codes of practice laid down for this type of work. Pipes run from the outlet side of the meter are often dictated by access available, convenience and neat appearance. Pipes above 20 mm in diameter may be buried in floor screeds but should be wrapped to prevent corrosion. Pipe sleeves should be used wherever gas pipes pass through walls and floors – not only for neatness, but also to ensure that settlement stresses and damage due to thermal movement are prevented.

Pipe supplies laid beneath suspended or intermediate floors must be clipped with saddle or holderbat clips. Galvanised clips or wire nail supports must not be used with copper pipes because of the possibility of corrosion by electrolysis.

Many gas appliances such as boilers and fires are connected directly to the pipework. In the case of others such as cookers and refrigerators, however, it is considered good practice to provide flexible connections to allow the appliance to be moved for cleaning purposes, as shown in Figure 1.8 (overleaf).

Controls

One of the main advantages of gas, as a fuel, is its ease of control. It can be turned up or down, off or on, simply and quickly, by manual or automatic means. An extensive range of devices has been developed and some of those used in domestic installations are dealt with in this section.

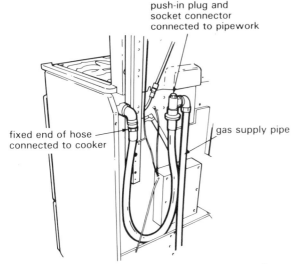

push-in plug and
socket connector
connected to pipework

fixed end of hose
connected to cooker

gas supply pipe

Figure 1.8   *Flexible gas connection to a cooker*

Controls may be used for a variety of purposes including:

1 Protection from the results of pilot flame failure,
2 Quick and safe cut-off in the event of danger, due to fire, pressure or supply failure,
3 Safe methods of ignition,
4 Control of pressure, temperature or time.

The majority of the extensive range of control systems used by modern gas appliances operate by the use of electricity, although there are many older appliances still in use which employ clockwork devices or gas pressure to give control.

The most important controls from the consumers' point of view are those which provide a means of switching appliances or other controls on or off, and those which control the temperature of heat produced. Most gas appliances house many of these controls on or within the appliance casing.

The basic form of manual control is by means of a valve, tap or cock. These three terms are widely used to describe most types of manual control.

A 'valve' controls gas flow through an orifice by the movement of a flap, disc or gate; it is generally larger than a tap or cock and usually fitted on service pipes and mains. Due to its method of construction it can withstand higher pressures than an ordinary cock or tap.

A 'tap' is usually fitted as an integral part of an appliance and it may have a plug or disc to control gas flow.

A 'cock' is a device fitted to a gas supply that usually controls the flow of gas by the rotation of a slotted or drilled, tapered plug (Figure 1.9). Gas cocks are made of brass. The tapered plug is turned by means of a thumb-piece, or by a lever which fits onto a square on top of the plug. The square head has a groove cut into it which indicates the direction of the drilling; most cocks employ an arrangement to ensure that the plug stops in the full on or full off positions. This is called the 'niting' and combines with the 'niting washer', which, to adjust the tightness of the tapered plug in the body, has a tab that engages with stops on the cock body to limit plug movement. Ninety-degree niting is usual although some larger cocks have 180° niting.

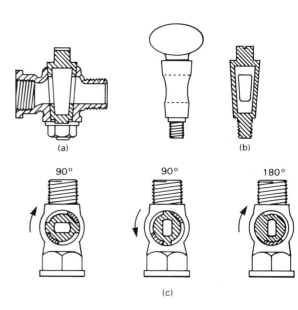

(a)

(b)

90°   90°   180°

(c)

Figure 1.9   *Plug cock*

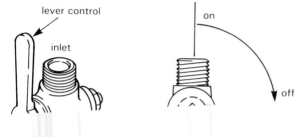

the meter control valve. In the event of fire or excessive heat, the solder melts and releases the plunger to seal the pipeline and cut off the gas supply to the meter, its connections and the complete internal gas installation. The solders

~~~~ whilst others modulate the fuel supply so that the main burner does not fully extinguish. Most water heaters have an on–off type of thermostat, whilst appliances such as gas fires and cookers have a thermostat which reduces the flow of fuel to the burner as the demand for heat is satisfied. A common type of thermostat is the rod-type as shown in Figure 1.12. This operates on the principle that metals expand at different rates, and if two metals such as brass and invar steel, which have high and low rates of expansion respectively, are used, a fine degree of control can be obtained. These thermostats operate in the following way: an invar steel rod is housed within a brass tube, one end of the rod being securely fixed to the tube. On the free end of the rod is a valve, which, due to the expansion of the brass tube when it is heated, carries with it the invar rod and the valve, thus causing the valve to close onto a seating and stop the flow of gas to the appliance burner. These thermostats are made with an adjusting knob (shown in Figure 1.12) which allows control through a range of temperatures. By turning this control to the left or right the position of the valve can be varied in relation to its seating. For example, if the distance is lengthened the brass tube will have to expand more before the valve can close, which has the effect of allowing for an increase in temperature before the valve can close. If the adjusting knob is turned the other way so that the valve

Figure 1.10 shows the normal type of valve used adjacent to the inlet of a domestic meter to control the supply of gas to a premises. This control has had several different names but is now called the 'meter control'.

Thermal cut-offs

These valves are only used in certain selected locations. There are several devices available which operate on a thermal basis. A typical device is shown in Figure 1.11. This consists of a malleable iron tee with a spring-loaded plunger fitted in the branch of the tee. The plunger is held open against the force of the spring by a low melting point solder. The device is fitted into the service pipe before

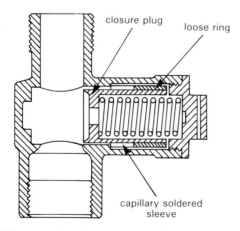

Figure 1.11 *Thermal cut-off*

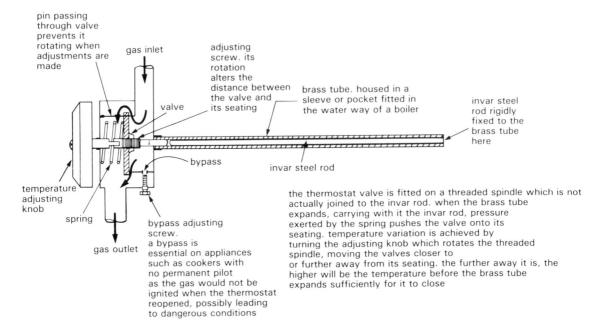

pin passing
through valve
prevents it
rotating when
adjustments are
made

gas inlet

adjusting
screw. its
rotation
alters the
distance between
the valve and
its seating

valve

brass tube. housed in a
sleeve or pocket fitted in
the water way of a boiler

invar steel
rod rigidly
fixed to the
brass tube
here

bypass

invar steel rod

temperature
adjusting
knob

spring

gas outlet

bypass adjusting
screw.
a bypass is
essential on appliances
such as cookers with
no permanent pilot
as the gas would not be
ignited when the thermostat
reopened, possibly leading
to dangerous conditions

the thermostat valve is fitted on a threaded spindle which is not
actually joined to the invar rod. when the brass tube
expands, carrying with it the invar rod, pressure
exerted by the spring pushes the valve onto its
seating. temperature variation is achieved by
turning the adjusting knob which rotates the threaded
spindle, moving the valves closer to
or further away from its seating. the further away it is, the
higher will be the temperature before the brass tube
expands sufficiently for it to close

Figure 1.12   *Invar rod-type gas thermostat*

is closer to its seating, it will close at a lower temperature. Many appliances fitted by the plumber have thermostats which are actuated by electricity. These operate in a similar way to those which control electric immersion heaters. Some work on the principle of a flexible bellows, which, by expansion or contraction (this being brought about by temperature rise or fall in the water), makes or breaks an electrical contact, or, as shown in Figure 1.13, controls the flow of gas directly. Other types of thermostat control an electric solenoid valve which regulates the flow of gas to the appliance burner.

Governors

Gas pressure in the main distribution system varies from area to area, and it is always higher than that required by gas-fired appliances. A gas governor is a fitting used for controlling the pressure and flow of gas to a whole installation or to an individual appliance. The main system governor is located on the inlet side of the gas meter, and its purpose is to reduce the mains pressure to a suitable working pressure for that particular system. Figure 1.14 illustrates a simple 'gas governor. An increase of the inlet pressure will exert force on the compensating diaphragm causing it to lift slightly and carry with it the stem which raises valve A towards

probe inserted into sleeve in
boiler water jacket

temperature
adjustment
screw

capillary
tube

spring

flexible
bellows

valve

seating

gas inlet

Figure 1.13   *Vapour expansion thermostat*

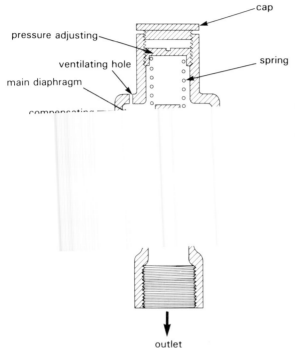

pressure adjusting—
ventilating hole
main diaphragm
compensating —

cap
spring

Figure 1.14   *Gas governor*

outlet

pendent governors. This ensures that in a system where several appliances may be used simultaneously that as long as pipes are correctly sized and an adequate supply of gas is available, pressure and flow fluctuations should not occur.

should then be ignited and allowed to burn for several minutes to allow for pressure stabilisation. When the U-gauge indicates a steady pressure, adjustment can be made to the pressure adjusting screw in the governor to obtain the pressure recommended by the manufacturer, which will be indicated in either millimetres water gauge or millibars. When all adjustments have been made the appliance burner should be turned off, the rubber hose removed from the test nipple and the securing screw or plug fitted to seal the test nipple.

its seating. This has the effect of reducing the aperture through which gas can flow, thus causing a pressure reduction. A lowering of the inlet pressure will allow the diaphragm to drop and valve A to open, thereby allowing a greater flow of gas through the aperture. The movement of valve A enables a fine balance to be maintained between inlet and outlet gas pressures. The outlet pressure can be increased by turning the pressure-adjusting screw clockwise, which compresses the spring. This increases the aperture between valve A and its seating and allows more gas to pass through. The ventilating hole must always be kept open to atmospheric pressure, which itself fluctuates and acts upon the main diaphragm to ensure constant and steady flow of gas to appliance burners regardless of atmospheric pressure variations.

To obtain maximum efficiency from a gas appliance a constant pressure of gas is required. The majority of modern gas appliances are provided with their own inde-

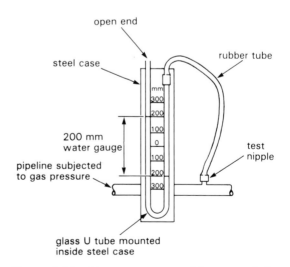

open end
rubber tube
steel case
mm
300
200
100
200 mm
water gauge
0
100
pipeline subjected
to gas pressure
200
300
test
nipple
glass U tube mounted
inside steel case

Figure 1.15   *U-gauge connected for commissioning an appliance*

Relay valves

A 'relay valve' is a pressure-operated valve controlled by a diaphragm. As this valve operates by gas pressure only it requires no electricity supply. As the name implies, the valve 'relays' signals from other controls fitted on the weep line to the main gas supply. The weep line is a small diameter copper tube that runs from the top of the relay valve and usually terminates at the base of the boiler adjacent to the burner assembly. The pipe derives its name from the very small quantity of gas which passes through it. In appearance the valve is similar to a gas governor. Figure 1.16 shows a relay valve and the controls which govern its action.

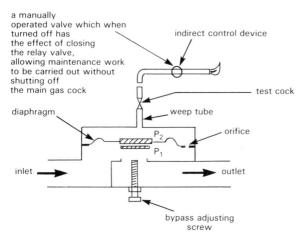

Figure 1.16   *Relay valve*

diaphragm is no longer supported and the valve closes, shutting off the appliance.

When the indirect control opens again, the pressure above the diaphragm is released and the differential pressures necessary to lift the diaphragm and open the valve are restored.

When the valve is used as a high–low control, some form of by-pass is incorporated. The simplest form is an adjustable screw in the base which is made to prop the valve off its seating and allow a small flow of gas to maintain flames on the burner. Some valves have a separate by-pass controlled by a needle valve to achieve this requirement.

Fail-safe relay valves

These valves were developed to overcome the possibility of the valve failing to close due to damage to the weep line. The operating diaphragm is in the lower part of the device and the valve and valve seating are located above (Figure 1.17). A secondary diaphragm

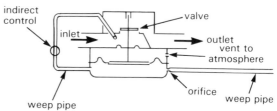

Figure 1.17   *Fail-safe relay valve*

When the control devices are all open, gas can flow through the orifice at full rate and pass on to the burner. Thus the pressure above the diaphragm (P_2) is considerably less than the inlet pressure under the diaphragm (P_1). The pressure difference lifts the diaphragm and opens the valve to gas flow, thus turning on the appliance. When any of the small indirect controls shuts off the weep line, the flow through the orifice slows down and finally stops when pressure above the diaphragm (P_2) has built up to be the same as that beneath the diaphragm (P_1). The

separates the two parts and the space between the diaphragms is vented to the atmosphere. The two diaphragms and the valve are connected to the valve spindle. A weep line passes the inlet side of the valve, through the indirect controls and back into the space underneath the operating diaphragm. As the line leaves this chamber on its way to the burner, it passes through the restrictor orifice. The effect of the restriction is that, with the controls open, gas can flow into the lower chamber faster than it can flow out. The pressure builds up and lifts the diaphragm, which opens the valve and allows gas to flow to the burner.

When the independent control closes, the flow of gas into the lower chamber is reduced until the pressure can no longer support the diaphragm and the valve closes. With the control fully shut no more gas enters the

shows a variation of a fail-safe relay valve connected with an on–off thermostat.

Solenoid valves
These valves are operated by electricity and act in the same way as an electromagnet.

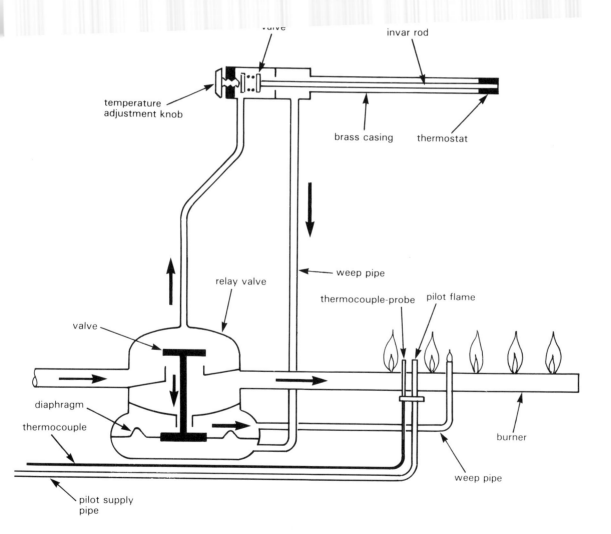

Figure 1.18   *On–off thermostat and relay valve*

be incorporated in a multifunctional control box or installed as a separate device as shown in Figure 1.19. When the solenoid is energised by electricity, it overcomes the pressure of the return spring and lifts the valve from its seating; when the electricity supply is stopped, the solenoid is de-energised and the pressure of the return spring returns the valve to its seating, thus closing the pipeline.

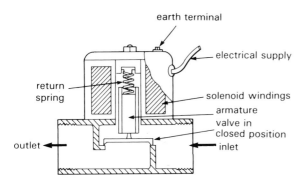

Figure 1.19   *Solenoid valve*

Ignition devices
In all modern gas appliances there needs to be some method or device which will ignite the gas in the main burner when the controls are calling for heat. Some gas appliances, such as those often used for space or water heating, employ a permanent pilot flame, while others, such as cookers, gas fires and some boilers, use a system whereby the appliance burner is lit by a spark or filament coil ignition. Some older appliances, particularly gas fires, cookers and water heaters, have a pilot jet which is easily accessible and can be lit manually with a match or taper.

Spark
These ignition systems require electricity, which may be supplied from a battery or taken from a mains supply via a transformer, as shown in Figure 1.20. The spark generator causes a number of high voltage electric impulses to be discharged across a small gap between two electrodes which incorporate a permanent or non-permanent pilot. The

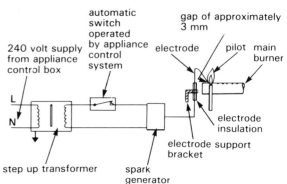

this system of ignition is usually employed with appliances having non-permanent pilots. its action is normally fully automatic, being part of the control system of the appliance

Figure 1.20   *Mains spark ignition*

permanent pilot arrangement means that the pilot flame is alight whether or not the main burner is alight and stays on indefinitely. The non-permanent system operates through a control system, which, when the thermostat calls for heat, sends a signal to the spark igniter causing it to operate and light the pilot flame. This then operates an automatic gas valve which opens to allow gas to pass through to the main burner where it is ignited by the pilot flame. When the main burner extinguishes the non-permanent pilot goes out also.

Piezo-electric
This system of spark ignition is similar to that previously described and differs only in the method used to produce the electrical energy needed to initiate the spark.

The piezo method uses the fact that certain types of metallic crystals possess the ability to produce electrical energy when they are compressed. Devices that use them usually consist of a crystal element to which pressure is applied by pressing or pulling a plunger (Figure 1.21). When the plunger is released by the spring or trigger mechanism the rapid change in pressure on the crystals causes a high voltage flow of electrons which in turn causes a spark to jump the points gap at the electrodes. This device operates independently of an outside source of electrical

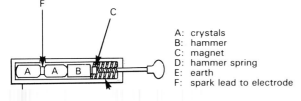

A: crystals
B: hammer
C: magnet
D: hammer spring
E: earth
F: spark lead to electrode

element out of position, or element burnt out.

Flame-failure devices

The purpose of a 'flame-failure device' is to prevent unlit gas passing into the combustion

manufacturer recommends. The high tension leads must be well insulated and not directly in contact with metal parts of the boiler.

Filament

A small heating wire or element is positioned in the vicinity of the pilot burner and connected via an ignition switch to a low voltage supply either from a battery (1.5 to 3.0 volts) or from a mains transformer. On pressing the ignition switch and completing the circuit the element will glow red hot and ignite the gas at the pilot flame. The diagrammatic sketch in Figure 1.22 illustrates the working aspects of the ignition system, which is basically simple. Faults which may arise include: no electrical supply (flat battery, blown fuse, etc.), broken or disconnected wiring, circuit shorted to earth,

flame protection device, must detect the presence of a flame to maintain the supply of gas to the burner and shut off the supply when the flame is not present. To do this, the device is usually actuated or brought into action by a pilot flame. The presence of the flame may be sensed in a number of ways, including:

1 Using heat from the flame,
2 By the flame conducting and rectifying an alternating current,
3 The effect of ultra-violet or infra-red rays on a photoelectric cell.

The devices described in this chapter use the methods outlined to control a gas valve situated in the supply to the main burner. All of them can, however, be made to operate relays and electrical switches. In this way they may be used in more sophisticated control systems, often giving complete automatic operation of the appliance.

Bimetallic

Metals expand when heated, and different metals expand by different rates for the same heat input. If two small strips of two different metals are joined together to form a 'bimetal' strip (Figure 1.23a) and heated, then if the top metal expands more than the one underneath, the strip will bend when it is heated (Figure 1.23b). The distance that the end of the strip will move when heated can be increased if the strip is already bent into a

240 volt supply from
appliance control box

fuse

push switch igniter button

contacts

pilot jet

L

N

main gas burner

earth

step down transformer reduced mains voltage

when the switch is operated, glow coil igniter achieves bright red heat due to its resistance to the flow of electricity. this will ignite the pilot flame when a supply of gas is available

Figure 1.22 *Mains filament ignition*

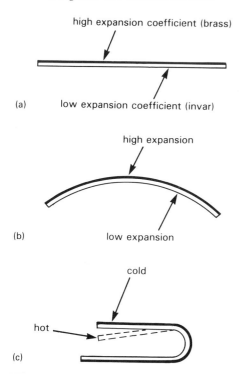

high expansion coefficient (brass)

(a)   low expansion coefficient (invar)

high expansion

(b)   low expansion

cold

hot

(c)

Figure 1.23   *The working of a bimetallic strip*

curve (Figure 1.23c). This will also show the amount of movement due to heating. If the strip is secured at one end and a valve spindle is attached to the other, the valve can be made to open the gas pipeline to the main burner, when it has become heated by a pilot flame (Figure 1.24). If the pilot is extinguished, or becomes blocked or shortened, the strip will cool down and straighten and so close the gas valve.

These devices are relatively simple and inexpensive and have been used on domestic water heaters and cookers for many years. Their main disadvantage is that they do not shut off the pilot if the flame goes out, and that they are slow in action, taking about 1½ minutes to close the gas valve following the elimination of the pilot flame.

Thermoelectric
This type of device has been used on cookers, water heaters and boilers for many years. As the name implies, it is an electrically operated valve, the electricity being generated by

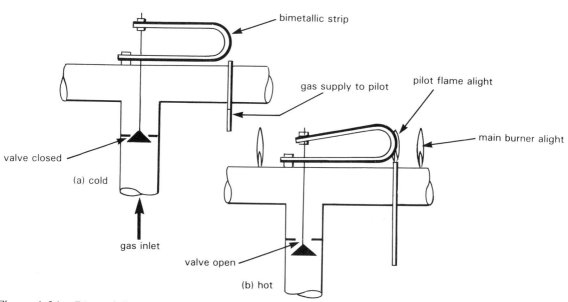

bimetallic strip

gas supply to pilot

pilot flame alight

main burner alight

valve closed

(a) cold

gas inlet

valve open

(b) hot

Figure 1.24   *Bimetal flame protection device*

the heat contact of the thermocouple when the pilot flame is alight. In its simplest form a thermocouple consists of a loop of two different or dissimilar metals joined together at one end and with the other ends connected to an electrical magnet or meter. When the held up as long as the magnet remains energised. If the pilot flame is extinguished, the thermocouple will lose heat quickly and cease to produce an emf, the coil will no longer be magnetised and the spring will close the valve.

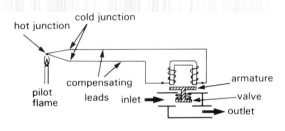

Figure 1.25 *Principle of the thermocouple connected to an electromagnet*

flame, the main gas valve F must be raised off its seating. This is done by pressing in the reset button A. When this is first pushed in it allows the flow interrupter valve E to come into contact with the lower valve seating, so closing off the outlet. Further pressure on the push button raises the spindle through the interrupter valve and lifts the main valve F off the top valve seating. This brings the armature H into contact with the pole pieces

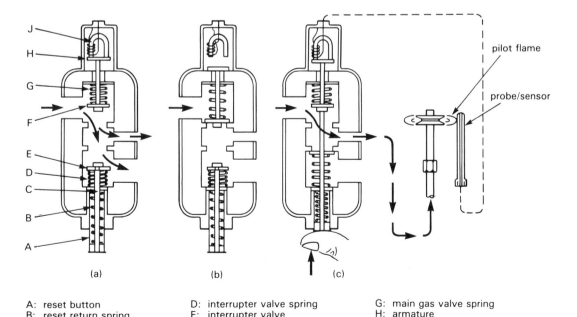

A: reset button	D: interrupter valve spring	G: main gas valve spring
B: reset return spring	E: interrupter valve	H: armature
C: spindle	F: main gas valve	J: electromagnet

Figure 1.26 *Thermoelectric flame protection device: (a) operating position; (b) off position; (c) setting position*

of the magnet and also allows gas to pass to the pilot connection (Figure 1.26c). The pilot can now be lit, heating the thermocouple and energising the electromagnet.

This process can take up to 60 seconds, during which time the push button must be held in. When the button is released (Figure 1.26a), the spring-loaded interrupter valve and push button return to their starting positions and gas can now pass through both valve seatings to the burner.

If pilot failure occurs or the gas supply is interrupted whilst the main burner is off, then the thermocouple will cool, the magnet will become de-energised and the main gas valve will shut off in about 30 seconds. The setting process must be repeated and the

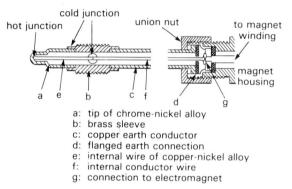

a: tip of chrome-nickel alloy
b: brass sleeve
c: copper earth conductor
d: flanged earth connection
e: internal wire of copper-nickel alloy
f: internal conductor wire
g: connection to electromagnet

Figure 1.27   *Thermocouple and lead connections*

pilot flame re-established before gas can pass to the main burner.

Because the thermocouple is remote from the magnet it is connected to it by means of a special electrical lead. The conductors are made of copper with the outer one in the form of a tube. The inner wire is insulated from the tube by a glass fibre sleeve and the two form a coaxial cable. At one end the conductors are brazed onto the thermocouple and at the other end they are connected to the magnet housing by a union nut (Figure 1.27).

Vapour pressure devices

When liquids are heated sufficiently, they turn into vapour or boil. The vapour has a much greater volume than the liquid and so causes a rapid increase in pressure which can be made to operate the valve in a vapour pressure flame-failure device (Figure 1.28).

Unlike the thermoelectric device, which requires a permanent pilot flame, the vapour pressure device can be used where the pilot flame is ignited only when the appliance is in use. It is generally used with a solenoid-type main gas control and this, when electrically energised, allows gas to flow to the inlet of the vapour valve and to the pilot jet. When the pilot is lit, the flame heats the phial

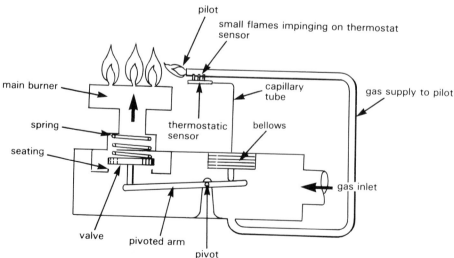

Figure 1.28   *Mercury vapour flame safety device*

(which contains liquid mercury) and the mercury vapour expands and extends the bellows, causing the lever to pivot and open the main gas valve to the burner, overcoming the pressure of the spring. When the appliance thermostat is satisfied, it operates

removed for renewal or servicing. The multifunctional device may include a

1 Main gas valve,
2 Flame protection device,
3 Solenoid valve,

thermoelectric valves. If the valve fails to open this is usually due to a leaking or damaged bellows unit, and a replacement unit will need to be fitted.

Photoelectric devices
These devices depend on the fact that some metallic substances do not conduct electricity when they are in the dark, but allow a current to pass when light shines upon them. Selenium is one such substance and is used in photoelectric cell devices for operating doors, detecting smoke and actuating alarm systems. It may also be used to switch on electricity when the level of light falls to a pre-selected value.

The devices used to protect gas flames are sensitive to either ultra-violet or infra-red rays and not to light. The infra-red detector can be made to accept only the pulsating rays from the flames and not the steady output from the combustion chamber itself. The infra-red detectors are used mainly on such appliances as boilers.

Multifunctional controls
A multifunctional control is a composite control which incorporates all the control devices required by a particular appliance. It consists of a chassis fitted in the gas supply to the appliance to which the individual control units are attached. The chassis can remain in the gas supply whilst the various units are

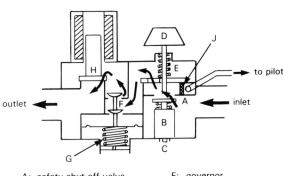

A: safety shut-off valve
B: thermo-electric valve unit
C: thermocouple connection
D: knob
E: disc-type cock
F: governor
G: governor spring
H: solenoid valve
J: pilot filter

Figure 1.29 *Multifunctional control*

The manometer or U-gauge

This piece of equipment is used for measuring both the soundness of installations and the working pressure of gas appliances. It usually consists of a glass or clear plastic tube 300 mm long bent in the shape of a U and fitted into a metal or wood case. The tube is filled with water and the device will measure pressures up to 30 mbar.

The tube has a scale fitted between the two upright parts or 'limbs'. One limb is connected to the gas supply and the other remains open to the atmosphere. The scale is usually capable of adjustment so that the zero can be lined up with the water level as

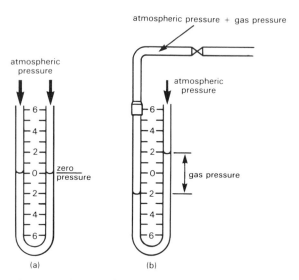

Figure 1.30   *U-tube pressure gauge*

marked in millimetres. Since 10 mm equals 1 mbar the scale can be read as millibars. It is necessary to add together the amount of rise and the amount of fall to read the total height of liquid. If the gauge has been zeroed correctly one side can be read and then doubled.

The half scale gauge (a) has a half size scale where 5 mm represents 1 mbar. As the scale is already doubled all that needs to be done is to zero it properly and then read off one side – usually the top one – to obtain the gauge reading.

The surface of the water in each leg is curved because it adheres to the sides of the tube. This curve is called the 'meniscus' and the gauge reading should be taken at the bottom of the curve as shown in Figure 1.32.

shown in Figure 1.30a. When gas pressure is applied (Figure 1.30b) the water will be displaced downwards in the left limb and upwards in the right by equal amounts. The total height of the column of water supported indicates the gas pressure.

U-gauges may be of the full scale (Figure 1.31b) type or of the half scale (Figure 1.31a) pattern. The full scale gauge has a scale

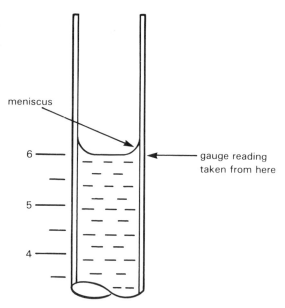

Figure 1.32   *Reading a U-gauge*

Soundness testing procedure for domestic gas installations

Soundness testing (Figure 1.33) should be carried out on every occasion that installation, disconnection, removal, alteration, replacement or maintenance of gas appliances, fittings, etc. is undertaken. A manometer to

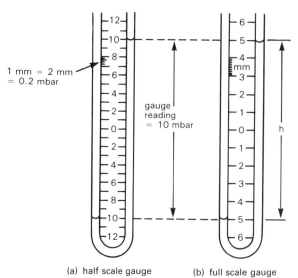

Figure 1.31   *U-gauge scales*

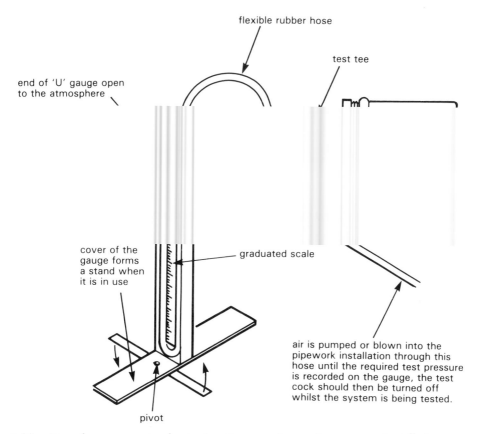

flexible rubber hose

test tee

end of 'U' gauge open
to the atmosphere

cover of the
gauge forms
a stand when
it is in use

graduated scale

air is pumped or blown into the
pipework installation through this
hose until the required test pressure
is recorded on the gauge, the test
cock should then be turned off
whilst the system is being tested.

pivot

Figure 1.33   *Use of a manometer for testing the soundness of a new gas installation*

measure a minimum of 30 mbar is required for this purpose.

Method of testing

Existing installations

1 With all outlets closed and a manometer attached to the system, fill the installation with gas to a pressure of 20 mbar (200 mm wg).
2 Turn off the gas and allow 1 minute for stabilisation of pressure.
3 Observe the manometer gauge reading. After a further 2 minutes the installation may be deemed sound if any pressure drop is within the limits shown in Table 1.2. This varies according to the meter size.

Table 1.2   *Pressure drop limits for various meter sizes*

Meter size	Permissible meter drop	
U6 (DO7)	4.0 mbar	(40 mm wg)
P1 (D1)	2.5 mbar	(25 mm wg)
P2 (D2)	1.5 mbar	(15 mm wg)
P4 (D4)	0.5 mbar	(5 mm wg)

Any additions to existing installations should be regarded as new installations and subjected to the test for new pipework.

Before commencing work the soundness of the existing installation should be tested at 20 mbar gas pressure. Any pressure drop should be measured and the additional pipework installation connected only if the drop is within the permitted limits.

On completion of the work, a pressure test should again be carried out and the results compared with the original test. If a presure drop is found it should not be in excess of that measured during the first test.

New installation pipework
1 With all the outlets closed and a mano-meter attached to the system, fill the system with air to a pressure of 30 mbar (300 mm wg).
2 Allow 1 minute for the stabilization of pressure.
3 Observe the manometer gauge reading. After a further 2 minutes the installation is deemed sound only if no pressure drop has occurred.

If a pressure drop has occurred then there is a leak in the system. Leaks are best detected by brushing soapy water around all joints and connections, a leak being detected by the emergence of air bubbles through the soap solution.

Gas pipework systems and gas ap-pliances should always include a test nipple or plug (Figure 1.34) to facilitate soundness testing, commissioning or service testing. The nipple allows for the connection of a rubber hose to the pipework system or gas appliance. It is important that every gas appliance should have a test nipple for commissioning purposes. System test nipples are usually located at or adjacent to the gas meter outlet connection.

Purging gas installations

When commissioning a new gas installation it is important to purge it of all air, for there is a danger of an explosion if gas and air mixes within the pipework system. This is why new installations are always tested for soundness with air pressure. The procedure for system purging is as follows.

The meter control valves should be turned off before any individual appliance is turned on. Then the largest capacity appliance or the one at the end of the main run of installation pipework should be turned on. First discon-nect the burner union, then turn on the meter control valve and allow air to escape via the disconnected union. It is essential that the space into which the gas/air mixture is discharging is well ventilated, and that there is no danger from naked flames or electrical controls. As soon as gas can be smelt re-connect the burner union and check joints for soundness with a brushed-on soap solu-tion. This procedure should be carried out until all appliances have been checked and gas is available at each burner. Only when all the air in the system has been removed and replaced by gas should any attempt be made to light the appliances.

Flues

Functions
When fuel is burned in an appliance, it combines with oxygen from the surrounding air to produce combustion products. Pro-vided that the appliance is correctly adjusted and serviced, and provided there is an adequate supply of fresh air, these combus-tion products will consist predominantly of carbon dioxide, nitrogen and water vapour, all of which are non-toxic. However, to avoid discomfort and condensation, excessive

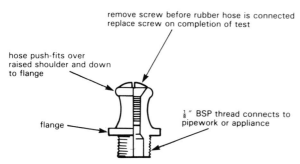

remove screw before rubber hose is connected
replace screw on completion of test

hose push-fits over
raised shoulder and down
to flange

flange

⅛″ BSP thread connects to
pipework or appliance

Figure 1.34   *Test nipple fitted to gas systems and appliances to facilitate testing and commissioning*

build-up of these products must be prevented. Furthermore, unless they are removed from the room containing the appliance, they cannot be replaced by a further supply of fresh air. If this continued long

operation of the appliance, ... *combustion products and inducing an adequate supply of fresh air.*

In addition to its main function, an open flue will promote the general ventilation of the room even when the appliance is not in operation. This is a consequence rather than a purpose, but is a significant benefit, contributing to the comfort of the occupants and, particularly in kitchens, minimising the occurrence of condensation.

Necessity
A flue is essential for most gas appliances and *all* solid fuel and oil-fired appliances. However, if the general level of ventilation in a room is sufficient to prevent undue build-up of products and to ensure sufficient combustion air, then flueless operation of a gas-fired appliance is acceptable. In practice, this means that flueless appliances are permissible, under the following conditions:

1 They are of very low rating, e.g. refrigerators.
2 Their periods of use are of inherently short duration, e.g. instantaneous sink heaters.
3 Conditions associated with their operation make it likely that the user will increase the room ventilation. For example, wash boilers and cookers cause steam or cooking smells, making it likely that the user will open the windows.
4 The room has forced ventilation which

operates in conjunction with the appliance and which is sufficient to ensure removal of the combustion products.

Gas appliances which generally satisfy the above conditions are

3 Wash boiler, except when used in the same room as a bath.
4 Storage water heaters, provided the heat input is less than 3 kW (10,000 Btu/h), or 4½ kW (15,000 Btu/h) when the storage capacity is less than 45 litres.
5 Circulators, provided the heat input is less than 3 kW (10,000 Btu/h) and provided they are not installed in a bathroom, airing cupboard, or other poorly ventilated enclosure.

Operating principles
The operation of a flue is governed by a simple physical law: to produce movement of a quantity of gas, it is necessary for a pressure difference to be applied. In the case of a flue this pressure difference may be mechanical in origin, as in a fanned draught flue or appliance, or it may be thermal, as in a natural draught flue.

In a natural draught flue, the upward movement of the combustion products results from the temperature difference between the hot gases and the cold ambient air. Referring to Figure 1.35 (overleaf),

Pressure at A (a point just outside the base of the flue)

= Atmospheric pressure at the top of the flue

+ Pressure due to a column H of cold air

Pressure at B (a point just inside the base)

= Atmospheric pressure at the top of the flue

+ Pressure due to a column H of hot gases

Thus, there is a pressure difference between A and B. This is known as the flue draught, and it is equal to the difference in pressure between two columns of height H, one consisting of cold air, and the other of hot combustion products. It produces a tendency for air to flow from A to B, into the base of the flue, thereby forcing the hot gases to move up the flue and out from the top.

The operating principles are the same both for open flue and for room-sealed flue systems. In a natural draught-balanced flue appliance the magnitude of the flue draught is limited by the height of the appliance and is therefore inherently small. This has placed great importance on the proper design of balanced flue terminals, in order to minimise the occurrence of out-of-balance pressures caused by winds.

Factors affecting performance of flues
The performance of a natural draught flue is influenced by a number of factors, including its height, cross-sectional area, thermal input, route, heat losses and wind effects (Figure 1.36).

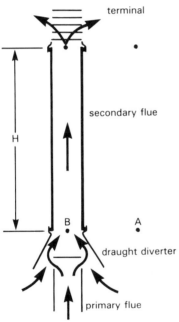

Figure 1.35   *The operation of a flue*

The upward movement in the flue, whether produced thermally or by fan power, is opposed by the resistance to flow – the friction of the flue walls, turbulence at bends, changes of section, etc. Under the action of these forces, the flow of gases settles down to a steady rate.

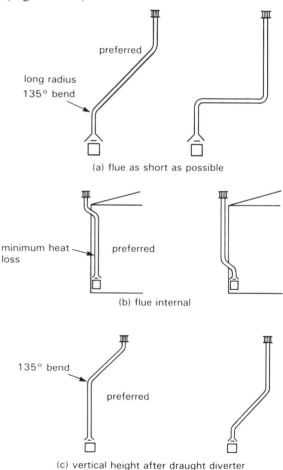

Figure 1.36   *Preferred flue routes*

Height

Raising the height of a flue increases the flue draught, but at the same time adds to the pressure loss due to friction. The net effect on the flow rate is not immediately obvious,

they are, mechanical extraction may be necessary.

Cross-sectional area

There is a more direct relationship between the flue flow and the cross-sectional area. The flue draught is unaffected by changes in the cross-section, but the frictional pressure losses decrease as the area is increased, resulting in a greater flow. As the flue area is increased, the flow induced in the flue increases approximately in proportion, but with a slight tendency for the flow per unit area of flue to increase.

Thermal input

The flue draught increases as the flue gas temperature is raised. The pressure losses are also increased as a consequence of the greater volume flow of the hot gases. The net result is that increased temperature generally leads to a greater flow rate but the effect becomes less marked at higher temperatures. Indeed, above about 260 °C (500 °F) the flow rate slows as the temperature is further increased.

Route

Horizontal runs of flue make no contribution to the flue draught; instead they increase the pressure losses, thus tending to reduce the flow rate. Bends and other flow resistances have a similar effect. It follows, therefore, that the ideal route for a flue is as near

vertical as possible, with a minimum of bends, changes of section and other restrictions (Figure 1.36a).

Where possible, flues should be vertical and as straight as possible. If changes of direction are necessary, bends having an

usually quite small; the increase in flow obtained by using a well-insulated flue in place of an unlagged one is only about 10%. It is nevertheless important to minimise heat losses if condensation is to be avoided (Figure 1.36b).

Wind effects

Wind blowing across a building is likely to produce a pressure difference between the bottom of a flue and the point of termination. This pressure difference will depend on the wind speed and direction, the positions of the top and bottom of the flue in relation to the building, and the presence of neighbouring structures or geographical features.

The wind effect may assist or oppose the natural flue draught, causing increased flow up the flue, or reduced flow up the flue, or downdraught. Wind pressure can be many times greater than the flue draught, and for this reason it is important to minimise its effect by careful attention to the terminal position.

Air supply requirements

However well designed an open flue may be, there will not be an adequate supply of combustion air to enter the room. An additional opening is required, usually a purpose-designed air vent.

For information on air supply requirements and size of opening, reference should be made to the manufacturer's fitting instructions, the appropriate code of practice and to the Building Regulations.

Condensation

The products of combustion of solid fuel, oil and natural gas contain water vapour, and if they are allowed to cool below their dew-point, condensation will occur. Although the prime consideration in flue design is to ensure an adequate flow of gases up the flue, an important secondary requirement is to discharge the gases before they condense. If this is not done, arrangements must be made to drain off the condensate, and to ensure that the flue will not deteriorate under conditions of continual wetting.

As the combustion products move up the flue, they lose heat through the flue walls. To minimise condensation, these heat losses must themselves be minimised. This may be achieved by

1   Keeping the flue as short as possible,
2   Avoiding the use of bends and horizontal lengths,
3   Insulating the flue,
4   Keeping the surface area as small as possible.

Some of the requirements for minimising condensation are in conflict with the criteria for good flue flow. Thus, increased height and increased flue diameter both lead to increased flue flow, but make condensation more likely, and a compromise solution is necessary.

Where possible, flues should be vertical and as straight as possible. If changes of direction are necessary, bends of not less than 135° are preferred. The starting and finishing points of a flue are determined by the appliance position and terminal location, respectively.

Installation

As mentioned earlier, flues should be vertical and as straight as possible. Where bends are necessary they should not be sharper than 135°, to reduce the resistance to the upward

flow of combustion products. Horizontal lengths of flue should be avoided in all circumstances. The diameter of a flue should never be less than the outlet socket connection of the appliance it is connecting to. The flue should be connected in such a way that it can be easily disconnected from the appliance, which is usually achieved with a split collar or sliding socket (Figures 1.37 and

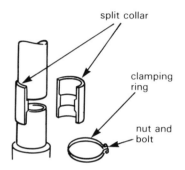

the two halves of the split collar are secured with a clamping ring prior to sealing joints with fire cement.

Figure 1.37   *Use of a split collar*

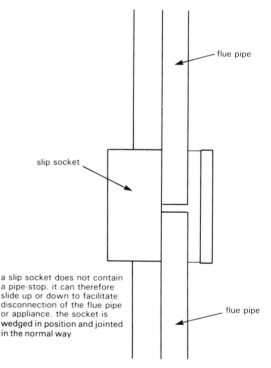

a slip socket does not contain a pipe-stop. it can therefore slide up or down to facilitate disconnection of the flue pipe or appliance. the socket is wedged in position and jointed in the normal way

Figure 1.38   *Use of a slip socket*

1.38). Flue pipes should be installed with the socket upward for two reasons:

1 This method avoids any condensation liquid running out of joints and down the ̶ ̶ ̶ ̶f̶ ̶ ̶ ̶ ̶ ̶ ̶p̶i̶p̶e̶ leaving an

Terminal location
The position chosen for the termination of a flue system can have a critical influence on the performance of that system. It is important that the terminal should be located in a position where the wind can blow freely across it at all times. The position should always be such as to avoid blockage of the flue by snow, leaves, etc. Terminals must not be sited adjacent to openable windows, or other air inlet openings.

The preferred positions for a terminal are shown in Figure 1.39 (overleaf).

1 At or above the ridge of a pitched roof (Figure 1.39a). Such positions are not generally subject to the build-up of wind-induced static pressure. Adverse effects are only likely to be encountered in situations where geological features or neighbouring buildings cause unusual wind effects.
2 Unobstructed flat roof (Figure 1.39b). If the building has a flat roof, and if there are no obstacles to wind flow over the roof, the base of the terminal should be a minimum of 0.25 m above the intersection with the roof.
3 Flat roof with obstacles. If there are obstructions on the roof, such as parapets or tank rooms, the base of the terminal should be a minimum of 0.25 m above a line joining the highest points of neighbouring obstacles. For example, in Figure 1.39c any terminal in the vicinity of A and

B should be at least 0.25 m above the line AB.
4 Unobstructed pitched roof (Figure 1.39d). The base of the terminal should be a minimum of 0.25 m above the ̶i̶n̶t̶e̶r̶s̶e̶c̶t̶i̶o̶n̶ with a roof having a pitch of

6 External flue (Figure 1.39f). If the upper run of a flue is outside the building, the terminal position should be at least 0.25 m above the level of the adjacent roof edge or parapet.

A summary of the preferred terminal locations is given in Table 1.3 on p. 27.

The presence of obstructions on the roof of a building may influence the performance of nearby terminals. Taller buildings in the neighbourhood may also affect performance, but whether or not they create major problems depends on a number of factors, including their lateral dimensions, the relative heights and the distance apart of the buildings, and the speed and direction of the prevailing winds.

There are so many possibilities that firm rules cannot be given, and removal of the terminal location out of the region of influence of the taller building usually introduces structural or aesthetic problems. In general, therefore, a compromise position must be accepted.

When termination above roof level would lead to a flue of excessive length, or have other disadvantages, termination of the flue on the face of a wall may be chosen. Such positions have been used in the past with varying degrees of toleration, but it must be recognised that they are much inferior to the preferred positions shown in Figure 1.39. Termination on or adjacent to the face of a

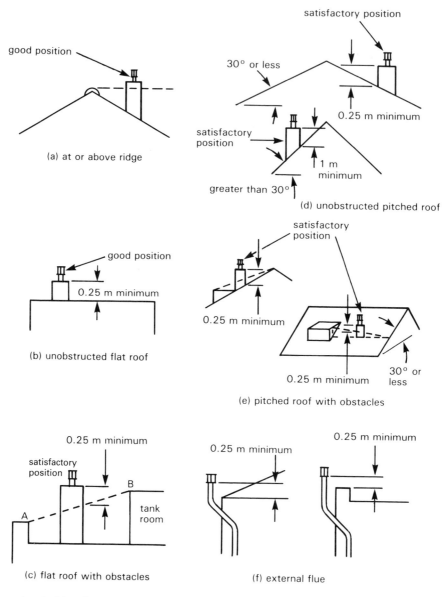

good position

(a) at or above ridge

satisfactory position

30° or less

satisfactory position

0.25 m minimum

1 m minimum

greater than 30°

(d) unobstructed pitched roof

good position

0.25 m minimum

(b) unobstructed flat roof

satisfactory position

0.25 m minimum

0.25 m minimum

30° or less

(e) pitched roof with obstacles

0.25 m minimum

satisfactory position

B

tank room

A

(c) flat roof with obstacles

0.25 m minimum

0.25 m minimum

(f) external flue

terminal locations which will ensure that winds can blow across the terminal from any direction without causing excessive downdraught.

Figure 1.39 *Terminal positions*

wall will result in significant periods of down-draught, the frequency of occurrence of which will depend on the direction of the prevailing wind.

The Code of Practice does not allow termination on the face of a wall, but it does allow termination adjacent to a wall in the case of an instantaneous water heater, or a circulator of input rating up to 4.5 kW (15,000 Btu/h). Wall termination must never be used for any other type of appliance. If, with an appropriate appliance, a wall posi-

Table 1.3 *Location of above-roof terminals for individual natural draught open flue systems*

Type of roof		Minimum height to base of terminal		
		Internal route		External route
Flat	With parapet	Not applicable	0.25 m above roof intersection (Figure 1.39c)	As above

tion is chosen, there must be a height of at least 1.2 m between the appliance outlet and the base of the terminal, and there must be a clearance of 0.25 m between the wall and the flue pipe.

Wall positions which must never be used include:

1 Immediately beneath the eaves or a balcony. The top of the terminal should be not less than 1 m beneath the eaves, and not less than 3 m below a balcony.
2 A re-entrant position on the face of the building.
3 Adjacent to any pipe or other projection on the face of the building.
4 Any position where wind effects may create a zone of high pressure.

Figure 1.40 illustrates three typical flue terminals commonly used with conventionally flued gas appliances.

Balanced flue (room-sealed) gas appliances

These appliances do not require a conventional flue or chimney for the discharge of combustion products because the flue is an integral part of the appliance. Air for

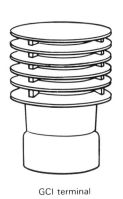

GCl terminal

terminal to replace
chimney pot (GC2)

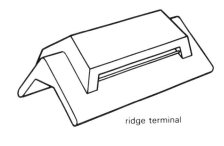

ridge terminal

Figure 1.40 *Typical flue terminals*

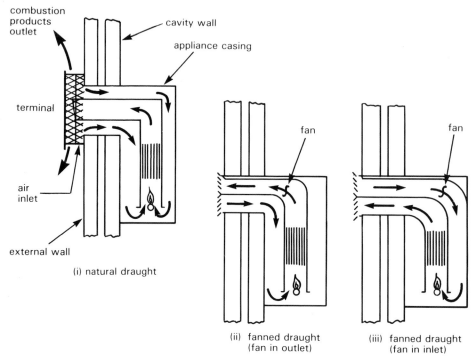

Figure 1.41   *Natural and fanned draught balanced flues*

combustion is drawn in from outside the building through a terminal which is part of the appliance and is mounted in a wall, usually behind the appliance. The burnt gases are discharged from the appliance through a section of the same terminal to the atmosphere outside the building.

The terminals for balanced flue appliances are manufactured in such a way that there is no danger of burnt gases re-entering the appliance. Figure 1.41 shows three illustrations of the balanced flue principle.

The main limitations in the use of balanced flue appliances are that they (a) must be fitted on or close to an external wall, and (b) the siting of the flue terminal must be such as to avoid the possibility of combustion products entering the building through open windows or air ventilation bricks, or causing damage to the fabric of the building. Figure 1.42 shows typical terminals.

Figure 1.43 shows the generally acceptable

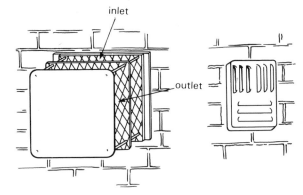

Figure 1.42   *Natural draught and fanned draught terminals*

positions for balanced flue terminals, although manufacturer's installation instructions should always be adhered to.

In locations where terminals may get hot and burn someone, a properly manufactured terminal guard such as that shown in Figure 1.44 should be used.

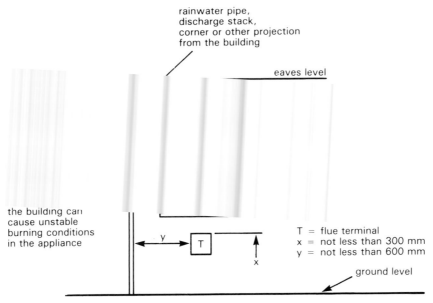

Figure 1.43 *Possible terminal positions for balanced flue appliances*

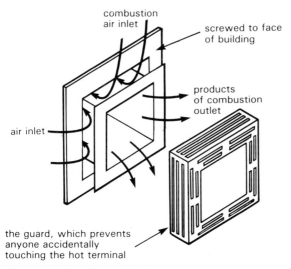

Figure 1.44 *Typical balanced flue terminal with guard removed to show ducts*

Chimneys

For independent boilers

Because modern boilers are highly efficient, they require properly designed chimneys if they are to perform satisfactorily without

hazard to health and safety or risk of structural damage from the effects of condensation.

Chimney design should aim to cut down heat losses in the flue, thereby increasing the buoyancy of the flue gases, raising the temperature of the flue surfaces and minimising the risk of condensation; the chimney fabric must be protected against the effects of condensation should it occur.

Functions

The functions of a chimney are to help induce the flow of air needed for complete combustion of fuel and to vent the products of combustion safely to the outside atmosphere. A badly designed chimney will fail in either or both of these duties, especially when the outside air temperature is only marginally different from that inside and there is little or no wind.

Insufficient draught to burn fuel completely will result in the formation of carbon monoxide and other dangerous substances that endanger health and safety if they are allowed to accumulate. The hazard may take the form of a flue explosion, with risk of damage to the chimney structure, or the leakage of gases into living areas with possible fatal consequences. If the flue surface temperatures are too low, combustion products will condense on the flue surfaces; in the absence of a protective lining, this may damage the chimney fabric and cause staining inside the dwelling.

Both types of malfunctioning can be prevented by designing to make the best use of the small quantities of heat entering the flue with boilers which have a high thermal efficiency. Account must be taken of differences in the mode of operation of domestic boilers with various types of fuel.

Modes of operation

Solid-fuel boilers operate continuously or occasionally, depending on the user's needs. The rate of burning is controlled by opening or closing a primary air inlet, either by hand or by a thermostat in the water-jacket. The fire-bed is highly resistant to the flow of air through it and so, unless the appliance is fan assisted, the flue draught is needed both to maintain the required burning rate and to vent the combustion products to the outside air. A small fixed opening for the admission of air above the fire-bed is a common design feature. This secondary air assists combustion and dilutes the products of combustion. A damper for manual control against wind effects is sometimes fitted at the appliance outlet.

Oil-fired boilers operate under thermostatic control either at two levels (high/low flame) or intermittently at one level (on/off). Burning rate depends on the rate at which oil is fed to the burner, which may be a pressure jet or vaporiser. Both types of burner can operate under natural or forced draught. Where the combustion process is fan-assisted, flue draught is only needed to vent the products of combustion to the outside air; under natural draught conditions, however, part is required to assist the combustion process. Draught in excess of that required

for these duties is admitted by allowing air from the room to enter the flue through an opening in the appliance flue-pipe. This opening may be pre-set manually or may include a draught stabilizer which adjusts automatically to compensate for variable wind conditions.

Gas-fired boilers operate intermittently in response to a pre-set thermostat coupled to a relay valve. When the valve opens, a pilot flame ignites the main burner which then operates at full output. Flue draught is not required for the combustion process but is needed to vent the products to the outside air. A fixed opening at the appliance outlet admits air into the flue to restrict draught in excess of that required; this opening is called a draught-diverter (Figure 1.45) and provides protection against flame failure should down-draught occur as shown in Figure 1.46a and b.

Combustion

Calorific value and air requirement

The heat given off when unit weight of fuel is completely burned is termed its heating or calorific value. There is a theoretical

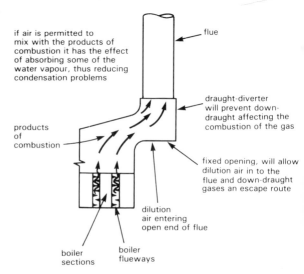

if air is permitted to mix with the products of combustion it has the effect of absorbing some of the water vapour, thus reducing condensation problems

flue

draught-diverter will prevent down-draught affecting the combustion of the gas

products of combustion

fixed opening, will allow dilution air in to the flue and down-draught gases an escape route

dilution air entering open end of flue

boiler sections

boiler flueways

Figure 1.45 *Admitting dilution air to appliance flues to restrict draught*

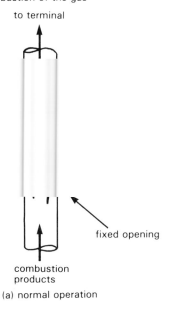

down-draught diverter: its purpose is to
prevent down-draught affecting complete
combustion of the gas

to terminal

fixed opening

combustion
products

(a) normal operation

combustion products
blown back into the flue
due to adverse
draught
conditions

combustion
products

(b) effect of down-draught

Figure 1.46   *Operation of a down-draught diverter*

requirement for the amount of oxygen, and therefore of air, required for the chemical process of combustion but, in practice, an excess of 25–50% over this amount is supplied to ensure good mixing and to assist combustion. Because of differences in the chemical composition of fuels, there are small variations in calorific value and therefore in theoretical air requirements, but the ratio of air required/unit of heat does not vary greatly.

Products of combustion
Water vapour and carbon dioxide are the chief combustion products. Depending on the type of fuel burned, sulphur oxides, nitrous oxides, ammonia, tar acids, free water and unburned particles of fuel may also be present and the flue gas system will contain excess air.

Condensation and chemical attack
Unlined chimneys of traditional construction have always been prone to chemical attack.

The temperature of the flue, particularly if serving slow-combustion appliances, was insufficient to prevent condensation and the condensate could act on sulphur compounds in the flue deposits, supplemented sometimes by sulphates contained in the bricks, to set up sulphate attack of the mortar. This caused the mortar to expand, and because the attack was usually uneven the stack would distort. Attack was progressive because many of the salts were hygroscopic and took up moisture from the air when the chimneys were not in use.

Building Regulations now require all new chimneys to be lined. Problems arising from condensation are consequently less acute but only if the flue linings are of suitable material and correctly installed. They should be resistant to acids and impermeable to liquids or vapours.

Lining existing chimneys
The recommendations for sizing and insulating new flues apply to existing ones and

should be followed as closely as possible when chimneys are repaired so as to avoid a recurrence of troubles, or when new appliances are to be fitted.

Composition cement flue-pipe is sometimes used in straight chimneys because the long lengths available require few joints. Several lengths are arranged socket uppermost and jointed with high alumina cement before being lowered into the chimney. The lining is centered within the brick flue and supported at the base by a plate inserted just above the soot box. (Composition cement flue-pipe is not permitted within 1.8 m of the junction of the flue with a solid-fuel or oil-fired appliance). An air space is sometimes left between the lining and the brickwork but it is more usual to fill the space with dry exfoliated vermiculite or a weak mixture of lightweight concrete. To prevent the formation of voids, the infill should be well tamped; it should be protected at the top by a cement flaunching to prevent rain entering the space and reducing the insulating properties of the material.

Clay and refractory concrete flue linings require temporary access holes to be cut through the brickwork for jointing. Both are available in various diameters and lengths and with rebated joints to keep any condensation inside the linings. A range of standard bends is available. Thermal insulation can be improved by filling the cavity between the lining and brickwork with suitable materials, as the work progresses.

Flexible metal linings are intended for use with gas or oil-fired boilers. The linings are corrugated and available in a range of diameters. They can be cut to any length and, being flexible, are particularly useful where bends in an existing flue have to be negotiated. The lining will usually be of stainless steel or aluminium alloy. Figures 1.47 and 1.48 show alternative methods of connecting an appliance flue to the liner. To provide additional thermal insulation, they may be wrapped with lightweight material such as glass-silk or mineral wool before

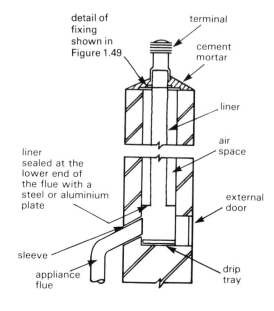

Figure 1.47   *Lining installed in flue*

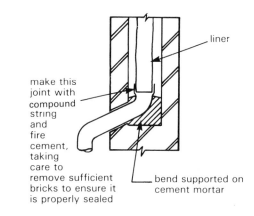

Figure 1.48   *Alternative method of connecting an appliance flue to the liner*

insertion into the chimney; alternatively, the space between lining and brickwork may be filled with a lightweight insulating material such as exfoliated vermiculite.

Care is needed during installation to avoid the lining being damaged by abrasion as it is pushed down the chimney. The lining is supported at the top of the chimney by a metal plate which also acts as a cover to prevent rain entering the space around the linings (Figure 1.49).

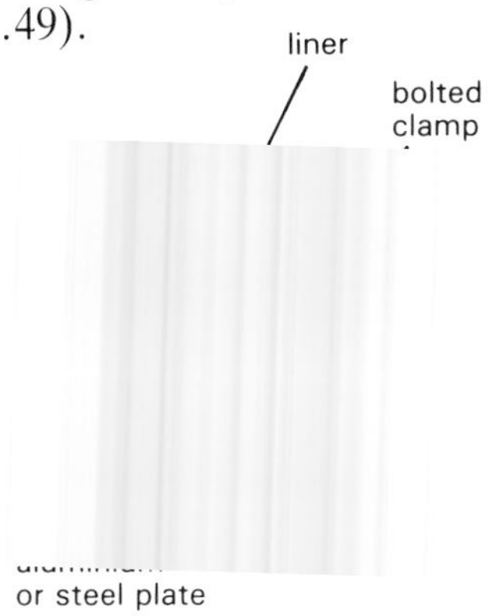

liner

bolted
clamp

or steel plate

Figure 1.49 *Detail showing how the liner is secured at the top of the flue*

For lightweight concrete infills, an inflatable rubber tube is inserted into the chimney and centred in the flue-way by metal spacers attached to it at points where bends occur in the chimney. The tube is then inflated to the ... diameter of the finished flue and a

This method gives a reduced size of flue with additional thermal insulation in one operation.

Self-assessment questions

1   The main constituent of natural gas is
(a)   nitrogen
(b)   oxygen
(c)   methane
(d)   carbon dioxide

2   The minimum depth for a below-ground gas service pipe is
(a)   200 mm
(b)   375 mm
(c)   600 mm
(d)   850 mm

3   The component of air which supports the burning of natural gas is
(a)   carbon monoxide
(b)   carbon dioxide
(c)   oxygen
(d)   nitrogen

4   The poisonous gas liberated because of incomplete combustion of natural gas is
(a)   carbon monoxide
(b)   hydrogen
(c)   methane
(d)   carbon dioxide

5   The minimum bore of a gas pipe to be buried in a floor screed should be
(a)   6 mm
(b)   12 mm
(c)   20 mm
(d)   25 mm

6   If the flue-ways of a gas-fired boiler regularly become blocked with carbon soot, a possible reason is
(a)   excessive use of the heating system
(b)   lack of use of the heating system
(c)   excessive gas rate to the burner
(d)   excessive air intake

7   One purpose of a temporary continuity bond on gas pipework is to
(a)   safeguard against the risk of fire
(b)   assist in pipework identification
(c)   help support heavy pipework
(d)   assist the flow of gas

8   The calorific value of a fuel refers to the
(a)   density of the fuel
(b)   quantity of gas it contains
(c)   heat produced when completely burned
(d)   price the customer pays for the fuel

9   A balanced flue gas water heater draws its air for combustion from
(a)   a high level air brick
(b)   the space around the heater
(c)   a point adjacent to the flue outlet
(d)   below-floor ducting

10 An accepted test standard for the soundness of a new gas pipework installation in a dwelling would be
(a)   air at 1 mbar for 1 hour
(b)   air at 30 mbar for 2 minutes
(c)   the gas at 10 mbar for 5 minutes
(d)   nitrogen at 5 mbar for 10 minutes

2 Drainage

3 Recognise and identify the various materials.

4 Select material suitable for given jobs and state reasons for selection.

5 Select method of jointing and fixing.

6 Make dimensioned sketches of pipes and fittings.

7 Have knowledge of the drain testing procedure.

8 Have knowledge of laying, supporting and protecting of drains.

9 Identify and name the various types of domestic drainage systems.

10 Have knowledge of the need for access and ventilation of drainage systems.

Introduction

It has always been considered the responsibility of the plumber to arrange for the delivery of potable water to a building and to arrange for the collection and discharge of all foul and rainwater from the same building, this being carried out by a system of pipework from the local authority's water main on the inlet side to points within the building and by the connection of another system of pipework connected to the authority's sewer on the outlet side. The plumber must therefore be fully conversant with the design requirements of drainage systems, all the different types of material in common use and installation procedure to conform with the relevant Building Regulations and Codes of Practice.

The materials in common use today are (a) clay, (b) cast iron, (c) concrete, (d) pitch fibre and (e) plastics. Underground drainage of clay or concrete systems have traditionally become the work of the bricklayer or drain layer, due possibly to the use of sand and cement for the method of jointing. The other materials are nevertheless firmly considered the responsibility of the plumber and he must therefore become fully conversant with the principles involved in drainage work.

Drainage materials

Table 2.1 (overleaf) lists the materials currently used for the conveying of effluents in drainage systems.

The following factors affect the choice of material:

1 Strength to meet loading requirements

2 Robust enough to withstand site handling

3 Durable enough to remain watertight for the anticipated life of the system
4 The pipes and joints should remain sufficiently watertight to prevent ingress of ground water and egress of effluent when subjected to ground movement and settlement
5 Diameter and lengths of pipes available
6 Ease of cutting and simplicity of jointing
7 Range of fittings available
8 Ease of handling.

Table 2.1   *Materials used to construct drainage systems*

Category of material	BS no.	Material and applications
Ceramics	65, 1196	Clayware pipes and fittings
	3921	Bricks and blocks of fired brick-earth, clay or shale
Concrete	5911	Concrete: ordinary Portland cement
		sulphate-resisting Portland cement
Metals	534	Steel pipes and fittings
	437	Grey iron pipes and fittings (gravity)
	4622	Grey iron pipes and fittings (pressure)
	4772	Ductile iron pipes and fittings
Pitch fibre	2760	Pitch fibre
Plastics	4660 5481 3506 5480	uPVC ⎤ gravity ⎥ drain and ⎥ sewer GRP ⎦ pressure

Rigid pipes

These pipes do not deform appreciably under their design load. A rigid pipe is able to support the load transmitted to it, the size of which is established by reference to actual crushing tests.

Composition cement

Composition cement pipes and fittings for gravity drainage systems are manufactured to BS 3656 in diameters from 100 mm, in lengths of 3 m, 4 m and 5 m, and to the strength classifications given in that standard. Pressure pipes are manufactured to BS 486 in diameters from 50 mm and in lengths of 3 m and 4 m.

Cast-iron fittings for use with these pipes are also available. Both the above standards include requirements for flexible joints.

Clayware

Clay pipes and fittings are manufactured to BS 65 in lengths of 0.3 m to 2.5 m in three strength classifications as given in that standard. The standard also includes requirements for flexible joints, perforated pipes and extra chemically resistant pipes.

Concrete

Plain and reinforced concrete pipes and fittings are manufactured to BS 5911 in diameters from 150 mm, in lengths of 0.9 m to 2.5 m and to the strength classifications given in those standards. The standard also includes requirements for flexible joints.

Concrete drainage pipes are suitable for use with normal effluents but may be attacked by sulphates or acids in the effluents or surrounding soil or ground-water.

Grey iron

Pipes and fittings in grey iron are manufactured to BS 437, in diameters from 50 mm. Standard lengths are obtainable as 1.83 m, 2.74 m, 3.66 m and 5.5 m (50 mm diameter pipes are in 1.83 m lengths only).

These pipes and fittings have run or caulked lead joints. BS 437 permits the use of flexible joints and proprietary flexible couplings.

Grey iron pressure pipes are manufactured to BS 4622 in diameters from 80 mm. They are available in standard lengths of 5.5 m for pipes with caulked lead or flexible joints. For pipes with screwed-on flanges the standard lengths are 4.00 m. In the case of cast-on flanges the pipe lengths are 0.75 m or 1.00 m.

pitch fibre and uPVC pipes are installed with bedding materials, properly compacted in accordance with this code, they will not generally be deformed by more than 5% of their original diameter, which is considered acceptable.

Ductile iron
Ductile iron pressure pipes and fittings are manufactured to BS 4772 in diameters from 80 mm and to BS 437 in diameters from 50 mm. They are available with flanged or flexible joints and in standard lengths of 5.5 m or 4.00 m.

Glass fibre reinforced plastics (GRP)
GRP pipes and fittings are manufactured to BS 5480. They are available in diameters from 25 mm and in 3 m, 5 m, 6 m, 10 m and 12 m lengths. Their use in building drainage is limited and their longevity may be adversely affected by the continuous conveyance of hot liquids. Since the term GRP covers a wide range of materials with differing characteristics, it is essential that the manufacturer be consulted regarding their use.

Pitch fibre
Pitch impregnated pipes and fittings and flexible joints are manufactured to BS 2760. They are manufactured in diameters of 50 mm and in standard lengths of 1.7 m, 2.5 m and 3.0 m. These pipes should not be used for pressure purposes nor for the continuous conveyance of hot liquids having a temperature of 60 °C or more.

Unplasticised PVC (uPVC)
uPVC pipes and fittings for drainage with either flexible or rigid (solvent welded) joints

the manufacturer.

The impact strength of uPVC pipes is reduced in cold weather conditions, and extra care in handling must be exercised. Further guidance on handling, support, transport and installation is given in BS 5955, Part 6.

Cast-iron drains

Figure 2.1 illustrates a cast-iron pipe with a socket on one end and a beaded spigot on the other. The effective length of the pipe is the overall length of the pipe less the jointing space accommodated within the socket.

Figure 2.2 shows a double-socketed pipe, this type is very useful in certain situations.

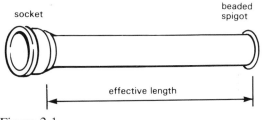

Figure 2.1

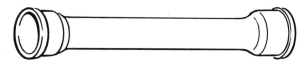

double-socketed pipe

Figure 2.2

Figure 2.3 is another variation of pipe available. In this case we have a plain-ended pipe, the pipe having either plain or beaded spigots.

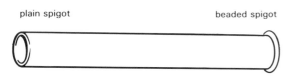

plain spigot   beaded spigot

Figure 2.3

Cast-iron drain-pipes are available in varying lengths, depending on the British Standard, and may be single or double-socketed, or plain-ended. Cast iron has the advantage of making good sharp castings, and is more resistant to corrosion than steel or wrought iron. Protection against corrosion can be achieved by hot dipping the pipes and/or fittings in a coal-tar-based solution (Dr Angus Smith's Solution). Care in handling the items is very important as the protection is only a surface one.

Modern casting methods and heat treatment have improved the basic flake graphite structure, but even so this flake formation still limits the strength of the metal and prevents ductility. For most drain purposes grey iron still has sufficient strength and is superior to uPVC, vitrified clay or pitch fibre when the situation requires pipe strength.

Drainage of premises

As stated previously the plumbing craftsperson of today must be conversant with the design and installation of all types of drainage system. The drainage system provided for any building depends upon the requirements of the Building Regulations, the local authority, and of the sewerage system in use in the district where the property is located.

The usual methods of dealing with the discharges from premises are:

1   Combined system,

2   Separate system,
3   Partially separate system,
4   Septic tank system,
5   Cesspool system.

The discharges received by the systems from the appliances are classified under the following headings:

1   Soil (any appliance that discharges urine and/or excrement),
2   Waste (any appliance that discharges washing and bathing water),
3   Surface water (all rainwater discharges).

The combined system

In this system (Figure 2.4) *all* the discharges, i.e. *soil, waste* and *surface* water, are discharged into one common sewer, usually belonging to the local authority, which conveys the effluent to the sewerage disposal point, where it is purified up to an acceptable standard before being discharged into a convenient river or other outfall. As Figure 2.4 shows, only one system of drainage pipes is required.

The separate system

In this system (Figure 2.5, overleaf), the *surface water* is kept entirely separate from the *soil and waste water*. There are therefore two sets of drains on the property, one drain taking all surface water (rainwater) and one taking all the soil and waste discharges. The local authority (LA) also provides two sewers to receive the respective discharges: the surface water is discharged untreated into the river or suitable water course, while the soil and waste discharges are conveyed to the sewerage treatment plant before discharge into possibly the same river.

The partially separate system

This system has the same characteristics as for the *separate system* except that in this system the LA has granted permission for certain *rainwater* points to be discharged into the *soil drain*. This is allowed where there are

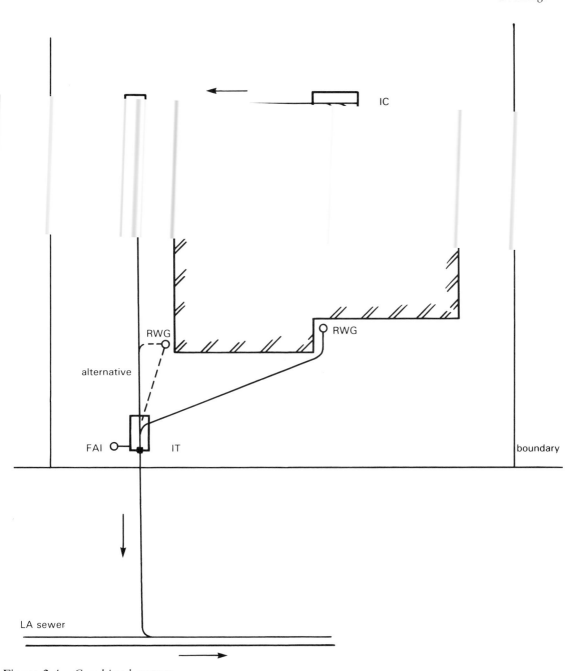

Figure 2.4 *Combined system*

Note It will be readily seen that there is only one set of drains on the property and only one sewer taking all the *soil*, *waste* and *rainwater* discharges, i.e. *combined system*.

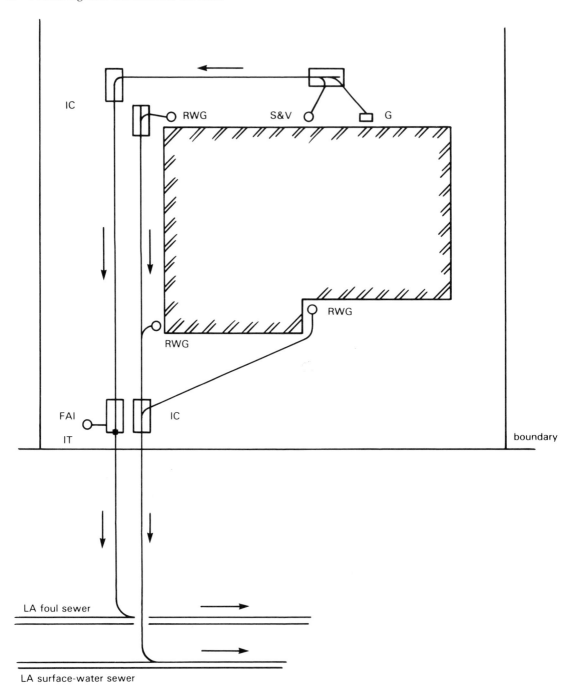

Figure 2.5   *Separate system*

Note   It must be noted that many local authorities (LAs) do not permit the use of interceptor traps in new drainage systems. The reasons for this change of regulation will be explained later in this chapter.

isolated rainwater points which would necessitate excessively long runs of pipe or
other installation problems.

Septic tank system

Cesspool system

This system is also used where there are no
main sewers available to receive the discharges from the appliances. The rainwater is
discharged into soak-aways, while the soil
and waste discharges are delivered into the
cesspool where they are stored for a period of
time prior to being collected by a tanker and
taken to a disposal point.

Table 2.2 *Classification of appliances*

Soil appliances	Waste appliances	Surface water
Water closets	Sinks	All rainwater
Urinals	Baths	
Bed-pan	Wash basins	
washers	Bidets	
	Showers	
	Washing	
	machines	
	Dish washers	

Drainage work

The design and layout of drainage systems

(a) Obtain from the LA the following
information:

   1 The size of the main sewer,
   2 The invert level,

3 The location of the sewer,
4 The type of system (combined or
   separate),
5 If intercepting traps are required,
6 The possibility of surcharge.

drainage system which is required by
the LA and must be approved by them
before work can commence.

Procedure

The function of a drainage system must be to
collect, convey and discharge all the soil,
waste and rainwater adequately and safely
from the respective property by whichever
system of drainage is used. The system must
be constructed and laid so as to be self-
cleansing and so reduce the risk of stoppages
to a minimum. Adequate ventilation must
also be provided to maintain the system in an
odourless condition. The drain pipes must be
laid in straight lines between access points,
which should be at every junction and at
every change of direction on foul drains. The
system should remain sound and water-tight
during its operation to prevent pollution of
the surrounding earth.

Material

The choice of material generally lies between
cast iron, clay, pitch fibre and polyvinyl-
chloride, cast iron being the choice where the
drain passes under buildings in made-up
ground and for shallow drains under roads.

Size of drain

The drain must be large enough to take the
maximum estimated flow from the appliances
and the surface water area. Drains for

domestic use must have a minimum diameter of 100 mm when conveying foul and waste water. This size of pipe, when laid at an incline of 1:40 (Maguire's rule), will give a discharge of approximately 1.14 m/sec when flowing one-third full.

Laying

Irrespective of the type of material used the following principles should be followed:

1   The pipes must be laid on adequate foundation.
2   They should always be laid in straight lines between access points.
3   Each run must be as short as possible.
4   Entry of all branch drains should be made in the direction of the flow.
5   The pipes should have an evenly maintained gradient.

Gradient

The gradient must be sufficient to give a self-cleansing velocity of flow; many LA's adopt Maguire's rule of:

1:40 for 100 mm pipe
1:60 for 150 mm pipe
1:90 for 225 mm pipe.

These gradients are often greater than needed and will achieve velocities of approximately 1.14 m/sec when flowing one-third full. The drains must always be laid at a self-cleansing gradient and where possible the drains should be laid with the natural gradient of the ground to economise in excavation. Where the slope of the ground is excessive the drain must drop vertically and be accommodated in back-drop chambers, then continue at the correct gradient.

The gradient board

The easiest method of laying drains to obtain the correct gradient is by the use of a gradient board. It is particularly useful when laying short lengths of drain, and it is a comparatively simple task to make one. The first operation is to establish the fall of the drain,

i.e.   100 mm pipe 1:40
             150 mm pipe 1:60.

This must now be converted into actual distances.

Example:

$$\text{Gradient} = \frac{\text{Fall}}{\text{Length}}$$

$$= \frac{\text{Highest level} - \text{Lowest level}}{(\text{Length of branch drain})}$$

Taking a 150 mm pipe laid to a fall of 1:60 means that the pipe will fall

1 mm in 60 mm or
1 m in 60 m.

Therefore the gradient $= \dfrac{1\,\text{m}}{60\,\text{m}}$

$$= 0.0166\,\text{m in each metre length}$$

There are 1000 mm in 1 metre. Therefore to convert 0.0166 m to millimetres:

gradient $= 0.0166 \times 1000$ mm

$$= 16.6 \text{ mm fall in each metre length}$$

The gradient board can now be set out according to the calculated gradient (see Figure 2.6). The length of the gradient board may be any convenient length. It is better to work in metre lengths and perhaps a 2 m length would be satisfactory. Therefore setting out the gradient to a given example the fall or gradient would be:

16.6 mm per metre

$\therefore$ 16.6 × 2 = 33.2 mm per 2 metre length of board

The trench to receive the drain is dug roughly to depth allowing for 150 mm of concrete or similar foundation. Pegs are then driven into the base of the trench as shown in Figure 2.7. The gradient board is then placed on the pegs, angled edge down, with a spirit

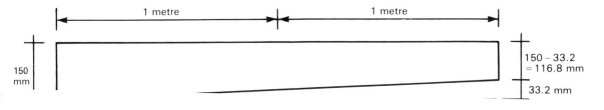

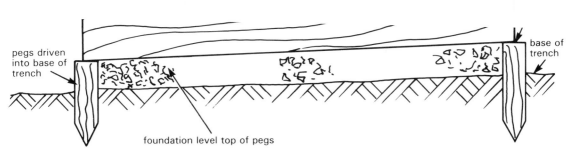

Figure 2.7   *Checking gradient*

level on the top edge; pegs are driven into the ground to give the necessary fall; the foundation material is then placed and drain laying commenced. It is also possible to place the gradient board on the top of the completed line of drain to obtain the same result. The more advanced methods of levelling drainage systems, using levelling equipment, are outside the scope of the craft student.

Access to drain

Drainage design requires pipes to be laid in straight lines between points of access. Suitable access points may be made by providing rodding eyes, access fittings and inspection chambers.

Rodding eyes

A rodding eye (see Figure 2.8) provides access at surface level for the clearance in one direction only of obstructions and debris, using the normally accepted manual rodding

techniques. The rodding eye should be constructed in pipework preferably of the same diameter as the drain it serves and should be connected to the drain at an angle not steeper than 45° to the horizontal. It should be carried up to ground level at the same angle to permit easy rodding and to reduce resistance to the passage of the rods.

Access fittings

An access fitting provides for rodding in more than one direction and for testing. On a

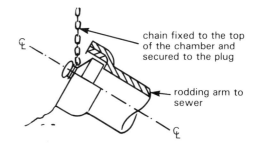

Figure 2.8   *Rodding eye*

buried drain they are used in three ways:

1   As an opening in the top of the drain having a sealed cover.
2   With a raising piece terminating with a suitable cover at surface level.
3   With a sealed cover located within an inspection chamber.

Inspection chambers
At junctions, changes of direction and at intermediate points, access to the drain is made by means of an inspection chamber. It is in fact a pit usually of brick construction, incorporated into the run of the drain at which point the drain becomes an open channel. In the case of cast iron drains, the inspection chambers are purpose-made with bolted-on access covers; the unit is housed in a brick-built or pre-cast concrete chamber.

Inspection chambers should be resistant to water penetration, be durable and designed to minimise risk of blockage. The size of the chamber will depend on the size and depth of the main drain, and the number, size and position of any branch drains. Recommended sizes are given in BS 8301. The detail set out below is an example:

Length   Allow 300 mm for each 100 mm branch on the side having most branches plus an allowance at the downstream end for the angle of entry (Figure 2.9).

Width   The sum of the widths of benching plus 150 mm or the diameter of the main drain (whichever is the greater).

Note   The width of the benching with branches = 300 mm
The width of the benching without branches = 150 mm

Length

$$\begin{array}{rl}
\text{‘A’ branch} = & 300 \text{ mm} \\
\text{‘B’ branch} = & 300 \text{ mm} \\
\text{Downstream allowance} = & 600 \text{ mm} \\
& \text{(approx.)} \\
\hline
\textit{Total length} = & 1200 \text{ mm}
\end{array}$$

Width

$$\begin{array}{rl}
\text{Benchings } 300 \times 2 = & 600 \text{ mm} \\
\text{Diameter of drain} = & 150 \text{ mm} \\
\hline
\textit{Total width} = & 750 \text{ mm}
\end{array}$$

Size of chamber

Length 1200 mm × width 750 mm

Ventilation
This is another very important feature of sewerage and it is most desirable to arrange for a current of air to pass through each drainage system. This is achieved by means of a fresh air inlet (Figure 2.10) at the lowest point of the system, this being at the intercepting chamber in the situation and area where they are still permitted, and a foul

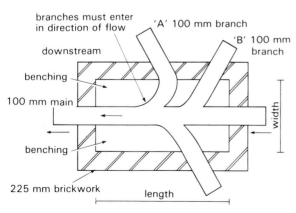

branches must enter in direction of flow
‘A’ 100 mm branch
‘B’ 100 mm branch
downstream
benching
100 mm main
benching
width
225 mm brickwork
length

Figure 2.9   *Inspection chamber dimensions*

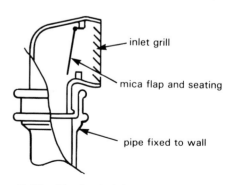

inlet grill
mica flap and seating
pipe fixed to wall

Figure 2.10   *Fresh-air inlet*

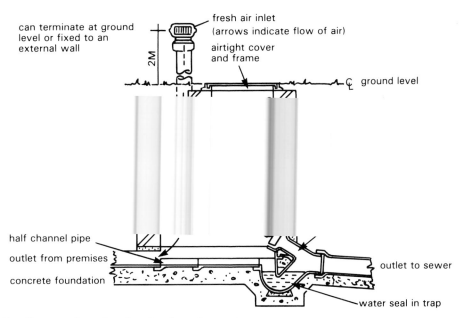

can terminate at ground level or fixed to an external wall

2M

fresh air inlet (arrows indicate flow of air)

airtight cover and frame

ground level

half channel pipe

outlet from premises

concrete foundation

outlet to sewer

water seal in trap

Figure 2.11 *Intercepting chamber in clay pipe system*

air outlet or vent at the highest point of the system. (This vent is usually known as the discharge pipe because it receives the discharges from the water closet and/or bathroom appliances.) The circulation of the air inside the system is by natural convectional currents, the cold, dense (heavier) air entering through the fresh air inlet and the warmer and less dense (lighter) air inside the system (due to the hot water discharges) rising up the vent where it is discharged into the atmosphere in a safe situation, i.e. above or away from any position where it may gain ingress into the building.

Where the local authority does not allow the fixing of intercepting traps (IT) the flow of air and foul gases passes from the sewer to each and every system. Therefore each property takes its share of venting the sewer.

Fresh-air inlet

This fitting is a form of non-return valve and is usually a hinged mica flap, allowing the ingress of fresh air to the drainage system but preventing the egress of foul air. The

problem arises when the hinge corrodes with age, fixing the valve in a fully open or closed position.

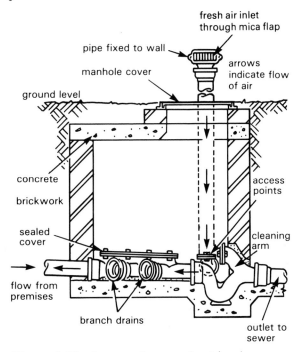

fresh air inlet through mica flap

pipe fixed to wall

manhole cover

arrows indicate flow of air

ground level

concrete

brickwork

sealed cover

flow from premises

branch drains

access points

cleaning arm

outlet to sewer

Figure 2.12 *Intercepting trap (cast iron)*

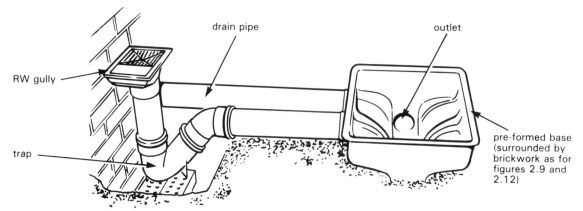

Figure 2.13 *Inspection chamber (Osma plastics)*

Note This type of chamber would be fitted at the head of the drain line. Intermediate chambers would have an inlet at one end and an outlet at the other.

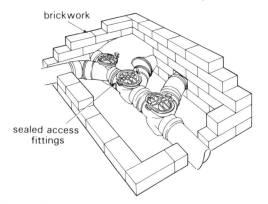

Figure 2.14 *Inspection chamber sealed system (Terrain)*

Rodding eye
Most blockages occur in drainage systems between the intercepting trap and the sewer connection. The rodding or cleaning arm facilitates the rodding of this section of the system.

Trenches
Drain trenches (Figures 2.15 and 2.16) must not be excavated so near to a building that they impair its stability.

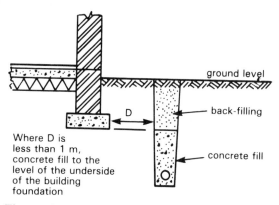

Figure 2.15 *Trenches for drains adjacent to buildings*

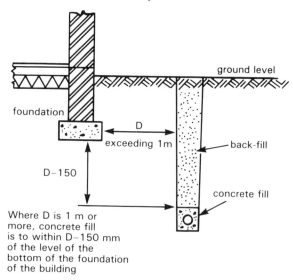

Figure 2.16 *Trenches for drains adjacent to buildings*

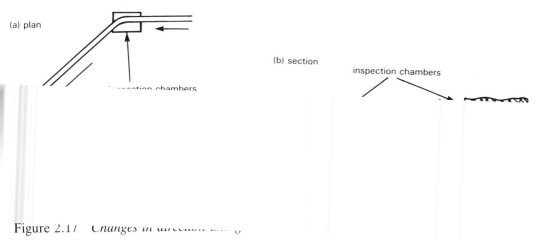

(a) plan

(b) section

inspection chambers

inspection chambers

Figure 2.17 Changes in direction along

Pipes should be laid in straight lines between changes of direction (Figure 2.17) and designed, constructed, sized and laid at a gradient to be self-cleansing and carry away the maximum estimated volume.

Maguire's rule for incline Incline is usually stated as 1 in distance L (Figure 2.18).

To find distance

$$L = \frac{\text{Diameter of drain in mm}}{2.5}$$

Example 100 mm drain $\div$ 2.5 = 40

Therefore incline = 1 in 40

This rule only holds good for short branch drains. The use of Maguire's rule could mean considerable and unnecessary excavation for some installations.

Access

All drains and private sewers shall have such means of access as may be necessary for inspection, cleaning and the clearing of possible stoppages. This is achieved by the use of inspection chambers arranged in the line of the drain and fitted at every change of direction and at specified distances in the case of long lengths of drains. It is now an acceptable practice to arrange the end of the line of drain and/or a branch pipe to the drain to be formed into a rodding point (Figure 2.21 overleaf).

As already stated, where a line of drain is being laid in a straight line without the introduction of branch drains, which would necessitate inspection chambers, then this drain must have fitted in its length access points with a maximum distance of 90 m as illustrated in Figure 2.20 (overleaf). This is necessary due to the fact that it would be extremely difficult, if not impossible, to clear a blockage manually should this length be exceeded. Regulations state that no part of a drain or sewer shall be more than 45 m from an inspection chamber (Figure 2.20).

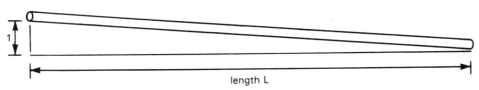

1

length L

Figure 2.18

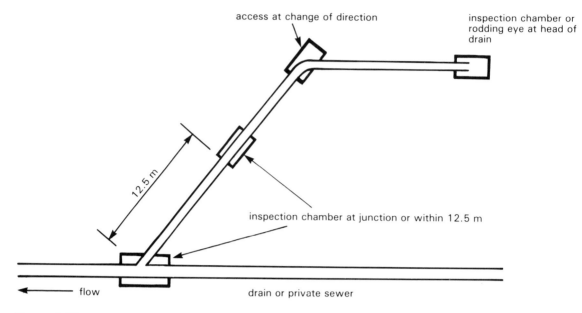

access at change of direction

inspection chamber or
rodding eye at head of
drain

12.5 m

inspection chamber at junction or within 12.5 m

← flow

drain or private sewer

Figure 2.19

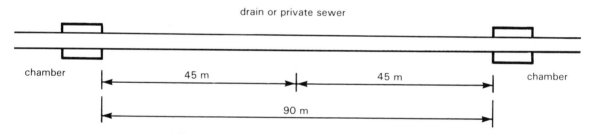

drain or private sewer

chamber

45 m

45 m

chamber

90 m

Figure 2.20   *Drain or private sewer*

Figure 2.21 illustrates a rodding point at the end of a line of drain as an alternative to an inspection chamber. The pipe is arranged by a number of purpose-made bends to rise and terminate near the surface of the ground where it affords access for rodding and cleaning purposes. The end of the pipe is sealed by a removable stopper or cap. The rodding point can also be fitted in the mid-point of a long line of drain by a junction or branch piece being fitted and the branch pipe being carried up and terminating as previously described.

In all cases it must be possible to rod each and every part of the drainage system. Where the drain passes under a building the drain must be provided with an inspection chamber at the points of immediate entry and exit to the building (Figure 2.22). It must also be

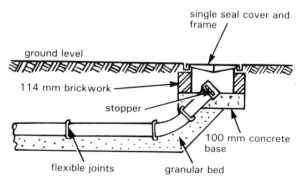

single seal cover and
frame

ground level

114 mm brickwork

stopper

flexible joints

granular bed

100 mm concrete
base

Figure 2.21   *Rodding point at head of drain*

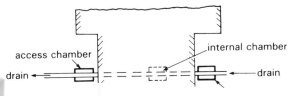

2 They must sustain any imposed loads.
3 Subsoil water should be excluded.
4 They must be made watertight in case of a blocked drain.
5 They should be of such size and form to permit access for inspection, cleansing

noted that any access chambers within the building must have bolted-on air-tight covers.

Inspection chambers should be designed and constructed with the following points in mind:

1 Suitable material, such as brickwork, concrete, PVC and cast iron must be used.

Inspection chamber covers

All chambers must have a cover and frame fitted which should be:

1 watertight,
2 airtight,
3 removable and non-venting,

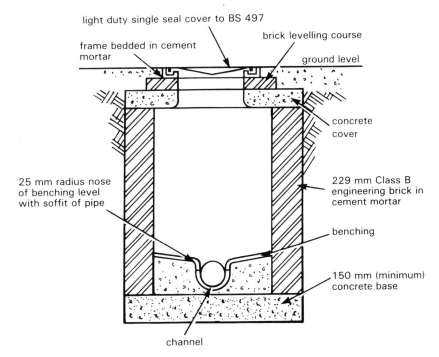

Figure 2.23 *Section through inspection chamber constructed with brick*

4 secured by corrosion resistant bolts (internal),
5 strong enough to withstand maximum estimated load (traffic).

The most common type of cover and frame is the cast iron single seal variety.

Figure 2.24 shows a metal cover with a non-skid surface finished level with the floor surface. This type is generally fitted in outside situations. The cover is usually of a loose fit, being held in place by its weight, although it can also be supplied secured to the frame by four countersunk brass studs. The covers are supplied in different weights, i.e. the heavier the cover the greater the load the cover will support before failure will occur. Therefore correct selection of weight is essential.

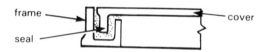

Figure 2.24   *Single seal cover and frame*

In situations where appearance is of some importance, a recessed cover is obtainable as shown in Figure 2.25. The recess is then filled with the same substance as that surrounding the area, with only a small amount of cast iron frame being visible.

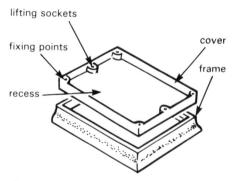

Figure 2.25   *Recessed single seal cover and frame*

Double seal covers and frames (Figure 2.26) are suitable for fixing in internal situations, or alternatively a double seal

Figure 2.26   *Double seal cover and frames*

recessed cover and frame may be fitted. The recess is filled with concrete or other material, suitable for internal location.

Another type of inspection chamber cover is the double cover and frame shown in Figure 2.27. This cover and frame has a single-seal outer cover. In addition a separate single-seal cover is fitted below the main cover. This second seal, when filled with grease, will render the cover and frame airtight, and will remain undisturbed by traffic, and uncontaminated by dirt and liquids working in from the outside.

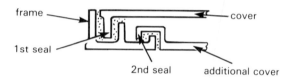

Figure 2.27   *Double cover and frame*

This double cover with its two separate seals must not be confused with the double seal cover with its double seal.

Cast-iron drainage
Access to a system of cast-iron drainage is by means of covers secured by gun-metal nuts and bolts bedded on greased felt gaskets. The access can be through either junctions, bends, or straight pipes. Figure 2.28 illustrates a typical access junction. These access

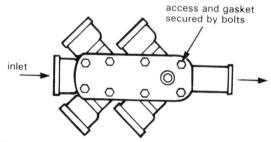

Figure 2.28   *Access to cast-iron system*

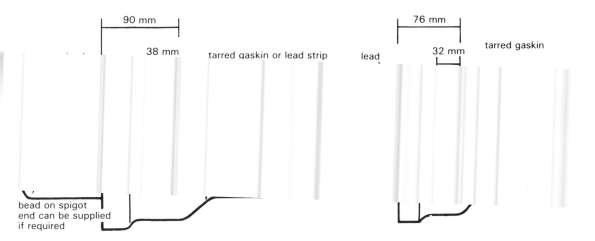

(a) Spun cast iron joint (plain spigot)   (b) Cast iron joint (beaded spigot)

90 mm

38 mm   tarred gaskin or lead strip   lead   76 mm   32 mm   tarred gaskin

bead on spigot
end can be supplied
if required

plain joint to BS1211 made with run pig lead   joint to BS437 made with run pig lead

Figure 2.29   *Rigid joints on cast-iron drains shown in half section and half elevation*

points are usually enclosed in brickwork or similar material chambers as shown.

Jointing of cast-iron drains

These joints are subdivided into:

1 rigid joints, and
2 flexible joints.

Rigid joints can be further subdivided into:

1 Poured molten lead, hand caulked,
2 Lead wool, hand caulked,
3 Cold caulking compound.

Making caulked joints

The spigot end of one pipe is placed in the socket of the other. A length of caulking yarn (jute gaskin) is then tightly twisted so that it will just enter the space between spigot and socket. The yarn is twisted around the top of the socket joint and driven securely to the bottom of the joint space with a yarning tool. Yarning continues until one-third of the socket is tightly filled. Molten lead is then poured into the remaining space to fill the joint completely.

When the lead has set and cooled, the metal must be consolidated in order to complete the joint. The metal in the joint is consolidated with a blunt-ended finishing tool (caulking chisel, see Figure 2.31).

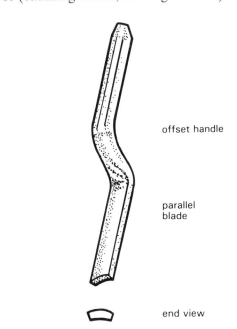

offset handle

parallel blade

end view

Figure 2.30   *Yarning chisel*

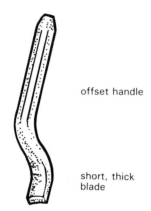

Figure 2.31   *Caulking tool*

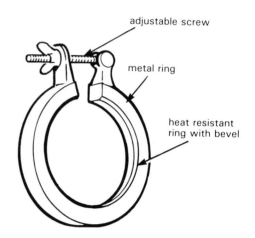

Figure 2.33   *Pipe caulking clamp*

To the uninitiated the running of molten lead into a horizontally placed socket might seem an impossible task, but for the experienced craftsperson it is actually a relatively simple one. The job is simplified by the use of a *squirrel tail pipe jointer* (Figure 2.32) or a *caulking clamp* (Figure 2.33), or a quantity of pliable putty or clay.

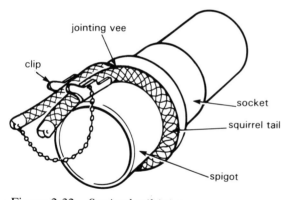

Figure 2.32   *Squirrel tail jointer*

The jointing space is partially filled and stemmed with yarn and the adjustable squirrel tail jointer is placed around the open socket and clipped into position. A small vee inlet is formed by the clip, which must be at the top of the pipe. Molten lead is then poured into the socket via the vee. The ladle should hold sufficient molten lead to ensure that the socket is filled in one operation. The use of molten lead in this instance is quite

safe, provided that the normal safety guidelines are followed:

1   Never place a cold or wet ladle in the molten lead. (Warm the ladle first.)
2   Never pour molten lead into a cold or damp socket. (Warm the socket before pouring the lead.)
3   Place a small quantity of tallow in the mouth of the vee socket before pouring the lead. (This helps to prevent the lead blowing back.)

An alternative method is to use the caulking clamp (see Figure 2.33), the method of jointing being as described for the squirrel tail jointer.

Another very simple practical method is to use either putty or clay. This is formed into a roll and carefully placed around the mouth of the socket, care being taken that the material is not pushed too far into the socket and that there is no chance of a leak of the molten lead. A vee is formed at the top to allow the lead to be poured in.

Yarning and caulking tools

These are specially manufactured steel chisel-like tools with an offset handle to enable the consolidation of the yarn, so keeping the hand of the user clear of the cast iron pipe. The blade of the tool must be thin enough to enter the jointing space yet long enough to reach the bottom of the joint. They have a parallel blade approximately 25 mm wide and slightly concave in section and are about 6 mm thick. Figure 2.30

the lead inside the socket.

Cold-caulking compounds

In some situations, wet conditions, for instance, it may be hazardous to use molten lead to make caulked joints on cast iron drain pipe. In such a situation the solution could be to use one of the cold-caulking compounds, such as lead wool or composition cement. The method of making a caulked joint with lead wool is much the same as with yarn, the difference being that instead of molten lead the socket is filled with the cold lead wool, each turn of the lead wool being firmly caulked home until the whole socket is filled.

Composition cement compound is a particularly useful alternative and can be applied in almost any situation. The material is very simple to handle and is caulked home in the same way as lead wool. The only point to remember is that the caulking tool must be constantly wetted during the caulking operation. The aim is to introduce just the correct amount of water to bring about a chemical reaction to unite the cement with the composition fibres, the result being a hard-setting, pressure-tight joint.

Flexible joints for cast-iron drains

These joints are classified under the following four headings:

1 Slip-fit seal joint,
2 Bolted gland joint,
3 Screwed gland joint,
4 Patent coupling joint.

There are several different types of flexible joints, each one offering some special merit. Broadly speaking, the advantages of flexible joints over rigid ones are:

1 Flexibility,

the retaining heel and bead. The gasket is bulbous in shape at this stage. The dotted line shows the completed assembled joint.

Figure 2.34 *Typical slip-fit ring seal drain joint*

This type of joint allows for the following deflection:

(a) Pipes up to 300 mm: 5° deflection.
(b) Pipes 350–400 mm: 4° deflection.
(c) Pipes 450–675 mm: 3° deflection.

Pipe assembly

One of the recommended methods of assembling long lengths of cast iron drain-pipe with flexible slip ring seal joints is to use the fork tool method (Figure 2.35). This

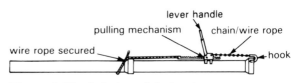

Figure 2.35 *Jointing of drain pipes*

consists of a hook, a wire rope and a fork tool which acts as a lever. The hook is placed over the end of the pipe, the wire rope is attached to the hook and along the length of the pipe and secured to the fork tool, which in turn is secured to the socket of the previously fixed pipe. Using the lever tool the new length of pipe is now drawn into the socket.

Two other types of joint are shown in Figures 2.36 and 2.37. The bolted gland joint (Figure 2.36) allows the following deflection:

1   Pipes up to 675 mm allow 4° deflection,
2   Pipes over 675 mm allow 3° deflection.

encountered. The pipes should not be subjected to too great a pressure; they cannot be obtained in such long lengths as cast iron or PVC and therefore require more joints and greater care in laying.

Figure 2.38 shows a straight pipe and identifies the important parts. The inside of the socket and the outside of the spigot are grooved to assist the cement to key to the material.

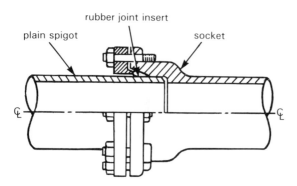

Figure 2.36   *Bolted gland joint*

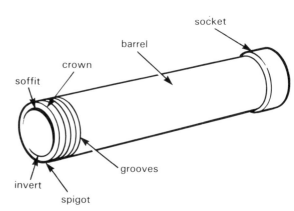

Figure 2.38

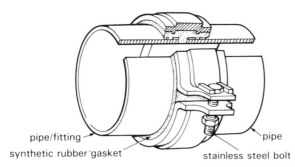

Figure 2.37   *Patent coupling Glynwed timesaver*

Jointing

The traditional gaskin and cement joints shown in Figures 2.39 and 2.40 are generally being replaced with flexible joints as illustrated in Figure 2.41.

Clay drain and sewer pipes

Clay pipes are now commonly used and are non-absorbent and completely incorrosible which makes them particularly suitable where acid effluents or acid subsoils are

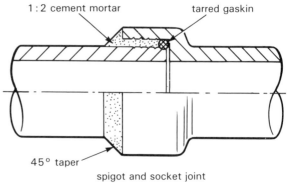

Figure 2.39   *Rigid sand and cement joint*

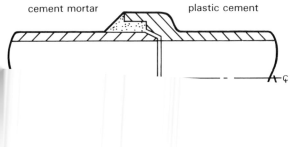

cement mortar   plastic cement

Cutting

The cutting of clay pipes can be very time- and materials-consuming unless care and knowledge are used. Wherever possible use a mechanical saw or pipe cutter. With skill and ... it is possible to cut the pipe by chisel

Rigid joints

These joints are made by compacting the base of the socket with spun yarn, then by filling the remainder of the socket with sand and cement mortar, carefully trowelling the mortar to a smooth 45° fillet, as in Figure 2.39.

The disadvantage of clayware as a material is that it is brittle and if rigid mortar joints are used the pipe-line is likely to fracture if subjected to the slightest movement.

Flexible joints

Clay pipes with flexible joints (Figure 2.41) are much quicker and easier to lay and can withstand a fair degree of movement without the pipe-line fracturing. Flexible joints are also available in both polyurethane and polypropylene.

forgetting to allow the distance ... up-g will enter into the socket.

3 It is essential to support the walls of the pipe; this is done by packing the pipe tightly with sand; the pipe can be cut in the vertical position (Figure 2.42) or, as is quite common practice, laid on a bed of sand or similar.

4 Using the chisel and hammer or the brick-hammer, gently cut a groove around the pipe on the mark; continue cutting and turning until the pipe separates.

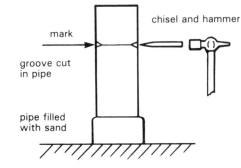

Figure 2.42 *Cutting a pipe*

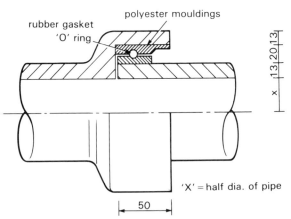

Figure 2.41 *Flexible joint on clay pipe (drawn in half section half elevation)*

Polyvinyl chloride (uPVC) pipes

uPVC pipes are relatively light in weight, which is a great advantage over most of the other materials during the handling, carrying and fixing operations (Figure 2.43). uPVC is

Figure 2.43   *uPVC pipes are easy to carry*

a tough resilient material but careless handling of the pipe and fittings may cause damage. Extra care is required in cold conditions, when the material is less pliable.

Storage   The pipes should be stored on flat, level ground free from large or sharp stones or on 75 mm square timbers at maximum 1.5 m centres. They should be stacked to a maximum height of six layers (Figure 2.44). When the pipes are fitted with couplings or sockets they should be stacked with the sockets protruding at alternate ends.

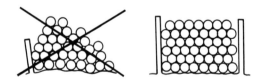

Figure 2.44

The sun has a detrimental effect on some plastics. Therefore when long-term storage in the open is envisaged, screening from the sun is recommended (Figure 2.45). The above recommendation also applies to the solvent weld cement and cleaning fluid. It must be kept in a cool place and out of direct sunlight.

Plastic pipes are fairly flexible when compared with other traditional materials such as cast-iron, clay, etc. This inherent flexibility, combined with flexible jointing

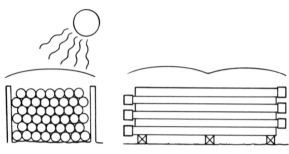

Figure 2.45

methods, provides a system of drainage which will accommodate ground movement to a fairly high degree (Figures 2.46 and 2.47).

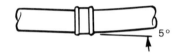

Figure 2.46   *Angular movement 5° per joint*

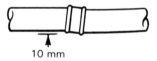

Figure 2.47   *Line displacement 10 mm per joint*

Behaviour under load

If we compare the contrasting manner in which drain-pipes bear their load, we find that rigid pipes primarily carry the imposed load by virtue of the pipe's own built-in strength. With a flexible pipe the imposed load pressure is transmitted through the pipe and is borne mainly by the passive resistance of the side in-fill, between the pipe and trench sides (Figure 2.48). This means that

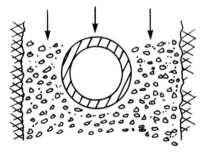

Figure 2.48   *Load on flexible pipe*

uPVC pipes, while they are capable of being deformed without fracture, rely for the retention of their true shape when under load upon the care exercised in the selection and ⌐ ⌐ ⌐⌐⌐ ⌐⌐⌐ in-fill and cover

1 Loose socket couplings, ⌐⌐
2 Socketed pipes, the sockets being integral or solvent welded to the pipe.

In Figure 2.49 the arrow indicates the point to which the pipe must be withdrawn from the socket to allow for the expansion of the material when subjected to heat.

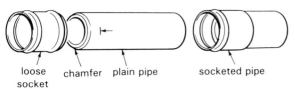

loose socket   chamfer   plain pipe   socketed pipe

Figure 2.49   *uPVC pipe with (a) loose socket and (b) socketed pipe*

Method
Where speed of fitting is a very important factor, then the 'ring seal' or 'push fit' method of jointing must be recommended as this type of joint can be made in seconds. Many of the manufacturers (Marley, Osma, and Terrain, to mention a few) have designed their joints with locked-in rubber sealing rings. This helps to prevent displacement while jointing, or the loss of the rings during transit. The following method should be used:

1 The pipe end must be cut square using a fine-toothed saw or a purpose-made cutter. The pipe should have a continuous line around the whole circumference as a guide or a jig should be used (Figure 2.50).

approximately ⌐⌐ ⌐⌐⌐ (according to the design of the joint) (Figure 2.51). In preparing for the ring seal joint, mark the insertion depth. There is not the same variation in temperature in underground drains as in exposed discharge pipes above ground. Provision for movement at the joint will however help to accommodate any ground movement as well as slight changes in pipe lengths due to expansion. Specially designed tools are manufactured to cut and form the chamfer if required.

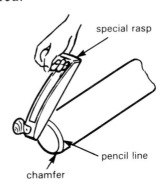

special rasp

pencil line

chamfer

Figure 2.51   *Cutting the chamfer*

3 It is customary to mark two points on the spigot end:

(a) The full depth of the socket,
(b) The insertion depth of the socket.

The difference between these two marks is the amount of expansion that must be allowed for as recommended by the manufacturer (usually 10 mm). Failure to make this provision will be disastrous because the system will fail. When this is completed a smear of lubricant is applied to the chamfered spigot end (Figure 2.52). It is now ready for insertion into the socket. Hand pressure coupled with a slight turning action will slide the spigot into the socket. Care should be taken to ensure that the ring seal is not dislodged from its seating.

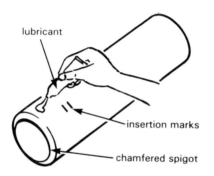

Figure 2.52   *Applying jointing lubricant*

4   The pipe is entered full socket, then withdrawn 10 mm so as to form an expansion gap (this is of paramount importance) (Figure 2.53). With the ring seal method of jointing the system can be tested immediately after assembly. Back-filling and reinstatement can then follow, making for a fast operation.

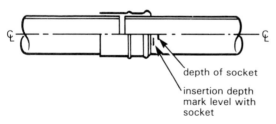

Figure 2.53   *Completed joint*

Examples of ring seal joints are shown in Figures 2.54 and 2.55.

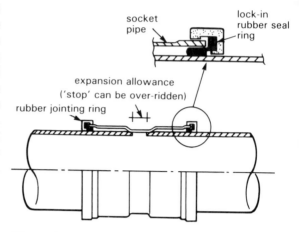

Figure 2.54   *Detail of plastic joint*

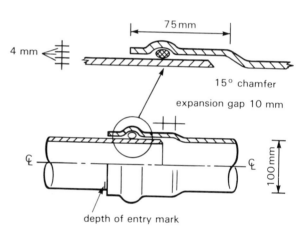

Figure 2.55   *Integral oval ring joint*

Solvent welded

Solvent welding of plastics is the name given to the joining of the plastic pipe involving the use of a liquid-type substance which has the ability to eat into and adhere to the pipes and/or fittings. Once the two parts are mated together they form a permanent union, known as a solvent welded joint. This is because of the action of the glue-like substance. Care must be taken not to use excessive amounts of the solvent cement and to remove all surplus cement from the joint as soon as possible.

Prior to the use of the solvent cement the material to be joined must be cleaned, this

cleaning in this manner.
(spirit) cleaning fluid to the outside of the pipe spigot and the inside of the socket with a clean brush or cloth. The cleaning fluid removes the surface oxide (skin), so exposing the plastic material to the action of the cement.

Solvent cements and cleaning fluids are highly volatile substances and should only be used in well-ventilated locations; the vapours from these fluids should not be inhaled.

To minimise evaporation and waste always replace lids or covers on their containers immediately after use.

Safety in the use of solvent weld cement and cleaning fluid

1   Do *not* use in a confined space.
2   Do *not* inhale the fumes.
3   Do *not* smoke when handling.
4   Do *not* use near naked flame.
5   Avoid direct contact with skin.

Method

1   Cut or rasp the end of the pipe true and square.
2   Mark the depth of entry of the socket on the spigot.
3   Deoxidise the inside of the socket and the outside of the spigot. This is achieved by applying the cleaning fluid to the mating parts, using a clean brush or cloth.
4   Apply the solvent cement with a clean brush to the inside of the socket and the

action if possible and
socket.

Note The operations of applying the cement and assembly of the joint must be performed as quickly as possible; it only takes seconds for the cement to begin to set on the plastic.

6   Do not disturb the joint for a short period of time (approximately 30 seconds).
7   Remove the surplus cement from the pipe and/or socket.

Note Joints may be handled after 5–10 minutes (allow a longer time in cold conditions), after which time air tests can be applied. Full strength of the joint will be attained after approximately 12 hours. Once a solvent welded joint has set it is impossible to undo it without physical damage to the material.

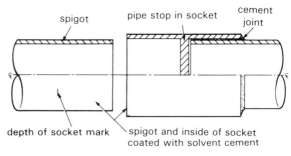

Figure 2.57 *Solvent welded joint (half section half elevation)*

Supporting and protecting drains

Building Regulations state: 'Any drain or private sewer shall be of sufficient strength having regard to the manner in which it is bedded or supported and the maximum loads and forces to which it may be subjected and protected against damage.'

Important points to be observed when laying drains in a trench (see Figure 2.58):

1 Limit length of open trench,
2 Backfill as soon as possible,
3 Width of trench to equal diameter of pipe plus 150 mm on each side,
4 Clay subsoils exposed to sun or rain may shrink or expand, which may lead to damage.

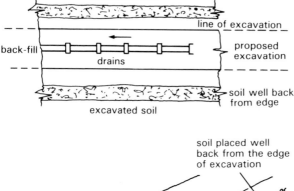

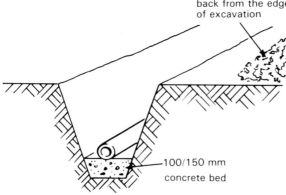

Figure 2.58 *Section through a trench*

The traditional method of bedding and jointing is by rigid jointing of the pipes laid on a bed of concrete. However, it is now quite common practice to lay drain-pipes

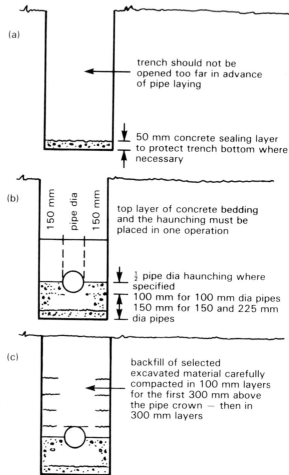

Figure 2.59 *Class 'A' bedding*

with flexible joints on a granular bed. The above methods are classified 'A' and 'B'.

Figures 2.59 and 2.60 show haunching to the drain pipe where class 'A' bedding is being used. This consists of adding more concrete along the side of the pipe and should be laid before the concrete bed has set.

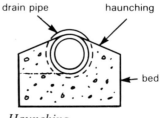

Figure 2.60 *Haunching*

Figure 2.61 shows the method of support and protection when the drain-pipe is subjected to load, e.g. where the pipe is:

1 Laid under buildings,
2 Laid under roads, or
3 Laid above ground.

Figures 2.63–2.65 show details of bedding for various types of drain materials.

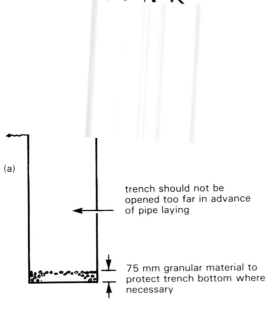

(a)

trench should not be opened too far in advance of pipe laying

75 mm granular material to protect trench bottom where necessary

(b)

150 mm | pipe dia | 150 mm

form holes for pipe sockets to allow pipelines to rest uniformly on the bed

100 mm min granular bed under pipe barrel

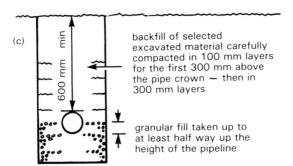

(c)

600 mm min

backfill of selected excavated material carefully compacted in 100 mm layers for the first 300 mm above the pipe crown — then in 300 mm layers

granular fill taken up to at least half way up the height of the pipeline

Figure 2.62 *Class 'B' bedding*

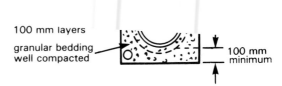

100 mm layers

granular bedding well compacted

100 mm minimum

Figure 2.63 *Class 'B' bedding for clay or cast iron pipes*

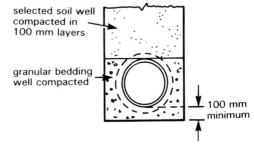

selected soil well compacted in 100 mm layers

granular bedding well compacted

100 mm minimum

Figure 2.64 *Class 'B' bedding for pitch fibre pipes*

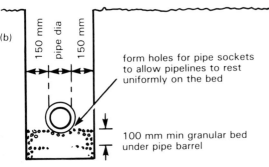

100 mm minimum

Figure 2.65 *Class 'B' bedding for PVC pipes*

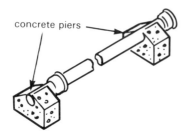

Figure 2.66   *Method of support of brick or concrete piers, used for cast-iron drains*

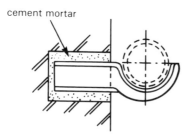

Figure 2.67   *Cantilever bracket built into the wall*

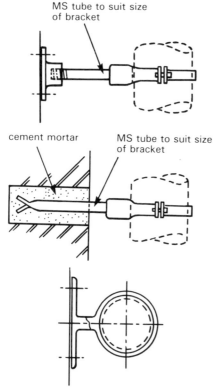

Figure 2.68   *Different kinds of holderbats used in supporting pipelines in various locations*

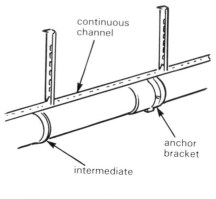

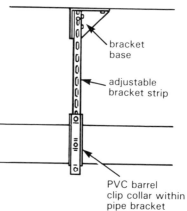

Figure 2.69   *Two methods of suspending PVC drains*

Exposed drainage pipework

Figures 2.66–2.69 show details of various methods of supporting exposed pipework.

Building regulations: Part H, drainage (1985)

This part of the regulations is concerned with the disposal of soil drainage and rainwater from buildings. Drainage systems are basically divided into two sections:

1   Those above ground,
2   Those below ground.

Drains which start below ground and then emerge are still treated as drains below ground.

Figure 2.70 shows a drain or private sewer part below ground, part supported above ground on piers.

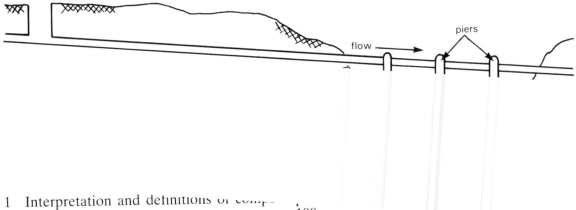

inspection chamber

piers

flow

1 Interpretation and definitions of components,
2 Minimum sizes of pipes,
3 Testing,
4 Installation,
5 Access.

Interpretation

Although there is some vagueness as to the
exact meaning of the word 'drain', the
following may be used as a suitable definition. A 'drain' means a pipe conveying soil,
waste, or rainwater discharges which is:

1 Wholly below ground, or
2 A continuation, in the direction of flow,
  of part of a drainage system that has been
  below ground.

The British Standard code of practice
BS.8301.1985 gives the following definitions:

1 A *drain* conveys sewage or surface water
  from within a single curtilage,
2 A *sewer* conveys from more than one
  curtilage.

Note (1) the term 'drain' is used in the code
for the wider purpose to indicate any pipeline
conveying drainage; (2) the term curtilage is
the area attached to a dwelling.

Minimum sizes of pipes

The internal diameter of any pipe must not
be less than the outlet diameter of any
appliance, pipe, or drain discharging its
contents through it, and in any case must

100 mm.

Testing

Drains must be capable of withstanding a
suitable test for water tightness after all the
work is done, including backfilling (see
Figure 2.71). Backfilling is the term given to
the refilling of the excavation with soil.

  BS 8301 states that testing should be
applied after laying and before backfilling or
placing a concrete surround. A test pressure
of 1.5 m head of water should be applied at
the high end, but not more than 4.0 m at the
low end. The head should hold steady for a
minimum of 30 minutes (see Figure 2.71),
with 2 hours being the usual requirement.

Installation

Drains and private sewers must be of
sufficient strength depending upon the
method of bedding, support, and maximum
loads, and where necessary protected against
damage, as shown in Figure 2.72. Precautions must be taken to prevent damage to
pipe-lines where they pass through or under
walls or under buildings (Figure 2.73).

  If considerable settlement is expected,
precautions are needed where the pipe
emerges from the concrete. A satisfactory
transition from rigid to flexible conditions
can be effected by surrounding the pipe with
at least 150 mm of good quality material, for
example, pea gravel. The material should fill
the trench base and extend about 600 mm
from the concrete face (Figure 2.73). Similar

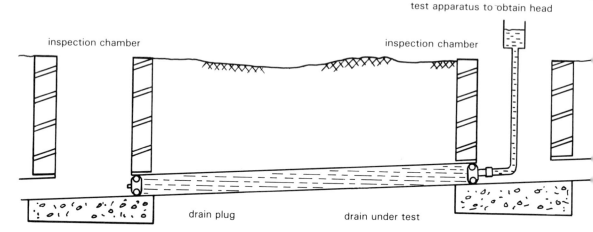

Figure 2.71   *Water test*

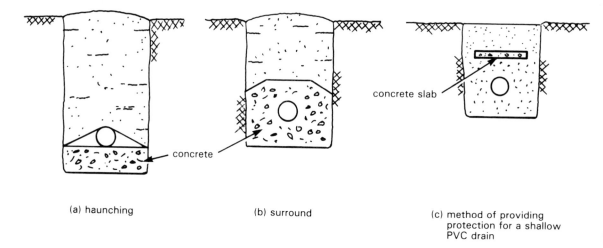

(a) haunching   (b) surround   (c) method of providing
                                              protection for a shallow
                                              PVC drain

Figure 2.72   *Protection of drains laid at different depths*

treatment is appropriate where a flexible pipe is jointed rigidly to a wall, such as the side of a manhole, but where a flexible pipe passes through a wall to which it need not be jointed, as for example, through a substructure, the hole should provide at least 50 mm clearance around the pipe and should be protected by sheeting against the entry of granular surrounding material (Figure 2.73).

Access

The drainage system is provided with access by means of inspection chambers (man-holes), rodding eyes, access pipes, etc. Access is required to all parts of the system for inspection, testing, and maintenance (see for example Figure 2.74). The regulations require that no part of the system shall be more than 45 m from a point of access and that a branch shall be not more than 12 m from a chamber.

Drainage fittings

This section is to enable the student to recognise and identify drainage fittings,

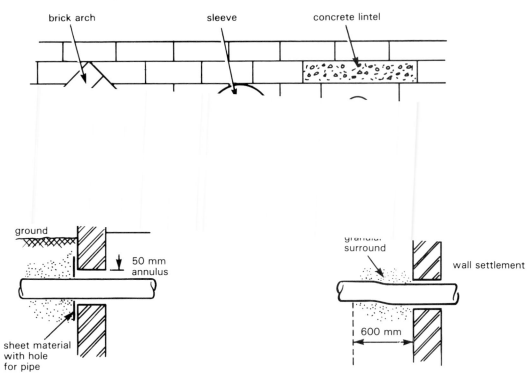

Figure 2.73 *Precautions taken where a pipe passes through a wall*

including types of material and relevant British Standard numbers for them.

Bends

At every change of direction, purpose-made bends must be fitted. The following are only a few of the many types and sizes that are manufactured. (For the full range of fittings available see the manufacturers' catalogues.) Bends are known according to the number of degrees contained in the angle of the bend, e.g.

$$360° \text{ in a circle.}$$
$$\text{a } \tfrac{1}{8} \text{ bend would be}$$
$$360° \div 8 = 45° \text{ (external angle)}$$

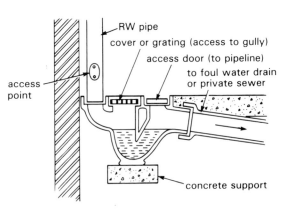

Figure 2.74 *Back-inlet trapped gully*

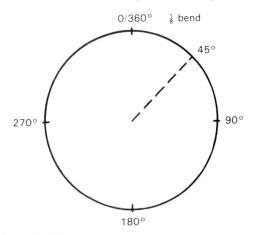

Figure 2.75

Some manufacturers make reference to the internal angle of the bends, i.e. the $\frac{1}{8}$ bend = 135°.

Clay
Figure 2.76 shows a 90° bend also known as a quarter bend. A bend with an angle of 45° is known as an eighth bend. Similarly, the $22\frac{1}{2}°$ bend in Figure 2.77 is a sixteenth (sixteen such bends would make a complete circle).

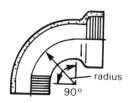

Figure 2.76   *90° short radius bend*

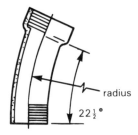

Figure 2.77   *$22\frac{1}{2}°$ bend or sixteenth*

The bend shown in Figure 2.78 incorporates a facility which allows access for rodding.

Figure 2.78   *Access bend*

Figure 2.79 shows the fitting to be placed at the base of a vertical discharge pipe. It is called a 'rest bend' because of the shape of the base or heel, which gives greater support and stability. It is also known as a duckfoot bend.

Figure 2.79   *Rest bend*

Channel bends (Figure 2.80) are manufactured either left hand or right hand. They are also made in half and/or three-quarter sections.

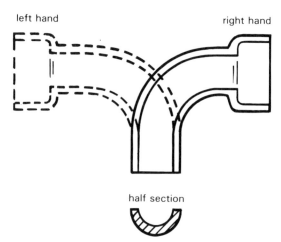

Figure 2.80   *Channel bends*

Concrete
Bends manufactured in concrete are similar to those in clay.

Cast iron
Bends with a radius of less than 250 mm are known as 'short radius bends'; above 250 mm radius they are classified as 'long radius bends'. Figure 2.81 depicts a typical cast iron bend.

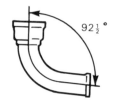

Figure 2.81   *Cast-iron bend*

Knuckle bends are available in various angles. Due to the sudden change in direction their use is limited and is not recommended.

Polyvinyl chloride
Examples of uPVC fittings are shown in Figures 2.85–2.87. Short radius bends are manufactured with or without sockets; channel bends are available in various angles, ... right hand.

Figure 2.82 *Long arm bend*

Pitch fibre
Angled couplings (Figure 2.83) are used where only a slight deflection is required.

Long radius bends (Figure 2.84) are manufactured in various angles and radii. Short radius or knuckle bends are also available.
Note A range of fittings suitable for pitch fibre pipes is manufactured in polypropylene.

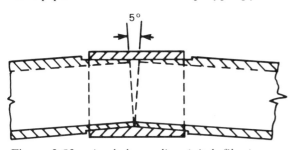

Figure 2.83 *Angled coupling (pitch fibre)*

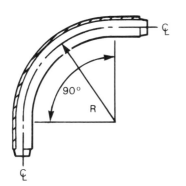

Figure 2.84 *Typical long radius pitch fibre bend*

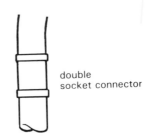

double
socket connector

Figure 2.85 *Long radius bend with two spigot ends jointed to pipe by means of sockets*

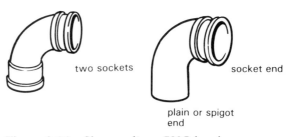

two sockets

socket end

plain or spigot
end

Figure 2.86 *Short radius uPVC bends*

Figure 2.87 *A channel bend*

Gullies
A gully is a drainage fitting fitted at the head of a branch drain to receive the discharges of waste and/or rainwater. In most cases the gully has incorporated in its manufacture a trap to form a water seal as a barrier to the

passage of foul gases and vermin from the drain.

Clay
Figure 2.88 shows the variations in the design of yard gullies. These are manufactured with square or rounded inlets and with 'P', 'Q' or 'S' trap outlets.

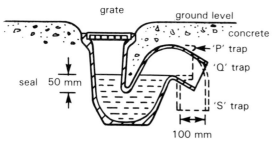

Figure 2.88   *Yard gully*

Back-inlet gullies (Figure 2.89) are manufactured as detailed in Figure 2.88 but with the addition of either a vertical or horizontal inlet to receive rainwater or waste discharges. (Also available with side inlet connections.)

Garage gullies (Figure 2.90) contain a large amount of water to allow any petrol to

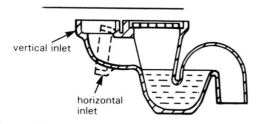

Figure 2.89   *Back-inlet gully*

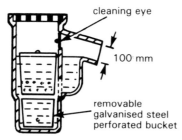

Figure 2.90   *Typical garage gully*

be retained and the fumes to evaporate. They also contain a removable silt bucket manufactured from galvanised steel. This will prevent mud etc. from gaining access to the drainage system.

A mud gully (Figure 2.91) is similar to the garage gully, the difference being that it is much smaller, retains less water and the receptacle is more like a tray than a bucket. The function of this fitting is to receive the washings from paved areas. The tray/bucket allows the easy removal of soil or mud from the gully. This should be carried out periodically.

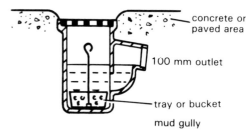

Figure 2.91   *Mud gully*

The rainwater shoe fitting shown in Figure 2.92 (not to be confused with the shoe fixed at the base of a rainwater stack) is the type fitted to receive surface water from a paved area. Others are available with vertical or horizontal socket to receive a rainwater discharge pipe.

Figure 2.92   *Rainwater shoe*

Note   The rainwater shoe illustrated has no water seal and must therefore not be connected to a foul water drain unless protected by a trap.

A trapless gully (Figure 2.93) can only be used to receive surface water from a paved area where the drain pipe is trapped before being connected to the foul drain.

Figure 2.94   *Typical cast-iron gully*

The function of the fitting shown in Figure 2.95 is to prevent flood water escaping from a gully fitted to a line of drains liable to surcharge during peak periods or storms. This is achieved by means of a seamless float inside the gully which is lifted on to a rubber seating by the flood water. When conditions return to normal and the back pressure is released the float drops, allowing water to pass through the gully again.

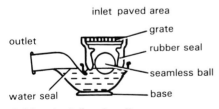

inlet paved area

outlet

grate

rubber seal

seamless ball

water seal

base

Figure 2.95   *Anti-flood gully*

Junctions

Where it is necessary to connect a branch drain into a main drain, this must be performed by a purpose-made junction (branch piece), entry always being made in the direction of the flow.

Branch entry may be either perpendicular

(Figure 2.96) or at an oblique angle (Figure 2.97). Double square and double oblique junctions are also available.

Figure 2.97   *Oblique junction (clay)*

Cast iron

Figure 2.98 shows a single oblique cast-iron junction. Similar junctions are available with a branch socket large enough to receive a clay pipe.

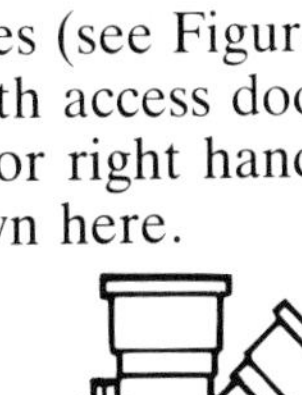

Figure 2.98   *Single oblique junction (cast-iron)*

Access branches (see Figure 2.99) are also manufactured with access doors on the side, either left hand or right hand, as well as on the back as shown here.

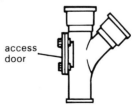

access door

Figure 2.99   *Access branch*

Pitch fibre

Typical pitch fibre junctions are shown in Figures 2.100 and 2.101.

Figure 2.100   *Pitch fibre junction with spigot tapered ends*

Figure 2.101   *Pitch fibre double junction with socket ends*

Intercepting traps

An intercepting trap is a fitting installed in the drainage system at the point where the system leaves the property before finally being connected to the authority's sewer (see Figure 2.102).

Note some local authorities have now banned the use of intercepting traps on new installations, the reasons being:

1   Less risk of stoppages,
2   Each house drainage system becomes a vent for the authority's sewer.

The purposes of fitting intercepting traps are:

1   To disconnect the house drain from the main sewer,
2   To afford access by means of the rodding eye to the section of drain to the sewer connection,
3   To prevent foul gases (by means of the water seal) from passing up the house drain,
4   To prevent vermin entering the house drain from the sewer.

The main disadvantage is that the trap tends to retard the flow with the possibility of stoppages.

Intercepting traps are manufactured in each of the materials used in drainage work. Figures 2.103 and 2.104 illustrate two of the most commonly used traps.

In Figure 2.103, the vertical drop (1) is known as the cascade; its function is to increase the flow of the water to assist in ensuring the trap is kept clear. (2) is the depth of water seal, the function of which is to act as a barrier between the house drain and the authority's sewer. The stopper in the

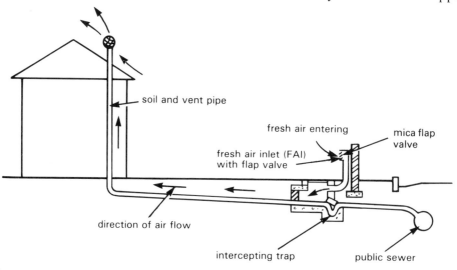

Figure 2.102

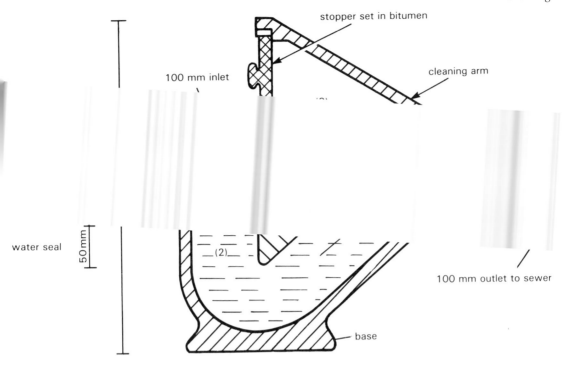

Figure 2.103 *Typical clayware intercepting trap with approximate sizes and angles*

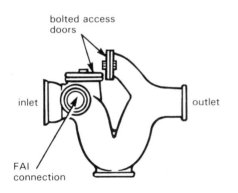

Figure 2.104 *Typical cast-iron intercepting trap*

rodding arm (3) is usually set and held in place by a bitumen seal. Some stoppers are held in place by a locking device.

Figure 2.104 shows an elevation of a cast iron intercepting trap with bolted on access doors and a connection point for a fresh-air inlet. In cast iron drainage systems the fresh-air connection must be made direct to the pipe and not to the inspection chamber.

Sewer connection

When a new sewer is laid, purpose-made junctions are fitted at the appropriate places. If additional connections are required in an existing system this is achieved by means of a fitting known as a saddle (see Figure 2.105).

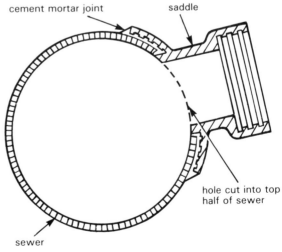

Figure 2.105 *Saddle connection to sewer*

Testing of drains

The testing of drains comes under three headings:

1 Alignment,
2 Soundness,
3 Tracing.

Alignment

For the system to operate satisfactorily the pipes should be laid in straight lines, at the correct gradient and without any obstruction inside the bore of the pipe, i.e. jointing materials. The alignment test is carried out in one of two ways.

Mirror test

This is carried out using mirrors and a light which is diverted by the angled mirrors. Figure 2.106 illustrates the setting up of this test which will indicate to the operator any obstruction inside the pipe or any deviation in the alignment. A true circle of light will be visible if the system is correctly laid and jointed.

Ball test

This consists of passing a purpose-made steel ball through the drain. The ball, which is just slightly under-size of the pipe, will roll along the drain unaided, provided that the alignment and gradient are correct and that there are no obstructions inside the pipe.

Soundness

Soundness tests on drainage installations must be performed on both existing and also new systems. Most local authorities require that new drains must be subjected to an hydraulic test of 1.5 m head. In the case of some installations the inspection chambers may also be filled with water to test for their soundness. New systems are tested twice, once on completion of laying but before backfilling, and again upon the final completion after the trenches have been consolidated and paths laid.

For old systems a less stringent test than that of water would be used, the most common one being the *smoke test*.

There are four methods of testing of drainage systems, each with its own particular advantage. Each test will be described and illustrated and their merits and demerits noted. The tests for soundness are:

1 Hydraulic (water),
2 Smoke,
3 Pneumatic (air),
4 Chemical (smell).

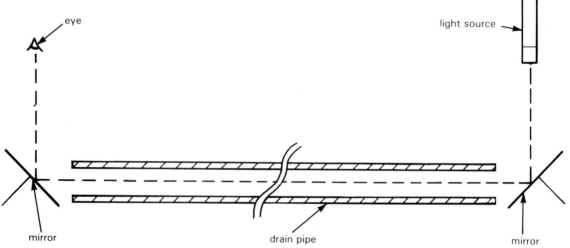

Figure 2.106   *Mirror test*

Hydraulic test

Water testing of drains requires that a 1.5 m head of water is applied to the system from the highest point of the section under test. .... out by plugging off the

by passing a small rubber hose through the trap and into the crown of the gully as shown in Figure 2.110.

When the system is fully charged with water it should be allowed to stand for a period of time as laid down by the local authority. Usually 2 hours (as per BS 8301) is satisfactory. If the water level in the first instance should fall, the head of water should be topped up and the test applied again because the loss of water could be due to the porosity of the joints, i.e. yarn, sand and cement, and/or the pipe. When the system is considered sound, remove the cap (only) from the expanding stopper (plug) at the lowest point of the drain being tested. This will release the considerable head of water pressure before the plugs are removed.

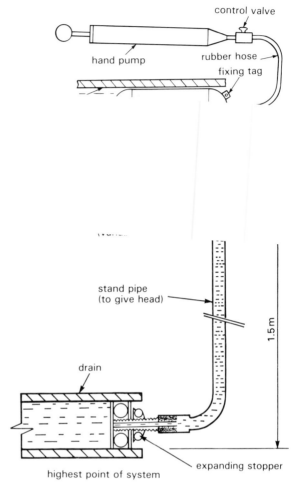

Figure 2.109 *Applying water test*

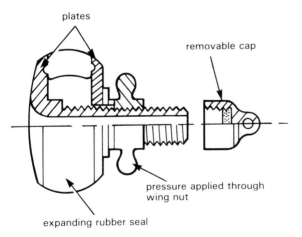

Figure 2.107 *Expanding stopper (plug)*

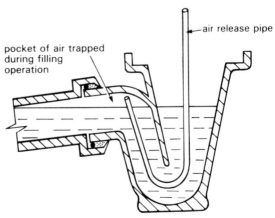

Figure 2.110 *Removing air from the system*

Note Do not leave the drains standing full of water for long periods in freezing conditions.

Smoke test

The smoke test is used both for testing the soundness of the system and for tracing a suspected leak. It can be used equally well for the testing of above ground soil, waste and vent pipes.

All water seals must be charged with water and all branch drains and vents must be sealed except one. Smoke is then pumped into the system through a test plug which is fitted in the lowest point of the drain or stack by means of a smoke generating machine as illustrated in Figure 2.111. The highest vent is left open until smoke begins to escape. At this point the vent is then sealed and pumping continues until sufficient pressure is built up inside the smoke machine to raise the dome approximately 50 mm. Pumping now ceases and the system remains under test for 5 minutes. If the dome remains in the elevated position the system is sound. Should the dome fall or fail to rise a leak is indicated. Pumping is continued while the system is checked for smoke leakage.

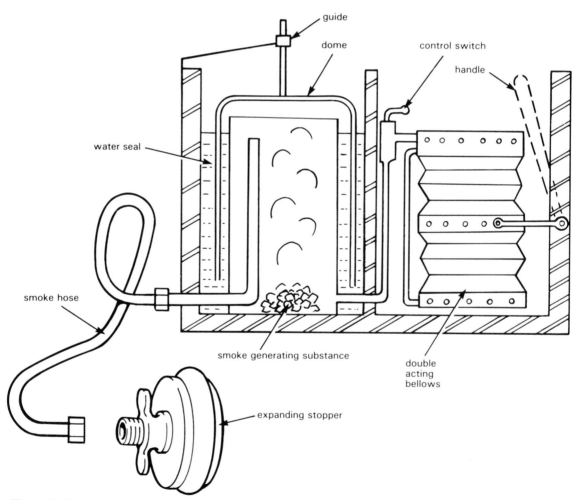

Figure 2.111 *Smoke generating machine*

Note The smoke test is actually an air test using smoke as a leak tracing element. This trace test should not be used on plastic systems, because of the detrimental action ~~the smoke and some types of plastic.~~

previously described. The main problem with the air test is that it is not easy to find any subsequent leak. The method used is to apply soap solution to each joint until the offending leak is located. Alternatively, should there be a leak indicated by the falling dome, smoke is then pumped into the system to find the leak visibly. As already said, the pneumatic test is actually a variation of the smoke test and should not be confused with the proper air test which consists of an air pump and a manometer and is applied as follows.

To apply the air test all open ends must be sealed and all water seals charged. A three-way test piece with valves is connected to a manometer ('U'-gauge), a hand pump and a hose as shown in Figure 2.112. The

hose is passed through the seal of the trap (Figure 2.113) with valves A and C open and valve B closed. Air is pumped into the system and the air pressure is checked periodically by opening valve B. When the test pressure is ~~reached close valve A and open valve B.~~

underground drainage systems, it is generally used for above-ground drainage work, i.e. sanitation systems. The pressure normally applied is limited by the depth of water seal in the traps and the fittings.

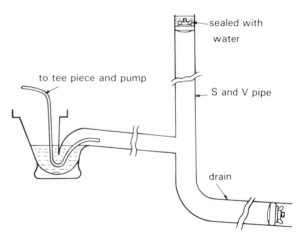

Figure 2.113 *Conducting an air test*

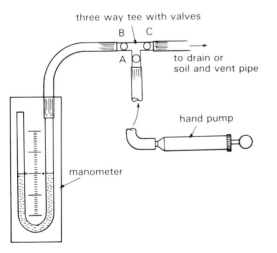

Figure 2.112 *Air test apparatus*

Chemical test (smell test)
The apparatus for the chemical test consists of a special grenade container filled with a pungent-smelling substance, i.e. calcium phosphide or similar. The container is manufactured in two halves, connected by a spring which tends to keep the container open. In use the container is bound with a long cord, one end of which is held firmly in

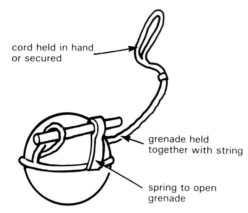

cord held in hand
or secured

grenade held
together with string

spring to open
grenade

Figure 2.114   *Chemical grenade*

the hand or, better still, attached to a fixed object. The container is then flushed down the drain through the water closet or a gully. As the container rolls down the pipe the cord unwinds, the grenade opens and the chemical is released into the drain. Detection is by smell only and no pressure is generated in the system. This method of testing is recommended for old systems where there are no inspection chambers on the system.

Table 2.3   *The comparative advantages and disadvantages of the four methods of testing for soundness*

Test	Advantages	Disadvantages
Hydraulic (water)	This test is a positive indication of soundness. The drain is subjected to a pressure at least equal to that caused by a stoppage. It is easily applied, leaks (if any) are visible and easily traced.	The pressure is uneven, i.e. a greater pressure is exerted at the lower end of the drain than at the top end. Water supply may not be readily available or disposed of after the test.
Pneumatic (air)	The pressure applied is of equal intensity on all parts of the system. This ensures a very severe test to all parts of the system. The test is easily applied.	If leakage occurs it is difficult to locate and may call for either a smoke or water test to be applied.
Smoke	This test possesses all the advantages of the previous tests with the addition that the blockage of a pipe can be easily recognised by the fact that smoke did not emit from that pipe. Easily applied. Leaks readily visible.	Special care required to prevent smoke escaping from the machine and entering the ducting, so nullifying the test. Smoke may cause damage to plastics.
Chemical	Used on systems where there are no inspection chambers.	Test is dependent on the user's sense of smell. No pressure exerted on system. Care must be taken to prevent any spillage.

Self-assessment questions

1 The minimum permitted size of an underground soil drain is:
   (a) 75 mm

   (b) 51 mm
   (c) 38 mm
   (d) 50 mm

3 Which one of the following correctly states the guiding principles to the siting of inspection chambers?
   (a) at changes of gradient and of ventilation
   (b) at all sewer junctions and rodding eyes
   (c) at private sewer connections and at 300 m intervals
   (d) at changes of direction and gradient

4 A combined drainage system is one which conveys the:
   (a) surface water from a number of dwellings
   (b) foul water and surface water in one drain
   (c) foul water in one drain and surface water in another
   (d) foul water from a number of buildings

5 A large radius bend at the base of a single-stack soil pipe helps to eliminate:
   (a) self siphonage
   (b) back pressure
   (c) induced siphonage
   (d) back siphonage

6 One method of eliminating negative pressure in long drain runs is by using a:
   (a) yard gully

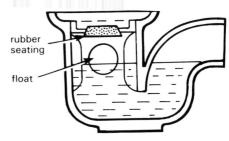

Figure 2.115

8 The recommended maximum distance between manholes on a straight line of drains is:
   (a) 50 m
   (b) 60 m
   (c) 90 m
   (d) 120 m

9 Which group contains only tests that would ascertain the water tightness of a drain:
   (a) ball test, smoke test
   (b) water test, obstruction test
   (c) hydraulic test, air test
   (d) reflection test, air test

10 Flexible joints are used on clay pipes to allow:
   (a) longer lengths of pipe to be used
   (b) slight movement without joint failure
   (c) greater pressures to be applied
   (d) interchangeability with cast-iron drains

3 Welding

After reading this chapter you should be able to:

1 Understand the safety requirements in the setting up and use of high pressure welding equipment.

2 Have knowledge of the safety measures when performing welding operations.

3 Have knowledge of the working principles of regulators and blowpipes, pressure adjustments and control.

4 Recognise and name component parts of high pressure welding equipment.

5 Have knowledge of the jointing processes by:
   (a) Soft soldering,
   (b) Hard soldering,
   (c) Fusion welding.

6 Demonstrate knowledge of the preparation and jointing of lead sheet and lead pipe.

7 Demonstrate knowledge of the preparation and jointing of copper tube by the bronze welding and brazing (silver soldering) techniques.

8 Have knowledge of and recognize the different types of welding flames and their uses.

9 Have knowledge of different types of welding fluxes, their use and removal.

Although the process of welding is a skill in its own right, and to become a qualified and certificated welder requires much skill and many hours of study and practice, the modern plumber must learn the basic requirements of this craft. Before welding was developed metals were joined together by riveting or by a blacksmith heating the metal to a very high temperature (but not to its melting point) then hammering or pressing it into unity. Today three methods of welding are in use in the plumbing craft:

1 Brazing,
2 Bronze welding,
3 Fusion welding.

All of them will be described in some detail in this chapter, but only enough to cover the basic requirements of the craft plumber. As already stated the skill of the welder is such that we do not intend to cover every aspect of welding here.

Safety is of paramount importance when setting up the welding equipment and carrying out the process of welding. Since high pressure welding equipment together with the combination of oxygen and acetylene are in the most common use in both site and college, this is the method every plumber must be conversant with.

Equipment

The plumber must first be able to recognise all the components of high pressure gas welding equipment as detailed below and shown in Figures 3.1 and 3.2:

4 Welding blowpipes – size and type depends on the size and type of welding operation.

5 Set of spanners:
   (a) Regulator spanner,
   (b) Outlet spanner

(b) Acetylene.

and neat,

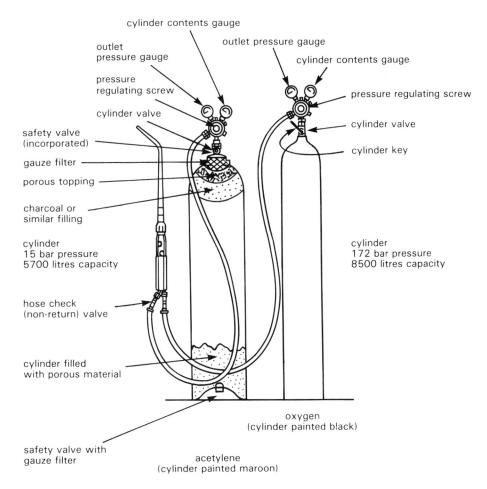

Figure 3.1 *High pressure welding equipment*

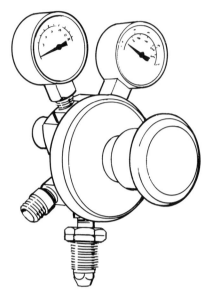

Figure 3.2   *Typical two-stage regulator*

    (b)   Aprons,
    (c)   Trousers and jackets,
    (d)   Skull cap.
 9   Wire brush.
10   Cylinder support.

In addition to the above list there are other items that are used in special welding situations and these will be described at the appropriate place. There are also numerous tools, some of a specialist nature, and these will also be described.

The craftsperson must always bear in mind that he/she is handling potentially dangerous equipment and treat it with great care and respect. Many accidents happen when the operator becomes complacent and thereby treats the equipment with contempt.

The setting up procedures are shown in Table 3.1 (opposite).

Regulators

The regulator is a very delicate and important piece of welding equipment and great care must be taken when handling and fitting gas regulators to the cylinders or gas lines.

The function of the regulator is to reduce the high pressure of the cylinder content to a working pressure at the blowpipe. By means of the regulator the pressure is controlled to give a steady flow of gas with no fluctuation of the flame, even if the gauge does not register correctly.

There are two types of regulators:

1   Single stage,
2   Two stage.

Single-stage regulators
Figure 3.3 shows a typical single stage regulator. This type of regulator is usually fitted to a line fed from a manifold which is already reduced in pressure, but it could of course be fitted directly to the cylinder. The gas from the line or cylinder enters through the inlet and the pressure is registered on one of the gauges. The working pressure is obtained by adjusting the control. This is screwed in to give a pressure on the diaphragm, which in turn opens the valve and allows gas to pass through the outlet to the blowpipe. A second gauge registers the working pressure. When the pressure from the cylinder overcomes the spring valve pressure the valve closes and shuts off the

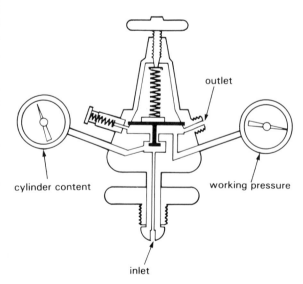

Figure 3.3   *Single-stage regulator*

Table 3.1 *Setting up procedures*

Procedure	Important points to note
Secure oxygen and acetylene cylinders in an upright position.	Fasten to a trolley or cylinder stand or similar place.
~~way round, no hose shown~~ .... ~~p p~~ gas will flow otherwise.	.... equipment is coloured *maroon* with left-hand threads.
Check that the regulator control is in the position that ensures it will not pass gas (the control will be rotated in an anti-clockwise direction). Slowly open the cylinder valve until gas is registered on the contents gauge. Turn the regulator control in a clockwise direction until a small amount of pressure shows on the line gauge. This will blow through the hose to ensure cleanliness. Turn the control anti-clockwise to stop the supply of gas. *Note* It should not be necessary to close the cylinder valve at this point.	1 Cylinder valves to be opened slowly and carefully otherwise damage to gauges will result. 2 Do not stand in front of gauges; the faces may blow out. 3 Ensure the gases released into the atmosphere will not prove a *hazard*, i.e. oxygen supports combustion; acetylene is a flammable gas.
Now fit the welding blowpipe to the other ends of the hoses taking care as before and observing the same salient points.	
Ensure acetylene blowpipe control valve is open, adjust regulator to give a pressure reading of 0.7 bar. Close valve, repeat for oxygen, check thoroughly using soap solution that the equipment is gas tight.	Soap bubbles will indicate leaks. Do not use excessive force should a leak be indicated.

supply of gas, and when the gas pressure under the diaphragm is reduced the valve opens to allow more gas to enter from the line or cylinder. When both forces are balanced a constant flow of gas will result.

Two-stage regulators
As Figure 3.4 shows, the working of the two stage regulator is very similar to that of the single stage type. The gas from the cylinder enters through the inlet and the pressure is measured on the first dial. It then passes through the first stage valve and diaphragm which is preset at approximately 20 bar

(atmospheres). The gas then passes through the second stage valve, the pressure being obtained and controlled by the second diaphragm and the adjustment control being set at the required working pressure.

The two stage regulator gives a smoother and more constant flow of gas to the blowpipe and is therefore the one that is recommended.

Welding blowpipes
There are basically two types of blowpipes, high pressure and low pressure, but they are made in a variety of sizes and designs

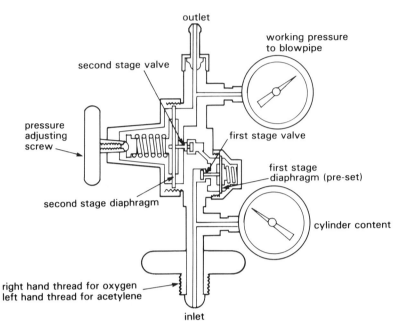

Figure 3.4   *Two-stage regulator*

depending upon the size and type of welding to be performed and also the manufacturer. We will be dealing with the high pressure type only in this book as this is the one in common use.

High pressure blowpipes
This type of blowpipe is designed for use with oxygen and dissolved acetylene from cylinders (Figures 3.5 and 3.6). The blowpipe is designed to use equal volumes of the gases. The gases enter the mixing chamber where they are thoroughly mixed before issuing from the nozzle (see Figure 3.7). The blowpipe is fitted with control valves for each of the gases and interchangeable nozzles of varying sizes for welding different thicknesses of metal.

Note   High pressure equipment cannot be used on a *low pressure system.*

Hoses
These are rubber-based with canvas reinforcement and are complete with brass or alloy connections for fixing to the regulators and blowpipes. The connectors are held in

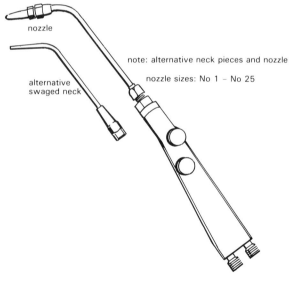

Figure 3.5   *Saffire (BOC) lightweight welding blowpipe*

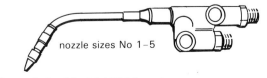

Figure 3.6   *Model 'O' blowpipe*

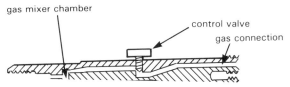

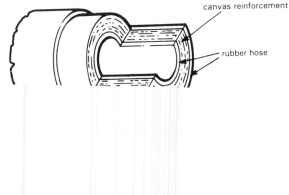

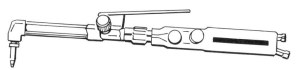

Figure 3.7 *Section through a high pressure blowpipe*

place by O-clips. The ends of the hoses connected to the blowpipes have 'hose check valves' fitted to them, which act as non-return valves in the case of a backfire taking place in the blowpipe. They are also known as 'hose protection valves'. Oxygen hose is *blue* in colour with right-hand connectors and acetylene hose is *maroon* in colour with left-hand connectors.

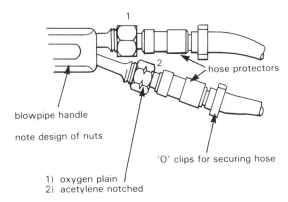

Figure 3.8 *Hose connection to blowpipe*

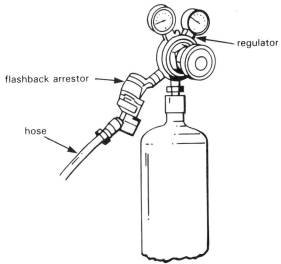

Figure 3.9 *A typical welding blowpipe with cutting attachment*

bursting pressure of four times working pressure. The colour code is *maroon* for acetylene, *blue* for oxygen and *black* for non-combustible gases.

Note Oxygen cylinders and **old** equipment are coloured black.

Safety

Flashback arrestor
The flashback arrestor can be fitted to the cylinder regulator (see Figure 3.11). It incorporates the following features:

1 Flame trap – a sintered stainless steel filter quenches the flame.

Figure 3.11 *Cylinder protection*

2 Non-return valve – a diaphragm is actuated under reverse pressure.
3 Safety valve – excessive pressures vented to atmosphere.
4 Flow cut-off valve – cuts off incoming gas supply.
5 Warning re-set lever – lever 'jumps out' indicating the fact that it has been triggered. Re-set after checking cause.

Backfires and flashbacks
Both these troubles are in many ways similar in their cause and also in the remedial methods required to correct them. They are caused by pre-ignition of the gases:

1 *Backfire*: the retrogression of the flame into the blowpipe neck or body with rapid extinction.
2 *Sustained backfire*: the gases ignite right back in the blowpipe and a loud squealing noise is emitted. The blowpipe itself will become red hot and if not turned off immediately will melt.
3 *Flashback*: the retrogression of the flame beyond the blowpipe body into the hose with the possibility of a subsequent explosion.

There are several ways in which these faults occur, mainly:

1 The nozzle overheating causes pre-ignition.
2 Welding in confined spaces (especially 'T' fillets).
3 Slag build-up on the end of the nozzle.
4 Nozzle too close to the weld.
5 Nozzle not correctly fitting into blowpipe.
6 Incorrectly set pressures.

Should either 'backfires' or 'flashbacks' occur:

1 Turn off both blowpipe valves immediately (oxygen first).
2 Check for causes 1–6 above and remedy.
3 Relight in accordance with correct procedure.

Note If the nozzle has become overheated turn on oxygen valve *only*, plunge the nozzle and blowpipe head into a bucket of cold water. The oxygen prevents water entering the blowpipe.

Nozzles
Any skilled craftsperson has a natural pride in their work and knows that to achieve a good welding technique only good equipment should be used. The welding process depends a great deal for its efficiency and accuracy on the nozzle selected.

Nozzles should be carefully chosen for each particular job. Their design and manufacture are the result of years of practical experience and research.

Great care should be taken to ensure the nozzle does not become damaged; being made of copper and/or brass or sometimes copper alloys, this is easily done. Therefore, to avoid damage, the nozzle must not be handled roughly, dropped on the floor, or used to remove slag etc. from welding jobs.

Should the nozzle become partially blocked this must be removed using only the proper nozzle cleaners manufactured for this job. Should the nozzle end become burred it should be cleaned and filed to return it to the proper shape and size. An imperfect nozzle will give a split or crooked flame, or an incorrectly burning flame, all of which will affect the welding process.

Figure 3.12   *Faulty flames caused by misuse or dirty nozzle*

Saffire welding blowpipe
This type of welding blowpipe can be used for fusion welding of steel up to 8 mm in thickness and also for bronze welding and brazing of steel, copper and brass. A number of interchangeable nozzles enable a large

Table 3.2 *Steel welding chart*

Material thickness (mm)	Nozzle size	Gas consumption (litres/hour)	Pressure (bars)
			0.14

range of welding to be performed covering most of the plumber's work.

Both the nozzles illustrated (Figures 3.13 and 3.14) are equally satisfactory, each

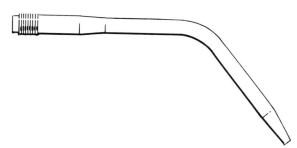

Figure 3.13 *Saffire swaged nozzle*

Figure 3.14 *An alternative nozzle (this type requires a shank piece)*

having minor characteristics of their own. The correct size of nozzle and gas pressures are shown in Table 3.2. It must be understood that these figures are only a general guide. The size of nozzle will vary according to many factors, the main ones being:

1 Skill of operator.
2 Type of material.
3 Mass of material.
4 Type of weld.
5 Position of job.
6 Welding technique.

When welding copper, particularly where the bulk is large, it may be necessary to use a nozzle one size larger than shown for steel. This is due to the material being a very good conductor of heat.

Table 3.3 *Flame temperatures*

Gas	Temperature (°C)
Oxy-acetylene	3200
Oxy-propane	2500
Oxy-hydrogen	2370
Oxy-coal gas	2200
Air-acetylene	2458
Air-coal gas	1871
Air-propane	1750

Model 'O' lead welding blowpipe
Lead welding is performed using a model 'O' blowpipe with interchanging nozzles depending upon the thickness of lead and the type of job, i.e. sheet or pipe, inside a building or outdoors (see Figures 3.6 and 3.15).

Figure 3.15 *Lead welding nozzle*

Gas welding

Gases

The atmosphere is a mixture of many gases. The principal ones are shown in Table 3.4.

Table 3.4   *Atmospheric gases*

Gas	Quantity (%)
Nitrogen	78.0
Oxygen	21.0
Argon	0.9
Carbon dioxide	0.03
Neon Helium Xenon Other gases	0.07

Production of gases for welding

Oxygen

Oxygen for commercial use is obtained from the atmosphere by a process known as liquefaction or distillation. The atmospheric air is compressed to a very high pressure and subjected to intense cold. The air first liquefies (approximately $-180\,°C$); after further cooling (approximately $-196\,°C$) all the other gases are removed leaving pure oxygen. The liquid oxygen is then allowed to evaporate into a gas when it is compressed into steel cylinders for storage, transportation and general commercial use. Pure oxygen must never be inhaled from these cylinders, nor must it be used instead of compressed air. The cylinders are painted black and have right-hand threads.

Acetylene

Acetylene for commercial use is manufactured by the action of *water* (H_2O) on *calcium carbide* (CaC_2).

Calcium carbide (CaC_2) is a chemical compound formed by fusing together lime and coke in an oven subjected to intense heat. This causes the calcium of the lime to combine with the carbon of the coke.

Calcium oxide and carbon
    = calcium carbide and carbon monoxide.

When water is brought into contact with the carbide immediate reaction takes place and acetylene gas (C_2H_2) is given off.

Calcium carbide and water
    = acetylene and calcium oxide

The acetylene gas produced is then filtered, purified and then compressed into steel cylinders for storage, transportation and commercial use. It is very important that the acetylene gas used for welding is free from impurities that may prove detrimental to the weld.

Possible impurities
Ammonia
Sulphur
Sulphuretted hydrogen
Phosphorus
Water

The purifying agents must not be corrosive, explosive, flammable or destructive to the acetylene gas. The cylinders are painted maroon and have left-hand threads.

Properties of welding gases

Oxygen

Oxygen is a colourless gas without taste or smell and is *non-combustible*. Although a non-combustible gas it readily supports *combustion* and it is this fact that makes it so important to the welding process; whichever combustible gas is used the addition of oxygen brings about additional heat and brilliance. The property of oxygen as a supporter of combustion can be seen when a glowing ember of wood is subjected to a stream of pure oxygen. The ember immediately bursts into flame. Without oxygen being present nothing would burn.

Acetylene

Acetylene is a colourless flammable hydro-carbon gas (C$_2$H$_2$) that has a disagreeable odour. It is lighter than air and has a specific

pressure or temperature it becomes unstable.

Storing gases

Oxygen

The oxygen is supplied in solid drawn steel cylinders at a pressure of 172 bar. The usual cylinder has a capacity of 8500 litres. The oxygen cylinders are painted black and are fitted with a valve with right-hand threads. The cylinders are usually examined at each filling and pressure tested periodically (every

4 years). Where large quantities are required to supply several benches it is necessary to couple a number of cylinders together in the form of a manifold. For the large industrial users oxygen is also supplied in liquid form

threads. They are subjected to periodical inspection and testing.

Acetylene cylinders are fitted with two safety devices, one in the domed base and the other in the outlet valve.

Because acetylene gas is very unstable when subjected to increased temperature or pressure, special arrangements are necessary to store the gas at the stated pressure. The cylinders are filled with a spongy mass of charcoal, asbestos, kapok or similar material

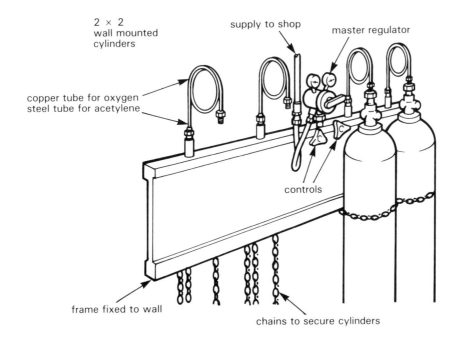

Figure 3.16   *Typical manifold system*

capable of absorbing a liquid (acetone). Acetone itself has the ability to dissolve 25 times its own volume of acetylene. It will absorb an additional 25 volumes for every bar rise in pressure. Acetone expands as the acetylene is dissolved and is compressed into the cellular structure of the filling material. Conversely as the gas is used and the pressure reduced, the dissolved acetylene is released. Because of the liquid acetone, acetylene cylinders must be supported in a vertical position to prevent the liquid being drawn into the blowpipe. Acetylene gas must not be drawn off at the rate of more than one-fifth cylinder capacity per hour for the same reason.

Safety

Welding and cutting

1 Use protective clothing. Wear eye shield, goggles and gloves.
2 Make sure the cylinders are clear of falling sparks.
3 Have fire extinguisher nearby.
4 Use surrounding screens if other workers are near.
5 Electric equipment – see that the work is properly earthed.

Gas cylinders

1 Handle all cylinders carefully – never violently.
2 Store oxygen and acetylene separately in a cool place.
3 Acetylene cylinders must be stored and used vertically.
4 Do not stack oxygen cylinders more than four high, check for stability.
5 Keep grit, oil and dirt out of valves, otherwise it is impossible to prevent equipment leaking at the joints.
6 Never leave gas cylinders exposed to excessive heat or cold.
7 Never test for leaks with a naked light or flame. Use soapy water.
8 *Never* allow oil or grease to come into contact with cylinder valves or fittings because in the presence of oxygen under pressure oil and grease will ignite and may result in an explosion.
9 Shut off the valve before disconnecting the hose.

Safety precautions (HSW Form 1704)

1 Cylinders must not be roughly handled.
2 Grease and oil must not come in contact with valves or fittings.
3 No jointing materials or washers to be made from flammable materials.
4 Cylinders must be kept cool.
5 Cylinders must be kept away from naked flames.
6 Frozen equipment must not be thawed out by flames but by the use of hot water.
7 Ensure gas tight system:
   (a) Leak of oxygen could endanger the operative by fire.
   (b) Leak of acetylene could cause an explosion or fire.
8 Oxygen must not be used in place of compressed air:
   (a) To clear fumes from an enclosed area.
   (b) To test any system.
9 Oxygen must not be inhaled direct from the cylinder – it is injurious to health.
10 Adequate protection must be worn by operative:
   (a) Eyes: tinted goggles.
   (b) Hands: leather gauntlets.
   (c) Head: leather skullcap or hat.
   (d) Body: leather apron or overalls.
11 Cylinders to be kept away from electric controls and switches to guard against possible arcing.
12 Excessive force must not be used when assembling welding equipment.
13 Precautions must be taken to prevent starting fires, i.e. remove or cover flammable materials, extinguishers to be available.
14 Ensure adequate ventilation when working in confined spaces.

Safe working

1 Always ensure the hoses are purged (cleaned out). This is achieved by allow-... of acetylene gas to

... nozzle is presented to a flame ... the flow of acetylene is established.
(b) If the gas velocity is too high the flame will blow off the end of the nozzle and be extinguished.
3 Do not use matches. These could be a hazard. Use some form of spark lighter or flint gun (Figures 3.17 and 3.18).

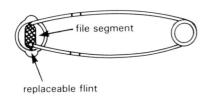

Figure 3.17 *Spark lighter*

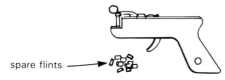

Figure 3.18 *Flint gun*

4 Only when you are sure the equipment is in a sound working condition can you proceed to the pressure adjustment, lighting up and flame setting required.

The three flames

Before any kind of brazing or welding can be performed the operator must be aware of the *three* different types of flames and also know the type of flame required to carry out the task that has been set.

The three flames can be obtained by adjusting the controls on the blowpipe and so regulating the amounts of gas being emitted. They are:

... Carburising (used for hard facing of ... wide variety ... welding, brazing, bronze welding, hard fac-ing, flame cleaning, heating and cutting.

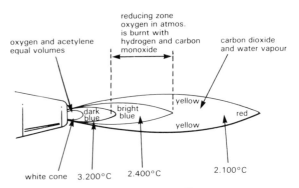

Figure 3.19 *The gas welding flame*

Carburising flame

Assuming the gases have been previously turned on and adjusted to the correct pressure for the size of the nozzle fitted:

1 Open acetylene valve on blowpipe and purge the air.
2 Apply spark lighter to nozzle.
3 Adjust acetylene to get rid of the smoke and soot – but not enough to cause flame to lift off nozzle.
4 Open oxygen valve on blowpipe (slowly).

As the oxygen supply is increased a white diminishing cone with a feathery edge will be noted. This is caused by unburned particles of carbon. The degree of carburising depends on the length of the acetylene feather.

Neutral flame

The procedure is the same as for the carburising flame, up to the production of the acetylene cone. Continue slowly to open the oxygen control on the blowpipe and observe the flame. As the oxygen supply increases the acetylene feather cone decreases. This continues until the acetylene feather almost disappears inside the small white cone. At this point the flame will be neutral. The moment the acetylene feather disappears the increasing of the oxygen must be stopped. Some people recommend that a very slight feather should be seen on the small cone as a safeguard against excess oxygen.

Oxidising flame

The process is the same as for the neutral flame. When this has been obtained the flame is changed into an oxidising one by *reducing* the flow of acetylene. When the acetylene is reduced it will be noticed that the size of small white cone also decreases and it appears to be very sharply pointed. For normal bronze welding it is recommended that the cone be reduced by one-third its length. It is better practice to reduce the acetylene from the neutral position to obtain an oxidising flame than to increase the flow of oxygen. The former gives a gentler and less noisy flame.

Flame characteristics

Carburising flame

Examination of this type of flame makes the difference in structure between it and the other two very obvious. In the oxidising and neutral flames there are only *two* really visible cones whereas the carburising flame clearly shows *three*. This effect is brought about by an excess of acetylene, which gives the intermediate cone known as an acetylene feather (see Figure 3.20).

This type of flame should not be used for ordinary welding. It is a dirty flame, the carbon not burned away being deposited on the weld metal. This process shows as a

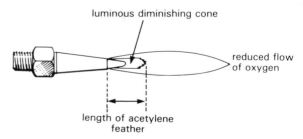

Figure 3.20 *Carburising flame*

boiling action and results in a hard brittle weld.

Carburising flames are used for hard-facing of metals.

Neutral flame

The neutral or normal flame is the one most frequently used in welding. It is called neutral because it neither oxidises nor carburises the parent metal (i.e. it does not add or take anything away).

A neutral flame requires equal volumes of oxygen and acetylene to be burnt in complete combustion.

The neutral flame is a clean flame: the metal remains clean and flows easily. It is used for most welding jobs that require the metal to be melted and mixed together.

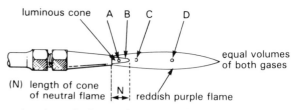

a) unburned mixture of oxygen and acetylene gases
b) primary combustion cone (slightly rounded)
c) hottest point of the flame
d) secondary combustion zone

Figure 3.21 *Neutral flame*

Oxidising flame

At first view, particularly to the beginner, this flame may be mistaken for a neutral flame. However, the cone is short and more pointed, and it is more noisy and fierce. The greater the imbalance between the gases, the

oxidising flame

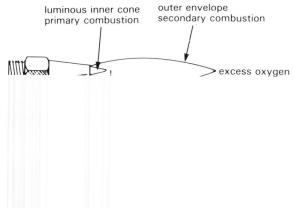

luminous inner cone
primary combustion

outer envelope
secondary combustion

excess oxygen

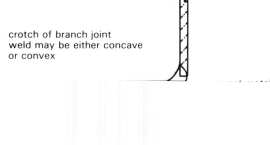

crotch of branch joint
weld may be either concave
or convex

fusion welding steel, as it causes the metal to boil and spark. The additional oxygen in the flame causes the metal to burn resulting in a brittle weld. A slightly oxidising flame is used for bronze welding, which is explained in detail on page 98.

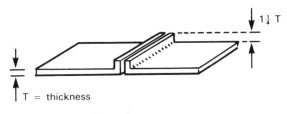

T = thickness

Figure 3.25   *Flanged*

Fusion welding

In fusion welding there is controlled melting of the two edges of the parent metals while a filler rod of the same or similar material is added, thereby producing a uniform mass along the length of the joint. The addition of the filler rod enables the welder to build up the weld face to give additional strength and the uniform finished bead.

Figure 3.26   *Square or open butt*

Figure 3.27   *Single vee*

Basic fusion welds
The two types of basic fusion welds are:

1 Butt weld (Figure 3.23),
2 Fillet weld (Figure 3.24).

All common joints utilise one or other of these welds.

Figure 3.28   *Double vee (used on thick plate)*

Features of a good weld

1 Fusion full depth of parent metal.
2 Equal fusion on both edges.
3 Even penetration at the root.
4 Regular bead profile and reinforcement.
5 Correct alignment of work.
6 Absences of inclusion and surface defects.

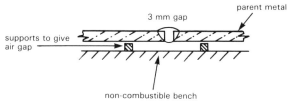

3 mm gap

parent metal

supports to give
air gap

non-combustible bench

Figure 3.23   *Butt weld*

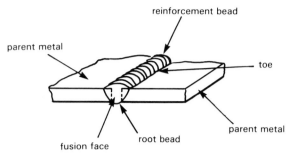

Figure 3.29   *A good weld*

Common defects in welds

Various welding defects are shown in Figures 3.30–3.34.

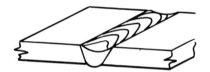

Figure 3.30   *Insufficient reinforcement*

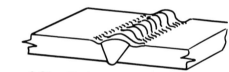

Figure 3.31   *Undercut*

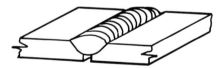

Figure 3.32   *Lack of penetration*

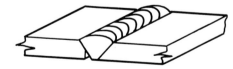

Figure 3.33   *Unequal fusion*

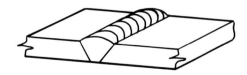

Figure 3.34   *Excessive penetration*

Steel

There are three welding techniques for this metal:

1   Leftward,
2   Rightward,
3   All positional rightward (too specialised for inclusion in this chapter).

Leftward technique

In this technique the welding commences at the extreme right with the blowpipe pointing to the left. The weld is progressed to the left; hence its name. The completed weld is behind the blowpipe. The technique is illustrated in Figures 3.35–3.37.

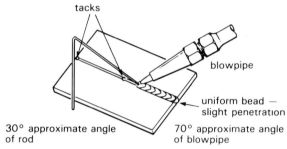

Figure 3.35   *Leftward technique*

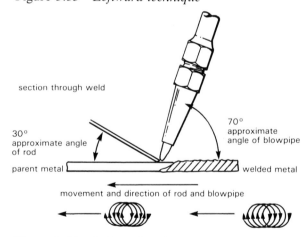

Figure 3.36   *Leftward technique*

The leftward technique is the recommended method for welding thin sheets of metal. It is also the easiest and the one most widely used in the industry for all kinds of welding.

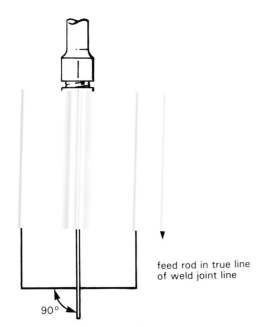

feed rod in true line
of weld joint line

90°

Figure 3.37   *Leftward technique*

Rightward technique
This method of welding is carried out in the opposite direction to the leftward method, i.e. from left to right. The blowpipe is directed towards the completed weld with the feed rod between the flame nozzle and weld pool (see Figures 3.38 and 3.39).

section through weld

approximate angles

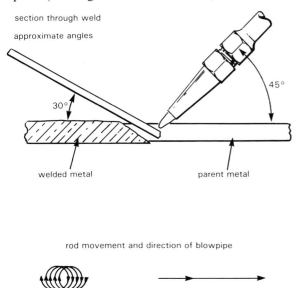

45°

30°

welded metal   parent metal

rod movement and direction of blowpipe

Figure 3.38   *Rightward technique*

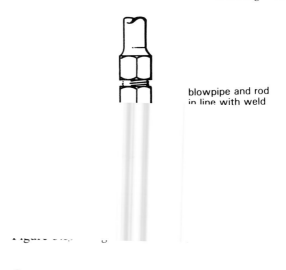

blowpipe and rod
in line with weld

Copper
Fusion welding of copper sheet and tube can be carried out advantageously on de-oxidised copper (oxygen has been removed). Special de-oxidised filler rods are used or alternatively the edge of the sheet or tube is turned out and used as the filler rod material as illustrated in Figure 3.42 (overleaf).

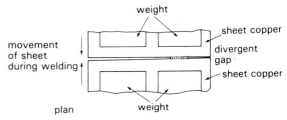

weight

sheet copper

movement
of sheet
during welding

divergent
gap

sheet copper

plan   weight

Figure 3.40   *Fusion welding of sheet copper*

note: flame envelopes
the weld area preventing
oxidation

neutral flame
70/80° angle to weld

wedge moved along
joint as welding
proceeds

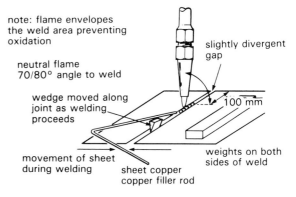

slightly divergent
gap

100 mm

weights on both
sides of weld

movement of sheet
during welding   sheet copper
copper filler rod

Figure 3.41   *Fusion welding of sheet copper*

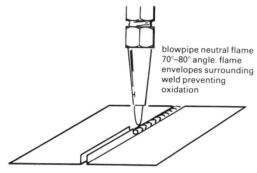

blowpipe neutral flame 70°–80° angle. flame envelopes surrounding weld preventing oxidation

sheet copper edges turned to form filling rod

note: a strictly neutral flame must be used

an oxidising flame would cause copper oxide to form resulting in a brittle weld

a carburising flame will cause porosity

Figure 3.42   *Alternative preparation for sheet welding copper*

A strictly *neutral* flame must be used because an *oxidising* flame causes copper oxide to form, resulting in a brittle weld, and a carburising flame will cause porosity.

Advantages

1   Recommended where colour match is essential.
2   Has equal expansion and contraction.
3   There is no electrolytic action.
4   Electrical and thermal conductivity is maintained.

Copper sheet

1   Thoroughly clean the weld area.
2   Set the sheet on an insulating type plate to conserve heat. Allow a slightly divergent gap, tapering 10 mm in 300 mm.
3   Hold in position using weights.
4   Choose a larger nozzle size than for steel, set a *neutral flame.*
5   Preheat weld area (due to high conductivity of copper).
6   Angle of blowpipe 70–80° to weld seam. The flame envelopes the weld area preventing oxidation. Rod angle 30°.
7   The *leftward method* of welding is used and it is recommended to commence

welding some little way in from the right-hand edge (approx. 100 mm). Weld this section last.

8   Lightly hammering the finished weld while it is still hot will improve the weld strength.

Copper tube

1   Thoroughly clean the weld area.
2   Choose nozzle one size larger than for steel.
3   Preheat the weld area.
4   Set a neutral flame.
5   Angle the blowpipe at 90° to the weld seam.
6   Using the leftward method fuse the edges of the tube together or alternatively add copper filler rod.

Figures 3.43 and 3.44 show how the tube walls can be turned out to serve as filler rods. Of course, a filler rod may be used on its own in either case.

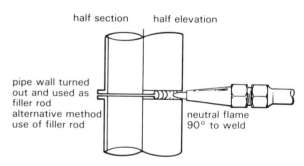

half section   half elevation

pipe wall turned out and used as filler rod alternative method use of filler rod

neutral flame 90° to weld

Figure 3.43   *Forming straight connector*

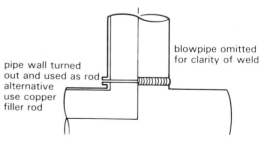

pipe wall turned out and used as rod alternative use copper filler rod

blowpipe omitted for clarity of weld

Figure 3.44   *Forming tee piece*

A note on brazing and bronze welding

These two techniques for the jointing of copper sheet and tubes are sometimes confused in the mind of the beginner, so let

only tinned (surface adhesion) by the welding rod and at no stage should the material be melted in either process. The hard solder used is one of many bronze alloys or silver solder.

Note Lead-free solders are now being manufactured to replace the existing lead–tin solders.

Brazing

Brazing relies on the phenomenon of capillary attraction in the jointing method. Capillarity is the movement of a liquid in all directions; in the case of brazing the liquid is the brazing rod or strip, which has a low melting point.

The success of a joint depends upon its correct preparation, which can be defined as the snugness of the fit between the two pieces of sheet or pipe. Recommended joint clearance is between 0.05 and 0.2 mm and

Rods and fluxes

Many different types of brazing rods are manufactured, each having its own particular advantage. Each type contains different proportions of the metals making up the brazing alloys and is suitable for a variety of jobs.

The brazing alloys are manufactured from mixtures of silver, copper, zinc, cadmium and tin. Some mixtures give an alloy with the ability to fill gaps in the work whilst others give greater fluidity.

In soldering the purpose of a flux is to remove oxides, and it is the same in brazing. It is not necessary to use fluxes in all circumstances, e.g. when using a copper

Table 3.5

Type of jointing	Jointing material	Examples
Soft soldering	Lead–tin solder	Wiped joints on lead pipes Capillary joints on copper pipes
Hard soldering	Brazing solder	Silver soldering Capillary joints on copper pipe
	Bronze solder	Bronze welding on copper pipe Bronze welding on steel
Fusion welding	As parent metal	Lead welding Steel welding Copper welding

phosphorus rod. This rod has the advantage of not containing silver which makes it a comparatively cheap one. Where fluxes are recommended use the manufacturer's guide and recommendation or the correct wetting (tinning) and bonding may not take place.

There are two basic types of flux:

1   Borax (used for higher range of temperature),
2   Fluoride (used for lower range of temperature).

Sheet brazing

Recommended joints

Figure 3.45 shows the interlaced method which restricts joint movement during brazing. The alternative method is the simple lap.

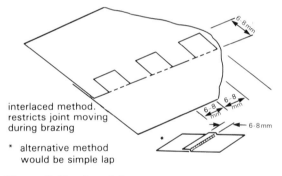

interlaced method.
restricts joint moving
during brazing

* alternative method
would be simple lap

Figure 3.45   *Lap joint*

A U-shaped joint (Figure 3.46) gives a receptacle for brazing material and a double sided contact.

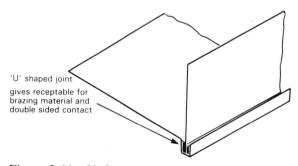

'U' shaped joint
gives receptacle for
brazing material and
double sided contact

Figure 3.46   *U-shape*

Figure 3.47 shows an upstand joint being made. A neutral flame is called for and the outer envelope of it is used. A large massy flame can be used with the bronze running ahead of the flame, or two blowpipes with smaller nozzles.

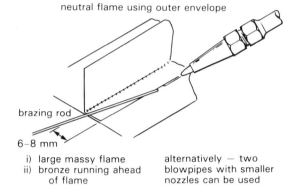

neutral flame using outer envelope

brazing rod

6–8 mm

i) large massy flame
ii) bronze running ahead
of flame

alternatively — two
blowpipes with smaller
nozzles can be used

Figure 3.47   *Upstand*

Preparation

The preparation of sheet for brazing is perhaps the easiest of all and is done as follows:

1   True lines and edges,
2   File all edges to remove burrs and sharp edges to prevent burning,
3   Thoroughly clean all surfaces (steel wool),
4   Ensure a snug fit to aid capillarity,
5   Select the correct rod and flux when required.

Technique

This is best carried out using a nozzle size larger than the one you would select for fusion welding. Adjust the flame to give a large neutral massy-type flame or alternatively use two blowpipes, one acting as a pre-heater, the other performing the brazing process. This is essential on copper which has a high rate of conductivity. The metal is brought up to the temperature at which the brazing rod will melt. The braze must be drawn the full distance of the joint between sheets.

The greatest danger when brazing is the temptation to use an ordinary welding approach, which often results in the metal being burned or a local heating effect and a ~~···~~ ~~In addition to the use of~~

5 Braze joint (as previously explained) taking care not to allow braze rod to overflow socket.
6 Direct flame around bottom of joint to draw filler metal to bottom of prepara-~~···~~ ~~··· ~~ ~~of joint afterwards~~

Straight connector

1 File one end of the pipe square and true. (This is known as the spigot.)
2 File the other end square and anneal (heat until red hot).
3 With the aid of a socket former and hammer, form capillary socket to required depth (Figure 3.48).
4 Clean outside of spigot, inside of socket and edge of same (mouth of joint).

(b) ~~Centre-pop (+) (Figure 3...),~~
3 Slit distance between points.
4 (a) With bent pin and hammer work up sides of socket. (Keep pipe red hot.)
   (b) As hole increases in size use a larger pin or pipe. Finish with pipe as near as possible to the diameter of the branch pipe. This ensures a good snug fit which will assist capillary attraction in the joint.

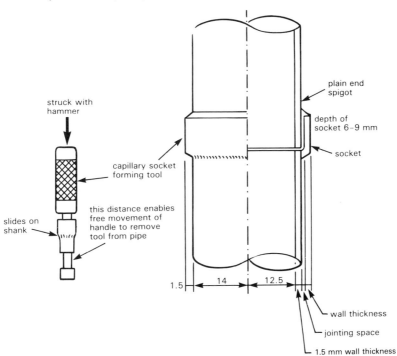

Figure 3.48 *Brazed straight connector (half section half elevation)*

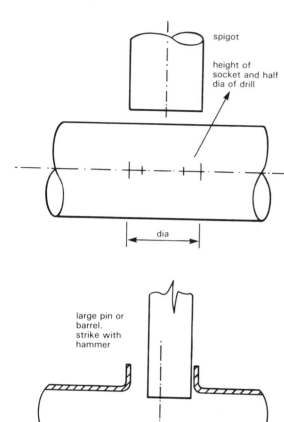

Figure 3.49   *Preparation of tee connector*

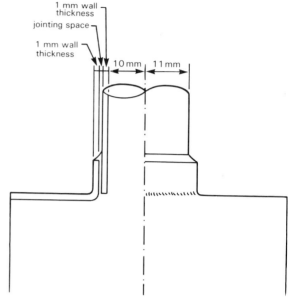

Figure 3.50   *Brazed tee connector (half section half elevation)*

5   Thoroughly clean inside and mouth of socket and outside of pipe.
6   Assemble and braze as previously described (Figure 3.50).
7   One important point is to ensure that the branch pipe does not drop inside the main pipe. Mark the branch before commencing to braze, tack, check again to ensure correct position.

Note   Always play heat on branch *first* to expand the pipe to keep it holding tight in prepared socket. Heating the socket first expands it and allows the branch pipe to drop inside.

Tools for joint forming
There are several types of tools on the market which can form the required sockets in a fraction of the time required to make them by hand:

1   Rothenburger tool,
2   Allen tool,
3   'T' Drill system

'T' Drill
Figures 3.52 and 3.53 illustrate one of several special tools on the market today used to prepare copper tube branch joints. It is a very simple and time-saving method. The special attachment raises the walls of the tee as illustrated in Figure 3.51.

Rast copper tube expanders
These are illustrated in Figures 3.54 and 3.55.

Bronze welding

Bronze welding differs from fusion welding in that the parent metal is only tinned by the

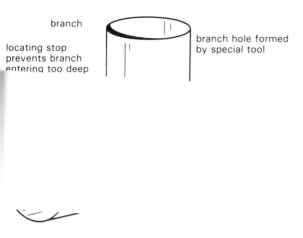

branch

locating stop
prevents branch
entering too deep

branch hole formed
by special tool

joint set up ready for soft or hard soldering

Figure 3.51 *Capillary type tee joint using 'T' Drill method. (The joint is set up for soft or hard soldering.)*

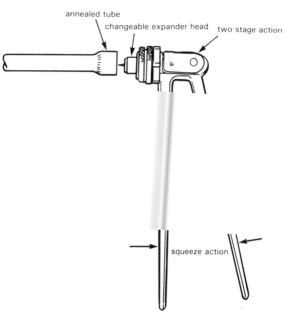

annealed tube

changeable expander head

two stage action

squeeze action

Figure 3.54 *Hand operated expander*

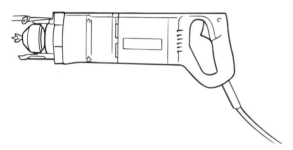

Figure 3.52 *Drill and branch hole attachment*

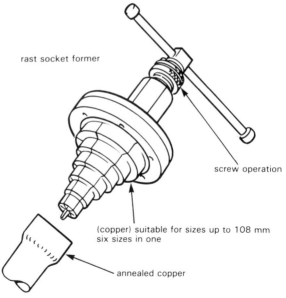

rast socket former

screw operation

(copper) suitable for sizes up to 108 mm
six sizes in one

annealed copper

Figure 3.55 *Screw operated expander*

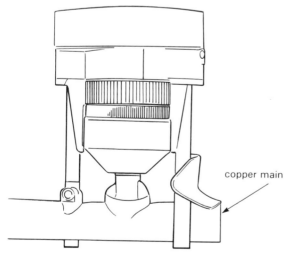

copper main

Figure 3.53 *Branch hole being formed*

bronze. It can be satisfactorily used on copper, cast iron, steels, brasses and galvanised steel. Bronze welding differs from brazing in needing a localised source of heat rather than a general spread.

In the bronze welding process the filler rods will flow onto correctly prepared metal surfaces which have a higher melting point and produce a bond with excellent properties. Although the parent metal is not melted the bond produced is equal in strength and comparable to a fusion weld.

Oxy-acetylene equipment is most satisfactory for this process being able to produce an intensely hot flame that gives controlled local heating.

The flowing of the bronze filler rod over the prepared surface is known as tinning and supplies great strength. As well as the tinning action a slight inter-alloying of the bronze and parent metal takes place and there is evidence that the heat can open up the grain structure of the parent metal and allow penetration of the bronze tinning.

Preparation

The joint on a sheet is known as the 'upset butt joint' (Figure 3.57).

1 The edges must be cut or filed true (a).
2 Turn 4–5 mm edge over the aid (b).
3 Complete 180° turn over a 1–2 mm piece of steel (c).
4 Thoroughly clean weld (steel wool or wire brush).

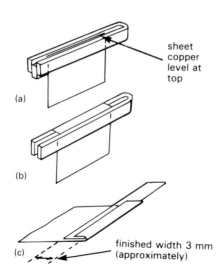

Figure 3.56 *Preparation of upset butt joint*

5 Repeat for both pieces. Place together and tack.

Technique

Details of the technique are shown in Figures 3.57 and 3.58.

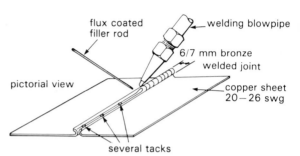

Figure 3.57 *Sheet bronze welding (upset butt joint)*

Pipe joints

Bell type

1 Cut or file end of pipes true.
2 File spigot (plain end) to 45° taper.
3 Anneal end of the other pipe (soften).
4 Hammer socket forming tool into pipe (keep pipe annealed).
5 Open socket to give minimum jointing space shown.
6 File socket level, radius outside edge. (This prevents the edge burning and aids tinning.)
7 Thoroughly clean with steel wool or wire brush.
8 Assemble and tack, ensure true alignment.

Note Copper is annealed (softened) by heating it until red hot. The manner of cooling makes no difference. Copper is worked hot because it hardens during the work process and would become brittle and may crack.

Saddle tee

1 Cut or file branch pipe true.
2 File end of branch to fit like a saddle on main (Figure 3.61).

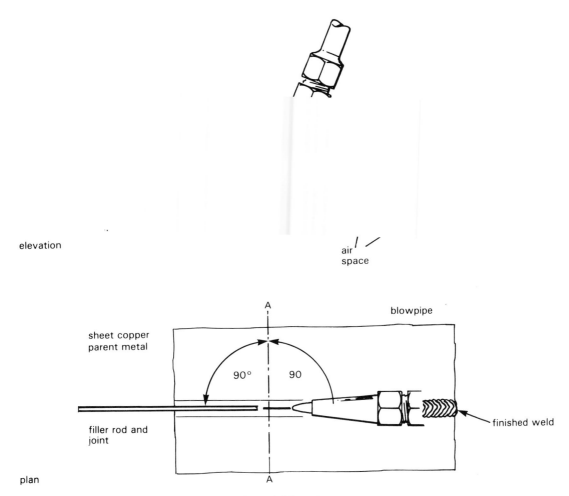

elevation

air
space

A

sheet copper
parent metal

blowpipe

90°   90

finished weld

filler rod and
joint

plan

A

Figure 3.58 *Position and angle of rod and blowpipe*

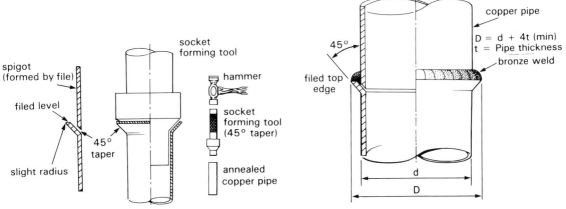

socket
forming tool

spigot
(formed by file)

hammer

filed level

socket
forming tool
(45° taper)

45°
taper

slight radius

annealed
copper pipe

Figure 3.59 *Preparation of bell type joint*

copper pipe

45°

D = d + 4t (min)
t = Pipe thickness

filed top
edge

bronze weld

d

D

Figure 3.60 *Finished bell type joint (half section half elevation)*

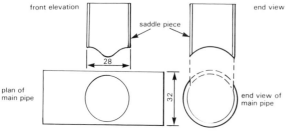

Figure 3.61   *Preparation of saddle tee joint (32 mm × 28 mm)*

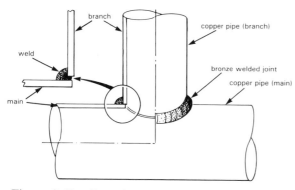

Figure 3.62   *Branch tee saddle joint*

3   Mark and centre-pop centre of branch hole.
4   Using correctly adjusted hole cutter drill branch hole.
5   File inside of hole to remove any burrs and to ensure hole is marginally larger than internal diameter of pipe (Figure 3.61).
6   Thoroughly clean joint area.
7   Assemble and tack, check alignment.

Diminishing

1   Cut or file both ends of copper pipe true.
2   Anneal one end of small diameter pipe and open to 45° by socket forming tool or steel turn-pin.
3   File edge of branch parallel (see Figure 3.63). This gives a larger area to the meeting surfaces.
4   Clean thoroughly.
5   Assemble and tack.

Diminishing type branch

Note   Always *commence* by preparing the *branch pipe first.*

1   Cut or file branch pipe true.
2   Anneal and open end to 45° as illustrated (Figure 3.65).
3   File edge of branch pipe parallel.
4   Place on main and mark outside diameter.

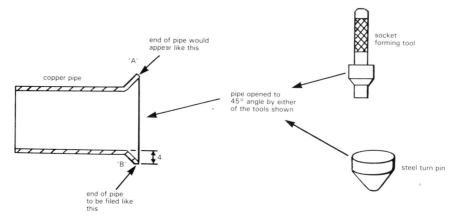

Figure 3.63

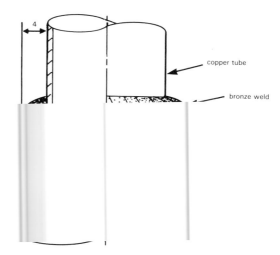

Figure 3.64   *Diminished joint*

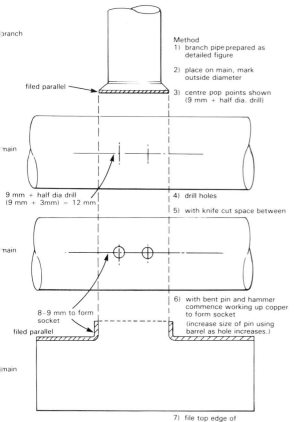

Figure 3.65   *Preparation of diminishing type branch joint*

5   Centre-pop points shown in Figure 3.65 (9 mm plus half diameter of drill). (This is most important – ensure 9 mm to form socket.)
6   Drill two small holes where indicated.
7   Anneal main and slit distance between holes with knife.
8   With steel pin and hammer work up copper to form sides of socket. Keep copper annealed and increase size of pin using steel barrel as hole increases until you have the required fit between branch and main pipe.
9   File top edge of the socket parallel with the main.
10   Thoroughly clean outside of branch, inside and edge of socket.
11   Assemble, check for alignment and tack.

Note   Always play heat on the branch pipe before heating the socket. This prevents the branch piece dropping inside the main pipe.

Angled branch
Preparation of this type of branch joint is as for the diminishing type except that in this case the branch is cut to the angle required and the main is opened to a corresponding angle.

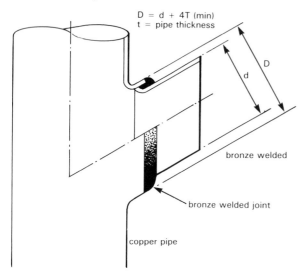

Figure 3.66   *Angled branch joint*

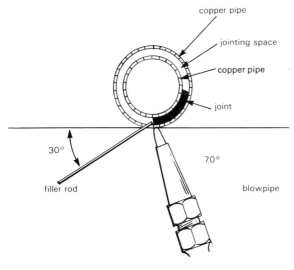

Figure 3.67   *Angle of blowpipe nozzle and filler rod*

Bronze welding technique

This type of hard soldering is performed using a blowpipe giving a high temperature concentrated flame which in turn enables a localised welding to be carried out. The addition of both suitable bronze filler rods and suitable fluxes is required. The work is heated up to the temperature where the bronze filler rod will melt and tin the parent metal. At no stage should the parent metal be melted. The correct temperature for bronze welding is indicated when the flux changes to a liquid and is seen to flow ahead of the flame. The filler rod is now added, which should also flow ahead of the flame tinning the parent metal. At the same time an additional rod is added building up a surface reinforcement bead. Mention has been made that a slightly oxidising flame is required. The setting and testing of this flame is very important to enable satisfactory welding to be carried out (see setting of oxidising flame, page 90).

The oxidising flame is necessary to prevent 'zinc volatilisation', which is the partial destruction of the zinc in the bronze filler rod by a fuming or boiling-off process, indicated by a white precipitation on the welded metal. The oxidising flame forms a skin of zinc oxide over the pool of metal, thus sealing in the molten zinc.

Before commencing to bronze weld it is advisable to test the flame on a spare piece of metal. Should fuming occur, decrease the acetylene until it stops. Now examine the weld for pitting or blowholes. If they are present decrease the acetylene still further. Test weld the metal again until you produce a weld free of blowholes or fuming and a bright shining bronze finish.

The key points to remember when bronze welding are:
1 Clean work.
2 Correct rod and fluxes.
3 Correct size of nozzle.
4 Equal and correct pressure setting.
5 Correct flame adjustment (set neutral flame then reduce acetylene).
6 Correct welding angles (rod and blowpipe).
7 Correct welding temperature:
   (a) Underheating is indicated by failure of bronze to flow and appearance of craters in the weld.
   (b) Overheating is indicated by flux becoming 'burnt' and taking on a black appearance.

8 Uniform welding bead.
9 Remove surplus flux from job.

Advantages of bronze welding:

1 Much easier to perform than fusion

Fluxes
Mention has been made of the importance of using the correct flux for the particular welding job in hand. The purpose of the flux is to:

1 Remove oxides from the metal to be welded (cleans),
2 Protect the edges of the metal from the oxygen in the atmosphere,
3 Float oxides and impurities to the surface,
4 Aid the fluidity of the bronze filler rod by lowering surface tension,
5 Have an affinity for oxygen and a lower melting point than the filler alloy.

Application

1 Have some rods impregnated with the correct amount of flux.
2 Heat part of a rod and dip in container of flux.
3 Mix with water to form a paste then apply to job.

Note Always use the minimum of flux.

Removal
There are several methods of doing this depending upon such factors as the type of work, job size, position of work, etc. The usual methods are:

1 Quenching in cold water immediately after completion of weld.

2 Scrubbing in alternate hot and cold water.
3 Wire brushing.
4 Soaking in 2% nitric or sulphuric acid solution.
5 Grit blasting.

ness is also of paramount importance; thorough washing of the hands and cleaning of the fingernails before having a meal is essential.

Shutting down procedure
This is a very simple yet extremely important task which must not be treated lightly for misuse or incorrent procedure can result in a serious accident.

1 Close acetylene valve on blowpipe. (The flame is extinguished leaving only oxygen gas flowing).
2 Close oxygen valve on blowpipe.
3 Close both acetylene and oxygen (cylinder) valves.
4 Re-open oxygen control valve on blowpipe to relieve the pressure in the blowpipe and hoses.
5 Repeat for acetylene.
6 Wind back pressure adjustment controls on regulator until they disengage the valve (do not remove). This also ensures no damage will occur to the diaphragm the next time the cylinders are turned on.
7 Finally close both controls on the blowpipe.

Lead welding (lead burning)

The controlled melting of lead and jointing together with or without the addition of more lead, i.e. filler rod, has for many years been practised by the plumber as lead burning.

Table 3.6 *Lead welding chart*

Lead welded seam	Lead code number	Size of nozzle
Flat butt	4–10	2 or 4
Flat lap	4–10	3 or 4
Inclined lap	4–10	3 or 4
Angle inclined faces	4–10	2 or 3
Upright lap	4–10	2 or 3
Vertical spigot joint	6–10	2 or 3
Lead to brass joint	6–10	3 or 4
Small brazing jobs	Metal (1.5 mm)	5

This title has now been generally dropped and superseded by the term 'lead welding'.

Lead welding is in fact the fusion welding (autogenous) of lead, generally with the addition of a filler rod of the same composition as the parent metal. Fusion welding is carried out using a blowpipe which produces a fine concentrated flame of immense heat which melts the parent metal and the filler rod into a locally controlled pool.

In almost every way lead welding can be likened to fusion welding of steel and is performed using the *neutral flame.*

Table 3.7 covers the most commonly used joints, the ones omitted being the underhand and the overhead, both of which are seldom used in normal plumbing work.

The nozzle sizes are given only as a guide, the skill of the operator and such factors as the position and climate (i.e. inside or outside of the building) will have a marked influence on the final choice. There is also a great range of flexibility in the setting of the flame for each nozzle size.

Preparation

The important points to be observed when preparing and welding lead sheet and pipe are:

1 *Clean surfaces.* All surfaces, including the edges, must be thoroughly shaved clean (shave hook recommended). The shaved area must not be touched. *No flux* is required, the work being carried out using a *neutral* flame. The flame as well as the metal must be clean (neither oxidising nor carburising). Keep preparation straight and neat using a straight edge.

2 *Correct penetration.* This is when the weld bead just penetrates the underside of the parent metal (flat butt joint) but in all

Table 3.7 *Joints on lead sheet and recommended nozzle size*

Joint	Lead thickness	Nozzle size	Gas pressure (bars)
Flat butt	4–7	2–4	0.14
Flat lapped	4–7	2–4	0.14
Angle	4–7	2–3	0.14
Horizontal lap	4–7	2–3	0.14
Lap on inclined surface	4–7	2–4	0.14
Upright	4–7	1–3	0.14
Inclined on vertical face	4–7	1–3	0.14

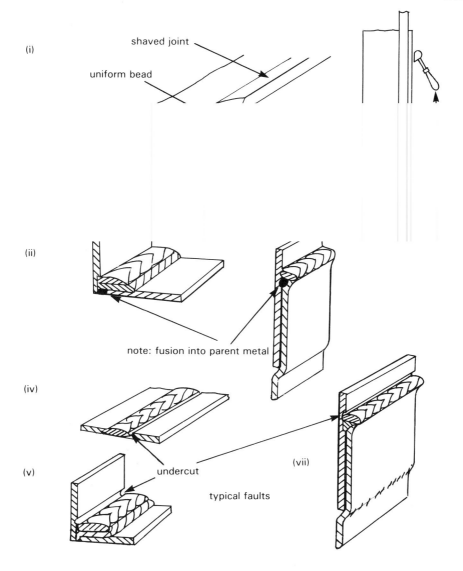

Figure 3.68 *Features of lead welding*

cases the filler rod must be melted (fused) into a homogeneous mass with the parent metal. Insufficient penetration is due to too cold a flame caused by incorrect setting or too small a nozzle size. Excessive penetration is due to too hot a flame, moving too slowly or unsupported work.

3 *Reinforcement bead.* Should be of herring bone pattern, even and uniform, extending to edge of shaved lead. Add approxi-

mately one-third thickness of lead as reinforcement.

4 *Undercutting.* This is the usual problem encountered by the beginner and is the melting away or thinning of the parent metal along the toe of the weld. It is generally caused by incorrect position or angle of blowpipe, too hot a flame or holding the flame in the same spot for too long.

Tacking

This is the holding together of the work prior to welding. It takes the form of individual tacks or a continuous tack (burning-in/fusing) performed with or without the addition of a filler rod (see Figure 3.69).

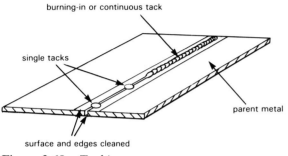

Figure 3.69   *Tacking*

Filler rods

These are coils of lead wire of varying diameter (usually 3–6 mm) or strips of lead sheet 6–12 mm wide according to the thickness of the work and the type of joint being welded. The filler rod must be shaved clean immediately prior to use.

Technique

Wherever possible the lead should be fully supported. The lead is cleaned and tacked as shown in Figure 3.69. The blowpipe is directed onto the lead with the tip of the cone just clear of the surface of the metal. As soon as the molten pool is formed the filler rod is added, sufficient rod being melted off to form the joint with a reinforcement of approximately one-third the parent metal thickness. Sufficient heat is applied to extend

the pool area to the width of preparation (sometimes by sideways movements of the blowpipe). The blowpipe should be directed down the centre of the seam with progress being made from right to left. There are two recognised methods:

1   Straight line progression,
2   Side-to-side progression.

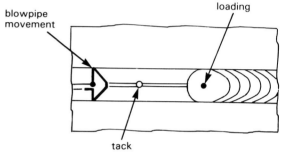

Figure 3.71   *Side to side progression*

The latter method is generally done with a cooler flame and the finished bead has a more rounded appearance. The straight line progression method with the hotter flame has a more herring-bone shaped bead.

Sheet joints

Various sheet joints are illustrated in Figures 3.72–3.79.

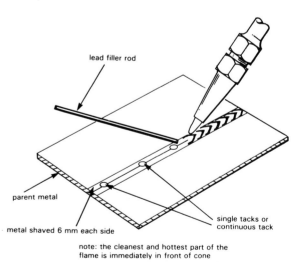

Figure 3.72   *Flat butt seam*

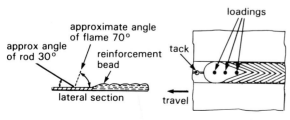

Figure 3.70   *Straight line progression*

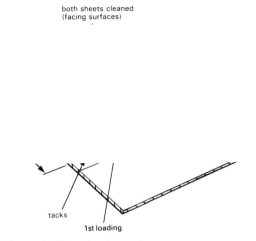

Figure 3.73   *Flat lapped seam*

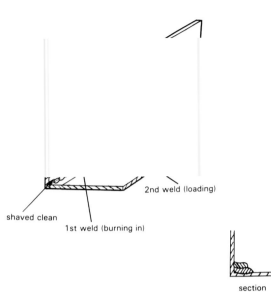

Figure 3.75   *Angle seam, one face vertical*

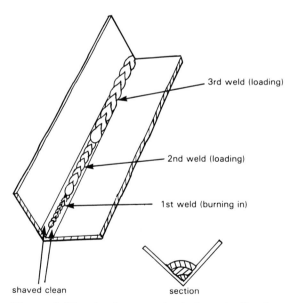

Figure 3.74   *Angle seam, both faces inclined*

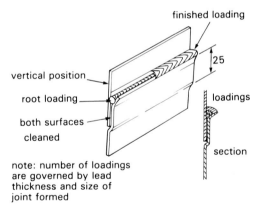

Figure 3.76   *Horizontal lapped seam*

Note   Number of loadings is governed by lead thickness and size of joint formed.

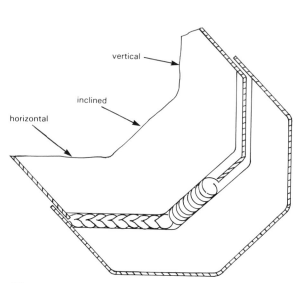

Figure 3.77   *Lap inclined surface*

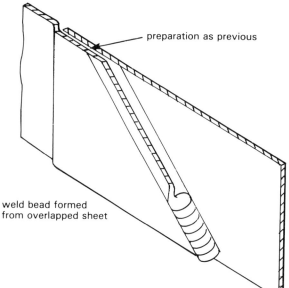

weld bead formed
from overlapped sheet

Figure 3.78   *Inclined on vertical surface*

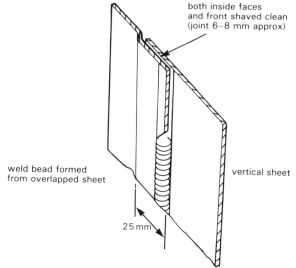

both inside faces
and front shaved clean
(joint 6–8 mm approx)

weld bead formed
from overlapped sheet

vertical sheet

25 mm

Figure 3.79   *Upright seam*

Pipe joints

On examination it will be seen that the joints used on lead pipes (Figures 3.80–3.83) are similar to the ones generally recommended for lead sheet, the set-up, tacking and welding procedure being identical.

Table 3.8   *Lead-welded pipe joints and recommended nozzle sizes*

Joint	Size of nozzle of oxy-acetylene blowpipe
Vertical spigot and branch joints	3 or 4
Lead to brass joint	3 or 4
Horizontal spigot joint	2 or 3

one or two loadings

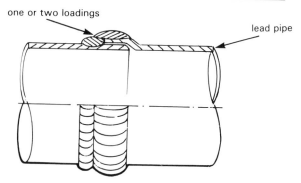

lead pipe

Figure 3.80   *Lead–lead horizontal joint*

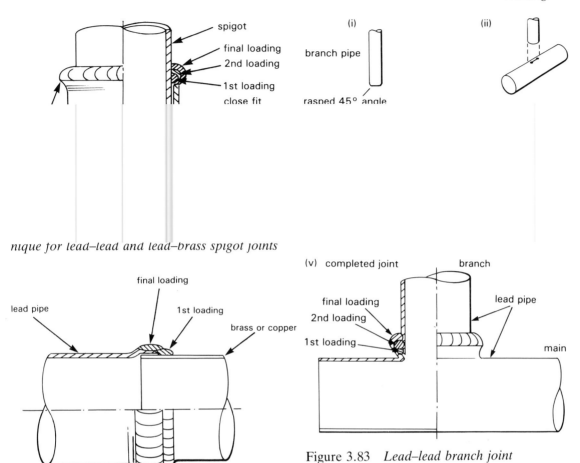

spigot

final loading

2nd loading

1st loading

close fit

(i)

branch pipe

rasped 45° angle

(ii)

nique for lead–lead and lead–brass spigot joints

(v) completed joint   branch

final loading

2nd loading

1st loading

lead pipe

main

Figure 3.83   *Lead–lead branch joint*

final loading

lead pipe

1st loading

brass or copper

Figure 3.82   *Lead–brass horizontal joint suitable for unions, w.c. ferrules and w.c. thimble joints*

Self-assessment questions

1 The acetylene cylinder must be used in a vertical position during the welding process to:
(a) Prevent the escape of acetone
(b) Allow the acetylene gas to leave the cylinder
(c) Enable safe erection of equipment
(d) Conserve floor space

2 An overheated blowpipe should be cooled by placing the blowpipe:
(a) In water with oxygen valve open
(b) In water with acetylene valve open
(c) Unattended on the bench to cool naturally
(d) In water with both valves open

3 An oxidising flame has:
(a) Insufficient oxygen
(b) An excess of oxygen
(c) Equal amounts of each gas
(d) A large inner cone

4 Bronze welding is:
(a) Silver soldering
(b) Soft soldering
(c) Hard soldering
(d) Autogenous

5 Before connecting regulators to gas cylinders you should:
(a) Clean the threads with oily waste
(b) Open the valve on the regulator
(c) Lay the cylinder on its side
(d) Open the cylinder valve momentarily to dislodge any dirt

6 For which type of joint is silver solder used?
(a) Wiped joint
(b) Gas pipe joint
(c) Bell type joint
(d) Capillary joint

7 When bronze welding copper pipes using an oxy-acetylene flame, it should be:
(a) Neutral
(b) Slightly carburising
(c) Slightly oxidising
(d) Feathered at the inner cone

8 The threads used on acetylene pipes and equipment are:
(a) Left-hand
(b) Right-hand
(c) Either left or right will do
(d) The same as those used for oxygen equipment

9 One of the purposes of using a flux is to:
(a) React with a base metal
(b) Lower the solder's melting point
(c) Increase the conductivity
(d) Prevent oxidation

10 Acetylene gas should never be conveyed in:
(a) Copper tubes
(b) Low carbon steel tubes
(c) Stainless steel tubes
(d) Pressure hose containing rubber

4 Science

3 Define 'stable equilibrium'.

4 Understand simple electric circuits.

5 Explain the effects of an electric current.

6 Demonstrate knowledge of common building materials.

7 Explain the difference between thermoplastic and thermosetting plastics.

8 Understand the differences between hardwoods and softwoods.

9 State common types and uses of adhesives and mastics in plumbing and building work.

10 Recognise and name craft materials associated with plumbing installations and systems.

The behaviour of gases

Gases, on the whole, behave in a simpler manner than liquids or solids. For example, the coefficient of expansion of all gases is (within certain limits) the same, while liquids and solids have different coefficients. The kinetic molecular theory was first developed from a study of gases. It explains the similar behaviour of all gases by the fact that the gas molecules are quite far apart, and that there are no attractive forces between them, so that it does not really matter what kind of molecules they are.

Two problems arise in the investigation of the behaviour of gases. First the gas has to be kept in some type of container. Any change in the volume of the container is very small compared with changes in the volume of the gas, so that it can usually be disregarded. A more serious problem arises from the fact that the volume of a fixed mass of gas (i.e. a fixed number of molecules) can be changed by altering either the pressure or the temperature, or both of these at the same time.

One of the most obvious properties of gases is that they are compressible. Robert Boyle investigated how the volume of a gas (air) altered when the pressure changed. Boyle trapped some air in the shortened closed limb of a U-tube and changed the pressure on the trapped air by pouring mercury into the long open limb, as shown in Figure 4.1 (overleaf). The pressure on the trapped air is equal to the atmospheric pressure plus the head of mercury in the long tube. It is clear from the results of this experiment that as the pressure on a gas increases, the volume of the gas decreases. The product of pressure times

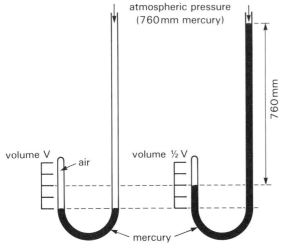

Figure 4.1 *Boyle's experiment*

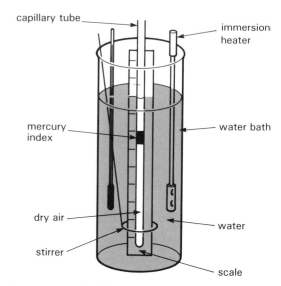

Figure 4.2 *Charles' Law apparatus*

volume was also seen to be constant within the accuracy of the readings taken and these results are summed up in *Boyle's Law* which states: '*The volume of a fixed mass of gas varies inversely as the pressure if the temperature remains constant*'.

Variation of volume with temperature

Experiments using different gases show that they all behave in a similar way, i.e. they expand uniformly and have the same coefficient of expansion. A French scientist, Charles, completed a series of experiments using dry air which was trapped in a capillary tube by a pellet of mercury and then gently heated. Readings of the volume of the trapped air were taken during warming up and subsequent cooling down to indicate the volume changes. The apparatus used is shown in Figure 4.2. When the volume (represented by the length of the column of trapped air) is plotted against the temperature, a straight-line graph is produced (Figure 4.3). This shows that air expands uniformly with temperature rise, but that the volume is not directly proportional to the temperature (measured in degrees Celsius) because the graph does not pass through the origin. Calculations show that the coefficient of expansion with respect to the gas volume at 0°C

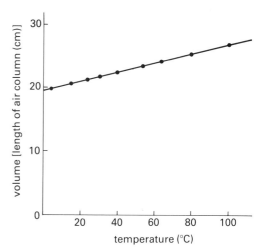

Figure 4.3 *Volume–temperature graph*

is $\frac{1}{273}$. The results of the experiments are summed up in *Charles' Law* which states: '*The volume of a fixed mass of gas increases by $\frac{1}{273}$ of its volume at 0°C for every degree Celsius rise in temperature, provided the pressure is constant*'.

Variation of pressure with temperature

To determine the variation of pressure with temperature the essential parts of the apparatus are a bulb to contain the air, and some

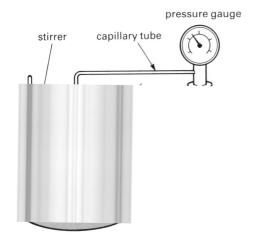

Figure 4.4   *Pressure–temperature apparatus using a pressure guage*

method of measuring the pressure. In one form of the apparatus, a pressure gauge is used (Figure 4.4). In another, more traditional form, the pressure is measured using a

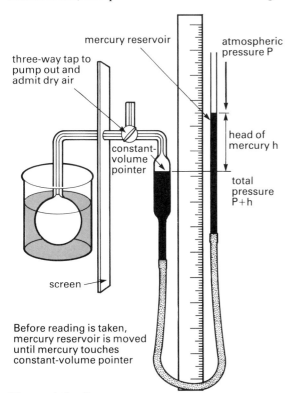

Before reading is taken, mercury reservoir is moved until mercury touches constant-volume pointer

Figure 4.5   *Pressure–temperature apparatus using a column of mercury*

column of mercury (Figure 4.5). In both cases the bulb is connected to the pressure recorder by a narrow capillary tube so that as little air as possible is unheated. A series of readings of pressure and temperature are

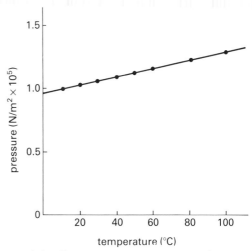

Figure 4.6   *Pressure–temperature graph*

Just as with the relationship between volume and temperature, when the experiment is repeated with different gases, the same result is obtained and this gives rise to the *pressure law*. This law states: '*The pressure of a fixed mass of gas increases by $\frac{1}{273}$ of its pressure at 0 °C for every degree Celsius rise in temperature, provided the volume is constant*'.

Centre of gravity and stability

The *centre of gravity* of a body is the point at which the whole weight of the body can be taken as acting, regardless of the position of the body. The centre of gravity of a body is in the same position as its *centre of mass*.

The centre of gravity may be regarded as the point of balance, and it is not difficult to guess where the centre of gravity, or balancing point, of a flat, circular piece of metal is. The centres of gravity of regular and uniform objects (made of the same material throughout), are at their geometrical centres, as shown in Figure 4.7.

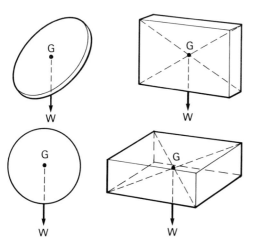

Figure 4.7   *Objects with their centres of gravity at their geometrical centres*

The centre of gravity of a triangle can be found by drawing lines from each corner to the mid-point of the side opposite that corner (see Figure 4.8). These lines are called medians. The centre of gravity of the triangle is at the position where the three medians intersect.

The centre of gravity of an irregularly shaped body must be found by experiment. When a body is suspended so that it can

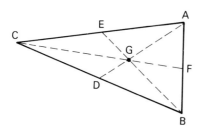

Figure 4.8   *Centre of gravity of a triangle*

swing freely, it will come to rest with its centre of gravity vertically below the point of suspension. Figure 4.9 shows an irregularly shaped piece of metal which is hung from a nail in three different positions. In each position a plumb-line is hung from the nail and its line marked onto the metal. The intersection of the lines from two points of suspension will determine the centre of gravity. The line from the third point can be used to check that the correct position has been found.

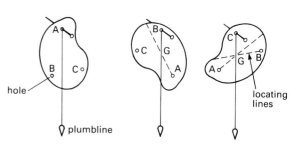

Figure 4.9   *Locating the centre of gravity of an irregularly shaped body*

Stability

A body is described as being in *stable equilibrium* if it returns to its original position after being given a small displacement. An acetylene cylinder standing on its base is an example of a body in stable equilibrium. The vertical line from the centre of gravity falls inside the base diameter (see Figure 4.10) and so, when the cylinder is displaced slightly to one side, its weight returns it to its original position. The lower the centre of gravity, the further the body can be displaced and still return to its stable position when the displacing force is removed. When the vertical line from the centre of gravity falls just outside the base, the body topples over. Objects with a wide base are not easily knocked over, although many building components do become 'top-heavy' as they are assembled, and care should be taken when working with unstable objects or moving irregularly shaped components such as boilers, wash basins, baths and WC pans.

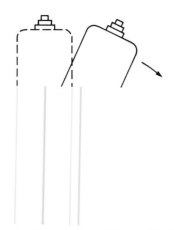

Figure 4.10 *Stable and unstable equilibrium*

Electricity: the electric circuit

In order to use electricity to perform a function such as lighting a lamp we must have a source of electricity, e.g. a dynamo or a battery. The lamp must be connected to the source and it is convenient to have a switch so that the lamp can be turned on and off. A simple circuit can be formed using a lamp, a battery, a switch and some connecting links. For an electric current to flow there must be a complete path for it, with no gaps. The circuit shown in Figure 4.11 is a simple *series*

circuit. The electric current flows through the series of objects connected one after the other. The order in which the pieces of equipment are connected does not matter; the switch will perform just as well on the

insulating material so that if two wires touch they will not cause a *short circuit*. Metals are good conductors, whilst non-metallic substances are usually insulators. Rubber and plastics are good insulators. Different materials can be tested by placing them across the test-gap of the equipment shown in Figure 4.12. If the bulb lights up, the material is a

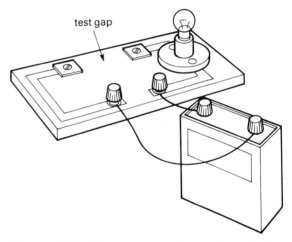

Figure 4.12 *Apparatus used to test conductors and insulators*

good conductor, but if the bulb shows no change, then the material is a good insulator.

Current

The word current means a flow or movement. The flow of an electric current round a wiring circuit is often compared with the flow

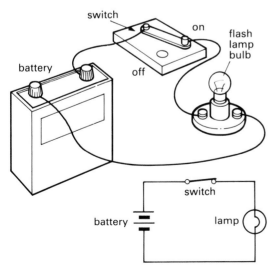

Figure 4.11 *A simple circuit and its circuit diagram*

of water through a pipework system. Water flows owing to either gravitational forces (head) or the pressure generated by a pump. A source of electricity such as a battery produces an 'electrical pressure' which causes electric current.

The instrument used to measure the magnitude of an electric current is called an *ammeter* and the unit of measurement is the *ampere* (A). The ammeter is connected in the circuit so that the current to be measured flows through it. In a simple series circuit, the current is the same at all points in the circuit (Figure 4.13).

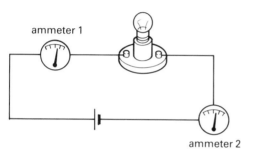

Figure 4.13   *Measuring current – both ammeters show the same reading*

Series and parallel circuits

Lamps can be connected in a variety of ways. Two examples are shown in Figure 4.14. In part (i) the lamps are connected in *series* and the same current flows through each lamp. In part (ii) the lamps are connected in *parallel*. In a series circuit when one lamp is removed the other lamps go out because the circuit is broken. If a lamp is removed in the parallel circuit, the other lamps remain alight.

A cell (or any other device which converts one form of energy into electrical energy) has an *electromotive force* (e.m.f.), which is a measure of its ability to drive a current through a circuit. The electromotive force is measured with a *voltmeter*. The unit of electromotive force is the *volt* (V).

In normal practice the electromotive force of a cell is called its voltage. The e.m.f. of a cell is also called the *potential difference* (p.d.), and when a current flows between two

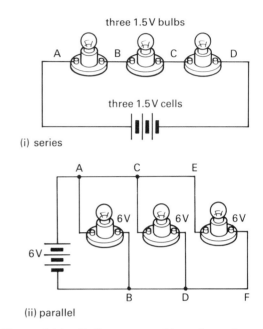

Figure 4.14   *Bulbs connected in series and parallel*

points in a circuit, there is said to be a difference in potential between them. A lamp (or any other electrical component) is designed to work at a particular voltage and this should match the electromotive force of the battery supplying it. In a series circuit of lamps and cells, the voltages of the cells are added together (Figure 4.15). When cells are

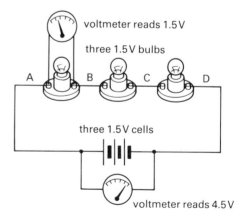

Figure 4.15   *Lamps and cells in series. Each lamp has its correct voltage supplied and lights normally*

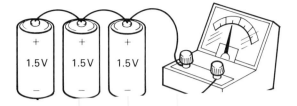

resistance and may be used as heating elements. Thin wires of tin and special alloys of lead and tin have a high resistance and also a low melting point. They melt and break the circuit when a large current flows through

... ..netism. This ability to switch magnetism on and off is very useful, particularly as the operation can be carried out at a distance. Electromagnets are employed in solenoid switches, relay valves and certain types of flame protection devices incorporated into modern boiler control systems.

connected in parallel (Figure 4.16), the voltage of the battery is the same as that of each of the single cells. The battery has three times the capacity of a single cell, but its e.m.f. is no greater.

The effects of an electric current

When an electric current flows in a conductor it produces certain changes in the space around the conductor and in the conductor itself. An electric current has:

1   A heating effect
2   A magnetic effect
3   A chemical effect if the conductor through which the current is passing is a solution.

As electricity is a form of energy it is able to change into other forms of energy, such as heat energy. When the current supplying an immersion heater is switched on the heating element increases in temperature and dissipates heat into the surrounding water. Electrical energy is being converted into heat energy in the heating element. At the same time the cable connecting the heater to the power supply remains cold. Some wires get hot when electricity passes through them; others do not. The heating effect depends on how large the current is, on the thickness of the wire and also on the material from which the wire is made. Wires which produce a large amount of heat when a given current passes through them are said to have a large

In an electric cell chemical changes take place and electricity is produced. Chemical energy is being converted into electrical energy. Many changes of this kind are reversible, and it is so in this case. An electric current can therefore bring about chemical change. Solutions of acids, alkalis and salts conduct electricity. Water itself is a poor conductor of electricity. Liquids which conduct electricity are called *electrolytes*. The liquid metal, mercury, is a very good conductor. When an electric current passes through an electrolyte, a chemical change takes place and the process is known as *electrolysis*.

This chemical effect is used in electroplating, in which a thin layer of one metal is deposited onto another metal (or sometimes plastic) in order to give a more attractive appearance, to increase mechanical strength, or to prevent corrosion. Electrolysis is used in the chemical industry to purify metals and extract them from their ores. Electrolysis can cause corrosion in plumbing systems where a combination of metals such as brass, zinc, copper, steel and lead often provide conditions likely to encourage the flow of an electric current.

Materials

Much of a plumber's work involves activities with or alongside other craft operatives. Knowledge of the installation procedure and practice and the materials used in these crafts is essential, and will enable a plumber to work with greater knowledge, skill, safety and understanding. This section of the chapter relates to materials used by craftsmen who work in close association with plumbers.

Adhesives

The development of adhesives has now reached an advanced stage. There is ample choice of available types and grades to meet all user requirements. The use of adhesives for joining structural members, especially in timber engineering, is proof of the strength and durability which may be achieved with modern adhesives. However, the adhesive used must always be suitable for the particular purpose, and the conditions and method of application appropriate to the grade of the adhesive used. The manufacturer's instructions should be studied carefully, since methods of application, curing times and performance vary according to formulation, and different grades of product of the same name are often manufactured to meet different user requirements. Mixing of different types of adhesives within a product also occurs, for example among the synthetic resin and solvent adhesives. Another factor is the large number of proprietary or trade names applied to products of any one class, although they can often be differentiated by their description, trade literature and performance.

Bonding is achieved most readily by mechanical adhesion, for example, on keyed, roughened or porous surfaces. For smooth, impervious surfaces only specific adhesion (inter-molecular attraction) can be relied upon. In these cases, it is essential to have a chemically clean surface and a suitable type of adhesive. An adhesive with a chemical set, a tack-drying solvent or a hot-poured mastic type would be best.

Types of adhesive
Animal glues   Animal glues are made from an extract from bones and hides. They are caused to set or harden either by cooling or by removal of moisture from the adhesive, or a combination of both. There is no chemical change involved. Moisture is usually removed by absorption into the material after it has been glued, or by evaporation. Removing the moisture or cooling the hot glue reduces the mobility of the liquid until it becomes rigid. The loss of moisture is accompanied by shrinkage. The whole process is reversible, so the hardened glue will soften and swell if moistened or if kept in air at high humidities, its strength being reduced accordingly. This makes such glues unsuitable for use externally or in damp conditions, unless measures are taken to exclude the damp. If damp, these glues are also liable to destruction by micro-organisms (moulds and bacteria). However, it is sometimes an advantage to use a glue which can be temporarily re-softened at an intermediate stage in the manufacture.

Animal glues are conveniently applied without special control measures and are relatively inexpensive. They are supplied in gel form for hot application, in liquid form for cold application and in powder, granular or cake form, for water addition and heating as required. They are particularly useful for wood-work.

Casein glues   Casein is a powder derived from milk curd and made water-soluble by the addition of an alkali. The casein glue powder is simply mixed with water for use, and sets partly by loss of water and partly by chemical action. The fact that chemical action is involved means that the glue must be used within a certain period of mixing, known as the pot life. This varies from several hours upwards and is reduced at higher temperatures. Joints are usually held under pressure during the setting period.

Casein glues resist moisture to a reasonable extent, but cannot withstand prolonged direct exposure to weathering and are therefore unsuitable for unprotected external use. When damp they are also liable to attack by micro-organisms. Some types have a staining action on wood, with which they are commonly used, but non-staining grades are obtainable

The thermosetting group includes the amino resins, e.g. urea formaldehyde (UF) and melamine formaldehyde (MF), the phenolic resins, e.g. phenol formaldehyde (PF) and resorcinol formaldehyde (RF), and the epoxy resins. The PVA glues, which are based on polyvinyle acetate, are thermoplastic types.

Amino and phenolic resins The setting action of amino and phenolic resins depends on the chemical action of polymerisation. These adhesives are not water-soluble. In general, they are highly resistant to moisture and can withstand exposure, but the different types are not equally efficient in these respects. These factors also depend on formulation and conditions of use and curing.

Amino and phenolic resins are supplied either in powder or viscous liquid form, and may or may not have to be used in conjunction with a hardener. Special glue film is available for use in the manufacture of plywood and other laminated products. A hardener may be mixed with the adhesive before application, or the two may be applied separately to the components to be joined and then brought together. The setting time can sometimes be adjusted by varying the amount of hardener added, and is also greatly accelerated by the application of heat. In viscous liquid form they cannot be stored indefinitely, since hardening will eventually occur without any hardener being

added, usually after many months or even years, depending on temperature.

Where the surfaces to be joined are not in very close contact during setting (i.e. more than 0.125 mm apart), a gap-filling grade of

dener.

PVA glues PVA glues consist of PVA resin emulsified in water. The setting action is not chemical, so the glue is supplied ready-mixed and has an indefinite storage and pot life if prevented from drying out. Water may be added if thinning is necessary. These features make PVA glues very convenient to use. These glues soften if exposed to moisture and are used mainly for internal work.

Other types of glues Solvent-type adhesives include adhesives based on such materials as bitumen, synthetic or natural rubbers, resins or gums, which harden by evaporation of their volatile solvent. Bitumen–rubber compositions are common. Solvent types are useful on non-absorbent materials, which must be dry to achieve their full adhesion. 'Contact' types, usually based on rubber, are allowed to become 'tack-dry' before mating the surfaces. The same base materials are also used as emulsions in water (e.g. rubber latex and bitumen emulsion adhesives) and these dry by evaporation of the water. Emulsion types are suitable for porous materials, and are not limited to dry surfaces.

Bitumen, pitch and tar are also used naturally, as hot-poured adhesives, and become hard as they cool.

Silicate adhesives, based on sodium or potassium silicate, are used for joining glass, or glass to metals.

Precautions

Many glues have to be used with great care because of their alkaline or acid nature. Alkaline types can cause staining of certain timbers (e.g. oak), which may be of importance to the work. Corrosion of metals can also occur. In addition, users may face the risk of dermatitis (skin afflictions), and appropriate precautions should be taken.

Mastics

Mastics are materials used to seal gaps or cracks, or to act as a joint filler or a jointing agent. They remain plastic or flexible to a sufficient degree to permit relative movement between the surfaces that have been sealed or jointed. It is essential that they are able to adhere firmly to the surfaces to prevent unsealing or loss of filler. In addition, they should not crack, run, blister or exude under normal temperature variations. Mastics for external use must in addition be weather resistant. The choice of a suitable mastic must also take into account special requirements, such as resistance to chemicals (e.g. alkalis or acids) and solvents (e.g. petroleum and oils). When used as a jointing medium, for example to fix tiles or glass, they are also acting as adhesives.

Materials used as mastics include plastic materials such as bitumen and tar, some natural and synthetic resins, as well as flexible (resilient) types, which include compositions based on oils, natural and synthetic resins. The flexible types are also referred to as elastomers.

Mastics may be applied by hand using a knife or trowel, extruded from a tube or pressure-gun, or applied in the form of tape or strip. Some may be heated and hot-poured. Some stiffen after application by loss of solvent or by chemical action. Others harden at the surface only, to form a protective skin. To obtain good adhesion, surfaces should be clean and dry and in some cases a special priming coat must be applied.

Many window putties harden and so are not true mastics. Glazing putties for wood frames are usually a mixture of linseed oil and whiting (powdered chalk), sometimes together with white lead. However, exceptions occur in the case of some glazing putties for metal frames which harden at the surface only, to form a skin enclosing a soft interior.

Summary of adhesives and mastics

Adhesives should be selected according to type and grade to meet the particular requirements of the work.

Types include animal and fish glues, casein and blood albumen, synthetic resins, starch and flour paste, cellulosic types, solvents and emulsions.

Animal glues, from bones and hides, harden by gelling and are re-softened by moisture, but are suitable as interior adhesives. Fish glues are similar.

Casein glues, derived from milk, set partly by loss of water and partly by chemical action. They are reasonably moisture resistant but require protection if used externally. Blood albumen and soya glues have similar properties.

Synthetic resin types may be thermosetting or thermoplastic. The amino resins (UF, MF) the phenolic resins (PF, RF) and the epoxy resins are all thermosetting, have a high resistance to moisture and are available for external use. PVA glues are thermoplastic synthetic resin (polyvinyl acetate) emulsified in water. They are re-softened by moisture but are popular for internal uses.

Bitumen, rubber and synthetic rubber-based adhesives are available both in solvent and emulsion forms. Solvent types require dry surfaces. Emulsions can be used on damp (or dry) surfaces.

Bitumen, pitch and tar are also used as hot-poured adhesives.

Silicate adhesives are used for joining glass.

Strength tests are made on adhesives, using beech test pieces, for dry strength and for wet strength (after immersion in cold, hot or boiling water or steam) to assess their moisture and weather resistance, and at the conclusion of mycological tests.

Mastics are of two kinds, plastic materials and flexible materials (elastomers). Both types are required to have good adhesive

in the building industry in Great Britain is the cement known as ordinary Portland, which got its name originally because of its resemblance, when set, to the natural Portland limestone from Dorset. The principal raw materials for making this cement are chalk (or limestone) and clay, both of which fortunately occur in extensive natural deposits in Great Britain.

The essential property of Portland cement is that it hardens by chemical action when mixed with water. This process is known as hydration. A paste of cement and water first undergoes gradual stiffening, called setting, but the hydration continues long after the paste has become rigid, resulting in a progressive increase in strength, called hardening.

In addition to ordinary Portland cement there are other types. Some are made from the same raw materials but manufactured to give slightly different properties, such as different rates of setting or hardening, or a greater resistance to chemical attack. These modified forms of cement, and ordinary Portland, together make up the Portland group of cements. There are also a number of special cements, including blends of Portland with other cementitious materials, as well as cements made from different raw materials.
Manufacture There are two methods of manufacture in use for producing Portland cements, the wet process and the dry process. The wet process was developed for the softer

clays and the dry process was developed for the harder clays and shales.

For the wet process the materials are chalk and clay, the proportions being roughly three parts of chalk (or limestone) to one part of

the horizontal, causing the contents to gravitate towards the lower end. The complete process takes several hours. Pulverised coal (or fuel oil) is blown in at the lower end of the kiln and burns continuously, causing the materials in the slurry to combine chemically. For this to occur a temperature of about 1250°C must be reached at the hottest part of the kiln (near its lower end). During the kilning the slurry first loses its free water content, then becomes dehydrated. The calcium carbonate decomposes to calcium oxide (quick-lime), and finally there is chemical combination between the quick-lime and the compounds in the clay to form cement. The cement leaves the kiln in the form of small nodules, known as cement clinker. The clinker is cooled by being passed through a ventilated rotating cylinder, similar to the kiln itself but of shorter length, and is finally ground in a tube mill to form the familiar grey powder, ordinary Portland cement. During the final grinding process a small quantity of gypsum (2–5%) is added to prevent the cement from setting too quickly after water has been added.

In the dry process the materials are crushed, dried, then ground in a tube mill to form a powdered mixture which is then burnt from the dry state.

Modified Portland cements
A number of different types of Portland cement with modified properties to suit

particular circumstances are available. While these may have different rates of hardening, it is useful to remember that they will all in time reach about the same strength.

Rapid-hardening cement   The main feature of this cement is that it is ground more finely than ordinary Portland, and its main use is in concrete work where greater early strengths are required than would be obtained with ordinary Portland.

Extra rapid-hardening cement   The rate of hardening of this cement is increased even further by adding an accelerator to rapid-hardening cement. The usual method is to add 2% of calcium chloride to the cement during its final grinding in manufacture. Alternatively, the same effect is obtained by adding the calcium chloride to rapid-hardening cement at the time of mixing, preferably in solution and added to the mixing water, to ensure good dispersion in the mix. This cement is used mainly for concreting work in winter conditions to counteract the reduced rate of hydration at low temperatures. As the cement is also quick-setting, the concrete should normally be placed in its final position within 20 minutes of leaving the mixer.

An increase in the rate of setting and hardening of cement is accompanied by an increase in the rate at which the heat of hydration is given off. In cold weather this lessens the likelihood of frost damage to new work. On the other hand, in mass concrete structures like dams, the heat of hydration is not easily lost and can cause overheating internally, resulting in cracking and even disintegration. For such cases, a low-heat Portland cement can be used.

Sulphate-resisting cement   This is a modified Portland cement with improved resistance to chemical attack by sulphates, which are salts found in sea-water, certain ground waters and (as impurities) in some building materials. Sulphates in solution can cause softening and considerable expansion of cement-based materials.

White cement   This is made by using china clay (kaolin), which is a pure clay, free of iron oxides. Iron oxides give ordinary Portland cement its grey colour.

Coloured cements   These are made by blending inert pigment powders with white, or grey, cement, depending on the colour required. The pigments may be added at the works, or, alternatively, by the user.

Water-repellent cement   This is produced by intergrinding the Portland cement clinker with a small proportion of a water-repellent substance, such as gypsum with tannic acid, or certain metallic soaps. These cements are used in water-repellent renderings and in base-coats where the background is of uneven suction (e.g. no-fines concrete), especially where a coloured finish coat is to be applied, in order to avoid patchiness. They are also used in dense concrete.

Gypsum building plasters

Gypsum building plasters are also known as calcium plasters, since calcium is a major chemical component of gypsum, the natural mineral from which they are made.

Manufacture of plaster

Gypsum plasters are made by heating gypsum to drive off part or all of the water of crystallisation. With strong heating, all the water is driven off and anhydrous gypsum plaster is formed. With less heat only three-quarters of the water is removed, giving a hemihydrate. If water is added to the powdered anhydrous or hemihydrate forms, conversion to the dihydrate (by hydration) takes place and a setting action occurs. It is this action on which the plasterer depends.

Whereas pure gypsum is white, the presence of traces of impurities in the raw material leads to gypsum plasters of different colours, such as grey, pink or brown. Their use is mainly for internal finishes to walls and ceilings, either on their own or with fine aggregate or lime added. The sand or lime is usually mixed in as required by the plasterer, but premixed plasters incorporating the light-

weight aggregates vermiculite and parlite require only the addition of water before use.
Anhydrous plaster   The crushed rock, calcined in a kiln at 400°C or above to drive off all the water of crystallisation, is ground to a

with an accelerator.
Hemihydrate plaster   The material first obtained in the heating of gypsum is plaster of Paris. This is the true hemihydrate and sets far too quickly for general use in plastering work, although it is useful for small areas and in making precast mouldings, such as cornices. To extend the setting time a retarder (e.g. keratin derivatives, or lime with an activator) is added during manufacture. The finished product is known as retarded hemihydrate plaster. In its manufacture the crushed rock is finely ground then heated for some hours at 150°C in a kettle (kiln) or open pan, or alternatively in a vessel called an autoclave heated by steam pipes.

Setting of plaster
The setting action of gypsum plasters results from the growth of crystals during the hydration. A slight expansion normally takes place as the setting advances and continues in the set material as the hydration proceeds and goes to completion.

The setting action (hardening) of most commercial plasters is normally complete within several hours, but the hydration usually occupies a longer period and for some products may still be incomplete after several days. In general, anhydrous types have a slower, more steady, rate of hydration than hemihydrate types. The absence of drying shrinkage means that there are no shrinkage cracks, and, in addition, a further plaster coat can follow.

Aggregates
An aggregate is a material in granular or particle form, such as sand or gravel, which is added to the class of materials known as binders (e.g. cements, hydraulic limes, plas-

2   The mechanical key or interlock which develops between the constituent particles by virtue of their shape, size and surface texture.
3   The strengths of the aggregate and binder respectively.

Reasons for mixing an aggregate with a binder may include one or more of the following:

1   To reduce material costs, using the aggregate as an extender (where the aggregate is less costly than the binder).
2   To offset either the drying shrinkage or setting expansion of a binder.
3   To obtain increased, or reduced, density (by using high or low density aggregates respectively).
4   To alter appearance, such as colour or texture.
5   To obtain better resistance to wear by abrasion or weathering (using hard, abrasion-resistant or non-absorbent aggregates).
6   To impart some other special property such as fire resistance, thermal insulation or acoustic characteristics.

Types of aggregate
Aggregates may be classified as fine or coarse, natural or artificial, dense or lightweight and so on. The correct type should be chosen, according to the requirements of the user.

The description fine or coarse refers to the largest size of particle present in substantial amounts. For general building purposes, a fine aggregate is one which will mainly pass a 5 mm square-mesh sieve, and a coarse aggregate is one which will be mainly retained on that sieve. An aggregate which has substantial amounts of both fine and coarse particles is termed an all-in aggregate.

Aggregates from natural sources include crushed or uncrushed stone or gravel, and sand, including crushed stone sand and crushed gravel sand. The crushing is done by machinery, usually at the pit or quarry. Artificial aggregates include crushed brick, blast-furnace slag and numerous lightweight and special aggregates.

Fine aggregates are used, together with an appropriate binder, to produce material for such purposes as rendering, plastering, floor topping and road surfacing. In addition to this, aggregates are used with a cement binder as jointing material for pipes, bedding for tiles, and mortars for brickwork and blockwork. For concrete, fine aggregates are normally used together with cement and coarse aggregate, or alternatively all-in aggregate can be used. Coarse aggregate is also used in some grades of asphalt.

Lightweight aggregates   These are composed of particles of high porosity, resulting in a low bulk density. The use of lightweight aggregates reduces the dead-weight of a structure, allowing the use of smaller supportive members and foundations at reduced cost. It also gives improved thermal insulation.

Clinker   This should be well-burnt sintered or fused furnace residue, substantially free of such impurities as sulphides and quick-lime, which promote unsoundness (expansive chemical action). Coke breeze is therefore not to be classified as a clinker, as it is unsintered and may contain harmful impurities.

Foamed blast-furnace slag   This is crushed and screened expanded slag, produced by water-cooling the molten slag obtained in the production of pig-iron. The expansion results from the bloating action of the resulting steam. This material is distinct from the heavier air-cooled slag, which is also used as an aggregate.

Pulverised fuel ash (PFA)   This is the ash of pulverised fuel (powdered coal), recovered from the flue gases of power stations. Its normal form is that of an extremely fine powder, but it is also obtainable in a processed, nodular form (sintered PFA).

Expanded clay, shale, slate, perlite and vermiculite   These are expanded forms of the natural materials produced by heating. Perlite is a glassy volcanic rock, giving expanded perlite, and vermiculite is a mineral of plate-like structure, like mica, giving exfoliated vermiculite.

Pumice   This is a natural, highly porous rock of volcanic origin.

Grading of aggregates

The classification of an aggregate as fine or coarse would give little chance of ensuring its suitability for a particular purpose. For example, a sand suitable for concreting work may be far too coarse to have any value as a material for use in plastering final coats. In practice we are concerned not only with the maximum particle size of an aggregate, but with the amounts of the various sizes present. This is known as the grading. The grading of an aggregate is found by shaking a sample through a series of sieves of different standard mesh size. The amount retained on each sieve is weighed and expressed as a percentage of the sample. It is conventional to convert these results to give the percentage weight of the whole sample to pass each sieve.

Mortars

Mortar may be defined as the bedding material used for bricks, blocks and masonry, in cases where the joints are of significant thickness (3 mm or more). This serves to distinguish a mortar from the more fluid grout or slurry used to fill the irregularities of a surface where units are butted against one another. The three basic types of mortar are cement mortar, cement–lime mortar and lime mortar, which each also contain sand.

Properties of mortar

4 Adequate adhesion to the bedded units both in the plastic and hardened state. The term bond is used for the adhesion in the hardened state.

5 Sufficient strength when hardened for the work concerned.

6 Sufficient durability with regard to the degree of exposure likely and any aggressive chemical agency.

7 Tolerable drying shrinkage and moisture movement where this is relevant to the proposed work.

In practice, an improvement in any one of these properties can readily be achieved by varying the mix proportions or constituents but usually to the detriment of one or more of the other characteristics. For example, an increase in cement content results in a stronger mortar with greater drying shrinkage. The use of a finer sand in a mix improves its cohesion, water retentivity and workability, but results in less strength and greater drying shrinkage. The question of the cost of the materials is also usually an important factor in these considerations. This results in a need to limit the cement content, as the cement is the most expensive compound, as far as is possible without causing too great a reduction in the strength.

Types of mortar
The strongest mortars are the cement mortars, but sand is also incorporated and the ratio of sand to cement should not normally be less than about three to one. Such mixes are confined to work which is below the ground level damp-proof course, to very exposed work, such as exterior free-standing walls and parapets, and to engineering construction with bricks of high strength: all are

duced workability (harshness) and less cohesion, and will produce a porous joint with a tendency for low frost resistance. However, these deficiencies can be rectified by the inclusion of a proportion of lime in the mortar, and this explains the importance of cement–lime–sand mortars. Another advantage of lime is that it increases the water retentivity of mortar, which prevents the excessive withdrawal of water by units of high suction. Water is necessary for laying the units and for hydration of the cement. By including lime the ratio of sand to cement can be increased to twice that of a cement mortar. In fact, the beneficial effects of lime may even be desirable when using the 1:3 cement–sand mortar referred to earlier, and this mix is often 'gauged' with up to one-quarter part of lime.

An alternative to the use of cement–lime–sand mortars is the use of a hydraulic or, more usually, a semi-hydraulic lime with sand. This type of mix is known as lime mortar, and one of its characteristics is continued strength development over long periods. This is considered to be a useful property in mortars for tall chimneys. However, for high early strength a cement-based mortar is preferable.

Lime mortars made with non-hydraulic lime can only harden very slowly by carbonation and are unsuitable except in special cases, e.g. internal work with very thin mortar joints, or externally in sheltered conditions where the mortar is protected by a frost-resistant pointing.

Other alternatives to cement–lime–sand mortars are plasticised, or aerated, mortars and masonry cements. In the case of plasticised mortar, lime is replaced as a workability aid by a proprietary plasticiser, added to the mix in a small quantity in powder or liquid form, usually in the mixing water. These plasticisers are mainly wetting agents, which act by reducing the surface tension of the mixing water, or air-entrainers.

Proportioning mortars
It is customary for the mix proportions of mortar to be stated as parts by volume. The strength requirements of mortars depend on the weather conditions during the construction and the degree of exposure to which the finished work will be subjected. For the sake of appearance, the sand used for masonry mortars is often crushed stone of the same variety as the units to be bedded, and it is also common for white or coloured cements to be used.

For units liable to undergo high drying shrinkage it is important to avoid the use of very strong mortars, unless permanently damp conditions are expected, in which case the drying shrinkage will be suppressed. This relates mainly to certain types of lightweight concrete blocks and some classes of sand–lime bricks, for which mortars stronger than about 1:2:9 cement:lime:sand should not be used for internal work. If stronger mixes are necessary, units with low drying shrinkage should be specified. In any event, adequate curing of concrete blocks is essential before they are used. For natural curing in air one month is recommended. Such units should not be laid wet and any initial adjustment of suction by damping should be kept to a minimum.

Mortar for tall chimneys should be limited to the weaker mixes as they more readily accommodate slight wind and thermal movements, and suitable mixes are 1:2:9 cement:lime:sand, 1:3 hydraulic lime:sand or a comparable mix with masonry cement (1:6 would be typical). Where internal units based on gypsum are to be bedded, a mortar with gypsum plaster as the binder may be used.

Mortar plasticisers and masonry cements
Mortar plasticisers, when used as an alternative to lime, permit the use of mortar mixes with aggregate:cement ratios comparable to those of lime-gauged cement:sand mixes for the same purpose.

Masonry cements give adequate workability when used only with sand although the amount of sand added is usually less than the amount added to a lime-gauged cement mortar to serve the same purpose.

In all cases where either plasticisers or masonry cements are used, it is important to follow the manufacturer's instructions regarding mix proportions, especially in relation to work in exposed positions.

Mixing mortars
Mortars can be mixed by hand or by mechanical methods. Uniform dispersion of the materials is essential, with just the right amount of water to achieve the required workability. Any mix containing cement should normally be used up within two hours of mixing, and the addition of further water after first mixing, known as retempering, should not be permitted. However, remixing (agitation without the addition of water) assists in maintaining workability of the mortar within the permissible working period, without detriment to the final strength of the mortar.

Renderings
The term rendering is used to describe a surface application of a cement–sand, or similar, mix to an external wall or other surface, either to give it a good appearance or to make it weather-proof, or both. It should not be confused with the term rendering coat, which is sometimes used to refer to the first coat applied in plastering on internal walls.

A rendering treatment may comprise one, two or even three coats. The first is termed the first or render coat, and the last is termed the final or finishing coat. The name floating coat is given to the undercoat immediately preceding the final coat. Variety in the finished appearance of a rendering may be

there must be a limited amount of suction; high suction is undesirable since the rendering must retain sufficient water to allow hydration of the cement. The reluctance of a mix to part with its water, its water retentivity, is

which allow water to penetrate and become trapped behind the rendering. This does not apply when a proportion of coarse aggregate is used, for example, in finishes such as roughcast or pebble-dash, which are consequently favoured where a high degree of impermeability is desired. However, these two treatments can only' be applied on strong, rigid backgrounds, otherwise loss of bond is likely.

Very smooth, highly trowelled rendered surfaces are also to be avoided, since they are liable to craze (develop a network of fine hair cracks at the surface). Excessive trowelling results in the accumulation of a skin of rich cement mortar with a high water content at the surface of the work. This skin is known as the laitance and has a high drying shrinkage relative to the remainder of the rendering, so that crazing occurs.

Workability

A proportion of high-calcium lime is commonly incorporated in the mix in order to limit the cement content and achieve the desired workability and durability. The alternative use of proprietary plasticisers or masonry cements has not yet found general approval for external use in renderings. Hydraulic limes may be used instead of cement and high-calcium lime mixtures, where they can give equivalent strength.

Background suction

For the wet mix to adhere to the background

otherwise the bond (adhesion of the hardened rendering) will be reduced.

Improving the bond

The achievement of a good bond between the hardened rendering and the background is facilitated by a rough-textured surface, rather than a smooth, dense surface. In some cases a specially grooved (keyed) surface will be available to give a mechanical key. For smooth, dense backgrounds, one or more of the following methods may be adopted to promote good bonding characteristics:

1 The raking out of mortar joints to about 10 mm depth.
2 Hacking the surface to provide a mechanical key.
3 The application of a preliminary spatter-dash treatment. This is a thin coat of cement–sand slurry, of proportions 1:2 approximately, thrown on wet to form an uneven layer of 3–6 mm thick. The spatterdash will also assist weather-proofing. The background must be damped before the application, and a further damping should follow some hours after the application to ensure hydration. A coarsely graded, sharp (angular-grained) sand is needed for this.
4 The preliminary application of a proprietary bonding agent, many of which are based on PVA (polyvinyl acetate) solutions. Alternatively, the bonding agent may be added to the mixing water of the

render coat. Similarly, it is sometimes mixed in with a spatterdash.

A method sometimes used on very difficult surfaces and in renovating old work is to apply the rendering onto metal lathing or expanded metal (6–10 mm mesh) fixed to battens plugged to the walls, or onto small-mesh galvanised wire netting fixed against the wall face.

Undercoat
An undercoat is normally between 10 mm and 15 mm thick. It is 'combed' or 'scratched' before hardening to provide a key for the subsequent coat, except where one of the thin machine-applied finishes is to be used.

Final coat
This will not normally be more than half the thickness of the preceding coat, and should not be stronger, except where coarse aggregate is included. Examples of different finishes are:
1 Floated finish.
2 Textured or combed finish.
3 Float textured finish.
4 Scraped finish.
5 Brushed finish.
6 Pebble-dash.
7 Roughcast.
8 Tyrolean finish.

In each case the lime can be replaced by another plasticiser, or a masonry cement can be used, following the manufacturer's recommended mix proportions. Coloured cement can also be used. Adequate drying time should be allowed between successive coats so that drying shrinkage is not transmitted through to the final coat.

Internal plastering
The object of plastering is to provide a finished surface for backgrounds. Internal plastering is usually classified as plastering which is based principally on one of two binders: Portland cement or gypsum plaster.

Hydraulic limes are alternatives to Portland cement. In each case sand and/or lime may be added. However, in adopting these simple classifications it should be remembered that in particular cases the amount of lime in the mix may exceed the amount of the binder. For example, a final coat might consist of non-hydraulic lime gauged with a small proportion of gypsum plaster. Also, there are some special thin-wall plasters in use, which consist of a finely ground mineral substance with an organic binder such as polyvinyl acetate (PVA).

Concrete
Concrete is an artificial material, similar in appearance and properties to some natural limestones. It is formed by binding together particles of natural or artificial stone, brick or other aggregate with cement. One of the important properties of concrete is the ease with which it can be moulded to any shape before hardening occurs.

Normal concrete is distinguished from mortar by the fact that it contains coarse aggregate, in addition to fine aggregate and cement. However, there are special types of concrete which dispense with either the fine, or the coarse, aggregate. The traditional type of concrete, made with normal-density fine and coarse aggregates, cement and water, is classified as dense concrete, and this is the type discussed below.

Water content and voids
The presence of coarse aggregate in concrete results in a hardened material which is far stronger than can be obtained using a mortar mix of the same cement content. This effect is achieved indirectly because less water is needed to produce a workable mix when coarse aggregate is added. This fact is fundamental in the study of concrete.

The setting and hardening of concrete is due to the hydration of the cement binder. This is a crystallisation process, and the aggregate can normally be considered as an inert constituent. The amount of water necessary for the complete hydration of 1 kg of ordinary Portland cement is roughly 0.25 kg but if these amounts of cement and water are mixed together, the resulting ce-

the workability necessary for handling and placing the mix. Unfortunately, the effect of this excess water for workability is to form voids, or pores, in the hardened mortar or concrete, as the material dries out. These pores (water-voids) cause a reduction in the density, strength and durability of the concrete. It follows that the water content of the mixes normally should be kept as low as possible, consistent with providing adequate workability to allow placing and full compaction. Compaction entails the removal of air from the concrete by vibration or punning (rodding), a practice made necessary because air-voids will equally reduce the strength of concrete.

Water:cement ratio

It is usual to express the amount of water in any mix as a ratio of the weight of cement present. If this rule is applied to the case where a cement paste with the minimum water is used to fully hydrate the cement, the equation will be:

Water:cement ratio

$$= \frac{\text{Weight of water in mix}}{\text{Weight of cement in mix}}$$
$$= \frac{0.25 \text{ kgf}}{1 \text{ kgf}} = 0.25$$

The range of water:cement ratios used in practice for ordinary dense concrete is between approximately 0.40 and 0.80.

Bricks, blocks and clay products
Clay as a raw material

disintegration of primary (igneous) rocks, and their composition varies. Clays are composed mainly of silica and alumina (aluminium oxide), together with other compounds, such as iron oxides, lime, magnesia and water. In raw clay the alumina is usually combined chemically with the silica as hydrated aluminium silicates, but silica may also be present in clay as intermixed sand. Clays containing large amounts of such sand are termed loams. Some other clays, containing chalk in quantity, are referred to as marls. Kaolin (china clay) is a clay consisting almost wholly of pure hydrated aluminium silicate, and is useful because it has special properties, e.g. it can be used in fire-resisting cement. Because of its white colour, it is also used in the manufacture of white Portland cement. Bauxite is the name given to clay that is rich in hydrated aluminium oxide. It is an ore of the metal aluminium and a raw material of aluminous cements.

A plastic or pure clay is one containing a high proportion of alumina, and this group includes the more workable raw clays. The texture of clays ranges from the more workable or plastic types to the very hard, laminated clays, termed shales, which approach the character of slates. Slates themselves are a highly densified form of clay. The wide variation in the composition and texture of raw clays leads to corresponding variations in the physical properties of fired clay, and the nature of the clay itself governs the types of product for which it is suitable.

Firing

Silica alone will not melt except at exceedingly high temperatures, but together with alumina and in the presence of a flux, such as lime or iron oxide, it will fuse at much lower temperatures. The firing of the raw clay entails heating it to at least the point of incipient fusion, which varies with the clay's composition, but is well over 1000 °C.

Plastic clays are not generally as suitable for firing at such high temperatures as clays with a high silica content, because the high shrinkage of the alumina gives them a tendency to warp and crack. As a result, plastic clays in general give a light, porous but strong product, quite suitable for most classes of bricks, blocks and roofing tiles. The higher temperatures at which clays of high silica content can be fired will produce the semi-vitrification and high density usually associated with engineering bricks, unglazed clay pipes, quarry tiles, terra-cotta and faience. Such clays are also used in some roofing tiles. The best clays in this category are those which formed earliest in the earth's history, since they are less liable to warp and crack during firing. Such clays are found near the coal measures of Great Britain.

Clays which can be fired satisfactorily at very high temperatures are, of course, used in the making of firebricks, which are able to resist temperatures ranging from about 1200 to 1800 °C. Products which can withstand these temperatures are called refractories, and suitable clays are known as fireclays. Their silica content ranges from about 70% for average refractory bricks to about 95% for bricks of the highest refractoriness, known as silica bricks.

Products which are underfired, in terms of temperature or time, are liable not to be durable, especially if used externally and in exposed situations.

Iron oxides, although their total extent in clays is only a few per cent, have an important influence on the colour of fired clay, as well as acting as a flux. The colour may vary from pink, through red to blue, in order of increasing maximum firing temperature, but depending also on the extent to which oxidation can occur under the particular kiln conditions. A yellow colour is usually associated with magnesia.

The influence of limestone, or chalk, as a flux has already been mentioned. However, this should not be present as lumps, as their conversion to quick-lime during firing would produce unsoundness in the finished product and might lead to lime-blowing at surfaces.

Expansion of clay products

After leaving the kiln, clay products take up moisture from the atmosphere and undergo slight expansion in the process. This action may continue, at a decreasing rate, over a number of years before the equilibrium condition is reached, during which the total expansion may be up to 0.1% or more. Since the greater part of this long-term expansion normally occurs during the first ten days after leaving the kiln, it is advisable not to lay bricks or other clay products until after this period. This expansion, which is regarded as irreversible, is distinct from the very slight moisture movement which can occur at any time.

Clay brick classification

Bricks may be classified in relation to their use, namely, as engineering bricks, facing bricks, common bricks and specials.

Engineering bricks are used mainly for their structural value and impermeability, and the essential properties are a high compressive strength, together with a very low water absorption. Associated characteristics are a high density and some degree of vitrification. Well-known examples are Staffordshire blue, Accrington red and Southwater, each named after their place of origin.

Facing bricks are bricks of good appearance or architectural value. They include sand-faced and rustic varieties, and some of the better stock bricks.

Common bricks are those which cannot be classified as engineering or facing bricks.

They include bricks for internal or external use, where neither high strength nor low water absorption is essential, and where appearance is relatively unimportant.

Special bricks are those made to serve spe-

8 Drying.
9 Firing.

The weathering stage is often omitted entirely, as it is nowadays only used for some of the best quality facing bricks.

Many natural clays are suitable for brickmaking without the addition of other materials, but some require blending to achieve a suitable composition. Clay bricks are moulded into shape while they are in the raw, plastic condition and are then fired. During firing, certain physical and chemical changes occur which cause the brick to solidify to its final shape. Substantial shrinkage of the brick occurs during this time, and this must be allowed for when moulding in order to achieve the desired finished size. Finished dimensions must conform to certain standard sizes and tolerances so that the bricks can be laid to the correct levels and with regular joints.

The sequence of operations used in preparing and processing the raw clay varies according to its composition and hardness. Any of the following stages may be included but not necessarily in the order given.

1 Clay digging (usually by mechanical methods).
2 Weathering (to break down the clay).
3 Washing and screening.
4 Grinding (for hard clays and shales).
5 Blending (addition of chalk, lime sand, breeze, etc.).
6 Tempering (addition of water and kneading to the required consistency).
7 Moulding (shaping) or extruding. This stage may include the sanding of one or more brick surfaces to produce a sand-faced brick.

masonry blocks, it is quite common to find the exterior, or interior, face of a building clad with thin stone facing slabs attached to brickwork or other backing, supported by a structural steel or reinforced concrete frame. This is a classic example of a balanced blending of natural and artificial materials to their best advantage.

Fixing stone cladding
In fixed stone cladding, the slabs are commonly fixed by metal cramps, anchors and dowels, let into grooves in the slab and built or cast into the backing, or bolted to the frame of the building. It is usual to leave a clearance of about 10 mm or more between the back surface of the facing slabs and the backing material. With thin slabs, up to about 50 mm thick, this gap is usually left unfilled, and by preventing capillarity over much of the area the weather resistance of an external wall is thus improved. The likelihood of salts passing from the backing into the stone facing to cause efflorescence is also reduced. A further precaution against this is to keep the work dry during the period of construction by covering it if necessary. If joints between slabs are left open this prevents water from being trapped behind the facings, otherwise special provision is required to deal with this. These thin facings are likely to undergo high differential thermal movements so that where jointing mortars are used these should not be too strong, and the inclusion of mastic expansion joints

is necessary. With thick facing slabs the clearance space is often filled with a grout. Modern methods of fixing stone cladding include the use of synthetic resin adhesives.

Painter's materials

Painting is the application of a thin coating of material in a liquid or plastic condition to a surface, as a decorative or protective measure. The applied coating is normally required to dry out or harden to a solid film. The coating applied can vary widely in its composition and chemical and physical properties, depending on the nature of the surface being coated, the method of application and the requirements with regard to decoration and protection of the work in hand. The materials used by the painter are of different classes, such as paints, varnishes, stains and preservatives.

The paint may be applied by brushing, spraying, dipping, or by roller. In the early days of the craft the painter mixed his own materials, and the exact ingredients and their proportions were regarded to a certain extent as secrets of the trade. Eventually, and inevitably, there appeared on the market the ready-mixed products, now made by specialist manufacturers to proprietary formulations, or to the larger customers' specifications.

The range of natural and synthetic (man-made) materials now being used in the making of paints, and the range of different products now available, is so vast that a simple classification of these would be very difficult. It is therefore important that the user should take careful note of the manufacturer's instructions and recommendations regarding selection, storage, preparation, application, subsequent treatment and maintenance of their products. Their advice should be sought when in doubt.

Paint composition

A paint consists essentially of one or more solid materials, called the pigment, and a liquid, known as the vehicle or medium.

Pigments The pigment is usually present in powder form, in suspension in the vehicle. Its function may be to provide the opacity ('hiding power') and colour of the paint film, or to confer durability or corrosion resistance to the surface painted, or both. Pigments are, in the main, inert white or coloured powders, such as metallic oxides or salts, although they may in some cases have a chemical influence on the hardening of the paint film. They are obtainable in powder form, or sometimes mixed with oil or water as a paste.

Paint vehicle The vehicle, or medium, is the liquid part of a paint. Its primary function is to facilitate application by giving the paint mobility (the ability to flow), but it often also serves as a binder for the pigment on drying, and gives adhesion to the surface painted. In fact, the nature of the vehicle will largely determine the characteristics and properties of the hardened (dry) paint film. The vehicle may also include a thinner, such as turpentine (a tree extract) or white spirit (a petroleum derivative), added to give increased mobility. Water, various volatile solvents (often with gum or resin content), emulsions, drying oil and oil varnish are used as vehicles.

A volatile solvent is a liquid which dissolves a substance (the film-forming constituent) but which readily evaporates, leaving behind the dissolved substance unaltered chemically. These include various alcohols (e.g. methylated spirit), naphthas and other coal-tar derivatives, and a very wide range of other organic chemicals.

Other paint ingredients Other special ingredients which may be present in small amounts include driers to assist hardening, plasticisers to improve the flexibility of the hardened paint film and extenders to improve working characteristics and film-forming properties, or to assist the suspension of the pigment.

Paint types

The main types of paint are emulsion paints, water paints and distempers, solvent paints, oil paints, hard gloss paints, enamels and synthetic resin paints.

Emulsion paints The typical emulsion paint is a synthetic resin, e.g. polyvinyl acetate (PVA), emulsified in water, but other emulsifiable binders are oils, oil varnish, resins, rubbers and bitumen. Other ingredients are

hardened films are washable, and some are suitable for external use. PVA emulsion paints are alkali-resistant and so may be used on cement, concrete, asbestos-cement and plaster. They are suited to roller and brush application.

Water paints These have a vehicle composed of a drying oil varnish or natural resin emulsified in water, usually together with a stabiliser, such as glue size or casein. Water paints are, in fact, emulsion paints, although they are not classified as such commercially. Pigments and extenders are added and the product is usually supplied in the paste form mixed with water, to be thinned with water by the user to the consistency required for application. These paints give a permeable paint film which is washable when hard, and most are unaffected by alkalis. They are used mainly for interior decoration but some are suitable for external use.

Distempers These differ from water paints in that they do not contain a drying oil, oil varnish or resin and they are not emulsified. They consist of a pigment and extender with a water-soluble binder such as glue size, and are supplied either in the mixed powder form or as a paste in water. They are prepared for use by adding water. As distempers are suitable for internal use only they are also known as soft distempers to stress the fact that they are non-washable and easily rubbed off. The main use is on ceilings, or as a temporary decoration for new walls.

Solvent-type paints These include various forms of rubber-based paint, such as cyclised rubber and chlorinated rubber varieties, bituminous and tar paints and cellulose enamels. These paints dry essentially by evaporation

Both rubber-based and bituminous paints are particularly resistant to water, water-vapour and most chemicals, but should only be applied on dry surfaces. Most are subject to gradual degradation when exposed to direct sunlight, resulting in colour-fading (or greying in the case of blacks), and to progressive reduction of film thickness due to weathering. They have been widely used on both metals and alkaline surfaces (concrete, rendering and composition cement).

The use of cellulose paints, based on nitrocellulose, is confined mainly to spray application on metals. These paints are characterised by the high gloss and wide range of colours obtainable, but have a comparatively thin finished film thickness.

Oil paints These have a vehicle consisting of a drying oil, or oil varnish, mixed with a thinner. They are typified by the group based on linseed oil mixed with white spirit, which constitute the traditional ready-mixed oil-based paints, but other natural and synthetic oils and thinners are also used. These paints are obtainable in a wide variety of colours and suit most purposes for both internal and external use.

Hard gloss paints These have a vehicle consisting of a specially treated oil varnish or drying oil (with or without resin) mixed with a thinner. They are capable of giving a better gloss than ordinary oil paints, and often dry more rapidly. They can be used externally, although their durability may not equal that of a good quality oil paint.

Enamel paints An enamel is a variety of hard gloss paint with special properties of drying to an exceptionally brilliant gloss finish, and possessing remarkably good flow characteristics in application. These are usually achieved by using best quality pale elastic (e.g. copal) varnish and limiting the amount of pigment added. They are not usually suited to external use, as they are less resistant to weathering than good quality oil paints.

Synthetic resin paints These have as their vehicle a synthetic resin, with or without drying oils and solvents. A good example is provided by the alkyd paints, which are paints based on alkyd resins, often with added drying oil, which can offer high gloss coupled with long life under severe exposure. These also have good flow properties in application and are quick-drying, with good adhesion and flexibility.

Other types are the epoxy and urethane paints based on epoxy and polyurethane resins, respectively. Both are obtainable as two-pack products, in which case one pack contains a curing agent which sets off the hardening action as soon as they are mixed together. Polyurethane types are also available as a one-pack product. These paints are obtainable in coloured forms, or clear for use as varnishes. They are highly resistant to water and chemicals and are capable of providing a very hard-wearing surface. Uses include their application to timber, concrete and metals.

Special paints

Silicate paints These are based on water-soluble alkaline silicates (e.g. sodium silicate), which become insoluble on drying. Their main uses are as a weather-protective coating on concrete, brick, asbestos-cement and similar surfaces, and as fire-retardants.

Neoprene paints These are based on a proprietary synthetic rubber. They are usually of a two-part type with a vulcanising agent acting as 'catalyst'. They are resistant to chemicals and weathering.

Cement paints These unconventional paints consist essentially of a white or coloured Portland cement, in powder form, to which water is added. They are used mainly on concrete and rendering.

Plastic paints This name is given to paints which are applied with the consistency of a thick cream, which allows them to be textured before they set or harden. They are based on such materials as gypsum, or whiting, with a gelatinous binding agent.

Thixotropic paints These are paints which have the character of a thick cream or gel when undisturbed, but which are free-flowing when subjected to a shearing action, as during brush application. They are also referred to as 'one coat', 'non-drip' or 'non-sag' paints.

Stoving paints/enamels These are paints designed to be cured (hardened) by baking, usually at a temperature above 60°C, after application, e.g. in an oven or by exposure to infra-red radiation. Included in this group are varieties of the thermosetting synthetic resin types.

Silicones These include a full range of synthetic paint types, based on silicon–oxygen compounds, including water-repellent solutions and emulsions, heat-resisting resin-based paints and silicone–organic copolymer types. Silicon liquids are also used as additives to organic synthetic resin paints as modifiers.

Other finishes

Stains These are used mainly to colour or tint new timber, without obscuring its natural grain or figure. They consist of dyes or translucent pigments in water, an organic solvent or a drying oil, sometimes with a preservative. Some are suitable for external use alone and can give protection equal to paint treatments; others can be over-painted with a clear varnish.

Oil varnish The use of oil varnish as a paint vehicle has already been mentioned. It is also used itself as a clear, or tinted finish, mainly on timber. For external use a suitable grade is required, and up to four coats may be specified for some types to give good durability.

Spirit varnishes These consist of a resin di-

natural and synthetic resins and are used mainly on interior timber surfaces, such as floors, to maintain gloss and provide protection against wear. Emulsified varieties are available.

Miscellaneous products

Knotting This is a sealer applied to the knots of resinous timber before painting. Usualy it consists of shellac dissolved in methylated spirit.

Size This is a solution of water-soluble glue of the animal extract, starch or cellulosic types.

Clearcole This is a prepared solution of size tinted with whiting. It is used to adjust the suction of a plastered surface before applying a size-bound distemper.

Petrifying liquid This is a water-paint medium, used either as a thinner for oil-bound water paint or to precede its application, in order to adjust suction.

Driers These are substances added to paints to reduce their drying times, e.g. compounds of lead, manganese or cobalt in the case of oil paints. For convenience they are usually blended with oils and solvents in a liquid preparation.

Paint schemes

Some paint treatments consist simply of applying one or more coats of a single material, possibly varying the amount of thinners in successive coats. Examples include the

solvent-type paints, and emulsion paints. In other cases successive coats may need to be of different compositions, in which case the whole process is referred to as a paint scheme. The need for a paint scheme arises

with an oil paint an increase in the ratio of pigment to oil will lead to greater opacity but with corresponding reductions in gloss and, usually, durability. In practice, a full paint scheme using one of the traditional finishes such as oil paint, hard gloss or enamel will normally require at least three coats, each of different composition and referred to respectively as the priming coat, the undercoat and the finishing or final coat.

Primer The function of the priming paint or primer may be to give protection against corrosion of metals or against dampness, especially of site-stored joinery. Priming paint can also be used to adjust the suction of a surface (e.g. of plaster, concrete or timber) and provide good adhesion for subsequent coats. Alternatively, it can act as a barrier coat to isolate one coat from a preceding coat, e.g. to prevent chemical interaction.

Undercoat paints The function of an undercoat is mainly to obliterate the background and provide a uniformly dense tone or colour to assist the finish. It is also required to provide good adhesion for the finished coat. It follows that undercoat paints tend to be heavily pigmented and usually need to be sealed against the weather by a finishing coat.

Finishing paints These give the required reflection characteristics to the painted surface (flat, eggshell or high gloss) and of course give the final colour. In the case of exterior paints, finishing paints must also seal the surface against the weather, and some elasticity may be desirable.

Plastics

Plastics are a group of materials which harden during manufacture from a condition in which they can be moulded to any desired shape. Plastics are formed from materials that are typically of organic composition by a process of molecular growth known as polymerisation.

Organic substances and polymerisation

Organic substances are compounds principally of carbon and hydrogen, often together with other elements, notably oxygen, nitrogen, sulphur and the halogens (fluorine, chlorine, bromine and iodine). Polymerisation is the linking together of like molecular units, termed monomers, to form a chain, or grid-like structure, known as a polymer. The polymerised substance is liable to possess physical and chemical properties which are vastly different from those of the monomer. In fact, it is possible to vary the final properties by controlling the size and arrangement of the molecular chains during manufacture. For example, increasing the length of the 'chains' results in a higher softening temperature and usually greater strength.

The process of polymerisation is usually brought about by subjecting the raw material (the monomer form) to the action of one or more influences such as light, heat, pressure or a catalyst (a substance which promotes a chemical reaction). Plastic materials produced in this way are synthetic, but some polymers also exist in naturally occurring substances. Examples include cellulose and starch, protein compounds, rubber latex and natural resins (e.g. shellac, copal and rosin).

Cellulose is the substance of the cell walls of plants and is a polymer of glucose. For commercial use, it is obtained from the cotton plant, which is the purest source, from wood and from straw. It is classified chemically as a carbohydrate, which means that it is composed of carbon, hydrogen and oxygen only.

Starch, like cellulose, is based on the glucose monomer, and is present in plants as a source of nutriment.

Proteins are a group of organic nitrogenous compounds in polymerised form, which make up the main structure of all plant and animal tissue. They are based on monomer of certain amino acids. Two sources of protein, which were important in the early days of the plastics industry, are casein, which comes from milk, and the soya bean.

Rubber latex is a tree extract based on a monomer called isoprene. Copal, rosin and rubber latex are extracts of certain species of trees, and shellac is an extract of certain insects.

All these naturally occurring polymers – cellulose, starch, proteins, rubber latex and resins – have what is described as straight chain, or linear, molecular construction which means that the monomers are linked end-to-end in a single row. The polymer is simply made up of a series of these chains lying together with their lengths parallel to a common axis, but with their ends overlapping. With this picture in mind, it is obvious that the ease with which these chains (the polymers) can be caused to slide over one another will depend to a great extent on the length of the individual chains and the amount of twist (the angle between alternate 'links' of each chain) in them. Such features profoundly influence the strength, flexibility and resistance to heat and moisture absorption of the plastic material.

Thermoplastic and thermosetting plastics

The straight-chain polymer plastics are softened by heat and will reharden on cooling, i.e. they are thermoplastic, and may therefore be reshaped or remoulded. This can be a useful property in the manufacture and working of the plastic materials. Other plastics are thermosetting, that is, once formed they cannot be resoftened by heat. In the thermosetting plastics the monomers are typically arranged to form a two- or three-dimensional, grid-like structure, or with the chains cross-linked. In general, the thermosetting plastics are more heat-stable and more resistant to solvent action than the thermoplastic ones.

erials which may be incorporated during the manufacture of a plastic material to serve some specific purpose include solvents, plasticisers, fillers and colouring agents. Solvents are used to give the material greater plasticity during the manufacturing stage, usually to facilitate moulding to the desired shape. Examples are acetone and chloroform. Plasticisers are usually non-volatile organic solvents with high boiling points, added to reduce the brittleness or increase the flexibility of the finished plastic material. Fillers are added to modify one or more properties of the finished plastic material; for example, as reinforcing agents to improve strength (e.g. glass fibre) or toughness (e.g. woodflour), or to confer heat resistance (e.g. asbestos). Colouring agents may be either dyes or pigments.

Present-day sources and properties of plastics
The majority of plastics in everyday use are produced from derivatives of coal-tar, mineral oil (petroleum) and natural gases. Plastics with a wide range of different properties are available. In general, plastics are resistant to water and chemicals, but are softened and expanded by organic solvents. Many thermoplastics have comparatively low softening points and high thermal expansion coefficients. They are easily moulded to complex shapes in manufacture, e.g. by casting, pressing, extrusion or injection moulding, and most can be foamed or expanded to lightweight cellular form. They provide products which are clean, comparatively light, easy to fix and in many cases, self-finished.

Types of plastics

cellulose acetate, which has similar properties and is formed by interacting cellulose with acetic acid and acetic anhydride together with a catalyst. This material finds a multiplicity of uses, mainly in small articles such as door furniture and fittings generally. It is useful for its clarity, when unpigmented, and its toughness, but it expands when exposed to moisture. Similar products, which were developed later, with greater moisture resistance include cellulose proprionate and cellulose acetate butyrate.

Casein plastics These plastics are made by immersing the thermoplastic casein in formalin (a solution of the gas formaldehyde in water), which cures (hardens) it by causing cross-linkage between the polymers. The curing process, known as formalising, is rather lengthy. These plastics are little used in the building industry.

Phenolic resins The name bakelite was given to the first fully synthetic plastic material to be made, by the interaction of phenol (carbolic acid) with formaldehyde. Both substances are obtainable from coal-tar. Phenol formaldehyde, often called PF resin, or simply 'phenolic' is a thermosetting plastic.

Phenol is the junior member of the phenol group of compounds, which also includes cresol and resorcinol. Any plastic made by the interaction of a phenol with formaldehyde (or other aldehyde) is classed as a phenolic resin. Phenolic resins are widely used for fittings and adhesives. They have high heat resistance but are not highly resistant to impact, unless specially reinforced.

Amino plastics Formaldehyde monomers are also interacted with urea to form urea formaldehyde (UF) and with melamine to form melamine formaldehyde (MF), both of which are thermosetting plastics. The fact that both contain the amine radical (NH_2) in their molecular formula results in their being termed amino plastics. They are obtainable in many attractive colours, and, apart from other uses, are popular as laminated plastic sheets, which consist of multi-layered plastic-impregnated paper, or when fabric bonded under heat and pressure. Melamine resins are renowned for their resistance to abrasion and heat, and are therefore used for wear-resisting surfaces. Both amino plastics are used as adhesives.

Vinyl plastics These are thermoplastics based on acetylene gas, and polyvinyl chloride and polyvinyl acetate are the typical examples.

Polyvinyl chloride, or PVC, made from the vinyl chloride monomer, is produced in both rigid (unplasticised) and flexible (plasticised) forms, and is widely used in the building industry. The plasticised form is a tough, rubber-like material which has high chemical resistance and is non-flammable. It is useful as a waterproof membrane and as a floor and wall covering in its tile and roll forms. The unplasticised form is used for roofing sheets, rainwater goods, plumbing fitments and pipes, although there is some limitation owing to its low softening point (70–80 °C).

Polyvinyl acetate, or PVA, is made from the vinyl acetate monomer. It can be emulsified in water for use as a paint base or adhesive, and is also mixed in with concrete to give it resilient properties. In addition, it can be added to plastering, rendering and floor toppings to improve their bonding properties.

Polystyrene The styrene monomer is made by reacting benzene with ethylene. The polymerised form, known as polystyrene, has also been called polyvinyl benzene, because it is structurally similar to the vinyl resins. This thermoplastic is a naturally transparent solid with high resistance to water and chemicals, and although it is somewhat brittle, it can be modified in manufacture to give tougher forms. It is perhaps best known in the building industry in its expanded (lightweight) form, in which it is used as insulating sheets.

Polythene Polythene, or polythylene, is made by heating ethylene gas under pressure, which causes polymerisation of the ethylene monomer. It is a thermoplastic, popular for pipes and plumbing fittings and as a damp-proof, curing membrane or weather-shield.

Polythene for general purposes is available in the density range 0.92–0.96, and its rigidity and softening point increase with density. Low-density polythene is softened by water near boiling point and so cannot be used for hot water services. In its natural, translucent form it degrades in sunlight as embrittlement and cracking are caused by ultra-violet rays, and it is consequently often heavily pigmented with carbon black in manufacture to prevent this happening. It has a relatively high coefficient of thermal expansion which varies with density, but has the advantages of flexibility (which prevents frost damage), lightness (it floats on water) and corrosion resistance.

Polypropylene This may be regarded as a close chemical relative of polythene, but is based on the propylene monomer. The important differences are that polypropylene has a higher softening temperature (135 °C) and greater resilience, and is used extensively for the manufacture of traps.

Polymethyl methacrylate (e.g. Perspex) This is classified as an acrylic resin, since the monomer (methyl methacrylate) is an acrylic acid derivative. It is a thermoplastic and is important because of its high degree of transparency to light. It is used for window glazing and as corrugated roof-light sheets, tiles and panelling, as well as for lighting fittings, some plumbing fittings (when reinforced) and as a base for a solvent-type adhesive.

Nylon This is a thermoplastic co-polymer, produced from phenol and ammonia, and is chemically a super (long-chain) polyamide. The length of the chain can be varied to produce grades of nylon with different prop-

Polyester and alkyd resins These plastics are usually thermosetting, but some forms are thermoplastic, depending on the form of the monomer. They are made by the interaction of certain organic acids with alcohols. Polyester resins are used in laminated construction, with glass fibre where high strength is required, e.g. as reinforced translucent sheeting. One class of polyesters, known as alkyd resins, is popular as a paint medium.

Epoxy resins These are made from certain petroleum derivatives and are extremely tough, with high heat and chemical resistance. They are used mainly as adhesives, in paints and as a binder in rendering and abrasion-resistant floor surfacing.

Polyurethanes These form a group of plastics with complex chemical structures. They have a number of specialised uses and can provide a hard, durable finish in paints, or act as a flexible mastic. They can also be foamed to give either a resilient or a rigid lightweight material.

Synthetic rubbers These are usually included in the class of flexible products known as elastomers, because of their special elastic properties. Elastomers are of particular importance as ingredients of mastics, adhesives and paints.

It is possible to synthesise latex (the natural raw material of rubber, obtained by tapping certain species of tree) by the polymerisation of isoprene, the monomer of which it is composed. In addition to polyisoprene, there are a number of other synthetic 'rubbers', each having slightly different characteristics, e.g. of softening point, hardness, flexibility, durability, flammability, chemical resistance and slipperiness when wet. Neoprene (polychloroprene) is a near relative to in its emulsified form in water, mixed with Portland, or other, cement and sand to provide resilient latex–cement flooring.

Silicones These form a distinctive group of polymeric substances based on both silica (silicon dioxide, SiO_2) and carbon compounds. The range of products from this source is considerable, and continues to increase. Important products are silicone waterproofing and fire-retardant solutions, silicone resin paints and mould-release agents, silicone elastomer sealants and silicone rubbers. All these products resist extremes of temperature and are water repellent.

The preceding list of plastics represents just a few of the many synthetic plastic materials in use at the present time.

Summary of plastics

Plastic materials are a group of polymeric substances, and may be organic or synthetic.

During manufacture, the monomer units are polymerised or co-polymerised by the application of heat or pressure, or by the use of a catalyst. Other components may be solvents, plasticisers, fillers and colouring agents.

Thermosetting plastics (i.e. those which will not be re-softened by heat) have the monomers arranged in a grid-like structure.

Straight-chain polymers are typically thermoplastic (i.e. they will be re-softened by heat), but if the chains are cross-linked, then they are thermosetting.

Naturally occurring polymers include cellulose, starch, protein (e.g. in casein and soya beans), rubber latex and resins.

Cellulose (a polymer of glucose) is used to make the cellulose plastics, e.g. the thermoplastics cellulose nitrate (celluloid) and cellulose acetate.

Casein plastics are made by formalising the moulded (thermoplastic) casein (an amino acid polymer) to cause cross-linkage.

Phenolic plastics are thermosetting and are made by interacting a phenol with an aldehyde. Examples are phenol formaldehyde (bakelite) and resorcinol formaldehyde, PF and RF respectively.

Amino plastics include urea formaldehyde (UF) and melamine formaldehyde (MF) types, and are thermosetting.

Table 4.1   *Materials used in various plastics*

Type of plastic	Raw material	Properties (or uses)
Vulcanised fibre	Absorbent unsized paper, rags or cellulose pulp	Resistant to abrasion; tough; large impact strength; resistant to oils, fats, fuels and other organic liquids; can be bent, drilled, cut, planed, machined, etc.
Cellophane	Beech or plywood Cellulose Caustic soda Carbon disulphide Sulphuric acid	Glass-like transparency; does not stick to flesh; does not dissolve in boiling water; dust-proof; impermeable to most solutions; non-flammable; weatherproof; high tensile strength
Celluloid	Pure wood pulp	Clear as glass; may be coloured; resiliently elastic; can be machined or formed under heat; stable in water, acidic or alkaline solutions
Casein plastics	Milk Formaldehyde	Odourless; tasteless; tough; stable in organic solvents; absorb water slightly
Phenoplasts	Phenol Formaldehyde	Typical thermosetting properties (e.g. bakelite); heat resistant; tough; may be laminated
Aminoplasts	Urea-formaldehyde	Typical melamine-like thermoplastic; heat resistant; as a foam may be used for thermal or acoustic insulation; used in production of lacquers and varnishes
Glass fibre reinforced plastic	Glass fibres Unsaturated polyesters	Composite material combining the strength properties of the glass fibre with those of the synthetic resin – production of large-sized parts under high stress; good tensile, flectural and impact strength; resistant to most common chemicals
Cross-linked polyurethanes	Polyesters Ethylene Phosgene	May be produced as a foam with either flexible, semi-rigid or rigid properties with a wide range of density and low thermal conductivity values
Polyamides Linear polyurethanes	Adipic acid Benzene	Tough, hard, stiff, thermoplastic material – used to make parts for machinery; soluble only in concentrated acids but absorbs moisture slightly if exposed to too high a relative humidity
Polycarbonates	Phenol Acetone	Transparent; high refractive index; very hard and tough with elastic properties over a wide temperature range; resistant to all acids
PVC	Vinyl chloride	White powder; may be plasticised; easily moulded; resistant to atmospheric attack; stable in most liquids; high tensile strength
Polystyrene	Styrene	Transparent, hard, brittle material; may be moulded above 120°C; stable in water, acids and alkalis; may be copolymerised to produce a material with a very high mechanical strength
Polymethacrylates	Propylene Acetone Hydrocyanic acid	Light transmission values comparable to best crystal glass; high impact strength; resistant to scratching; light with good loadbearing characteristics; good electrical insulator; stable in water, alkalis, concentrated acids and most organic solutions
Polyolefines Polyethylene Polypropylene	Acetylene Petroleum Alcohol	Combustible; themoplastic; density can be varied during manufacture to increase impact strength, permeability, transparency, etc.; large degree of chemical stability
Silicones	Silicon compounds	Fluids are clear liquids with variable viscosity; good temperature stability; suitable as release agents in processing of plastics; as a water repellant; to add glass to wax polishes; to prevent pigment separation in lacquers; may be produced as an emulsion or a rubber

Polyvinyl chloride (PVC) and polyvinyl acetate (PVA) are vinyl plastics made from the monomers vinyl chloride and vinyl acetate, prepared using ethylene. They are thermoplastic PVC may be plasticised (rubbery)

compressing the heated gases ethylene and propylene respectively. Polythene is made in medium and high densities, often carbon-pigmented to resist sunlight. Polypropylene has a higher softening temperature and greater resilience than polythene.

Polymethyl methacrylate (Perspex) is a thermoplastic acrylic resin, useful because of its high natural transparency.

Nylons are thermoplastic polyamides which can have high softening temperatures, and high degrees of strength and toughness. They are self-lubricating.

Polyesters, made by reacting certain organic acids and alcohols, can be thermosetting or thermoplastic. Those used in paints are called alkyd resins.

Epoxy resins and polyurethanes are used mainly in paints and coatings, because of the toughness, flexibility and adhesion which they provide.

Synthetic rubbers include the polymers polyisoprene, polychloroprene (neoprene), polybutadiene (buna) and the co-polymers acrylonitrile-butadiene (nitrile rubber), iso-butylene-butadiene (butyl rubber), styrene-butadiene and ethylene-propylene.

Silicones are polymeric compounds based on silicon and oxygen. They are highly water repellent and resist extremes of temperature.

Plastics are tested for colour fastness, dimensional change and loss of volatile matter on heating, curling, indentation, deflection and impact, and also for their resistance to chemicals, oils and organic solvents.

Timber

Timber is valuable as a building material for a number of reasons. It is structurally useful because of its high strength in relation to its density. It is comparatively easy to work to a

Timber is an organic material (i.e. composed of carbon compounds) produced in the growth processes of a living tree. The main source of timber used in the building industry is the trunk (main stem) of the tree. The girth (circumference) of the trunk increases as the tree develops, and when the tree is thought to have reached maturity it is felled and the raw timber is converted (cut to baulks and planks) and seasoned (partially dried) before use.

The growth and structure of timber is most clearly illustrated by the three principal trunk sections (Figure 4.17) – the cross-section (or transverse section), radial section and

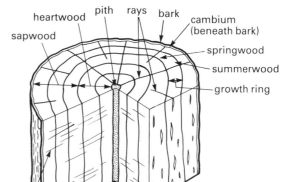

Figure 4.17 *The three principal trunk sections*

tangential section. The terms used in Figure 4.17 are explained below.

Growth

Growth takes place outwards from the centre of the trunk (except in bamboo and palm tree types, with which we are not concerned) and a new outer sheath of wood tissue is deposited during each growth period, or season. Each sheath, or layer, is termed a growth ring, and these concentric rings are in some cases clearly visible on inspection of the cross-section.

In temperate climates, as in the British Isles, growth takes place mainly in the spring and summer months, so that each growth ring normally represents one year's growth, and may then be referred to as an annual ring. In some tropical climates, however, the growing season is almost continuous and it is possible to have more than one growth ring during a year. Trees of rapid growth will tend to have wide growth rings, whereas slow growth is associated with narrow growth rings.

Growth in summer is slower than it is in spring, and this results in the summer wood (also called late wood) being stronger, and usually darker, than the spring wood (early wood). This variation in colour, or texture, is one means by which the growth rings are rendered distinguishable.

The pith, or heart centre, is a fibrous core of woody tissue forming the core of the trunk.

The sapwood is the more recently formed wood tissue, comprising the outer growth rings. It contains a large amount of sap (aqueous solution) and nutriment (food) for the growing tissue, and furnishes timber which has a somewhat lower natural durability than heartwood.

The heartwood is the inner part of the trunk, which provides the main strength to support the living tree, and which is substantially free of both sap and nutriment. Heartwood is often darker in colour than the surrounding sapwood, owing to chemical changes in certain substances (e.g. starch) present in the wood. In the growing tree the heartwood has ceased to contain living cells.

The cambium is an extremely thin, glutinous layer which forms a film at the outer surface of the sapwood, beneath the bark. It is the cambium which produces the wood tissue of the new growth ring, in addition to the much smaller proportion of bark required.

The bark is a protective outer layer of woody fibre, which periodically scales off as the trunk increases in girth, being renewed from its inside surface by the cambium.

Wood composition

Wood tissue is composed of various types of cells (the units of which living matter is composed). These cells have various shapes, but all consist of a wall enclosing a cavity. In the living tree the cavity will usually contain liquid matter. The living cells of the cambium are filled with a watery liquid called protoplasm. Cells produced by the cambium undergo a process known as lignification, in which the cell walls thicken, to form wood.

There are essentially three functions to be performed by the various types of wood cell. These are to conduct the sap, to provide storage space for food, and to provide the mechanical strength necessary for the support of the tree. To produce the substance of which the cells and foodstuffs are composed, the tree must first of all manufacture its own organic matter, the stuff of which all living tissue is made, and it achieves this by rather fascinating means. In the spring, sap, which is water containing various mineral salts in solution, is taken up from the soil by the roots of the tree and passes up through the sapwood into the branches. From the branches it passes into the leaves, where it is converted into carbohydrates (organic compounds of carbon, hydrogen and oxygen which are the tree's raw materials for foodstuffs) by a process known as photosynthesis. In this process, carbon dioxide is absorbed from the atmosphere and undergoes chemical action with the sap, using the sun's light as energy and the green colouring matter of the leaves (chlorophyll) as the catalyst (activator). Food material in solution then passes from the leaves back down the trunk through

Chemical nature of wood

The cell walls of wood are composed of cellulose, which, like starch and sugars, is a carbohydrate, and a substance called lignin (the non-carbohydrate constituent). The lignin acts as a cement, binding together the cellulose material in the cell walls to give the wood its strength and rigidity.

Softwoods and hardwoods

Commercially timbers are divided into two broad classes, according to whether they are from conifers (pine trees or firs), or from broadleaf trees. The conifers, which have needle-like leaves and are cone-bearing, furnish softwood timbers. The cones are exposed seeds. Hardwoods are furnished by broadleaved trees which have covered seeds. The two terms can be misleading, since although most hardwoods are in fact mechanically harder than most softwoods, this is not invariably the case. For example, pitch pine, although classified as a softwood, is mechanically harder than some hardwoods, whereas balsa and willow are notable examples of very soft hardwoods. Another distinction is that the hardwood trees are mainly deciduous (lose their leaves in winter) whereas the softwood ones are mainly evergreen.

Apart from the differences mentioned in defining softwoods and hardwoods, there are important differences in the cellular structure of the two groups.

Softwood structure
The softwoods have the more primitive structure, with only two types of cell, tracheids and parenchyma cells. Enlarged sections of these are shown in Figures 4.18 and 4.19. The tracheids are pod-like,

Figure 4.18 *A tracheid (section)*

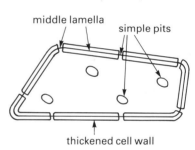

Figure 4.19 *A parenchyma cell (section)*

form the bulk of the timber, and are longitudinally arranged in the trunk and radially distributed about the pith. They have the dual role of conducting the sap and providing the tree's mechanical strength, and the cells develop thicker walls for this purpose. Parenchyma cells provide storage space for foodstuffs. They are brick-shaped and butt against one another to form chains, which are mainly horizontal and lie radially about the pith and are therefore called rays. However, they may also be in vertical chains, known as wood, or strand, parenchyma. Tracheids sometimes occur lying horizontally, in association with rays, and are then called ray tracheids.

Conduction between the different cells takes place through pits, which are areas of the cell walls that, because they have not undergone thickening during the process of lignification, are permeable to fluids. The two basic forms of pit are the simple pit and the bordered pit. Figure 4.20 shows these as

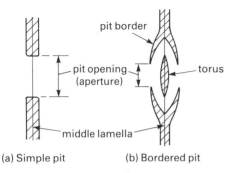

Figure 4.20   *Section through a cell wall at pits*

sections through the cell wall. They are seen in elevation at a smaller scale in Figures 4.18 and 4.19.

Simple pits have different shapes according to the species of timber in which they occur and it is these features which allow the positive identification of a particular species under microscopic examination. Bordered pits, which occur only in tracheids, can act as valves controlling the flow of sap or food-stuffs by movement of the disc-shaped thick-ened central region (the torus) in response to pressure.

Hardwood structure   There are four types of cell in hardwoods, i.e. fibres and vessels, in addition to parenchyma cells and tracheids. The fibres, which are needle-like in form (Figure 4.21) make up the bulk of the timber, and act as mechanical tissue. The vessels are cylindrical tubes (Figure 4.22) forming continuous vertical chains in the trunk to allow sap conduction. The circular or oval section of a vessel, as seen at a cross-section, is termed a pore. The parenchyma cells are of the same type as those in softwoods, with the same function of providing food storage. Tracheids are only occasionally present in

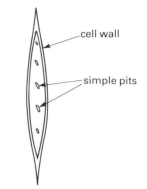

Figure 4.21   *A fibre (section)*

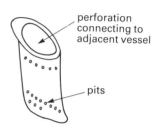

Figure 4.22   *A vessel*

hardwoods and are distinguished by their bordered pits.

Identification
Since the structure and composition of a particular timber will determine its properties and uses, identification of the species can be important. Apart from the commercial classification into softwoods and hardwoods, there is the botanical method of classification, in which each timber, or rather the tree from which it comes, belongs to a family, and within each family to a genus. Finally, each genus may give rise to a number of different species, which may be given a common, or local, commercial name.

Plywood, board and slab materials

Plywood
In spite of the fact that there is a tendency for the term plywood to be applied collectively to several forms of timber board (see Figure 4.23), for classification purposes and to avoid ambiguity in specification, a distinction must

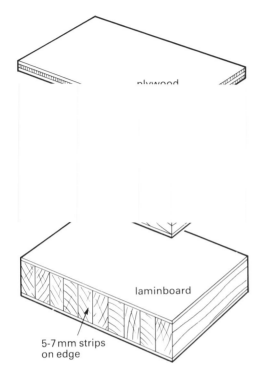

Figure 4.23 *Plywood, blockboard and laminboard*

be made between plywood of the traditional type and products such as blockboard and laminboard.

Plywood is a timber product consisting of a number of thin sheets or veneers of wood bonded together with an adhesive. Finished thicknesses vary from about 3 to 25 mm. The important characteristic of plywood is the vastly improved strength characteristics which result from bonding alternate veneers with the grain aligned in different directions, normally at right angles. Another benefit obtained by alternating the grain direction is a reduction in the maximum movement due to moisture changes, since the greater movement across the grain is restrained by the very small movement along the grain of adjacent veneers. A balanced construction, using an odd number of veneers (3, 5, 7 and so on), is usual, although not invariable, and reduces any tendency for distortion. Boards with more than three veneers are termed multiply.

The use of specially selected or expensive timbers for the surface plies only is economical. Veneers are always sorted for quality before they are used so that different grades of plywood can be manufactured to suit different purposes. The natural durability of the

of any size can be manufactured, which is a very important consideration to the user. The procedures of the remaining stages of manufacture – glueing, assembling, pressing and final conditioning – are fairly standard, but the amount of initial conditioning of the veneers before glueing varies. In general, the best quality boards are obtained by carefully drying the veneers to between 5 and 15% moisture content before glueing. Glueing 'wet' or 'semi-dry' veneers produces boards of lower quality and can cause an imbalance in the finished board, with possible warping, checking or splitting. In all cases, the boards should be finally conditioned to about 12% moisture content before dispatch.

Faced plywood Plywoods are obtainable with bonded facings of insulating, sound-absorbent, fire-resistant, abrasion-resistant or purely decorative sheeting (for example, of metals, plastics, or cork). Impregnated plywoods treated with preservatives and fire retardants are also available. Composite plywood boards have special core materials, such as foamed plastics or cork, to impart specific properties to the boards.

British Standards requirements Whenever plywood or similar products are needed it must be remembered that large quantities of these boards are imported and may not comply with the relevant British Standards. This does not, however, mean that they are inferior, and most manufacturers will support the quality of the material and give advice on its uses whenever necessary.

Blockboard

Blockboard is a board consisting of a core of wood strips about 25 mm wide sandwiched between outer veneers laid and glued with the grain at right angles to the core strips (Figure 4.23). The strips, usually of softwood, may be left unglued (stripboard) or may be glued together. The construction described is of three-ply blockboard (core and two single veneers), but five-ply blockboard (core and two double veneers) is also made. The finished thickness is from about 15 to 30 mm.

Laminboard

Laminboard is of similar construction to blockboard but has core strips of width 3–7 mm, glued together (Figure 4.23). The boards are usually heavier than blockboard, owing to the greater amount of adhesive used, and, in some cases owing to the use of denser timbers, often hardwoods.

Particle boards

Particle board, formerly called wood chipboard, consists of size-graded wood chips bonded together, usually under pressure and heat, by an adhesive which is normally a thermosetting synthetic resin. Adhesives of the urea formaldehyde type are often used, in which case the board is not suitable for external use. Boards of different thicknesses up to about 40 mm are obtainable in large sizes. Lower density boards are sometimes produced by an extrusion process instead of mechanical pressing, and these may be used to form a coreboard, which then has outer veneers of timber or other sheet materials applied to it. Boards with various facings and applied finishes are obtainable.

Wood wool slabs

Wood wool slabs are made by shredding timber into long fibres and binding these together with a cementing agent, usually ordinary Portland cement. The open-textured surface offers good sound absorption if left unfaced, or alternatively, provides good key for plaster and rendering. Slabs are made to various sizes, and are between 30 and 100 mm in thickness. Speical heavy duty grades and reinforced slabs are available to meet structural requirements.

Strawboard

Strawboard boards consist of compressed straw between millboard (a paper product) or other sheet materials and are usually about 50 mm thick. They can be supplied specially surfaced to receive plastering. The material normally has a high moisture movement, and should not be used in damp conditions.

Fibre building boards

Fibre building boards are made by pulping fibrous materials of vegetable origin, mainly timber, straining the mass to remove excess water and then pressing it with applied heat to cause binding of the fibres. The binding action may result from the lignin content of the wood alone, or other bonding agents may be added.

These boards are commonly classified as insulating boards, wallboards or hardboards, mainly according to their density and thickness, which govern their normal uses.

Insulating boards Insulating boards have low densities, up to 400 kg/m^3, and are not less than 10 mm thick. The three main types are (a) homogeneous insulating boards, used for their good thermal insulation, sound absorbency and anti-condensation properties, (b) bitumen bonded types, which are highly resistant to moisture, and (c) bitumen impregnated types, which are either grey (lightly impregnated) or black (heavily impregnated, e.g. for use in expansion jointing).

Wallboards Wallboards are very similar to insulating boards but may be slightly heavier, with density up to 480 kg/m^3, and are thinner, offering greater economy. Homogeneous types, termed building boards, are usually 8–10 mm thick, and laminated types are about 5 mm thick.

Hardboards Hardboards come in three grades, according to their density. Standard hardboards, with densities over 800 kg/m^3 and thicknesses of approximately 3–5 mm are general purpose building boards and

plastics, cork or glass fibre.

Corkboard
Corkboard is made by compressing granulated cork and applying steam heat. This

[...] able with different facing materials or surface treatments. Some are impregnated for fire resistance or perforated for sound absorbency and for use as peg-board. Composite types of board may contain a core of foamed

[...] condensation. It can also be used as a flooring material, as its texture deadens sound and it provides a decorative finish, either plain or patterned.

Self-assessment questions

1   Substances which allow electricity to flow through them are called:
    (a)   resistors
    (b)   insulators
    (c)   conductors
    (d)   convectors

2   Two materials that are good insulators are:
    (a)   polystyrene, fibreglass
    (b)   plywood, blockboard
    (c)   cement paints, hard gloss paints
    (d)   natural stone, gypsum plaster

3   The instrument used to measure the magnitude of an electric current is called a:
    (a)   voltmeter
    (b)   ammeter
    (c)   electromagnet
    (d)   monometer

4   Solvent cement joints may be formed on pipes made from:
    (a)   acrylinitrile butadiene styrene (ABS)
    (b)   pitch fibre
    (c)   polythene
    (d)   low carbon steel

5   A cold water pipe in a hotel kitchen may be insulated to prevent:
    (a)   electrical earthing
    (b)   condensation
    (c)   heat loss to the kitchen
    (d)   surface corrosion

6   Which one of the following groups of materials is potentially the most dangerous to health?
    (a)   hardwood, emulsion paint, plywood
    (b)   plastic, softwood, cork
    (c)   brick, plaster, concrete
    (d)   lead, mercury, asbestos

7   The abbreviation PVC refers to:
    (a)   polyethelene rubber
    (b)   protective varnish
    (c)   polyvinyl chloride
    (d)   polyethelene

8   Which of the following groups of materials is used to seal cracks or gaps or to act as a joint filler or jointing agent?
    (a)   cement, clinker, fine aggregate
    (b)   asphalt, bitumen, slate
    (c)   adhesives, mastics
    (d)   sand, lime, plaster

9   From which of the following does plywood derive its strength?
    (a)   direction of face grain
    (b)   type of timber used
    (c)   cross-banded veneers
    (d)   type of glue used

10   Concrete is formed by the binding together of:
    (a)   cement, sand, water
    (b)   cement, aggregate, water
    (c)   lime, water, sand, cement
    (d)   burnt clay, water, cement

5 Calculations

Introduction

In Books 1 and 2 the student was introduced to the basic knowledge required to understand and perform simple arithmetical problems up to and including the calculation of areas and volumes. Although it is not necessary for craft students to be able to perform involved calculations in order to pass the Craft Examination, it is both necessary and desirable for *all* students progressing to Advanced Level Studies and for practicing plumbers to be able to calculate correctly the requirments of a job for both the material required and for the costing of the work. The use of tables and calculators is now common practice in schools and colleges, as these enable the work to be simplified and are accepted generally for most examinations; never-the-less it is still of paramount importance for the student to be able to perform calculations using basic fundamental rules and methods. The calculations in this chapter will take the student past the syllabus requirement of the craft student and will introduce the work of the advanced student and/or craftsperson. If the step by step method illustrated is learned it should make the sometimes tedious work of calculation easier and more meaningful.

Good practice

1 Careful reading of the question is vital, for unless you comprehend the requirements clearly you will be unable to work out the problem satisfactorily.

2 It is worthwhile making a sketch of the object of the calculation; the solution is often much easier to understand when viewed this way.

3 Always start the solution by stating what you are proposing to do and by writing down the appropriate formula.

4 The worked solution should not be just a series of numbers but should in fact be laid out in clearly defined statements.

5 Each part of the work should be shown on a separate line with each equals sign ($=$) immediately below the preceding one.

6 It is also necessary to ensure that all the dimensions are given in the same units, i.e. all in millimetres or all in metres.

7 When performing calculations it is also good practice to develop the habit of drawing a line down the paper to form a margin and placing all the working out of the calculation in this margin exactly opposite the corresponding part for easy reference for yourself or for anyone who may have to check your work. A faint line should be drawn through this work to show that it is not part of the finished calculation.

Temperature

Since the introduction of SI units, the use of the British Fahrenheit scale for reading temperature has been superseded by the Celsius (centigrade) scale. Owing to the length of time required to complete the change-over and because there are still a great many components that are calibrated in degrees Fahrenheit it is desirable, if not even essential, to explain each of the scales, including the conversions from one scale to the other.

Conversion by mathematics

The fixed points on a thermometer are the freezing and boiling points of water. Other important and useful temperatures are shown in Table 5.1.

Table 5.1 *Useful temperatures*

Celsius	Location	Fahrenheit
0°	Freezing point (water)	32°
4°	Maximum density (water)	39.2°
20°	Average room temperature	68°
36.8°	Blood temperature	98.4°
43.3°	Bath water	110°
60°	Washing-up water	140°
65°	Primary return	149°
85°	Primary flow	185°
100°	Boiling point (water)	212°

As stated previously it may be necessary to convert degrees Celsius to degrees Fahrenheit or vice versa. By examination of the thermometers in Figure 5.1 it will be seen that on

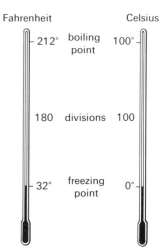

Figure 5.1 *Fahrenheit and Celsius thermometers*

one thermometer there are 180 divisions while on the other there are 100 divisions,

i.e. 180 divisions Fahrenheit
    100 divisions Celsius

$$\frac{\cancel{180}^{9}}{\cancel{100}_{5}} = \frac{9}{5}$$

This means that 9 divisions (degrees) Fahrenheit are equal to 5 divisions (degrees) Celsius, or that one degree Celsius is $\frac{9}{5}$ times greater than one degree Fahrenheit. It must also be understood that the Fahrenheit scale starts at 32° whereas the Celsius scale starts at 0° (freezing point).

1 The rule when converting a Fahrenheit temperature to Celsius is:

degrees Celsius
$$= \text{degrees Fahrenheit} - 32 \times \frac{5}{9}$$

2 The rule when converting degrees Celsius to Fahrenheit is:

degrees Fahrenheit
$$= \text{degrees Celsius} \times \frac{9}{5} + 32$$

These statements may be better understood once the following examples have been studied.

Example 1

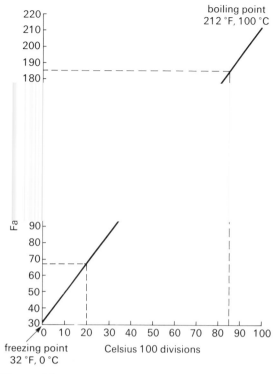

Figure 5.2   *Temperature conversion graph*

$$= 100° \text{ C}$$

Answer 212 °F = 100 °C

Example 2
Convert 20° Celsius to degrees Fahrenheit.

Rule   Degrees Celsius $\times \dfrac{9}{5} + 32$

$$\overset{4}{\cancel{20}} \times \dfrac{9}{\cancel{5}} + 32$$

$$= 4 \times 9 + 32$$

$$= 36 + 32$$

$$= 68 °\text{C}$$

Answer 20 °C = 68 °F

Solve the following problems:

1   Convert 85° Celsius to Fahrenheit.
                    (Answer = 185 °F)
2   Convert 140° Fahrenheit to Celsius.
                    (Answer = 60 °C)

Conversion by graph
An alternative method to that of solving the problem by the use of mathematics is to use a simple straight line graph. The accuracy of the graph will depend on the size of the graph, i.e. the scale of the drawing, and also on the accuracy of the drawing itself.

Figure 5.2 shows a possible graph with 100 divisions Celsius on the horizontal axis and 180 divisions Fahrenheit on the vertical axis.

Remember that the fixed points on the thermometer are the freezing point, 0° Celsius and 32° Fahrenheit, and the boiling point, 100° Celsius and 212° Fahrenheit. A straight line is drawn through the intersection of these two points. It is now an easy matter to read off any other temperature, as shown by the dotted lines, i.e. 20° Celsius is equivalent to 68° Fahrenheit and 185° Fahrenheit is equivalent to 85° Celsius.

Formulae

A formula is simply a shorthand method of writing down how several different terms are related to one another when solving calculation problems.

Example 3
Let us take a very simple formula such as the volume of a tank. To obtain the volume of the tank we must multiply the length by the

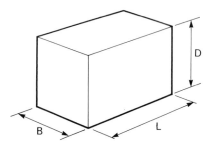

Figure 5.3

breadth by the depth. This is abbreviated to the formula:

$$V = L \times B \times D$$

where V = volume in cubic measure, L = length of tank, B = breadth of tank and D = depth of tank.

Example 4
The volume of a cylinder is obtained by multiplying the area of the base by the height of the cylinder. This is abbreviated to the formula

$$V = \pi \times r^2 \times h$$

where V = volume in cubic measure, π = pi (standard value of π is 3.142), r = radius of cyclinder and h = height of cylinder.

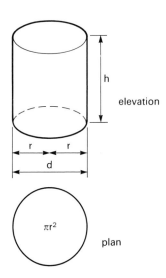

Figure 5.4

Transposing formulae
Transposing simply means changing the formula to make it simple to obtain the required unknown value. The following rules should make this sometimes troublesome procedure very simple to perform.

Let us take once again the simplest formula: V = L × B × D. The two very significant parts are:

(a) 'V' which is known as the subject of the formula
(b) '=' which is the equals or balancing point.

The important point to remember is to imagine that the formula is like a pair of scales and each side of the equals sign must be kept in balance (equilibrium) as shown in Figure 5.5.

Figure 5.5

Rule when transposing
1 An item which is moved from one side of the equation to the other *changes* its *sign*.

    (a) Multiplication becomes division.
    (b) Division becomes multiplication.
    (c) Addition becomes subtraction.
    (d) Subtraction becomes addition.
    (e) Roots becomes powers.
    (f) Powers becomes roots.

In other words, each becomes the exact opposite, or 'change the side, change the sign'. An alternative way of memorising the procedure is '*What you do to one side of the equation you must also do to the other side to maintain equilibrium*'.

Example 5
Let us return to our simple formula

$$V = L \times B \times D$$

Transpose the formula to make 'D' the sub-ject.
Rule: What you do to one side you must also do to the other side to maintain equilibrium.

so we divide by 'L' on the other side also.)

still in
equilibrium
$$\frac{V}{L \times B} = \frac{B \times D}{B}$$

(as above but with 'B')

still in
equilibrium
$$\frac{V}{L \times B} = D$$

('D' is now the subject of the formula.)

$$Answer\ D = \frac{V}{L \times B}$$

Let us now use the same formula but this time giving the letters simple values.

$$V = L \times B \times D$$

$$V = 4 \times 3 \times 2$$

equilibrium $24 = 4 \times 3 \times 2$

equilibrium $24 = 24$

Determine the value of 'D' in the formula.

equilibrium $\quad \dfrac{24}{4} = \dfrac{4 \times 3 \times D}{4}$

equilibrium $\dfrac{24}{4 \times 3} = \dfrac{3 \times D}{3}$

equilibrium $\dfrac{24}{4 \times 3} = D$

equilibrium $\quad 2 = D$

$$Answer\ D = 2$$

Having satisfactorily solved this simple prob-lem we can now attempt a slightly more diffi-cult formula.

Example 6

$$\frac{V}{\pi h} = \frac{\pi r^2}{\pi}$$

$$\frac{V}{\pi h} = r^2 \quad \text{(Remember powers become roots)}$$

$$\sqrt{\frac{V}{\pi h}} = r$$

$$Answer\ r = \sqrt{\frac{V}{\pi h}}$$

Example 7
Make 'h' the subject of the formula:

$$V = \pi r^2 h$$

$$V = \pi r^2 h$$

$$\frac{V}{\pi} = \frac{\pi r^2 h}{\pi} \quad \text{(Divide each side by } \pi)$$

$$\frac{V}{\pi r^2} = \frac{r^2 h}{r^2} \quad \text{(Divide each side by } r^2)$$

$$\frac{V}{\pi r^2} = h$$

$$Answer\ h = \frac{V}{\pi r^2}$$

Evaluation
Evaluation means the substituting of known values in a formula to find an unknown quan-tity.

Example 8
The volume of a rectangular tank is 1.8 m³. If the length is 2.0 m, and the width is 750 mm, calculate the depth of the water.
Note 1000 mm = 1 m
Formula: Volume of tank = L × B × D

$$1.8 = 2.0 \times \frac{750}{1000} \times D$$

Transpose to make D the subject of the formula.

$$1.8 = 2.0 \times 0.75 \times D$$

$$\frac{1.8}{2.0 \times 0.75} = D$$

$$\frac{1.8}{1.5} = D$$

$$1.2 = D$$

Answer D = 1.2 m

Example 9
A cylinder contains 150 litres of water. If its height is 915 mm, calculate its diameter.

Rule: (a) Convert litres to cubic metres.
     (b) Convert all the dimensions to the same unit (metres in this instance).
     (c) Transpose to obtain 'r' as the subject.

(a) $\frac{150}{1000}$ litres = 0.150 m³

(b) $\frac{915}{1000}$ mm = 0.915 m

(c) Formula for the volume of a cylinder = π × r² × h. Transpose to obtain 'r' as the subject of the formula.

$$V = \pi \times r^2 \times h$$

$$r = \sqrt{\frac{V}{\pi \times h}}$$

Evaluate $r = \sqrt{\frac{0.15}{3.142 \times 0.915}}$

Radius   = 0.23 m

Diameter = 0.46 m
         = 0.46 × 1000
         = 460 mm.

Answer Diameter of cylinder = 460 mm

Logarithms

By the use of logarithm tables the work of performing difficult and tedious calculations can be speeded up and with care, a little knowledge and practice, the tasks of *multiplication, division,* and finding *powers* and *roots* are made easier and more accurate. In logarithms all numbers are expressed by the power of a number called the base, which will be taken as 10 here. Various logarithm tables are available depending upon the type and accuracy of the work involved. In construction work four figure logarithm tables are the ones usually adopted. Logarithms consist of two parts:

(i) the *characteristic*, which is the number on the left-hand side of the decimal of the logarithm number.
(ii) the *mantissa*, which is the number on the right-hand side of the decimal point of the logarithm number and is obtained from the logarithm table.

The characteristic
Understanding and obtaining this part of the logarithm may be a little difficult at first but after carefully reading and following the worked examples no problems should remain. When working a calculation using logarithm tables the first operation is to fix the characteristic. This basically indicates how may 10s (tens) are involved and is determined by the position of the decimal point in the number. Conversely, it also fixes the position of the decimal point in the final answer.
    The characteristic of a number greater than unity is positive and is one less than the number of figures on the left of the decimal point.

Example 10
The characteristic of 42.00 = 1.
Count two digits on the left of the decimal point, less one = 1. Now follow the further
~~examples (note the decimal point)~~

~~The characteristic of a number less than unity~~
is negative and is one larger than the number of zeros on the right-hand side of the decimal point.

Example 12
The characteristic of 0.012 = $\bar{2}$.
Note the *bar* sign above the 2. This indicates a *minus* sign or *bar* sign. The characteristic is always one greater than the number of zeros after the decimal point. Now follow these further examples (note the decimal points).

Example 13

	Number	Characteristic
(i)	4.0	0
(ii)	0.40	$\bar{1}$
(iii)	0.040	$\bar{2}$
(iv)	0.004	$\bar{3}$

Until you are really familiar with this part of the work it may be good practice to make a small table starting with positive numbers and reducing to negative numbers.

Table 5.2

Number	Characteristic	Mantissa
100	2	.0000
10	1	.0000
1	0	.0000
0.1	$\bar{1}$	.0000
0.01	$\bar{2}$	.0000
0.001	$\bar{3}$	.0000

The mantissa
This is always positive and is *read directly* from a set of *logarithm tables* (see Table 5.3).

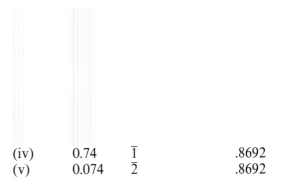

(iv)	0.74	$\bar{1}$	.8692
(v)	0.074	$\bar{2}$	.8692

Method of reading logarithm tables

Example 15
Find the logarithm number of 4234.0.

(i) Obtain the characteristic (one less than the number of figures to the left of the decimal point). There are 4 figures, therefore the characteristic is 3.

(ii) We now ignore the decimal point and take the first two figures, i.e. 42. Locate this number in the first column of the table.

(iii) The next figure, 3, is located on the top line in the first set of numbers 1–9, with the aid of a straight edge (rule) placed horizontally on number 42. By dropping down vertically from the figure 3 we obtain the figures 6263.

(iv) We now need to find the value of the fourth figure, which is 4. This is found in the mean difference columns situated on the right-hand side of the tables and numbered 1–9. With the straight edge still on 42 move along until you arrive at figure 4 in the difference column and obtain the figure 4.

(v) Add this figure to the first number found, i.e. 6263 + 4 = 6267. The logarithm number of 4234 will be 3.6267.

(vi) There are several different methods of

Table 5.3   *Logarithms*

	0	1	2	3	4	5	6	7	8	9	1	2	3	4	5	6	7	8	9
10	0000	0043	0086	0128	0170						4	8	13	17	21	25	30	34	38
						0212	0253	0294	0334	0374	4	8	12	16	20	24	28	32	36
11	0414	0453	0492	0531	0569						4	8	12	15	19	23	27	31	35
						0607	0645	0682	0719	0755	4	7	11	15	18	22	26	30	33
12	0792	0828	0864	0899	0934						4	7	11	14	18	21	25	28	32
						0969	1004	1038	1072	1106	3	7	10	14	17	20	24	27	31
13	1139	1173	1206	1239	1271						3	7	10	13	16	20	23	26	30
						1303	1335	1367	1399	1430	3	6	9	13	16	19	22	25	28
14	1461	1492	1523	1553	1584						3	6	9	12	15	18	21	24	27
						1614	1644	1673	1703	1732	3	6	9	12	15	18	21	24	27
15	1761	1790	1818	1847	1875						3	6	9	11	14	17	20	23	26
						1903	1931	1959	1987	2014	3	6	8	11	14	17	19	22	25
16	2041	2068	2095	2122	2148						3	5	8	11	13	16	19	21	24
						2175	2201	2227	2253	2279	3	5	8	10	13	16	18	21	23
17	2304	2330	2355	2380	2405						3	5	8	10	13	15	18	20	23
						2430	2455	2480	2504	2529	2	5	7	10	12	15	17	20	22
18	2553	2577	2601	2625	2648						2	5	7	10	12	14	17	19	21
						2672	2695	2718	2742	2765	2	5	7	9	12	14	16	19	21
19	2788	2810	2833	2856	2878						2	5	7	9	11	14	16	18	20
						2900	2923	2945	2967	2989	2	4	7	9	11	13	15	18	20
20	3010	3032	3054	3075	3096	3118	3139	3160	3181	3201	2	4	6	8	11	13	15	17	19
21	3222	3243	3263	3284	3304	3324	3345	3365	3385	3404	2	4	6	8	10	12	14	16	18
22	3424	3444	3464	3483	3502	3522	3541	3560	3579	3598	2	4	6	8	10	12	14	15	17
23	3617	3636	3655	3674	3692	3711	3729	3747	3766	3784	2	4	6	7	9	11	13	15	17
24	3802	3820	3838	3856	3874	3892	3909	3927	3945	3962	2	4	5	7	9	11	12	14	16
25	3979	3997	4014	4031	4048	4065	4082	4099	4116	4133	2	3	5	7	9	10	12	14	15
26	4150	4166	4183	4200	4216	4232	4249	4265	4281	4298	2	3	5	7	8	10	11	13	15
27	4314	4330	4346	4362	4378	4393	4409	4425	4440	4456	2	3	5	6	8	9	11	13	14
28	4472	4487	4502	4518	4533	4548	4564	4579	4594	4609	2	3	5	6	8	9	11	12	14
29	4624	4639	4654	4669	4683	4698	4713	4728	4742	4757	1	3	4	6	7	9	10	12	13
30	4771	4786	4800	4814	4829	4843	4857	4871	4886	4900	1	3	4	6	7	9	10	11	13
31	4914	4928	4942	4955	4969	4983	4997	5011	5024	5038	1	3	4	6	7	8	10	11	12
32	5051	5065	5079	5092	5105	5119	5132	5145	5159	5172	1	3	4	5	7	8	9	11	12
33	5185	5198	5211	5224	5237	5250	5263	5276	5289	5302	1	3	4	5	6	8	9	10	12
34	5315	5328	5340	5353	5366	5378	5391	5403	5416	5428	1	3	4	5	6	8	9	10	11
35	5441	5453	5465	5478	5490	5502	5514	5527	5539	5551	1	2	4	5	6	7	9	10	11
36	5563	5575	5587	5599	5611	5623	5635	5647	5658	5670	1	2	4	5	6	7	8	10	11
37	5682	5694	5705	5717	5729	5740	5752	5763	5775	5786	1	2	3	5	6	7	8	9	10
38	5798	5809	5821	5832	5843	5855	5866	5877	5888	5899	1	2	3	5	6	7	8	9	10
39	5911	5922	5933	5944	5955	5966	5977	5988	5999	6010	1	2	3	4	5	7	8	9	10
40	6021	6031	6042	6053	6064	6075	6085	6096	6107	6117	1	2	3	4	5	6	8	9	10
41	6128	6138	6149	6160	6170	6180	6191	6201	6212	6222	1	2	3	4	5	6	7	8	9
42	6232	6243	6253	6263	6274	6284	6294	6304	6314	6325	1	2	3	4	5	6	7	8	9
43	6335	6345	6355	6365	6375	6385	6395	6405	6415	6425	1	2	3	4	5	6	7	8	9
44	6435	6444	6454	6464	6474	6484	6493	6503	6513	6522	1	2	3	4	5	6	7	8	9
45	6532	6542	6551	6561	6571	6580	6590	6599	6609	6618	1	2	3	4	5	6	7	8	9
46	6628	6637	6646	6656	6665	6675	6684	6693	6702	6712	1	2	3	4	5	6	7	7	8
47	6721	6730	6739	6749	6758	6767	6776	6785	6794	6803	1	2	3	4	5	5	6	7	8
48	6812	6821	6830	6839	6848	6857	6866	6875	6884	6893	1	2	3	4	4	5	6	7	8
49	6902	6911	6920	6928	6937	6946	6955	6964	6972	6981	1	2	3	4	4	5	6	7	8

Table 5.3   (*Continued*)

	0	1	2	3	4	5	6	7	8	9	1	2	3	4	5	6	7	8	9
60	7782	7789	7796	7803	7810	7818	7825	7832	7839	7846	1	1	2	3	4	4	5	6	6
61	7853	7860	7868	7875	7882	7889	7896	7903	7910	7917	1	1	2	3	4	4	5	6	6
62	7924	7931	7938	7945	7952	7959	7966	7973	7980	7987	1	1	2	3	3	4	5	6	6
63	7993	8000	8007	8014	8021	8028	8035	8041	8048	8055	1	1	2	3	3	4	5	5	6
64	8062	8069	8075	8082	8089	8096	8102	8109	8116	8122	1	1	2	3	3	4	5	5	6
65	8129	8136	8142	8149	8156	8162	8169	8176	8182	8189	1	1	2	3	3	4	5	5	6
66	8195	8202	8209	8215	8222	8228	8235	8241	8248	8254	1	1	2	3	3	4	5	5	6
67	8261	8267	8274	8280	8287	8293	8299	8306	8312	8319	1	1	2	3	3	4	5	5	6
68	8325	8331	8338	8344	8351	8357	8363	8370	8376	8382	1	1	2	3	3	4	5	6	
69	8388	8395	8401	8407	8414	8420	8426	8432	8439	8445	1	1	2	2	3	4	4	5	6
70	8451	8457	8463	8470	8476	8482	8488	8494	8500	8506	1	1	2	2	3	4	4	5	6
71	8513	8519	8525	8531	8537	8543	8549	8555	8561	8567	1	1	2	2	3	4	4	5	5
72	8573	8579	8585	8591	8597	8603	8609	8615	8621	8627	1	1	2	2	3	4	4	5	5
73	8633	8639	8645	8651	8657	8663	8669	8675	8681	8686	1	1	2	2	3	4	4	5	5
74	8692	8698	8704	8710	8716	8722	8727	8733	8739	8745	1	1	2	2	3	3	4	5	5
75	8751	8756	8762	8768	8774	8779	8785	8791	8797	8802	1	1	2	2	3	3	4	5	5
76	8808	8814	8820	8825	8831	8837	8842	8848	8854	8859	1	1	2	2	3	3	4	5	5
77	8865	8871	8876	8882	8887	8893	8899	8904	8910	8915	1	1	2	2	3	3	4	4	5
78	8921	8927	8932	8938	8943	8949	8954	8960	8965	8971	1	1	2	2	3	3	4	4	5
79	8976	8982	8987	8993	8998	9004	9009	9015	9020	9025	1	1	2	2	3	3	4	4	5
80	9031	9036	9042	9047	9053	9058	9063	9069	9074	9079	1	1	2	2	3	3	4	4	5
81	9085	9090	9096	9101	9106	9112	9117	9122	9128	9133	1	1	2	2	3	3	4	4	5
82	9138	9143	9149	9154	9159	9165	9170	9175	9180	9186	1	1	2	2	3	3	4	4	5
83	9191	9196	9201	9206	9212	9217	9222	9227	9232	9238	1	1	2	2	3	3	4	4	5
84	9243	9248	9253	9258	9263	9269	9274	9279	9284	9289	1	1	2	2	3	3	4	4	5
85	9294	9299	9304	9309	9315	9320	9325	9330	9335	9340	1	1	2	2	3	3	4	4	5
86	9345	9350	9355	9360	9365	9370	9375	9380	9385	9390	1	1	2	2	3	3	4	4	5
87	9395	9400	9405	9410	9415	9420	9425	9430	9435	9440	0	1	1	2	2	3	3	4	4
88	9445	9450	9455	9460	9465	9469	9474	9479	9484	9489	0	1	1	2	2	3	3	4	4
89	9494	9499	9504	9509	9513	9518	9523	9528	9533	9538	0	1	1	2	2	3	3	4	4
90	9542	9547	9552	9557	9562	9566	9571	9576	9581	9586	0	1	1	2	2	3	3	4	4
91	9590	9595	9600	9605	9609	9614	9619	9624	9628	9633	0	1	1	2	2	3	3	4	4
92	9638	9643	9647	9652	9657	9661	9666	9671	9675	9680	0	1	1	2	2	3	3	4	4
93	9685	9689	9694	9699	9703	9708	9713	9717	9722	9727	0	1	1	2	2	3	3	4	4
94	9731	9736	9741	9745	9750	9754	9759	9763	9768	9773	0	1	1	2	2	3	3	4	4
95	9777	9782	9786	9791	9795	9800	9805	9809	9814	9818	0	1	1	2	2	3	3	4	4
96	9823	9827	9832	9836	9841	9845	9850	9854	9859	9863	0	1	1	2	2	3	3	4	4
97	9868	9872	9877	9881	9886	9890	9894	9899	9903	9908	0	1	1	2	2	3	3	4	4
98	9912	9917	9921	9926	9930	9934	9939	9943	9948	9952	0	1	1	2	2	3	3	4	4
99	9956	9961	9965	9969	9974	9978	9983	9987	9991	9996	0	1	1	2	2	3	3	3	4

Table 5.4   *Antilogarithms*

	0	1	2	3	4	5	6	7	8	9	1	2	3	4	5	6	7	8	9
0.00	1000	1002	1005	1007	1009	1012	1014	1016	1019	1021	0	0	1	1	1	1	2	2	2
0.01	1023	1026	1028	1030	1033	1035	1038	1040	1042	1045	0	0	1	1	1	1	2	2	2
0.02	1047	1050	1052	1054	1057	1059	1062	1064	1067	1069	0	0	1	1	1	1	2	2	2
0.03	1072	1074	1076	1079	1081	1084	1086	1089	1091	1094	0	0	1	1	1	1	2	2	2
0.04	1096	1099	1102	1104	1107	1109	1112	1114	1117	1119	0	1	1	1	1	2	2	2	2
0.05	1122	1125	1127	1130	1132	1135	1138	1140	1143	1146	0	1	1	1	1	2	2	2	2
0.06	1148	1151	1153	1156	1159	1161	1164	1167	1169	1172	0	1	1	1	1	2	2	2	2
0.07	1175	1178	1180	1183	1186	1189	1191	1194	1197	1199	0	1	1	1	1	2	2	2	2
0.08	1202	1205	1208	1211	1213	1216	1219	1222	1225	1227	0	1	1	1	1	2	2	2	3
0.09	1230	1233	1236	1239	1242	1245	1247	1250	1253	1256	0	1	1	1	1	2	2	2	3
0.10	1259	1262	1265	1268	1271	1274	1276	1279	1282	1285	0	1	1	1	1	2	2	2	3
0.11	1288	1291	1294	1297	1300	1303	1306	1309	1312	1315	0	1	1	1	2	2	2	2	3
0.12	1318	1321	1324	1327	1330	1334	1337	1340	1343	1346	0	1	1	1	2	2	2	2	3
0.13	1349	1352	1355	1358	1361	1365	1368	1371	1374	1377	0	1	1	1	2	2	2	3	3
0.14	1380	1384	1387	1390	1393	1396	1400	1403	1406	1409	0	1	1	1	2	2	2	3	3
0.15	1413	1416	1419	1422	1426	1429	1432	1435	1439	1442	0	1	1	1	2	2	2	3	3
0.16	1445	1449	1452	1455	1459	1462	1466	1469	1472	1476	0	1	1	1	2	2	2	3	3
0.17	1479	1483	1486	1489	1493	1496	1500	1503	1507	1510	0	1	1	1	2	2	2	3	3
0.18	1514	1517	1521	1524	1528	1531	1535	1538	1542	1545	0	1	1	1	2	2	2	3	3
0.19	1549	1552	1556	1560	1563	1567	1570	1574	1578	1581	0	1	1	1	2	2	3	3	3
0.20	1585	1589	1592	1596	1600	1603	1607	1611	1614	1618	0	1	1	1	2	2	3	3	3
0.21	1622	1626	1629	1633	1637	1641	1644	1648	1652	1656	0	1	1	2	2	2	3	3	3
0.22	1660	1663	1667	1671	1675	1679	1683	1687	1690	1694	0	1	1	2	2	2	3	3	3
0.23	1698	1702	1706	1710	1714	1718	1722	1726	1730	1734	0	1	1	2	2	2	3	3	4
0.24	1738	1742	1746	1750	1754	1758	1762	1766	1770	1774	0	1	1	2	2	2	3	3	4
0.25	1778	1782	1786	1791	1795	1799	1803	1807	1811	1816	0	1	1	2	2	2	3	3	4
0.26	1820	1824	1828	1832	1837	1841	1845	1849	1854	1858	0	1	1	2	2	3	3	3	4
0.27	1862	1866	1871	1875	1879	1884	1888	1892	1897	1901	0	1	1	2	2	3	3	3	4
0.28	1905	1910	1914	1919	1923	1928	1932	1936	1941	1945	0	1	1	2	2	3	3	4	4
0.29	1950	1954	1959	1963	1968	1972	1977	1982	1986	1991	0	1	1	2	2	3	3	4	4
0.30	1995	2000	2004	2009	2014	2018	2023	2028	2032	2037	0	1	1	2	2	3	3	4	4
0.31	2042	2046	2051	2056	2061	2065	2070	2075	2080	2084	0	1	1	2	2	3	3	4	4
0.32	2089	2094	2099	2104	2109	2113	2118	2123	2128	2133	0	1	1	2	2	3	3	4	4
0.33	2138	2143	2148	2153	2158	2163	2168	2173	2178	2183	0	1	1	2	2	3	3	4	4
0.34	2188	2193	2198	2203	2208	2213	2218	2223	2228	2234	1	1	2	2	3	3	4	4	5
0.35	2239	2244	2249	2254	2259	2265	2270	2275	2280	2286	1	1	2	2	3	3	4	4	5
0.36	2291	2296	2301	2307	2312	2317	2323	2328	2333	2339	1	1	2	2	3	3	4	4	5
0.37	2344	2350	2355	2360	2366	2371	2377	2382	2388	2393	1	1	2	2	3	3	4	4	5
0.38	2399	2404	2410	2415	2421	2427	2432	2438	2443	2449	1	1	2	2	3	3	4	4	5
0.39	2455	2460	2466	2472	2477	2483	2489	2495	2500	2506	1	1	2	2	3	3	4	5	5
0.40	2512	2518	2523	2529	2535	2541	2547	2553	2559	2564	1	1	2	2	3	4	4	5	5
0.41	2570	2576	2582	2588	2594	2600	2606	2612	2618	2624	1	1	2	3	3	4	5	5	5
0.42	2630	2636	2642	2649	2655	2661	2667	2673	2679	2685	1	1	2	3	3	4	4	5	6
0.43	2692	2698	2704	2710	2716	2723	2729	2735	2742	2748	1	1	2	3	3	4	4	5	6
0.44	2754	2761	2767	2773	2780	2786	2793	2799	2805	2812	1	1	2	3	3	4	4	5	6
0.45	2818	2825	2831	2838	2844	2851	2858	2864	2871	2877	1	1	2	3	3	4	5	5	6
0.46	2884	2891	2897	2904	2911	2917	2924	2931	2938	2944	1	1	2	3	3	4	5	5	6
0.47	2951	2958	2965	2972	2979	2985	2992	2999	3006	3013	1	1	2	3	3	4	5	5	6
0.48	3020	3027	3034	3041	3048	3055	3062	3069	3076	3083	1	1	2	3	4	4	5	6	6
0.49	3090	3097	3105	3112	3119	3126	3133	3141	3148	3155	1	1	2	3	4	4	5	6	6

Table 5.4   (*Continued*)

	0	1	2	3	4	5	6	7	8	9	1	2	3	4	5	6	7	8	9
0.50	3162	3170	3177	3184	3192	3199	3206	3214	3221	3228	1	1							
											1	2	3	4	5	6	6	7	8
0.61	4074	4083	4093	4102	4111	4121	4130	4140	4150	4159	1	2	3	4	5	6	7	8	9
0.62	4169	4178	4188	4198	4207	4217	4227	4236	4246	4256	1	2	3	4	5	6	7	8	9
0.63	4266	4276	4285	4295	4305	4315	4325	4335	4345	4355	1	2	3	4	5	6	7	8	9
0.64	4365	4375	4385	4395	4406	4416	4426	4436	4446	4457	1	2	3	4	5	6	7	8	9
0.65	4467	4477	4487	4498	4508	4519	4529	4539	4550	4560	1	2	3	4	5	6	7	8	9
0.66	4571	4581	4592	4603	4613	4624	4634	4645	4656	4667	1	2	3	4	5	6	7	9	10
0.67	4677	4688	4699	4710	4721	4732	4742	4753	4764	4775	1	2	3	4	5	7	8	9	10
0.68	4786	4797	4808	4819	4831	4842	4853	4864	4875	4887	1	2	3	4	6	7	8	9	10
0.69	4893	4909	4920	4932	4943	4955	4966	4977	4989	5000	1	2	3	5	6	7	8	9	10
0.70	5012	5023	5035	5047	5058	5070	5082	5093	5105	5117	1	2	4	5	6	7	8	9	11
0.71	5129	5140	5152	5164	5176	5188	5200	5212	5224	5236	1	2	4	5	6	7	8	10	11
0.72	5248	5260	5272	5284	5297	5309	5321	5333	5336	5358	1	2	4	5	6	7	9	10	11
0.73	5370	5383	5395	5408	5420	5433	5445	5458	5470	5483	1	3	4	5	6	8	9	10	11
0.74	5495	5508	5521	5534	5546	5559	5572	5585	5598	5610	1	3	4	5	6	8	9	10	12
0.75	5623	5636	5649	5662	5675	5689	5702	5715	5728	5741	1	3	4	5	7	8	9	10	12
0.76	5754	5768	5781	5794	5808	5821	5834	5848	5861	5875	1	3	4	5	7	8	9	11	12
0.77	5888	5902	5916	5929	5943	5957	5970	5984	5998	6012	1	3	4	5	7	8	10	11	12
0.78	6026	6039	6053	6067	6081	6095	6109	6124	6138	6152	1	3	4	6	7	8	10	11	13
0.79	6166	6180	6194	6209	6223	6237	6252	6266	6281	6295	1	3	4	6	7	9	10	11	13
0.80	6310	6324	6339	6353	6368	6383	6397	6412	6427	6442	1	3	4	6	7	9	10	12	13
0.81	6457	6471	6486	6501	6516	6531	6546	6561	6577	6592	2	3	5	6	8	9	11	12	14
0.82	6607	6622	6637	6653	6668	6683	6699	6714	6730	6745	2	3	5	6	8	9	11	12	14
0.83	6761	6776	6792	6808	6823	6839	6855	6871	6887	6902	2	3	5	6	8	9	11	13	14
0.84	6918	6934	6950	6966	6982	6998	7015	7031	7047	7063	2	3	5	6	8	10	11	13	15
0.85	7079	7096	7112	7129	7145	7161	7178	7194	7211	7228	2	3	5	7	8	10	12	13	15
0.86	7244	7261	7278	7295	7311	7328	7345	7362	7379	7396	2	3	5	7	8	10	12	13	15
0.87	7413	7430	7447	7464	7482	7499	7516	7534	7551	7568	2	3	5	7	9	10	12	14	16
0.88	7586	7603	7621	7638	7656	7674	7691	7709	7727	7745	2	4	5	7	9	11	12	14	16
0.89	7762	7780	7798	7816	7834	7852	7870	7889	7907	7925	2	4	5	7	9	11	13	14	16
0.90	7943	7962	7980	7998	8017	8035	8054	8072	8091	8110	2	4	6	7	9	11	13	15	17
0.91	8128	8147	8166	8185	8204	8222	8241	8260	8279	8299	2	4	6	8	9	11	13	15	17
0.92	8318	8337	8356	8375	8395	8414	8433	8453	8472	8492	2	4	6	8	10	12	14	15	17
0.93	8511	8531	8551	8570	8590	8610	8630	8650	8670	8690	2	4	6	8	10	12	14	16	18
0.94	8710	8730	8750	8770	8790	8810	8831	8851	8872	8892	2	4	6	8	10	12	14	16	18
0.95	8913	8933	8954	8974	8995	9016	9036	9057	9078	9099	2	4	6	8	10	12	15	17	19
0.96	9120	9141	9162	9183	9204	9226	9247	9268	9290	9311	2	4	6	8	11	13	15	17	19
0.97	9333	9354	9376	9397	9419	9441	9462	9484	9506	9528	2	4	7	9	11	13	15	17	20
0.98	9550	9572	9594	9616	9638	9661	9683	9705	9727	9750	2	4	7	9	11	13	16	18	20
0.99	9772	9795	9817	9840	9863	9886	9908	9931	9954	9977	2	5	7	9	11	14	16	18	20

setting down the figures. The correct one to use is the one you understand best, providing it can be easily followed.

Number	Logarithm
4234	3.6267
Answer	3.6267

Example 16
Obtain the logarithm numbers of the following.

(i)   3676
(ii) 1089
(iii) 60.89
(iv) 10.29
(v)   6.063

Practice makes perfect.

Having achieved proficiency in obtaining the logarithm numbers let us now work through a problem to the final stage.

Example 17
Multiply 4201 by 14.

Number	Logarithm
4201	3.6233
14	1.1461
	4.7694
Antilog.	4.5880
	58800.0

(When multiplying *add* the log. numbers). (Change characteristic into a decimal point: 4 becomes 5 places of decimal.)

Answer = 58800.00

It will be observed that we have now added an additional term known as an antilogarithm. This number is obtained from the set of figures in Table 5.4. The reading of these antilogarithms is exactly the same as explained for logarithms, the only difference being that in changing back to the actual numbers we ignore the characteristic until we have obtained the antilogarithm number. We then use the characteristic to fix the decimal point in the answer. Because we are reversing the process to obtain the correct decimal place we must add one to the characteristic figure and count the decimal places from the left-hand side of the final number.

Example 18
Multiply 324 by 25

Number	Logarithm
324	2.5105
25	1.3979
	3.9084
Antilogarithm	3.8098

(When multiplying add the log. numbers) (Change characteristic into a decimal point: $3 + 1 = 4$ places of decimal)

Answer = 8098.0

Important basic rules
Before commencing to perform calculations using logarithm tables, the following basic rules must be clearly understood.

1 It is only possible to perform the following mathematical functions.
   (a) Multiplication of numbers (in this case, add the logarithm numbers).
   (b) Division of numbers (in this case, subtract the logarithm numbers).
   (c) Involution, i.e. raising to a power such as x^3 (in this case, multiply the log. number by the index number).
   (d) Evolution, i.e. obtaining the root of a number such as $\sqrt[4]{x}$ (in this case, divide the log. number by the index number).
2 To obtain the *characteristic*, use the method explained earlier, e.g. the characteristic of the number 42356.0 is 4.
3 To obtain the *mantissa*, ignore the position of the decimal point and use only the first four numbers (four figure log. tables.). Should the fifth figure be 5 or greater, add one to the previous number.

Example 19
Obtain the characteristic and log. number of 42356.0.

Number	Characteristic	Logarithm
42356.0	4.	.6269

The full log. number of 42356.0 = 4.6269.

Worked examples. Follow carefully the following worked examples covering the four operations of multiplication, division, involution and evolution.

Example 24
Find the square of 153.5.
(This may also be written as 153.5^2, the small two being known as the index or power. In this case you need to find this number to its second

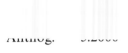

Antilog.

Answer = 200000.0   (approximately)

Answer = 23560.0

Example 21
Multiply 1250 by 2.5.

Number	Logarithm	
1250	3.0969	
2.5	0.3979	(add log. numbers)
	3.4948	
Antilog.	3.3125	

Answer = 3125.0

Example 22
Divide 200000 by 3125.

Number	Logarithm	
200000	5.3010	(subtract
3125	3.4949	log. numbers)
	1.8061	
Antilog.	1.6398	

Answer = 63.98

Example 23
Divide 150 by 0.034.

Number	Logarithm	
150	2.1761	(Negative characteristics: change the bottom sign to positive and add.)
0.034	$\bar{2}$.5315	
	3.6446	
Antilog.	3.4412	

Answer = 4412.0

Example 25
What is 0.034215^4?
(The small 4 is the index and means that in this case you have to find this number to its fourth power.)
Convert to 4 significant figures: 0.03422^4

Number	Logarithm	
0.03422	$\bar{2}$.5343	
4th power	$\times 4$	(multiply by index)
	$\bar{6}$.1372	
Antilog.	.000001372	

Answer = 0.000001372

Example 26
Find the square root of 153.3.
(This is also written as $\sqrt[2]{153.3}$, the small 2 being known as the index.)

Number	Logarithm	
153.3	2.1856	
$\sqrt[2]{}$	2)2.1856	(divide by index)
	1.0928	
Antilog.	1.1238	

Answer = 12.38

Example 27
Find the cube root of 1089.5.

(This may also be written as $\sqrt[3]{1089.5}$.)

Number	Logarithm
1089.5	3.
1090	3.0374 (characteristic only)
$\sqrt[3]{1090}$	3)3.0374
	1.0124 (divide by index)
Antilog.	1.1029

Answer = 10.29

Plumbing mechanics (levers)

A plumber needs to know a great deal about the properties of different materials and the basic rules which govern their behaviour. All materials are inert, that is, the material cannot move of its own accord, and it is important to remember that water and air in particular will not move unless some force (or forces) makes them move.

Force is not a property of a material; it is something *which moves* or *tries to move* an object and is usually defined as 'that which changes, or tends to change, a body's state of rest or uniform motion in a straight line' (Figure 5.6). The *force* in levers is also known as the *effort*.

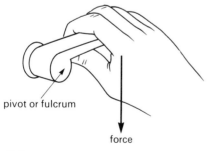

pivot or fulcrum

force

Figure 5.6

Load is the term given to the work to be overcome by the effort, i.e. moving an object, closing off the water by the valve in a tap, etc.

A *lever* is a form of simple machine, and may be defined as 'a rigid bar free to rotate or move about a fixed point known as the fulcrum'. The fulcrum is also known as the pivot.

A lever is used to magnify a force applied to move an object (Figure 5.7). Its length is

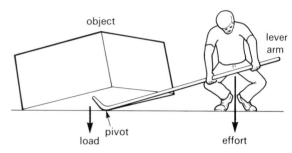

object

lever arm

load   pivot   effort

Figure 5.7

measured from the point where the force is applied to the centre of the fulcrum. The simplest (machine) form of lever is a straight rigid bar; the handle of a pipe wrench (stilson) is such a lever. When the wrench is held by the end of the handle (see Figure 5.8) the amount of pressure that can be exerted on the pipe or fitting gripped by the wrench will be much greater than if the wrench was held in the middle of the handle (lever).

The amount by which the lever increases a force depends partly on where the pressure is applied in relation to the fulcrum, and partly on the position of the object to be moved, in relation to the fulcrum. The lever magnifies the effort applied to move an object, and is said to give a *mechanical advantage*. Mechanical advantage is defined as the ratio of the load (L) to the effort (E). Therefore

$$\text{Mechanical advantage} = \frac{\text{Load}}{\text{Effort}}$$

Mechanical advantage is a ratio of like quantities and therefore has no units.

Example 28
A simple machine requires an effort of 20 N to raise a load of 160 N. What is the mechanical advantage?

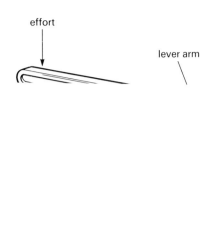

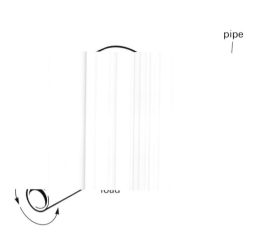

Figure 5.8

Mechanical advantage $= \dfrac{\text{Load}}{\text{Effort}}$

$= \dfrac{160}{20}$

$= 8$

Answer $= 8$ N

Example 29 (see Figure 5.9)
A crowbar requires an effort of 12 N to move a boiler which weighs 132 N. What mechanical advantage does the crowbar give?

Mechanical advantage $= \dfrac{\text{Load}}{\text{Effort}}$

$= \dfrac{132}{12}$

$= 11$

Answer $= 11$ N

As the above examples show, a lever is an instrument used to overcome resistances, or to lift a load to the advantage of the person operating the lever.

Calculations involving levers

Load × Length of lever arm
$\qquad$ = Effort × Length of lever arm

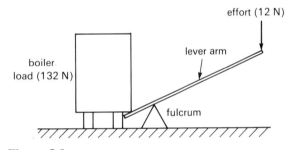

Figure 5.9

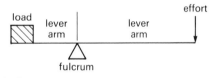

Figure 5.10

Levers are classified according to where the fulcrum, load and effort are situated. There are three kinds, known as first-order, second-order and third-order levers. Figure 5.11 (overleaf) illustrates examples of each kind found in everyday use. After careful examination of the diagrams you should be able to identify and appreciate how each lever works.

As previously stated, the purpose of a lever is to make work easier to do and this will be demonstrated by the following examples.

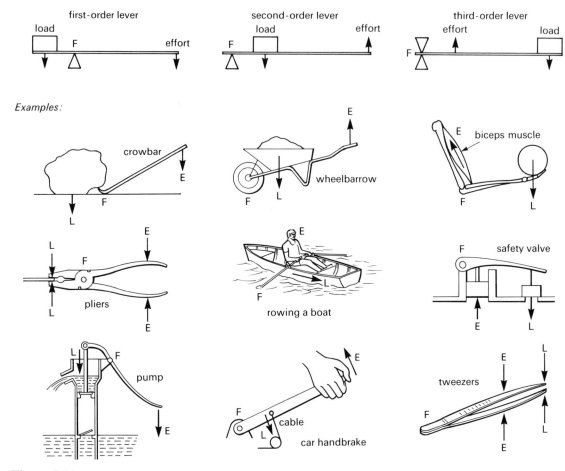

Figure 5.11

Example 30

Using the first order of levers as shown in Figure 5.12, calculate the effort required to raise a boiler weighing 132 N.

Effort × Lever arm = Load × Lever arm

E   × 2.5 m   = 132 N × 0.5 m

$$E = \frac{132 \times 0.5}{2.5}$$

E   = 26.4 N

Answer Effort = 26.4 N

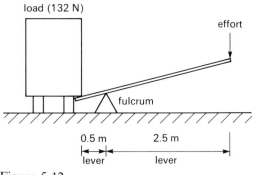

Figure 5.12

It can be easily proved and seen that by increasing the length of the lever arm, less effort will be required to lift the load as shown in Example 31.

Example 31
Again using the first order of levers and the same load, calculate the effort required if the fulcrum is moved 0.25 m nearer to the boiler.

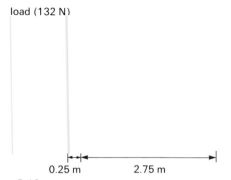

load (132 N)

0.25 m   2.75 m

Figure 5.13

Effort × Lever arm = Load × Lever arm

$E \quad \times 2.75 \text{ m} \quad = 132 \times 0.25$

$E \qquad\qquad = \dfrac{132 \times 0.25}{2.75}$

$E \qquad\qquad = 12 \text{ N}$

Answer Effort = 12 N

Example 32
Using the second order of levers as shown in Figure 5.14, calculate the effort required to raise the same load.

Effort × Lever arm = Load × Lever arm

$E \qquad = \dfrac{\text{Load} \times \text{Lever arm}}{\text{Lever arm}}$

$E \qquad = \dfrac{132 \times 0.5}{3.00}$

$E \qquad = 22 \text{ N}$

Answer Effort = 22 N

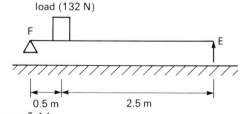

load (132 N)

F

E

0.5 m   2.5 m

Figure 5.14

Example 33
Calculate the effort required using the third order of levers to balance a weight (load) of 132 N as shown in Figure 5.15.

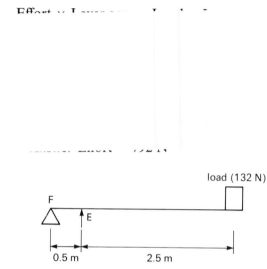

load (132 N)

F

E

0.5 m   2.5 m

Figure 5.15

The principle of the lever is used to advantage in many plumbing components. A good example of this is a ballvalve, as illustrated in Figure 5.16 (overleaf), which clearly shows the relevant parts with assumed lengths and loads.

Example 34
Calculate the effort required to close the ballvalve as shown in Figure 5.16 (overleaf).

lever   lever
W 25 mm F   300 mm   E

Effort × Lever arm = Load × Lever arm

Transpose: $\text{Effort} = \dfrac{\text{Load} \times \text{Lever}}{\text{Lever}}$

$\qquad\qquad = \dfrac{7 \times 0.025}{0.3}$

$\qquad\qquad = 0.583 \text{ kgf}$

Answer Effort = 0.583 kgf

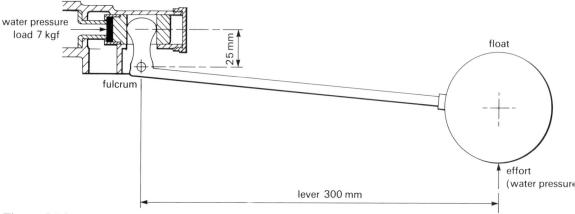

Figure 5.16

Note: To convert kgf to Newtons multiply by 9.81.

Effort = 0.583 × 9.81 N

= 5.719 N

Example 35

An effort of 2.5 N is exerted upwards by the float connected to the ballvalve arm as shown in Figure 5.17. Calculate the force produced at the piston.

Effort × Lever arm = Load × Lever arm
(*Note*: Load = Force)

Transpose to find the required term.

Effort × Lever = Force × Lever

$$\frac{\text{Effort} \times \text{Lever}}{\text{Lever}} = \text{Force}$$

$$\frac{2.5 \text{ N} \times 0.320 \text{ m}}{0.020 \text{ m}} = \text{Force}$$

40 N = Force

Answer Force = 40 N

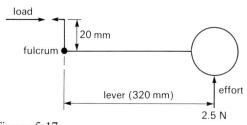

Figure 5.17

Water pressure and flow

It is often necessary to calculate the weight of water contained in tanks or cisterns. It is also necessary to be able to calculate the flow rate and the intensity of pressure created under various working conditions. To be able to perform these tasks it is important to be familiar with the units listed in Table 5.5 and to understand a little of their origin.

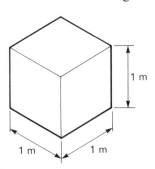

Figure 5.18

Note: 1m = 1000 mm

Area of base = 1 m × 1 m
= 1 m² (1 000 000 mm²)

Volume = 1 m × 1 m × 1 m
= 1 m³ (1 000 000 000 mm³)

Mass and force

It is important to distinguish between the mass of a body and its weight. When a piece of lead is dropped the force of gravity acts upon it

Table 5.5 *Units and symbols*

Item	Units	Symbol
Area	Square metres	m^2

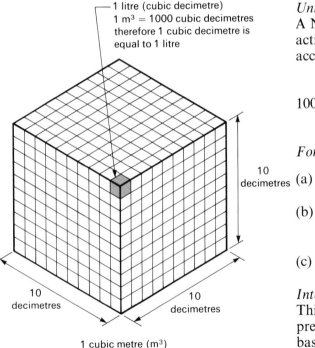

1 litre (cubic decimetre)
1 m³ = 1000 cubic decimetres
therefore 1 cubic decimetre is
equal to 1 litre

10 decimetres

10 decimetres

10 decimetres

1 cubic metre (m³)

1 cubic metre (m³) contains 1000 litres
1 litre (l) contains 1000 millilitres (ml)

Figure 5.19

pulling it to the ground and the size of the *force* is the *weight* of the object.

Example 36
A mass of 3 kg has a weight of 3 kgf (kilogrammes force).

Unit of force
A Newton is defined as that force which when acting on a mass of 1 kilogramme gives it an acceleration of 1 metre per second per second.

$$1 \text{ Newton} = 1 \text{ kg} \times 1 \text{ m/s}^2$$

$$1000 \text{ Newtons} = 1 \text{ kiloNewton}$$

$$= 1 \text{ kN}$$

Formulae

(a) $\text{Pressure} = \dfrac{\text{Force}}{\text{Area}}$

(b) $\text{Force} = \text{Pressure} \times \text{Area or}$
$\text{Mass} \times \text{Acceleration}$

(c) $\text{Area} = \dfrac{\text{Force}}{\text{Pressure}}$

Intensity of pressure
This is the term used to indicate the force or pressure exerted on a stated area such as the base of a cistern, cylinder or a valve seating. When this is required it is necesary to divide the answer obtained in kN by the area the water is resting on, i.e. the base of the cistern.

Unit of mass
In the SI system the unit of mass is the kilogramme.

Kilogramme force (kgf)
This is defined as that force which will move

1 kilogramme with an acceleration of 9.81 m/s².

9.81 Newtons = 1 kgf

1 kilogramme force is the force produced by 1 kg mass of water.

Head of water
This is usually expressed in metres head. 1 cubic metre = 1000 kg of water acting on the base of the vessel (head of water). It may be necessary to express the head of water in kN/m².

$$\text{Pressure} = \frac{\text{Force}}{\text{Area}}$$

$$1 \text{ metre head of water} = \frac{1000}{\text{m}^2} \text{ kgf}$$

$$= 1000 \text{ kgf/m}^2$$

$$= 1000 \times 9.81 \text{ N/m}^2$$
$$\text{(as 1 kgf} = 9.81 \text{ N)}$$

$$= 9810 \text{ N/m}^2.$$

Just as when using lengths the millimetre is a very small dimension and we tend to divide by 1000 to convert into a larger dimension, i.e. metres, so with the gramme and the Newton also being small we divide by 1000 to convert them into kilogrammes and kiloNewtons.

Note: (a)   1000 mm = 1 metre

(b) $\dfrac{9810 \text{ g}}{1000} = 9.81 \text{ kg}$

(c) $\dfrac{9810 \text{ N}}{1000} = 9.81 \text{ kN}$

Gravity The force of gravity is the pull that is exerted on all matter. In the United Kingdom the figure used was 32.18 ft/s². With the introduction of the SI units which are used today the figure used is 9.81 m/s².

Note: 1 metre = 3.28 ft

$$\text{Gravitational pull} = \frac{32.18 \text{ ft/s}^2}{3.28}$$

$$= 9.81 \text{ m/s}^2$$

Example 37
Calculate the force in Newtons acting on the base of a cold water cistern measuring 650 mm × 500 mm × 450 mm.

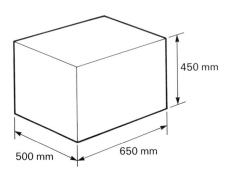

Figure 5.20

Method
Volume = L × B × D (in cubic metres)

$$\text{Volume} = \frac{650}{1000} \times \frac{500}{1000} \times \frac{450}{1000} \text{ m}^3$$

$$= 0.65 \times 0.5 \times 0.45 \times 1000 \text{ litres}$$

$$= 146.25 \text{ litres}\quad \text{(or kgf)}$$

$$\text{Force} = \text{Mass} \times \text{Acceleration}$$

$$= 146.25 \times 9.81 \text{ N}$$

$$= 1434.7 \text{ N}$$

Note: Should the answer be required in kilo-Newtons, divide by 1000.

$$\text{Force} = \frac{1434.7}{1000} \text{ kN}$$

$$= 1.435 \text{ kN}$$

Answer = 1.435 kN   (or 1434.7 N)

Intensity of pressure

Example 38
Calculate the intensity of pressure on the base of a cold water cistern measuring 650 × 500 × 450 mm (see Figure 5.20).

Note: for simplicity and speed we are using the same dimensions as for Example 37.

Force $= \dfrac{\text{Mass} \times \text{Acceleration}}{\text{Area of base}}$

$= \dfrac{0.65 \times 0.5 \times 0.45 \times 1000 \times 9.81}{0.65 \times 0.5} \text{ N/m}^2$

...base of a hot water cylinder 1.00 m high with a diameter of 374 mm.

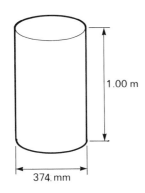

1.00 m

374 mm

diameter = 374 mm
radius = 187 mm

Figure 5.21

Volume $= \pi \times r^2 \times h$

$= 3.142 \times \dfrac{187}{1000} \times \dfrac{187}{1000} \times 1.00 \text{ m}^3$

$= 3.142 \times 0.187 \times 0.187 \times 1.00 \times 1000 \text{ litres}$

$= 109.87 \text{ litres (or kgf)}$

Force $=$ Mass $\times$ Acceleration

$= 109.87 \times 9.81 \text{ N}$

$= 1077.8 \text{ N}$

$= 1077.8 \div 1000 \text{ kN}$

$= 1.078 \text{ kN}$

Answer $= 1077.8 \text{ N or } 1.078 \text{ kN}$

Example 40
Calculate the intensity of pressure on the base of the cylinder shown in Figure 5.21.

$= 1.00 \times 1000 \times 9.81 \text{ N/m}^2$

$= 9810.00 \text{ N/m}^2$

$= 9810.00 \div 1000 \text{ kN/m}^2$

$= 9.81 \text{ kN/m}^2$

Answer $= 9.81 \text{ kN/m}^2$

Example 41
Calculate the force in Newtons on the seat of a 22 mm tap fed from a cistern producing a head of 6 m.

Volume of water $= \pi r^2 \times h$

$= 3.142 \times \dfrac{11}{1000} \times \dfrac{11}{1000} \times 6 \times 1000 \text{ litres}$

$= 3.142 \times 0.01 \times 0.01 \times 6 \times 1000 \text{ litres}$

$= 1.885 \text{ litres or kgf}$

Force $=$ Mass $\times$ Acceleration

$= 1.885 \times 9.81 \text{ N}$

$= 18.49 \text{ N}$

To convert Newtons to kiloNewtons, divide by 1000

Force $= \dfrac{18.49}{1000} \text{ kN}$

$= 0.018 \text{ kN}$

Answer $= 0.018 \text{ kN or } 18.49 \text{ N}$

Example 42
Calculate the intensity of pressure on the seat of a tap using the same dimensions as for the previous example (see Figure 5.22).

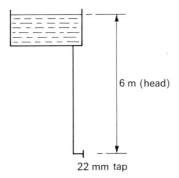

6 m (head)

22 mm tap

Figure 5.22

$$\text{Intensity of pressure} = \frac{\text{Mass} \times \text{Acceleration}}{\text{Area of tap}}$$

$$= \frac{3.142 \times 0.01 \times 0.01 \times 6 \times 1000 \times 9.8}{3.142 \times 0.01 \times 0.01}$$

$$= 6 \times 1000 \times 9.8 \text{ Newtons/m}^2$$

$$= 58800 \text{ N/m}^2$$

Divide by 1000 to convert to kN

$$\text{Intensity of pressure} = \frac{58800}{1000} \text{ kN/m}^2$$

$$= 58.8 \text{ kN/m}^2$$

$$\textit{Answer} = 58.8 \text{ kN/m}^2 \text{ or } 58800 \text{ N/m}^2$$

By examination of the problems involving the intensity of pressure it will be seen that the *area of the base* on the top line of the problem is cancelled out by the *same area* on the bottom line. Once the method and understanding is appreciated this step can be omitted as shown in the following example.

Example 43
Calculate the intensity of pressure in N/m^2 on a 25 mm valve having a head of 8 m.

(Intensity of pressure = Force)

Original formula

$$\text{Force} = \frac{\text{Mass} \times \text{Area}}{\text{Area of valve}}$$

$$= \frac{\cancel{\text{Area of valve}} \times \text{Head} \times 1000 \times \text{Acceleration}}{\cancel{\text{Area of valve}}}$$

Revised formula

$$\text{Force} = \text{Head} \times 1000 \times \text{Acceleration}$$

$$\text{Force} = 8 \times 1000 \times 9.81 \text{ N/m}^2$$

$$= 78480 \text{ N/m}^2$$

$$= 78480 \div 1000 \text{ kN/m}^2$$

$$\textit{Answer} = 78.48 \text{ kN/m}^2 \text{ or } 78481 \text{ N/m}^2$$

Air pressure

Air pressure is generally recorded in a unit known as a bar, which is the equivalent of one atmosphere of pressure. It may be necessary in certain types of work and operations to have a smaller unit of measurement. In this case the unit is the millibar. There are 1000 millibars (mb) in one bar.

1 bar (1000 mb)	$= 100 \text{ kN/m}^2$
1 bar	$= 760 \text{ mm mercury}$
1 millibar (mb)	$= 100 \text{ N/m}^2$
1 pascal (pa)	$= 1 \text{ N/m}^2$
S. G. mercury	$= 13.6$
1 bar	$= (760 \times 13.6)$
	$= 10336 \text{ mm water}$
	or 10.336 m water
	$= (10.33 \times 9.81)$
	$= (101.33 \text{ kN/m}^2$

Example 44
A test reading on a drainage pipeline shows a reading of 50 mm of water. What would the reading be in millibars (mb)?

Note: 1 m head = 9.81 kN/m² (known fact)

manometer reading of 50 mm

$$= \frac{50}{1000} \times 9.81 \text{ kN/m}^2$$

where H = head in metres, L = length in metres, q = discharge in litres/second and d = internal diameter in millimetres.

By transposing the formula as shown earlier it

$$q = \sqrt{\frac{Hd^5}{25 \text{ L } 10^5}}$$

Example 45
If the reading on a pressure gauge is 50 kN/m² what would the reading be in mb and m.

$$L = \frac{H d^5}{25 q^2 10^5}$$

Note: reading from table of known facts

  1 kN/m² = 10 mb

 or 1 m head = 9.81 kN/m²

Therefore

(a) 50 kN/m² = 50 × 10 mb

  = 500 mb

(b) 50 kN/m² = 50 ÷ 9.81 m head

  = 5.1 m head

 Answers = 500 mb and 5.1 m

Size and flow related to pipes and channels

There are several formulae that can be used to obtain the discharge of pipes and channels. Perhaps the two most commonly used are the 'Box' formula and the 'Chezy' formula. By transposing the formulae it is possible to rearrange them to obtain not only the discharge but also other factors such as diameter of pipe, head of water etc.

The formula by Thomas Box states:

$$H = \frac{25 \text{ Lq}^2}{d^5},$$

Example 46
Calculate the diameter of a pipe 20 m in length required to discharge 2 litres of water per second with an effective head of 8 m.

Box formula

$$d = \sqrt[5]{\frac{25 \text{ L q}^2 \, 10^5}{H}}$$

$$d = \sqrt[5]{\frac{25 \times 20 \times 2^2 \times 10^5}{8}}$$

$$d = \sqrt[5]{\frac{25 \times 20 \times 4 \times 100\,000}{8}}$$

$$d = \sqrt[5]{\frac{200\,000\,000}{8}}$$

$$d = \sqrt[5]{25\,000\,000}$$

$$d = 30.0 \text{ mm}$$

Answer = 30 mm

Flow of water in drains or channels

Perhaps the most common formula used for this type of calculation is the one known as the Chezy formula and, with normal care, little trouble should be experienced in transposing and solving this form of problem.

The Chezy formula states:

$$V = c\sqrt{Mi},$$

where V = velocity in metres per second, c = a constant (coeffecient of friction), M = hydraulic mean depth in metres and i = inclination of pipe.

The constant

The constant, unless otherwise stated, is taken as 55, which is the figure used for stoneware drains, and is obtained by using the formula

$$c = \sqrt{\frac{2 \times g}{f}},$$

where c = a constant, g = gravitational acceleration and f = frictional resistance (0.0064 for stoneware).

$$c = \sqrt{\frac{2 \times 9.81}{0.0064}}$$

$$c = 55.36$$

Hydraulic mean depth

The hydraulic mean depth is calculated using the formula

$$M = \frac{\text{Wetted area (in m}^2)}{\text{Wetted perimeter (in m)}}$$

The above formula may be understood more easily by referring to Figures 5.23 and 5.24.

Hydraulic mean depth of a channel
(a)   Wetted area = Cross-sectional area of water
(b)   Wetted perimenter = Channel in contact with the water

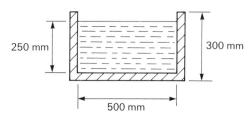

Figure 5.23

Using Figure 5.23:

(a)   Wetted area

= Cross-sectional area of water

$$= \frac{500}{1000} \times \frac{250}{1000}$$

$$= 0.5 \times 0.25 \text{ m}^2$$

$$= 0.125 \text{ m}^2$$

(b)   Wetted perimeter

= Channel touching water

= Base + 2 sides

$$= \frac{500}{1000} + \frac{250}{1000} + \frac{250}{1000}$$

$$= 0.5 + 0.25 + 0.25 \text{ m}$$

$$= 1.00 \text{ m}$$

$$\text{Hydraulic mean depth} = \frac{(a)}{(b)}$$

$$= \frac{0.125}{1.00}$$

$$= 0.125 \text{ m}$$

Hydraulic mean depth of a pipe

(a) Wetted area = Cross-sectional area of water

(b) Wetted perimenter = Pipe in contact with the water

Wetted area of water

$$= \frac{\pi \times D^2}{4} \quad \text{(area of a circle)}$$

Wetted perimenter

Figure 5.24

(a) Wetted area $= \dfrac{\pi r^2}{2}$

(b) Wetted perimenter $= \dfrac{\pi D}{2}$

∴ Hydraulic mean depth $= \dfrac{\dfrac{\pi r \times r}{2}}{\dfrac{\pi \times D}{2}}$

$$= \frac{0.5 \times \pi \times r \times r}{0.5 \times \pi \times 2 \times r}(D = 2 \times r)$$

$$= \frac{r}{2}$$

The figure used in the formula is exactly twice this figure hence

$\dfrac{r}{2} \times 2 = \dfrac{D}{4}$ (diameter in m)

and to further simplify the problem we use a different formula for the area of the water, i.e.

Area of a circle $= \pi r^2$ or $\dfrac{\pi D^2}{4}$.

The hydraulic mean depth of a pipe running full or half full is the same, i.e. $\dfrac{D}{4}$, and this can be proved as follows:

Example 47

Calculate the velocity flow of a 150 mm pipe flowing half full at a fall of 1:60.

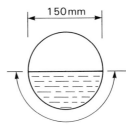

Figure 5.25

Formula $V = c\sqrt{Mi}$

where V = velocity of flow in m/s, c = a constant, M = hydraulic mean depth and i = inclination

$$V = 55\sqrt{\frac{CSA \times i}{WP}}$$

$$V = 55\sqrt{\frac{D}{4} \times \frac{1}{60}}$$

$$V = 55\sqrt{\frac{0.15}{4} \times \frac{1}{60}}$$

$$V = 1.375 \text{ m/s}$$

Answer = 1.375 m/s

Example 48
Calculate the discharge in litres per second from a 150 mm pipe running full, if the velocity of the water is 1.25 m/s.

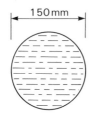

150 mm

Figure 5.26

This is the next progression using the formula.

Formula q = A × V × 1000
where q = quantity discharged in litres/second, A = cross-sectional area of the flow of water in metres, V = velocity of flow in metres/second and 1000 = number of litres in 1 m³.

$$q = A \times V \times 1000 \text{ l/s}$$

$$q = \frac{\pi D^2}{4} \times 1.25 \times 1000 \text{ l/s}$$

$$q = \frac{3.142}{4} \times 0.15 \times 0.15 \times 1.25 \times 1000$$

$$q = 22.09 \text{ litres/second}$$

Answer q = 22.1 litres/second

6 Examinations, assignments and

1 ~~Demonstrate~~ knowledge of examination procedure.

2 Successfully prepare for tests, examinations, projects and assignments.

3 State important aspects of job planning and organisation.

4 Write a short technical statement or report.

5 Understand different methods of communicating information.

6 State the necessary criteria to establish good customer relations.

7 Prepare and write a formal letter.

8 Understand the need for good quality and high standards of work when installing plumbing systems and components.

9 Competently fill-in and complete various types of forms and documents.

10 Describe the basic structure of the plumbing industry and understand the role of associated organisations.

The Plumbing Craft Certificate Scheme

The Plumbing Craft Certificate Scheme is one of several related to Construction Crafts, and is called the City and Guilds of London Institute 603 Plumbing. This scheme supersedes the 596 scheme which has been in operation for several years.

The courses in Construction Crafts are technical education designed for student craftspersons – apprentice or trainee – in the building and construction industry. They have been prepared by Joint Advisory Committees of the City and Guilds of London Institute and the Regional Examining Bodies.

Background to the 603 Plumbing Syllabus

In March 1985, a committee of the City and Guilds of London Institute undertook a review of the syllabuses for plumbing craft courses. At the first meeting of the committee it was agreed that the committee would concentrate its attention on the review of the syllabus for the Craft Certificate in Plumbing and would on completion of this review consider the requirements for Advanced Craft syllabuses.

Manpower Services Commission initiatives, aimed at producing education and training systems responsive to change, directed the committee's attention to the production of a syllabus that differs significantly from previous plumbing schemes.

The revised syllabus (603) is based upon an extensive analysis of the skills and further education requirements of plumbing craft occupations. This analysis was carried out and completed by the Joint Industry Board and its various constituent bodies, the aim being to determine the training standards and further education commensurate with employment at the three craft levels: Trained Plumber, Advanced Plumber and Technical Plumber. The content of the revised Craft Certificate syllabus emphasises the role of the plumbing craftsperson at Trained Plumber level as an 'installer' of mechanical engineering services systems.

The whole of the syllabus content has been grouped into two sections:

A   *Processes.* Content relating to material and installation skills and technology.
B   *Systems.* Content relating to the basic design and layout of mechanical engineering services systems, appropriate to the installation and operation of these systems and their components.

Assessment procedures

The revised system consists of four related elements:

603–1–01   A multiple choice paper designed to test the achievement of objectives related to industrial studies and process studies.

603–1–02   A multiple choice paper designed to test the achievement of objectives related to system studies.

603–1–03   A set of assignments designed to assess planning, communication, installation and problem solving skills.

603–1–04   A coursework assessment of practical activities designed to assess the candidate's competence to perform project work tasks related to the processes and systems.

Issue of examination results and certificates

Each candidate will receive a written record of performance for the components taken (01, 02, 03, 04). There are four grades obtainable: either *distinction, credit, pass* or *fail.* Where a candidate is successful in one or more components but not in all, the grade *referred* will replace *fail* and a referral number will be given to allow the carrying forward of component success.

Certificates are awarded to candidates who pass all four assessment components of each examination. The certificates indicate the grade of performance attained for each component.

The results and certificates are issued through the examination centre (college or skill-centre) at which the examination was taken.

Construction craft studies

The programmes of study in all crafts have been designed with the following considerations in mind.

1   Rapid changes in technology. It has become increasingly important that craftspersons should be educated and trained in the scientific and technological principles employed in industry so as to be able to understand, appreciate and apply new techniques as they are introduced.

2   The importance of the 'Industrial Relations' factor:

   (a)   Changing technology may increase the overlap between craft activities without necessarily removing the need for specialist and traditional craft skills and knowledge; individual craftspersons need, more than ever, to study their own craft, not only to understand their own function, but also to be able to cooperate with other craftspeople in the industry.

   (b)   Understanding your job makes job satisfaction more probable; the ability to communicate enables craftspeople to do their job better and attain a satisfactory personal status within the community.

Programme structure

one or two days' duration depending on their chosen craft, to be awarded a Certificate of Craft Recognition. This test will normally be taken during the third year of study.

Examinations and tests

Multiple-choice tests consist of a series of items. Each item is made up of a question and four answers, of which only one is correct. Candidates are required to study each item and choose the correct answer.

The question is usually called the 'stem'; each of the answers is an 'option' but only one of these options, known as the 'key', is correct. The other three options, known as distractors are incorrect but appear plausible

to many candidates. In the following example the components are identified.

Stem   A plastic cold water storage cistern installed in a roof space should be placed on

the answer correctly, or at least give them the chance to eliminate the distractors.

City and Guilds of London Institute multiple-choice examinations are produced to an examination specification which ensures that the test includes items that are a representative sample of the syllabus objectives (or topics) which it is to assess, and that this coverage remains constant in successive examinations.

The total number of items in a question book varies between different examinations, and in most construction crafts City and Guilds normally uses between fifty and sixty items. The time allowed for these tests is usually generous, for it is not intended that

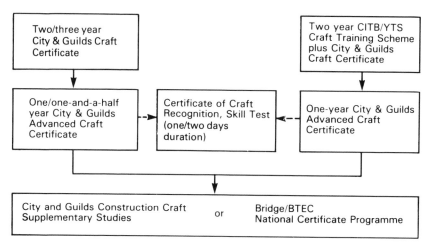

Figure 6.1   *Typical training programme structures*

the test be used as a measure of the candidate's speed of work.

City and Guilds have produced a leaflet for students titled 'Taking Your Tests: How to Do Your Best', which contains useful information for candidates taking either practical or written multiple choice tests and examinations. The leaflet is reproduced on pages 181–184 for your information.

Examination candidates are required to record their choice of answer on an answer sheet and simply do this by underlining either the letter a, b, c or d in line with the question number. Figure 6.2 shows a typical multiple-choice answer sheet.

Examination procedure is always fully explained prior to the examination by examination officials or invigilators.

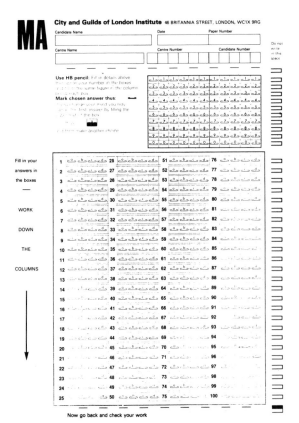

Figure 6.2

Assignments related to Craft Theory and Industrial Studies

Students are required to successfully complete a set of assignments related to Craft Theory and Industrial Studies during their course of study; this element usually consists of five three-hour assignments in total: four are based on Craft Theory and one is based on Industrial Studies. The four Craft Theory assignments are set by the Institute/Advisory Council; the Industrial Studies one is set by the institution offering the course (college or skill centre). These assignments are marked by course tutors and given one of the component grades which makes up part of the assessment for the Craft Certificate.

The Craft Theory assignments are based on common areas of plumbing technology, for example:

1 Roofwork and sheet weatherings,
2 Sanitation,
3 Drainage,
4 Hot and cold water systems,
5 Gas services and supplies.

The assignments set vary each educational year, although the format of the assignments remains constant. The time allowed to complete each assignment is 3 hours (maximum) and during this time students may consult books, catalogues or other craft-related literature.

Each assignment is broken down into six sections (A–F) which are:

A Planning,
B Measurement,
C Setting out,
D Communications,
E Fault diagnosis,
F Problem solving.

Students are advised to read all the assignment questions and study any drawings carefully before commencing writing and it is essential to answer the questions in each section in the order which is necessary to ensure sound and logical decisions and

Taking Your Tests: How To Do Your Best

will pass

● the examiners are *not* required to fail a certain number of candidates for each test.

Your test is a chance for you to give the examiner a true picture of what you know and what you can do.

To help you do your best, here are some tips on how to prepare yourself for your test.

Before your test

● Look at your course notes, and if possible the syllabus, and devise a revision programme — consult your tutor if necessary.

● Start your revision early.

● List the facts and techniques that are essential for your subject.

● Check for gaps in your skills and knowledge and work on them.

● Make sure you know how much time you will be given and how many questions you should answer.

● Read past papers or sample papers to become familiar with the style of the tests.

● Talk questions through with tutors and classmates.

● The more you practice, the more confident you will feel and the more easily your thoughts will flow in the test.

Practice and revision will increase your confidence. You'll know what to expect, what you are to do, what materials are to be used, where you are to work and how much time you'll have.

Figure 6.3   *City and Guilds leaflet*

The day before

- Get ready — collect all the equipment you'll need and a spare for each. Don't rely on old pen cartridges or old calculator batteries.

- Have a relaxing day and a good night's sleep.

- Whatever the temptation, don't drink alcohol before taking a test.

- Don't cram — last-minute revision may confuse you.

- Double-check that you have correct details of where and when the test will take place.

The day of the test

- Arrive at the test room early and try to relax.

- Once in the test room listen carefully to everything the invigilator says. He/she has important instructions to give you.

- If you don't understand the instructions, *ask*.

- Use all the time you are given — you don't get extra marks for finishing early and you may lose marks by rushing.

- Pace yourself, plan your time.

City and Guilds has two kinds of test, *practical* and *written* multiple choice (short answer or structured question). Here are some separate suggestions about these different kinds of test.

Practical tests

- Make sure you are familiar with all the materials and equipment you will be expected to use.

- Make sure you have available everything you will need for the test, and suitable clothing if required.

- Before the test begins, if you don't understand exactly what you have to do, ask the examiner.

- At the start of the test, plan your sequence of work using all your training and experience.

- Don't rush or you'll make mistakes. The test has been designed to allow sufficient time for the task to be completed.

- Avoid short-cuts that could be regarded as bad practice.

- Be safe. Work to Health and Safety guidelines.

Figure 6.3 *(continued)*

Written tests (all)

- Make sure you write in information requested, such as your name, candidate number, the centre number, the name of the paper, the date and your signature

should block it out according to the instructions on the answer sheet.

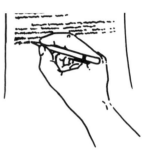

- Use space on your question paper for rough work — *not* your answer sheet.

- Be very careful *not* to lose your place on the answer sheet.

- There is only one correct answer to each question.

- You do *not* have marks taken off for wrong answers.

- Attempt all questions.

- Don't get stuck on a question you find difficult. Move on but return to it later, taking care to keep your answers in proper order.

- For any questions you find difficult, use your knowledge to eliminate the less likely choices one by one.

- There is *no* set pattern of how many times a, b, c or d comes up as the correct answer.

- If your test is shorter than the answer sheet *don't* cross through the unused section.

Written tests (short answer or structured question)

- Read through the whole paper before starting to answer.

- Make sure you know how many questions you have to answer and whether the paper has sections (these details will be shown on the front sheet of the question paper).

- Make sure you answer compulsory questions and the correct number of questions overall.

- You can answer the questions in any order you prefer, though compulsory questions are best tackled first.

- Underline the key words in the question to help you keep to the point in your answer.

- Don't waste time by repeating the question in your answer.

Figure 6.3   *(continued)*

- Look for instruction words in the question such as 'describe' and 'explain'. These tell you the type of answer to give. Common instruction words are

List/Name	Give list or name facts required rather than sentences
State	Give the relevant fact(s) briefly and to the point
Describe/Detail	Give a full account with examples of the procedure, term etc specified in the question
Outline	Briefly give all the essential points
Compare/Contrast	Point out similarities and differences, advantages and disadvantages, of the items mentioned in the question
Define	Give the exact meaning (eg of a term, principle, procedure)
What is meant by . . .?	More than just define — give a definition but go on to give some explanation and discuss its significance and limitations
Explain why . . .	Give the reason(s) for
Sketch	Do a freehand drawing
Draw	Do a fine-line-ruled drawing — to scale if required.

- If you start to 'dry up' on one question leave a space and move on. You are likely to gain more marks on the next question than you will by struggling on with the present one.

- If you feel your answer is incomplete, leave sufficient space below, so you can come back to it later and keep it all together.

- With structured questions, answer all the parts — each part carries marks.

- Write down the answers the examiner has asked for, not all the things you can possibly tell the examiner on the subject. For example, if you are asked to list *THREE* items, list *THREE* — you won't get extra marks for listing more.

- Help your examiner by numbering your answers clearly. Show all your working on your answer book. If you make a mistake, don't rub out — cross through.

- Make your sketches and drawings good-sized, label them clearly and include all essential points.

- If you start to run out of time, write short accurate notes instead of sentences.

- If you have the time, read through your answers and check any calculations you have made.

And finally

Remember, doing your best is not about luck. Success in tests is based on sound knowledge, practised skills and thorough preparation.

Figure 6.3   *(continued)*

choices. The section headings are to a degree self-explanatory of the activity within that section and the following gives examples of typical student activity.

Planning

ials.

5   Selecting materials or components.
6   Drawing additions in the form of pipe-work or components onto a given drawing.

Measurement
1   Calculating distance from given dimensions.
2   Measuring lengths with the aid of a scale rule.
3   Calculating area or volume.
4   Listing materials or components.
5   Calculating costs of labour or materials.

Setting out
1   Showing the position or location of components on a given drawing.
2   Making a diagrammatic sketch of pipe-work or components.
3   Naming parts or components of plumbing systems.
4   Describing methods of carrying out work.
5   Drawing with the aid of a scale rule or compasses.

Communications
1   Writing a list of instructions for another craftsperson.
2   Writing a letter to a client or an employer.
3   Explaining the operation of various plumbing components.
4   Listing materials and components for a supplier.
5   Stating first aid procedure.

Fault diagnosis
1   Stating causes of failure and suggesting remedial action.
2   Listing faults or defects.
3   Stating how faults may be rectified

procedures.
4   Describing correct installation procedures.

The three following assignments are typical examples of Craft Theory exercises based on common areas of plumbing technology.

Assignment No. 1
You will need the following:

1   Sheets of A4 lined paper,
2   Drawing paper,
3   Drawing instruments,
4   Metric scale rule.

You may consult the following:

1   Your text books,
2   Your note books,
3   Catalogues and other material on display.

You are advised to read all the questions and study the drawing carefully before commencing writing. Answer the questions in the order which is necessary to ensure sound and logical decisions and choices.

Attempt *all six* sections (A–F) of this assignment (i.e. *ten* questions in all).

Figure 6.4 (overleaf) shows a section through a dwelling. It is proposed to fix the sanitary fitments and heating components in the positions shown. The boiler is a gas fired balanced flue model situated in the kitchen, the hot water storage vessel is a single feed indirect cylinder (manufactured to BS 1566,

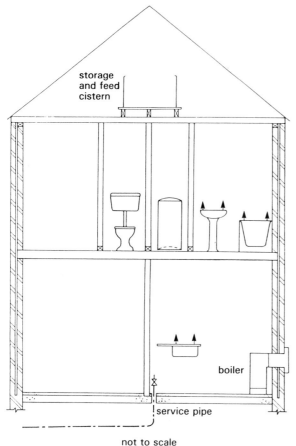

storage
and feed
cistern

boiler

service pipe

not to scale

Figure 6.4

Part II 1972) and is located in the first floor airing cupboard. There is an immersion heater fitted to the cylinder.

Section A – Planning
1   Show on Figure 4.4 the arrangement of the primary and secondary pipework for the hot water system.
2   Show on Figure 4.4 the arrangement of the service and distribution pipework for the cold water system.

Section B – Measurement
3   Calculate the actual capacity of the galvanised mild steel storage cistern which has internal dimensions of 914 mm × 612 mm × 580 mm high. The water

level is set 110 mm below the top edge of the cistern.
4   The hot water storage vessel has a capacity of 127 litres. The diameter of the cylinder is 450 mm. Calculate the height of the cylinder.

Section C – Setting out
5   With the aid of scale drawings show the setting out necessary to the storage and feed cistern to enable it to be drilled and cut ready to receive all the pipework connections.

Section D – Communication
6   The client is worried about the effectiveness of a single feed cylinder as compared with an indirect annular pattern. Using sketches to illustrate your answer, explain for the benefit of the client how the single feed cylinder works.

Section E – Fault diagnosis
7   During the summer months the thermostatically controlled immersion heater is used in preference to the boiler. The occupier has complained that the water drawn off at the taps is too hot and that noise is produced within the cylinder during the final stages of the heating up period.
(a)   State the remedial action necessary to lower the temperature of the stored hot water.
(b)   (i)   Give the recommended temperature for stored hot water in domestic premises.
      (ii)   State why this temperature is recommended.
(c)   State the present wiring code colours of a three core electrical supply to an immersion heater (earth, neutral and live).
8   Whilst you are working on this contract, the occupier complains that the WC flushing cistern is slow in filling. State:
(a)   The likely causes of this fault,
(b)   How these could be overcome.

Section F – Problem solving

9 The cold water service pipe which passes through the kitchen is often wet on its surface.
  (a) State the probable cause of this

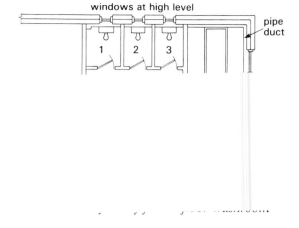

windows at high level

pipe duct

1 2 3

Assignment No. 2

You will need the following:

1 Sheets of A4 lined paper,
2 Drawing paper,
3 Drawing instruments.

You may consult the following:

1 Your text books,
2 Your note books,
3 Catalogues and other material on display.

  You are advised to read all the questions and study the drawing carefully before commencing writing. Answer the questions in the order which is necessary to ensure sound and logical decisions and choices.
  Attempt *all six* sections (A–F) of this assignment (i.e. *six* questions in all).

  An older style four storey building previously used as an office block has been acquired by the local authority and is to be converted into a hostel. The existing toilet accommodation, which will be close to several bed-sitting rooms, is to be modernised including the installation of siphonic wc suites.
  Figure 6.5 shows the proposed layout on the fourth floor.

Section A – Planning

1 Assuming that the uPVC discharge pipework and stack have been previously installed, and that copper tube is to be used:
  (a) List the sequence of operations involved in installing *one* of the WC suites,
  (b) List the tools that would be required to install the WCs, cold water supplies and warning pipes.

Section B – Measurement

2 The contract includes the installation of 12 siphonic WC suites. Calculate the total cost of purchasing these suites using the following information:
  (a) List price £160.00 each,
  (b) Trade discount 20%,
  (c) VAT 15%.

Section C – Setting out

3 On WC number 3 it is difficult to discharge the warning pipe from the cistern because of an external obstruction. Sketch and describe a suitable method of discharging the warning pipe internally which does not contravene the water by-laws.

Section D – Communication

4 The warden of the hostel is concerned about the cost of the siphonic pans. For his benefit state the advantages of the siphonic pan when compared with the wash down pan.

Section E – Fault diagnosis
5   After several months it is found that the contents of one pan are not removed by normal operation.
    (a)   List *two* possible causes of this,
    (b)   State how *each* of these may be rectified.

Section F – Problem solving
The WCs have 'S' trap outlets and it is found that the existing drain sockets are 25 mm too high to receive the outgo.

6   Sketch and describe a suitable method of overcoming this problem.

Assignment No. 3
You will need the following:

1   Sheets of A4 lined paper,
2   Sheets of A3 drawing paper,
3   Metric scale rule,
4   Drawing board and tee square.

You may consult the following:

1   Your text books,
2   Your note books,
3   Catalogues and other material on display.

    You are advised to read *all* the assignment questions and study the drawing carefully before commencing writing. Answer the questions in the order which is necessary to ensure sound and logical decisions and choices.
    Attempt *all six* sections (A–F) of this assignment (i.e. *eight* questions in all).

    Figure 6.6 shows a 450 mm × 450 mm brick chimney stack passing near the ridge of a 45° pitched roof of a two storey dwelling, to which you are to fix weathering and flashing. The roof is covered with standard 165 mm × 275 mm tiles laid to a gauge of 100 mm. All questions relate to this drawing.

Section A – Planning
1   (a)   Select from the following list of materials the *one* you would prefer

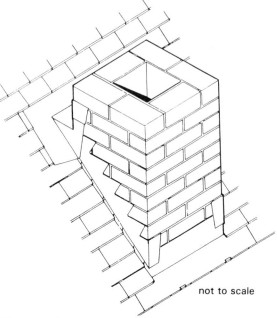

Figure 6.6

to use:
    (i)   Lead,
    (ii)   Copper,
    (iii) Semi-rigid bitumen sheet (Nuralite).
    (b)   State clearly the advantages of using this particular material.
2   List the names of all the pieces necessary to complete the weathering of the chimney stack in the correct order of fixing.
3   Fusion welding, bronze welding, seaming and delamination are methods of fabricating the pieces:
    (a)   Select the method suitable for your chosen material,
    (b)   List the tools required to complete the operation.

Section B – Setting out
4   Draw to a suitable scale the setting out necessary to make the back gutter. Show all cut lines and fold lines.

Section C – Measurement
5   Calculate the minimum size of sheet required to make the back gutter.

Section D – Fault diagnosis

6 Soon after the chimney has been weathered, it is found that water is entering the house. The owner suspects that the weathering is defective

removed and is no longer available.

7 List the minimum equipment necessary to gain access to the stack, and ensure safe working conditions at all times.

Section F – Communication

8 Because of the problems outlined in question 7, the work will take longer than expected. Write a note to your employer claiming extra time and giving reasons why he should allow it.

Assignments related to practical activities

Assessment of a student's practical ability is usually based on the completion of several practical exercises or projects. The projects are usually contained in a booklet called a Scheme of Work and are based on common areas of plumbing craft practice such as the manufacture of sheet weatherings, the cutting, bending and jointing of pipework and the fixing and testing of plumbing fittings and components.

The following examples are typical exercises of plumbing craft practice. You will see that each practical assignment also contains areas of related theory which have to be completed by the student.

Practical assignment no. 1: Roofwork – non-metallic sheet

Introduction

Read this paper carefully and complete the assignment in the most practical order.

Information

The roof of a bungalow is to be weathered with tiles and non-metallic sheet. You are required to make the detail shown in Figure 6.7 which incorporates similar features to the

being applied prior to working on the scaffold.

2 What first aid treatment would you render to the tiler who requests your help after having cut his hand with a saw?

Materials

State:

1 The size of a standard sheet of 'Nuralite',
2 The weight of $1\,m^2$ of 'Nuralite',
3 The optimum moulding temperature of this material.

Measurement/setting out

1 Calculate the area of a rectangular shaped roof measuring 7.8 m wide $\times$ 4.5 m in the direction of the fall.
2 Calculate how many standard size sheets of 'Nuralite' will be required to cover the roof in 1, allowing 150 mm of material on each of the four sides for upstands, drip edges, etc. The sheets are to be jointed using the D12C jointing strip system.

Tools/equipment

Sketch approximately half full size two different types of sealing irons which may be used on non-metallic sheet.

Components

1 Describe the uses of 'Nuralite' jointing compound No. 1 and 'Nuralite' adhesive No. 10.
2 Name the two main constituents of 'Nuralite' sheet.

material: A   600 × 400 mm
          B   600 × 300 mm
          C   600 mm D12C jointing strip

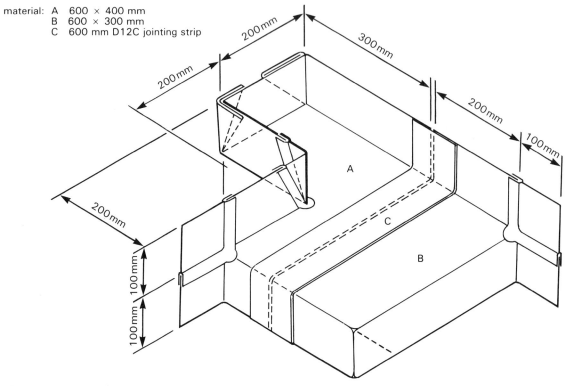

Figure 6.7   *Non-metallic sheet*

Produces/installs

Make the weathering detail to the shape and dimensions given in the diagram. The fabrication methods employed are to be in accordance with the manufacturers' recommendations.

Preserves/protects

1 Give details of the preparation and treatment necessary to timber roofs to ensure satisfactory performance and life of non-metallic sheet.
2 State the type of nails which should be used to secure non-metallic sheet.

Commission/test/find faults

A gutter 12 m long which was lined with non-metallic sheet approximately four years ago is reported to be giving trouble. Inspection reveals that the material has 'bubbled' and is starting to crack between the joints which are of the delaminated type. State:

1 The probable cause of failure,
2 How the failure could have been prevented.

Practical assignment no. 2: Roofwork – sheet lead

Introduction

Read this paper carefully and complete the assignment in the most practical order.

Information

A timber boarded roof of 7° pitch is to be weathered with sheet lead. You are required to make by bossing and lead welding a part of the weathering for this roof, the details of which are shown in Figure 6.8.

Safety

Work safely with due regard to others working around you.

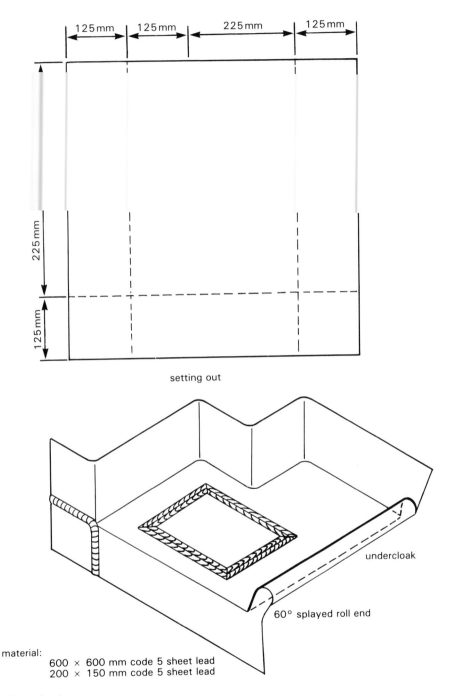

125 mm   125 mm   225 mm   125 mm

225 mm

125 mm

setting out

undercloak

60° splayed roll end

material:
600 × 600 mm code 5 sheet lead
200 × 150 mm code 5 sheet lead

Figure 6.8   *Sheet lead*

List *eight* safety and health precautions you would observe before, during and on completion of a job which involved using sheet lead and oxy-acetylene lead welding equipment.

Materials
Set out a table showing the BS code number, thickness in mm, and colour code for milled sheet lead to BS 1178 for code numbers 3–8 inclusive.

Measurement/setting out
Draw twice actual size a section through a wood-cored roll showing how the roll should be weathered. Indicate on your drawing how the undercloak is secured to the roll, and how the edge of the undercloak should be finished.

Tools/equipment
1 Sketch approximately one-third actual size *three* of the tools you will be using to manipulate the sheet lead to the required shape and dimensions.
2 Make a drawing showing the oxy-acetylene equipment required to perform lead welding on a site. Indicate on your drawing the essential components of this equipment.

Components
Describe or sketch a method of jointing the roofing material across the pitch of this roof. The method chosen must retain the lead sheet in position without any undue restriction on natural movement.

Produces/installs
Boss and lead weld the weathering detail to the shape and dimensions shown in Figure 6.8.

Preserves/protects
Prior to this roof being weathered the boarding is to be covered with inodorous felt. What is 'inodorous felt', and for what purpose is it used?

Commission/test/find faults
1 Explain the term 'creep' as applied to lead roofwork and state how it may be prevented.
2 With the aid of sketches explain:
   (a) Neutral flame,
   (b) Oxidising flame,
   (c) Carburising flame.
3 Which is the hottest part of a correctly adjusted oxy-acetylene flame?
4 State the melting point of milled sheet lead.

Practical assignment no. 3: Sanitation, hot and cold water

Introduction
Read this paper carefully and complete the assignment in the most practical manner.

Information
A range of three washbasins is to be fitted to a workboard. Part of the workboard surface has been extended forward for the washbasins, so that the main surface of the workboard simulates the internal wall of a plumbing services duct. You are required to install the washbasins complete with hot and cold supplies, wastes and vent all as per working drawings provided (Figures 6.9 and 6.10). All work is to conform with current Building Regulations, Water Authority By-laws and British Standard Codes of Practice.

When your board has been assembled it is to be connected to the existing hot and cold water services, drainage and sanitation system, and then commissioned and tested. You are advised to check the dimensions and positions of the existing workshop services and sanitation systems prior to commencing setting out and installation of your workboard project.

Safety
Work safely with due regard to yourself and others working around you.

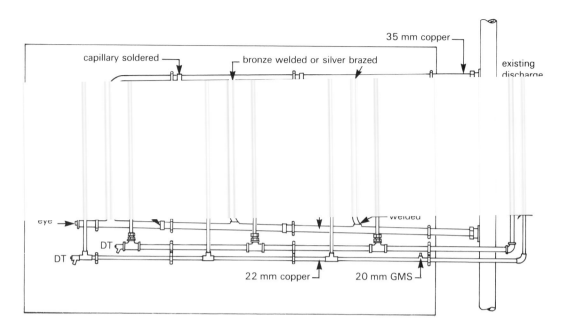

Figure 6.9   *Sanitation, hot and cold water*

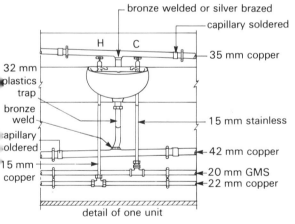

Figure 6.10   *Sanitation, hot and cold water*

1 Describe the first aid treatment you would carry out to relieve minor burns and scalds.

2 State *four* basic precautions for the prevention of fire which should be observed on a building site.

Materials

1 Name *four* materials from which sanitary appliances are currently manufactured.

2 Give a brief description of the characteristics of each material and state any advantages or disadvantages it may possess.

3 Describe what is meant by the following terms as related to properties of metals used by the plumber:
 (a) Ductility,
 (b) Malleability,
 (c) Thermal conductivity,
 (d) Specific gravity.

Measurement/setting out

1 State the recommended fixing heights for the following appliances:
 (a) Kitchen sink,
 (b) Cleaner's sink,
 (c) Wash basin,
 (d) High level flushing cistern.

2 (a) Draw to a suitable scale an isometric projection of a storage cistern which measures 1100 mm × 800 mm × 800 mm high.
 (b) Calculate the actual capacity of this cistern, assuming that the water level is set 100 mm below the top edge of the cistern.

Tools/equipment
1 Sketch or describe two pieces of equipment which may be used to seal the end of a drain or discharge pipe prior to testing.
2 List the tools and equipment required to perforate and then joint a strap boss onto an existing 100 mm PVC discharge pipe.
3 List *four* points that should be checked before using a hacksaw to cut a piece of low carbon steel tube secured in a tripod vice.

Components
1 Describe *two* methods and name the materials you would use in fitting a pillar tap into a wash-basin.
2 Draw full size a section through a suitable trap for a wash-basin. Show clearly the inlet and outlet connection details and indicate the depth of trap seal and the points between which the seal is measured.
3 Describe what is meant by the following terms:
   (a) Slotted waste fittings,
   (b) Unslotted waste fittings,
   (c) Combination waste.

Produces/installs
Complete the installation of the *three* wash-basins with all the relevant services as shown in Figures 6.9 and 6.10.

Preserves/protects
1 State *three* precautions which should be observed in order to allow for the thermal movement of pipework within a building.
2 List and describe *four* properties which should be possessed by a good thermal insulation material.

Commission/test/find faults
1 Describe what is meant by the term 'air lock' and list the possible causes of this in a cold water distribution system in a dwelling.
2 Describe an approved method of commissioning a cold water distribution system in a building where possible contamination may have occurred within the system.
3 Describe the initial procedure and method of carrying out a pneumatic test (air test) on a single stack sanitation system.

Practical assignment no. 4: Drainage, sanitation

Introduction
Read this paper carefully and complete the assignment in the most practical order.

Information
Figure 6.11 shows the plan of a proposed drainage installation to be assembled in the external project area. Under the direction of the Course Tutor you will be required to complete a section of this installation working on both cast iron and uPVC material. It is required that you apply hydrostatic and pneumatic tests to the section of the system which you have installed.

Safety
Work safely with due regard to yourself and others working around you.

1 State the posture which should be adopted when lifting heavy equipment from floor level.
2 Briefly describe the precautions you would take when using materials which involve a health hazard (e.g. lead, solvents, oil and asbestos).

Materials
1 State *four* materials suitable for below ground foul or surface water drainage pipework.
2 Sketch or describe a method of jointing which may be used for each material.

Measurement/setting out
1 If a drain 150 m long is laid to a fall of 1 in 40, what is the difference in invert levels between the two ends of the drain?

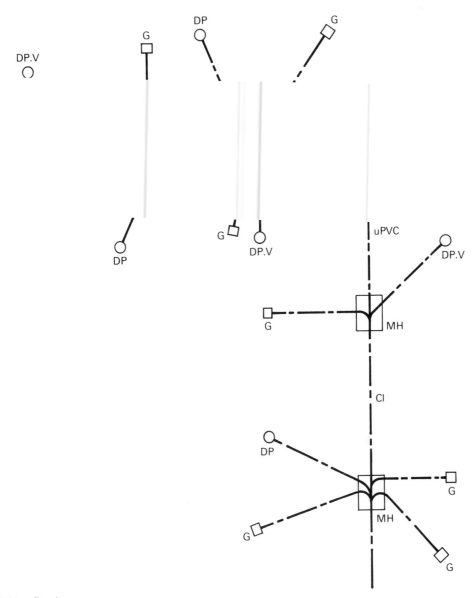

Figure 6.11 *Drainage*

2 Describe the use of 'boning rods' for setting out.

Tools/equipment

1 Make a complete list of the tools and equipment required for making a caulked lead joint on a horizontal cast iron drain pipe.
2 Make a list of the tools and equipment required to carry out a soundness test on a completed single stack sanitation system in a three-storey town house.

Components

1 Draw half full size a section through a type of flexible joint suitable for cast iron drainage pipework.
2 List or describe the locations where access should be provided on a sanitation system.

Produces/installs
Complete the installation of the drainage pipework and components as directed.

Preserves/protects
1 Sketch or describe what is meant by the following:
   (a) Surround,
   (b) Bed,
   (c) Haunching.
2 Describe or sketch how a drain should be protected when it passes through a foundation wall.

Commission/test/find faults
1 Explain with the aid of sketches suitable tests which may be carried out on an existing drain for:
   (a) Obstruction,
   (b) Alignment.
2 Describe what is meant by the term 'performance test', related to sanitation or drainage.
3 Following the connection of additional appliances to an existing combined system of drainage it is found that during heavy rainfall the system 'surcharges':
   (a) What is meant by the term 'surcharge'?
   (b) Suggest possible remedies to prevent this from recurring.

Communication

Speaking to people
The basic method of instructing people or passing on information is by speaking to them.

Few people know for certain if they speak well or badly, for our families and friends are inclined not to hurt us with comments or criticism about our speech. Success can be achieved only by practice and adhering to basic fundamentals. These fundamentals are:

1 Knowing your subject and what you want to say,
2 Developing the ability to say it,

3 Learning to say it in a way that is understood and of interest to the listener.

Whatever the subject or topic might be it is essential that you have reasonable knowledge and that you are interested in it. This should not be difficult for technical people such as plumbers who have such a wide-ranging and interesting craft.

It is often useful to jot down any important ideas or facts you may wish to pass on; this allows you to put the content in a logical sequence so that the discussion will run smoothly – particularly important if instruction is being delivered on technical matters. It is then important to rehearse the details in your mind so that you are sure of what you will say and how you will say it. This time spent on rehearsal will give you confidence. Before you commence speaking, think about and remember the good points which have impressed you when listening to more experienced talkers. Be aware of the need to make eye contact, to sit or stand in a correct posture, make gestures when necessary or applicable, and to modulate your voice to an acceptable level for the listener.

Speaking is something we all do from an early age, but it is necessary to be aware that we must hold the interest of those listening. Part of this holding technique comes from developing self-control, self-confidence and showing conviction and sincerity whilst talking. Most of these skills and attitudes are learnt from others or are self-taught by observation and continual practice.

Writing letters and reports
It is a mystery why writing is so easy for some people, but so difficult for others. Many students think that writing is speech copied down onto paper and they tend to write as they talk. The difference between talking and writing to communicate is considerable although their objective is essentially the same. The degree of control, thought and style required for each is radically different.

General conversation or speech is by its

nature usually formless, unstructured and low in content, but at the same time is wonderfully flexible and intimate. And it *does* make sense, because generally the

Like any other craft, writing requires a careful and hard-working period of traineeship; it means acquiring a mastery of the basics and an appreciation of the different uses it can be put to, the different forms and styles, the proven techniques and short cuts which make the job easier – all the know-how about their trade any craftsperson must acquire before they can consider themselves competent.

Writing is a technical skill that you should work hard at, and it can be an art you create.

Students should approach writing in a similar frame of mind to any other technical skill, because it is demanding and requires a good deal of serious application. It can be systematically mastered if you have enough information and put the information into controlled practice. Knowing how to use the skills you have, and how to gradually extend them is what it's all about.

The problems listed below will make the reader aware of some of the causes of communication problems.

1 Illegible or poor writing,
2 Bad spelling,
3 Poor sentence structure,
4 Bad punctuation,
5 Cramped or confused layout,
6 Bad expression of ideas,
7 Contradictory or confused statements,
8 Too short, incomplete information,
9 Too long, contains irrelevant information.

Dealing successfully with a writing task means working out *what* message you want to send, *whom* you intend to send it to, and *how* you should compose the message while

with:

1 Report writing,
2 Letter writing.

Report writing
A report is usually a statement of the results of an investigation or an action on which definite information is required by some person or organisation, or may be produced by the writer's own initiative. Before sitting down to draft the report, the writer needs to decide on the sequence of headings which will lead the reader through the report.

A short report on a technical matter can probably be produced under three headings:

1 Introduction,
2 Body of report,
3 Conclusion and/or recommendations.

The introduction will include any background history, the terms of reference, scope and limits of the report and a lead-in to the main content of the report. The body of the report will contain all the main points necessary, set out in a logical sequence or order for the reader to understand. The conclusions of a report are the critical part in the sense that it is here that the report writer delivers his or her verdict, although this may involve comparing different possibilities. Conclusions should look forward to recommendations and give the reasons for one course of action rather than another. Conclusions have to be persuasive; the reader must be convinced by any argument and go along with the writer. Recommendations are best written as though they were to be detached from the report. In this way they can be kept as short and factual as possible, avoiding any overlap with the conclusions. If the recommendations are extensive it may be worth subdividing them, for instance into long term or short term, or by the different people or agencies who should implement them.

Letter writing

Before commencing letter writing there are several things you will need to determine; these are:

1 To whom are you writing?
2 What do you want to include?
3 In what order do you want to say it?
4 Do you want to sound pleased, angry, formal?

If you are writing a formal letter to a materials supplier or the local council, for example, it is necessary to choose your words carefully to be sure that your letter is not misunderstood. In formal letters you need to include only the information necessary to get the reaction you want. The order in which you set out the letter is important particularly when writing a letter of complaint. You need to set out the facts in the order in which they happened, then say what you want done about your complaint.

When you write a letter it is usual to put your own address in the top right-hand corner of the page and to include all details, particularly the post code. If you are writing on behalf of a company you may use their own pre-addressed or 'headed' paper; the address used should be the one where you wish a reply to your letter to come to.

After the address you should write the date of the day that you are writing the letter, and also any reference number or letter which you wish to code or identify your letter by. If you do not know the name of the person you are writing to it is usual to start with 'Dear Sir or Madam'. If you do know the person's name you use it with their title, for example 'Dear Mr Jones', 'Dear Ms Bright'.

If you are writing a formal reply to a letter you have received it helps to refer to the date of that letter and any reference code or number used in that letter.

As you write you will need to consider how you want the reader to feel and what you want the reader to do. This will affect the way you put things and the words you choose. When you have completed writing do the following:

1 Read it through carefully.
2 Does it make sense?
3 Will the person who is going to read it understand it?
4 Does it convey the relevant information?

If you are not happy with it, you may want to make changes and copy it out again.

When you are satisfied with the layout and content of your letter it is necessary to finish. If you began your letter by using 'Dear Sir/Madam' it is usual to finish with 'Yours faithfully' and your signature followed by your name in block capitals.

If you know the name of the person you are writing to, it is usual to finish the letter with 'Yours sincerely' and your signature, followed by your name in block capitals.

It is good practice to file formal or business letters you receive; this provides a useful check as to exactly what was said or agreed in any earlier communication. This is particularly important with certain kinds of letters, for example from:

1 An employer,
2 A landlord,
3 A solicitor,
4 Anyone making a complaint against you.

One good way of filing letters is to make or buy a folder with sections for each topic or subject, and within each section file the letters in date order, i.e. the sequence in which they were received. As well as keeping the letters you receive, it is often wise to retain copies of important letters you send;

then, if your letter is lost or mislaid or someone telephones and asks you about it, you will have your copy of the letter for ~~reference. Copies may be made with the use~~

extra forms to practise on.

Most plumbers will have to fill in a weekly time sheet (Figure 6.12). The kind of information you may need to write on forms is:

1 Your full name,
2 Names of members of your family,
3 Your address and telephone number,
4 Date of birth (d.o.b.),

5 Place of birth,
6 Nationality,
7 Job or occupation,
8 Name and address of employer,

~~all times. If you have a serious accident,~~ information will help the police or the hospital to contact your family quickly.

It is important to keep written records, since they:

1 Save you having to try to remember lots of information,
2 Can help you not to make mistakes when you are asked for information,
3 Can help you prove that something belongs to you,
4 Can help to prove that you are telling the truth,
5 Provide a useful record of events and happenings.

It's sensible to keep certain kinds of information, for example *bills* you have paid, particularly for services provided, or tools and materials purchased; you should also keep *receipts*. This is so you can prove that you have paid. You may need to produce a receipt if you want to make a complaint or change something.

Applying for a job

When you apply for a job or a change of employment you may need to fill in an application form or write a letter. You are often asked to provide details about the employment you have had in the past, or about your previous education. Most employers keep an Employee's Record Card as shown in Figure 6.13 (overleaf). You need to be able to write:

LB construction weekly time sheet

Name _____

Craft _____

Week commencing _____

Registered office

	Job title	Description of work	Time: start/finish	total
MON				
TUE				
WED				
THUR				
FRI				
SAT				
SUN				

Details of expenses (attach receipts)

Authorized by _____ Position _____

For office use only

Standard hours	_____ at _____	=	_____
Overtime hours	_____ at _____	=	_____
Overtime hours	_____ at _____	=	_____
Overtime hours	_____ at _____	=	_____
		TOTAL =	_____

Figure 6.12 *Time sheet*

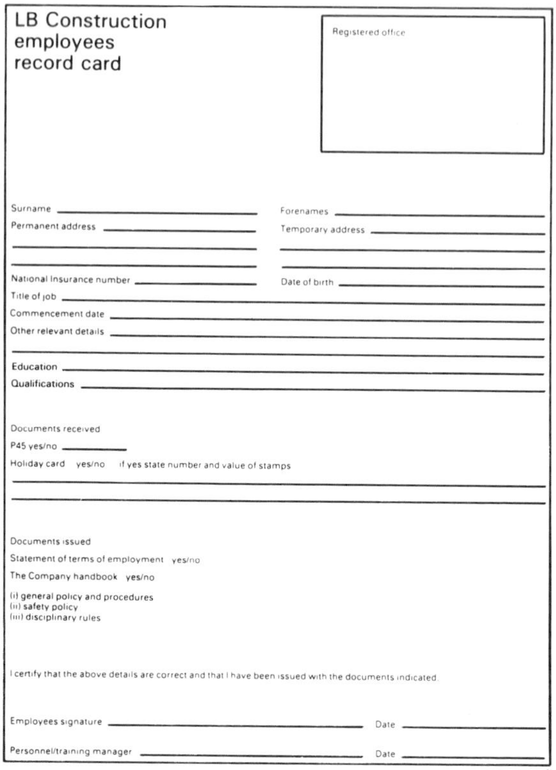

LB Construction
employees
record card

Registered office

Surname
Forenames
Permanent address
Temporary address
National Insurance number
Date of birth
Title of job
Commencement date
Other relevant details
Education
Qualifications

Documents received
P45 yes/no
Holiday card yes/no if yes state number and value of stamps

Documents issued
Statement of terms of employment yes/no
The Company handbook yes/no
(i) general policy and procedures
(ii) safety policy
(iii) disciplinary rules

I certify that the above details are correct and that I have been issued with the documents indicated.

Employees signature
Date
Personnel/training manager
Date

Figure 6.13 *Employee's record card*

1 The name of each firm you have worked for;
2 What sort of job you did,
3 The date you commenced employment with each firm,
4 The date you ceased employment with each firm,
5 The name of educational establishments where you have studied,
6 The title or name of the course or subjects completed,
7 The dates you commenced and finished your studies,
8 Qualifications obtained and examination results.

You may also be asked how much you were paid by different employers. It is very difficult to remember all this information, and writing it down saves you having to remember. Some people keep a special notebook or personal log book for information like this and update it at regular intervals or when they start or finish a job or a course of study.

Writing is an important communication skill, and one which needs to be practised at regular intervals, although like many other skills once it is mastered it is never forgotten. A person's writing is often considered as a reflection of their character or personality. Its importance in giving people an impression of the writer and as a means of communication should never be underestimated.

Job planning and organisation

Most plumbing contracts, whether for a new building or refurbishment of an existing structure, are priced to very tight margins and the difference between employers making a profit or a loss depends on the quality of the craftsperson on site. It is important, therefore, that craftspersons organise themselves and others to ensure the smooth running of any job. A well-run contract is a credit to all concerned with it. It is no use expecting high standards from others if you do not work to high standards yourself.

To start with, establish a work programme. This will enable you to plan ahead and build confidence. A good organiser always looks ahead and knows exactly what is to be done next. To avoid unnecessary delay and prevent wastage of materials, make certain that all materials are ordered for delivery at the time they are required, and that a suitable space has been designated for their storage. When materials arrive they must be checked to determine that they are of the right quantity and quality and not damaged in any way. Suppliers usually require you to sign a delivery receipt or note to this effect and so checking is important.

Always provide protection for materials before they are used. Plumbing components are expensive and some are easily damaged, therefore safe and secure storage areas where materials can be stacked and covered with a tarpaulin or dust sheet are essential.

Whatever the type of job good organisation will help to ensure smooth progress throughout the contract. As the work progresses and different stages are completed they must be protected from damage by

unheated buildings, thermostatic control valves and other sensitive components should not be fitted in position until necessary, and then protected by masking.

Pipework systems, whether for hot (Figure 6.14) or cold water, gas or waste water (above or below ground discharge pipe systems) should be tested for soundness and other appropriate tests should be carried out as each section of the system is completed. The dates of these tests and the names of the persons who applied the tests and who enforced the tests standard should be recorded in the site or job diary for future reference. A site log or job diary is a very useful document for recording items such as:

1 Dates when deliveries of material or equipment were received,
2 Stages of progress of the work,
3 Visits to the site by the Local Authority or other inspectors.

recorded). The snagging procedure is usually carried out by the clerk of works or a representative of the client.

If you are asked to provide a snagging list a sensible system is to start inside the building and work your way around the project in a methodical manner, so ensuring that all details are examined. Depending on the nature of the works a useful check-list could be as follows:

1 Test cold and hot water systems for leaks and efficiency.
2 Test heating system. Check components to ensure correct operation.
3 Test and check above ground discharge pipe system.
4 Test and check below ground discharge pipe system.
5 Inspect and check sanitary appliances for possible damage and correct operation.
6 Inspect and check roof weatherings, gutters and rainwater pipes.

All systems and components should be left in working order when testing and commissioning has been completed unless instructions in the specification state otherwise. Surplus and redundant materials and equipment should be removed from the site and all work areas cleaned and left tidy. Leaflets and user's instructions for components should be handed over to the client before leaving the site.

Quality work, satisfaction in a job well done at a competitive price and a satisfied

Figure 6.14 *Checking for soundness*

customer go together to ensure good public and customer relations for the plumber.

Customer and public relations

From the operative's point of view it is unlikely that lengthy meetings with the customer or client will be encountered, but, in the event, the craftsperson should be seen to be capable, suitably attired (Figure 6.15),

Figure 6.15

conscientious and polite. On no account should an operative make any derisory comments regarding his or her employer to the client.

The reason for good customer relations is fairly obvious since a satisfied customer is generally a customer who will provide future enquiries and possibly be prepared to negotiate the cost of an installation with a known contractor rather than go for a competitive tender.

Many contracting organisations employ staff specially skilled in the art of soliciting enquiries from potential customers.

Presentation plays a major part in negotiations. Many clients are non-technical and rely on agents such as architects or consulting engineers to handle negotiations on their behalf. A good presentation of drawings and documents, together with a prompt and efficient service, will be a major advantage to the contractor. In most cases, first impressions count, and a good front person backed up with an efficient service and well turned-out documentation will win the day.

Working in occupied buildings, whether domestic, industrial or commercial, requires a more demanding code of conduct from the craftsperson than when working in an empty building or on a new site.

It is important to consider the impression you give to the householder or user of the building – consider how you would expect a worker to perform in your home or place of work. The following list includes items for consideration, although these will of course vary depending on the nature of the work, i.e. routine or breakdown visit, service call, emergency call, replacement or refurbishment contract, installing a new heating system, etc.:

1 Arrive on time.
2 Obtain user's opinion of problem (breakdown visit).
3 Lay down dust sheets to protect floors, carpets, etc.
4 Advise the building occupier if and when you are going to turn off any service such as water, gas, electricity.
5 Keep the client informed of your progress.
6 Inform the building occupier if you have to leave the site for any reason.
7 Ask permission if you wish to use a telephone.
8 Do not borrow tools or other items from the building occupier.
9 Work to a planned sequence of operations which causes the minimum inconvenience.
10 Clean up as you complete various stages of the work.
11 Test all disturbed unions and joints.
12 Test all new components for soundness and satisfactory operation.
13 Instruct the user on the operation of the appliance or component.
14 Leave all appliances and components

commissioned and working unless instructed otherwise.

15 Clean up, and leave the job in a clean satisfactory condition.

16 Hand over any users' instructions or

that it is in your own interest to do a good job at a price acceptable to the customer. Everyone in the plumbing craft should work to achieve better standards of work.

Plumbing organisations

There are several organisations and institutions associated with the plumbing industry:

The Worshipful Company of Plumbers
The Institute of Plumbing
The Electrical Electronic Telecommunication and Plumbing Union
The Joint Industry Board for Plumbing Mechanical Engineering Services in England and Wales
The Confederation for the Registration of Gas Installers

On the following pages the history and

Figure 6.16

functions of these various organisations are described.

The Worshipful Company of Plumbers

restored in the reign of William and Mary. The Ordinances governing how the Company should operate are much older, the first being laid down in 1365 and subsequent further Ordinances in 1488. In 1532 the Company shared a Hall with the Vintners' Company and in 1639 the first Court Meeting was held in the Plumbers' own Hall in Chequers Yard. This Hall was destroyed by fire in 1666 and when rebuilt was occupied until 1863. At this time, the Hall was compulsorily purchased in order to build Cannon Street Railway station and from that date the Company held its meetings in other Livery Halls. There is a plaque at the station entrance commemorating the Company's former home. The Company has never lost its connection with the Art and Mysterie of Plumbing and was the instigator of the concept of a Register of Plumbers, a logical successor to the medieval role of the Company. The Register of Plumbers was inaugurated in 1886 and efforts to get 'The Plumbers' Registration Act' through Parliament occupied the activities of the Company in the 1890s. In 1893 the Company equipped a laboratory in King's College, London, during the Mayorality of Alderman Sir Stuart Knill, who was Master of the Company. Today the Institute of Plumbing carries on the tradition. The Company maintains close links with the Institute of Plumbing, Copper and Lead Development Associations, and all branches of Industry. The award of a gold medal to one of the top six students in the

City and Guilds of London Institute Plumbing examination demonstrates current interest in the profession and further education.

In addition, the Company sponsored and equipped a museum which is housed in the 'Court Barn'⁄ at the Weald and Downland Open Air Museum, Singleton, near Chichester, West Sussex. Every summer, plumbing students and staff from colleges of further education demonstrate their skills at the Plumbers' Museum by working with lead and other traditional materials.

Role of the Company
The Company exists to:

1   Foster, maintain and develop links with the plumbing craft and allied disciplines in the construction and other industries.
2   Promote as appropriate youth activities in the craft by financial and technical contributions to educational and vocational ventures.
3   Contribute to the City of London Charities.
4   Support the 'pursuit of excellence' so that through contact with other organisations the Company is able to call on past experience for the benefit of future enterprises.
5   Provide a pleasant social ambience for those in the Company.

The Institute of Plumbing
The Institute is an independent organisation embracing all interests in the plumbing industry.

The Institute sees its prime role as the identification and promotion of competence, skill, workmanship and standards for the public benefit.

Whereas most other professional institutions are somewhat élitist in outlook and cater only for those above craft level, the Institute's requirements for entry are broad in scope, reflecting the largely practical nature of the UK plumbing industry.

Figure 6.17

Figure 6.18

The Institute encourages young people to progress up the ladder of qualification it offers from apprentice to technician engineer.

History
The Institute was founded as the Institute of Plumbers in 1906 by the National Association of Master Plumbers with the objective of developing both the industrial and technical

aspects of the plumbing trade. Membership was limited to Master Plumber members of the Association.

In 1925 that Association became the

bers was revised in 1957 and the Institute of Plumbing then came into existence under the name which it still proudly enjoys. In that year, for the first time, membership extended to plumbers holding technical qualifications irrespective of their position in the industry.

In the late 1960s discussions began between the Institute and the Registered Plumbers' Association with the object of effecting a merger of the two bodies. The main role of the RPA was to manage a voluntary register on behalf of the Worshipful Company of Plumbers.

After considerable negotiation, the IOP/RPA merger was completed in 1970, when it was realised there was a pressing need for a single organisation to establish the technical authority of the plumbing industry in the wider field of building services and to manage the Register of Plumbers.

Today, the Institute is an independent, non-political organisation pursuing its major objectives of raising the science and practice of plumbing in the public interest and managing the Register of Plumbers, with compulsory registration in mind.

In 1979 the Institute became a Registered Charity, thereby acknowledging that its aims and objectives are primarily in the public interest.

Activities
The Institute's activities reflect its role as both a qualifying body and learned society. A wealth of information and expertise exists

within the membership and this is used to great effect when the Institute is called upon by Government Departments, technical and educational institutions to give its views on a wide range of topics.

drafting of standards and codes of practice affecting plumbing work, subsequently published by the British Standards Institution.

It supports the work of other voluntary organisations which promote high installation standards, namely the Confederation for the Registration of Gas Installers (CORGI), of which it is a founder constituent organisation, and the National Inspection Council for Electrical Installation Contracting (NICEIC).

There is an excellent relationship between the Institute and the manufacturing and distributing sectors of the plumbing industry. Communication is through the Industrial Associate category of membership and its Liaison Committee of representatives nominated by Industrial Associate members.

The Institute's historical close links with the Worshipful Company of Plumbers continues today. There is contact through regular meetings and the Institute is an active supporter of the Company's Plumbers' Workshop and Museum, established in the Weald and Downland Open Air Museum at Singleton, near Chichester, Sussex.

In the education and training field the Institute gives help and guidance to the Plumbing Examinations Committee of the City and Guilds and the relevant committees of the Technician Education Council and the Scottish Technical Education Council. It is also represented on the Mechanical Engineering Services Committee of the Construction Industry Training Board, as well as several regional and local committees dealing with construction training. Many lecturers of plumbing at colleges are members of the Institute.

At local level, the Institute's District Councils arrange lectures, visits and other events to increase the knowledge and expertise of members and Registered Plumbers, updating their appreciation of new materials and methods, etc. and broadening their interests. They also arrange events that enable like-minded people to meet socially.

The Institute regularly stages exhibitions in major towns and cities throughout the country and these often attract large attendances, not only of plumbers, but also of architects, engineers, merchants and others with an interest in plumbing. There is also an annual conference, when significant papers are presented and important topics discussed.

The Register of Plumbers
In 1883 the Worshipful Company of Plumbers inaugurated a voluntary system for the national registration of plumbers.

A congress was held at the National Health Exhibition and as a result the registration scheme became established and a register was instituted in 1886.

Statutory registration of plumbers
As part of its policy to achieve better plumbing standards, the Institute condemns the present system in the UK which permits incompetent persons to practise as plumbers. The Institute considers this presents a constant threat to the health, safety and well-being of the community. There is ample evidence to support this belief and the dangers are increasing as plumbing services become more sophisticated and complex. With the advent of fully pressurised hot and cold plumbing systems the risks will multiply and become even more serious in nature.

The Institute believes that all those who install plumbing work for gain should be

registered and required to perform to the highest standards of workmanship.

Application for membership
Applicants for admission to the Fellow, Member, Associate and Affiliate categories who can produce adequate evidence of practical competence in plumbing are automatically enrolled to a class of the Register of Plumbers appropriate to their training, qualifications and experience.

Existing members who wish to apply for transfer, and Registered Plumbers who wish to apply for a category of membership, are requested to do so on the appropriate form whenever possible.

Application forms can be obtained from:

The Institute of Plumbing
64 Station Lane
Hornchurch
Essex RM12 6NB

Electrical Electronic Telecommunication and Plumbing Union (formerly Plumbing Trades Union)
Local societies of plumbers are known to have existed before 1800 and there is evidence that Francis Place, a London tailor largely responsible for the repeal of the Combination Acts in 1824, had drafted rules for such societies in the closing years of the eighteenth century.

The Operative Plumbers appears to have existed as a regional society in 1831. This society covered only the north of England. An attempt was made to organise London

Figure 6.19

plumbers at the beginning of 1834, but the society disappeared.

There is certainly adequate surviving proof ... Operative Plumbers' and Glaziers'

was the practice of moving headquarters from one town to another at intervals varying from 2 to 5 years and changing the Executive Committee on each occasion. This nomadic existence continued with monotonous and disruptive regularity until 1921. Other unions with 'no fixed abode' in those early years included the carpenters and the bricklayers.

The existing national Union of Plumbers dates from 1865. The Manchester Society of Plumbers entered into negotiations with their Liverpool counterparts and at a conference held at the Star and Garter Hotel, St John's Lane, Liverpool, in December 1865 the rules of the new organisation were endorsed by delegates from thirteen towns. Total membership of the United Plumbers' Association, at the time of inauguration, was 892 and the secretary of the Liverpool Society, J.H. Dobb, was installed as 'Corresponding Secretary' with a salary of about £20 per annum.

After the first twelve months the Association had increased its membership to more than 1500 in 31 lodges throughout Great Britain and Ireland. The average weekly wage for a craftsman plumber was then 25s. (125p) for a 55-hour working week: his union contribution was 3d. (approximately 1½p).

The Operative Plumbers' Association made steady progress during the later Victorian years, although on more than one occasion its stability was seriously threatened by internal strife. The 'parent of the Association' (Manchester Lodge) withdrew in 1870 after a bitter dispute with the Executive

Council over voting returns on proposals to increase the weekly contribution to 4d. (2p) and limit payment of unemployment benefit to eight weeks. Two years later Glasgow ... succeeded in estab-

Association's finances were under constant strain, caused largely by increasing industrial conflict and heavy payments of strike benefit.

Adversity, however, frequently produces saviours. The dire state of affairs in the Plumbers' Association in 1879 led to the resignation of the General Secretary W.J. Barnett and his replacement by George Barker Cherry of Hull. Cherry's task was twofold: to rescue the union from extinction and, simultaneously, to protect its members from the worst effects of the industrial depression which then gripped Victorian Britain.

Raymond Postgate says that with the appointment of Cherry, the United Operative Plumbers' Association gained something in strength and much in reputation. 'He was an official of the older type, obstinate and narrow in many ways but energetic, of enormous force of character, able and unquestionably honest. Cherry gave the Society stability and some rudiments of a coherent policy.' George Cherry was destined to lead the plumbers through good times and bad for nearly 25 years.

The Victorian craftsman was a proud worker. Characteristic of the artisan class in general were a deep-routed conservatism and a large measure of snobbery, which were reflections of the social and moral climate of the period. They were epitomised in a remark made by George May, UOPA General Secretary from 1868–76, that plumbers were 'the most independent class in the building trade'. A top-hat and moleskin trousers still formed part of the plumber's customary regalia when he paraded in late Victorian times.

Cherry's only notable failure in all his years of leadership was his inability to break down this prejudice and persuade the plumbers that the range of admission to the Union should be extended beyond the narrow confines of the craft. As industry developed new trades were emerging on all sides – whitesmiths, iron fitters, gas fitters, and many more. In spite of his repeated appeals at successive delegate meetings, Cherry's members were obdurate in restricting membership to plumbing craftsmen and apprentices. Thus were sown the seeds of future conflicts with younger (but often more powerful) unions which sprang up in the latter part of the nineteenth century to assimilate workers whose spheres of operation gradually encroached upon and overlapped those of the plumber.

This inter-union demarcation warfare reached its fiercest point in the years immediately preceding the First World War, when the acrimony engendered between the plumbers and other tradesmen – notably the heating engineers – was so deep that it endured for nearly half a century.

During the first great European conflict the plumbers strengthened their ties with other building unions within a federal body, established as the National Wages and Conditions Council and later to become the National Federation of Building Trades Operatives. With a substantial membership in the shipbuilding industry, the UOPA was also a member-union of the Confederation of Shipbuilding and Engineering Unions and the plumbers have twice provided the Confederation with a President: Sir John W. Stephenson (plumber's General Secretary from 1929–49) in the 'thirties and Brother Fred McGuffie (EETPU Division Executive Officer) in 1973.

In 1921 the plumbers took possession of the premises in Clapham in south-west London which were to remain their permanent headquarters until amalgamation with the ETU in 1968. The post-war delegate meeting of 1919 had also decided that members of the Executive Council should be full-time officers, elected every five years. At last the days of itinerant government were over: the Union was given a permanent home and a stable administration.

When the Plumbing Trades' Union (as it became in 1946) celebrated its centenary in 1965 it was firmly established on the British industrial scene with a membership of 55,000.

The EETPU is a powerful organisation of over 420,000 members in every industry and area of the country. It was founded in the last century and has a great deal of experience in representing members. But the organisation and service is right up-to-date, using modern techniques and employing highly qualified staff.

The total membership now stands in excess of 420,000 and covers perhaps every single major industrial sector of the economy. In addition to the recruitment of skilled and apprentice electricians and plumbers, the Union also has in membership both male and female production workers, storemen, etc. and is at present rapidly expanding into those areas of technical and administrative employment where for many years it has represented the interests of skilled manual employees.

The members are serviced by a structure of officials headed by the Union's General Secretary and Executive Council. National Officers cover nationwide those members employed in specific industries whilst Area Officials and Full-time Branch Officials represent the members within their own geographical area. District shop floor liaison between members and the Union is made via the shop steward or convenor and the various officials.

The Union provides a number of financial benefits to its members, including accident benefit, funeral benefit, disablement grants and strike benefit. In addition the Union provides convalescence facilities to members at the Union's convalescent home at Torquay and makes a grant towards holidays for long ̲ ̲ ̲ ̲ ̲ ̲ Training for shop stewards

from its officials and by way of the benefits and facilities, firmly established the EETPU as one of the most progressive unions in the country.

For more details write to:

EETPU
Hayes Court
West Common Road
Bromley
Kent

The Joint Industry Board for Plumbing Mechanical Engineering Services in England and Wales

The JIB's main function is to establish national conditions of service for the Plumbing Mechanical Engineering Service Industry in England and Wales. After negotiations between the organisations representing the employers of plumbing and labour operative plumbers, the JIB lays down rates of pay, hours of work, holidays, etc. The JIB is also a registered body for the plumbing industry craft apprenticeship scheme and is involved in the design and operation of courses of further education and specialised training courses for the plumbing industry. The JIB's constituent bodies are:

The National Association of Plumbing, Heating and Mechanical Services Contractors
The Electrical, Electronic, Telecommunication and Plumbing Union
The Building Employers' Federation

Plumbing is no longer concerned just with working in lead as the name would suggest, but has developed into an important component of both environmental and mechanical engineering, embracing a wide variety of systems, services and complex equipment. ̲ ̲ ̲ ̲ ̲ in the scope of training and installations. The Board's grading system provides sections of the industry with the opportunity of management status for those undertaking the available courses of further study.

The apprenticeship scheme

In order to provide and maintain the skilled workforce required by the industry the JIB has laid down an apprenticeship scheme which encourages apprentices to study for qualifications which will permit them to progress through the industry's career structure and qualify for additional allowances.

It is essential to those young people entering the industry that their apprenticeship is registered under a Training Service Agreement with the Joint Industry Board.

This ensures that the apprentice will be employed under the correct terms and conditions and that the employers will support college attendance.

Apprenticeships served under a JIB Training Service Agreement are recognised by all industrial bodies and are insisted upon by some countries for immigration purposes.

The grading scheme

This scheme is designed to ensure that entrants to the industry have the opportunity to progress within the industry as their qualifications and experience increase. The industry pay structure is linked to the Grading Scheme so that progression through the Grading Scheme leads to increased rates of pay.

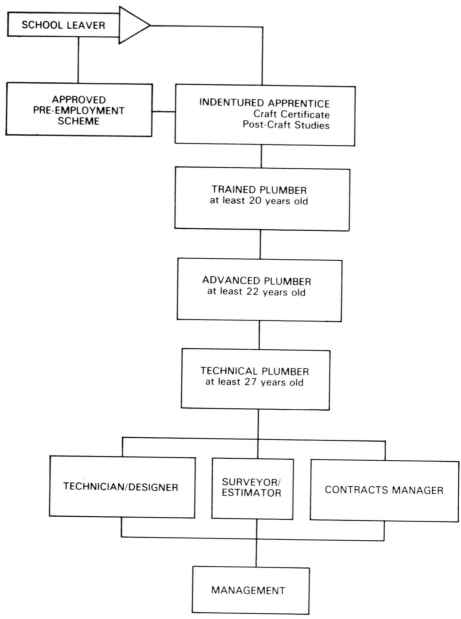

Figure 6.20   *Typical career pattern*

Pay allowances and benefits

1   All operatives and apprentices enrolled in the Industry's Benefit Scheme are entitled to Sick Pay additional to that provided by the State Scheme. They are also covered for accidental loss of limbs and permanent disability.

2   A weekly Tool Allowance is paid by employers to all apprentices and operatives who possess the full range of tools as stipulated by the JIB.

3   Operative plumbers in possession of JIB Certificates of Competency in Welding are entitled to an hourly pay supplement.

4   Travelling time and expenses are paid by employers to apprentices and operatives when and where appropriate.

5   All operatives and apprentices employed

operated by Plumbing Pension (UK) Ltd.

Additional information on the Plumbing Mechanical Services Industry can be

Rochdale,
Lancs   OL12 9EN
Telephone Number: 0706–522849

Telephone Number: 0532–786172

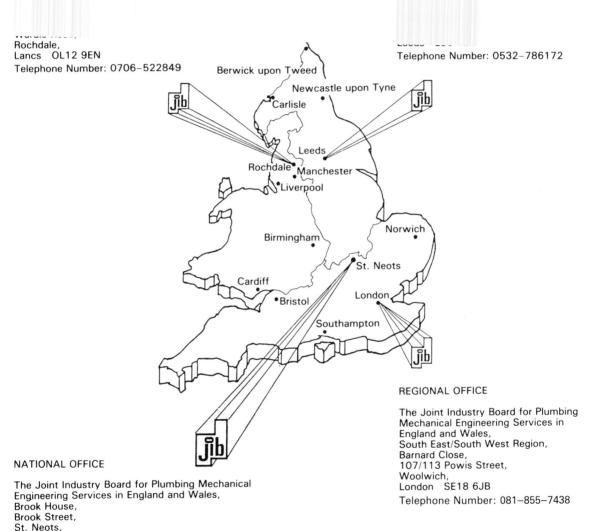

Berwick upon Tweed

Newcastle upon Tyne

Carlisle

Leeds

Rochdale   Manchester

Liverpool

Birmingham

Norwich

St. Neots

Cardiff

Bristol

London

Southampton

REGIONAL OFFICE

The Joint Industry Board for Plumbing
Mechanical Engineering Services in
England and Wales,
South East/South West Region,
Barnard Close,
107/113 Powis Street,
Woolwich,
London   SE18 6JB
Telephone Number: 081–855–7438

NATIONAL OFFICE

The Joint Industry Board for Plumbing Mechanical
Engineering Services in England and Wales,
Brook House,
Brook Street,
St. Neots,
Huntingdon
Cambridgeshire,
PE19 2HW
Telephone Number: 0480–76925

Figure 6.21

CORGI

CORGI (Confederation for the Registration of Gas Installers) was formed at the instigation of the Government in 1970 after a series of incidents involving gas explosions and/or fatalities in which the cause had been traced back to faulty installation of gas equipment.

Figure 6.22

A voluntary registration scheme was, at the time, considered to be the most workable and most acceptable to the trade, and so CORGI came into being as a self-governing body with the following organisations as current members:

Institute of Plumbing
Master Gasfitters' Association
Federation of Master Builders
Heating and Ventilating Contractors' Association
Building Employers' Confederation
National Association of Plumbing, Heating and Mechanical Services Contractors
Scottish and Northern Ireland Plumbing Employers' Federation
Society of British Gas Industries
British Gas Corporation

How CORGI works

The prime function of CORGI is to promote safe and satisfactory standards in the installation of pipes, fittings and appliances used in connection with the supply of gas by the British Gas Corporation. It does this by maintaining a Register of installing firms which regularly achieve the necessary standards. By this means, gas customers can make their selection from traders whose work is performed to safe and satisfactory standards.

In this way, as more and more customers employ only CORGI-registered installers for their gas work, it is hoped to squeeze out those who have for so long bedevilled the gas installing trade and its reputation.

CORGI's general policy is formulated by a National Council comprising representatives of the constituent bodies and is carried out by twelve Regional Committees made up of the regional representatives of the same bodies.

Regulations applicable from 30 March 1991 introduce a statutory registration scheme for gas installers. This requires every gas installation business and self-employed gas installer undertaking work subject to the Gas Safety (Installation and Use) Regulations 1984 to belong to a class of persons approved by the Health and Safety Executive (HSE).

Overall administration is in the hands of a small headquarters' staff in London.

For further details telephone your local CORGI Regional Secretary or write to:

CORGI
St Martin's House
140 Tottenham Court Road
London W1P 9LN

7 Glossary

tive and so used to separate gases, e.g. removal of carbon dioxide from air by an alkaline solution.

Accelerator Inorganic or organic substance added to speed up any chemical reaction.

Acetone A liquid with the ability to dissolve 25 times its own volume of acetylene for each atmosphere of pressure applied to it.

Acetylene A gas produced from calcium carbide and water. It is combustible and is used with oxygen in welding processes.

Air A mixture of gases with an average composition of nitrogen 78%, oxygen 21%, argon 0.9%, carbon dioxide 0.03% plus smaller quantities of other gases.

Anti-freeze A substance added to cooling systems to reduce freezing point below probable ambient temperatures (often ethylene glycol).

Anti-flooding valve A drain fitting incorporating a mechanical non-return device as a means of giving a measure of protection to a drain or sewer against surcharge.

Asbestos A mineral substance consisting of thin, tough fibres which can withstand high temperatures. The Asbestos (Prohibition) Regulations 1985 prohibit the importation of raw asbestos fibres, or products containing them, into Britain, and also their use in the manufacture and repair of any other product. Asbestos spraying and the installation of new asbestos insulation are not allowed.

Autogenous A welded joint in which two parts of the same metal are joined together with or without a filler rod of the same metal.

Backing bars Pieces of metal placed on the underside of a weld to assist in obtaining the required penetration and root fusion of the weld. They are temporary and are removed after completion of the welded joint.

Baffles Pieces of metal fitted inside a gas burner by its manufacturer to prevent more gas reaching one part of the burner than another.

Base Substance which in aqueous solution reacts with an acid to form a salt and water only.

Basement A storey where the floor is at some point more than 1.2 m below the surface of the adjoining ground.

Bauxite An ore of aluminium.

Bedding The material on which an underground pipe is laid and which provides support for the pipe. Bedding for drainage pipelines can be concrete or granular material.

Benching The sloping surfaces on either side of a channel at the base of an inspection chamber, for the purpose of confining the flow of sewage.

Blende Zinc sulphide, the chief ore of zinc.

Blinding A material used to fill irregularities in an exposed trench bottom, which when compacted will create a firm uniform foundation on which to place the pipe bedding material. Hoggin, sand, gravel, all-in aggregate or lean concrete are commonly used.

Bore The internal diameter of a pipe or fitting.

Branch drain   A line of pipes installed to discharge into a junction on another line or at a point of access.

Brass   A large group of alloys based on copper and zinc.

Brazing   The joining of metals using a low melting point bronze rod as in capillary or silver soldering (hard soldering).

Bronze welding   The joining of metals using a bronze filler rod with a high melting point. The deposited rod forms a built up joint pattern (also known as hard soldering).

Butadiene   A colourless gas, which polymerises to give a type of synthetic rubber.

Butane   A gas which is present in natural gas and is sold compressed in cylinders for industrial and domestic purposes.

Butt weld   A weld joining two pieces of metal, both pieces being in the same plane.

Calorific value   The heating power of a fuel.

Capillary attraction   A general term covering surface tension phenomena, e.g. the rise or fall of liquids in capillary tubes, fibres and materials.

Carburising flame   A flame in which an excess of acetylene is being burned.

Cast iron   Iron containing 2.5–4% carbon in the form of graphite. Cast iron is brittle but heat resisting.

Cathode   A negative electrode.

Caulked joint   A spigot and socket joint in which the jointing material is compacted by means of a caulking tool.

Chamfer   The edge of a piece of metal or pipe shaped off to form an angle other than a right angle.

Change of state   Transformation of a substance from one of the physical states of matter (solid, liquid, gas) to another, i.e. melting, freezing, boiling or condensing.

Channel   A half section semi-circular pipe.

Chemical change   A change in a substance involving a rearrangement of the atoms in the molecules to produce a different substance or substances.

Chromium   A hard white metal, widely used in the production of alloy (stainless) steels and as a plating metal.

Clay   A material used in pottery, sanitary ware and drainage pipeline manufacture.

Cleaning eye   An access opening in a pipe or pipe fitting arranged to facilitate the clearing of obstructions and fitted with a cap, plug or cover plate.

Combined system   A drainage system in which foul water and surface water are conveyed by the same pipes.

Concave fillet   A fillet weld with an inward curve.

Convex fillet   A fillet weld with an outward curve.

Cracking   Thermal splitting of substances, especially petroleum hydrocarbons into substances of lower molecular weight. Mineral oils can be converted into petrol using this method.

Detergent   A surface active agent which combines good wetting power with the ability to remove grease and dirt from surfaces.

Deposited metal   The actual metal deposited by the filler rod during a welding operation.

Diffusion   The tendency of molecules of a gas to spread out and fill a container or space, or to intermingle with another gas; many liquids also mix by diffusion.

Distillation   The process of converting a substance into vapour, leading off the vapour, and converting it back into liquid by cooling. It is used to separate a liquid from substances that are soluble in it, or to separate liquids of differing boiling points.

Double branch   A branch fitting used to connect two branch pipes or channels from opposite sides to a main pipe or channel.

Double collar   A pipe fitting usually in the form of a sleeve for joining the spigot or plain ends of two pipes in the same alignment.

Downhand weld   A weld made in a flat, gravity position.

Drain   A line of pipes normally underground, including all fittings and equipment such as inspection chambers, traps and gullies, intended to convey foul water and/or surface water.

Drain chute A tapered drain fitting fitted to the inlet or outlet of an inspection chamber

Edge preparation The shaping of the edges of the parent metal prior to welding.

Fatigue, metallic Failure of a metal sheet or component brought about by repeated stress. It is related to changes in the crystal structure of the metal.

Feldspar A material used in the manufacture of ceramics and enamels.

Filler metal The material that is added to the weld pool to assist in filling the joint space. It forms an integral part of the weld.

Flames

Neutral flame A clean flame burning equal amounts of oxygen and acetylene.

Oxidising flame A flame with an excess of oxygen.

Carburising flame A flame with an excess of acetylene gas.

Flange A projecting flat rim which may be cast, screwed or welded onto a pipe, fitting or vessel, and is used for making a joint.

Flash-back arrestor A safety device fitted to a cylinder regulator (outlet).

Flexible joint A joint designed and made to permit small angular deflection and small changes in the length of a drain without loss of watertightness.

Fluorescein A dye used in water for drainage pipeline tracing purposes.

Foul water Any water contaminated by soil, waste or trade effluent.

Fresh air inlet A fitting, usually with a hinged flap, used to allow air to enter a system of drainage.

Fusion welding Welding of metals which are in a molten state without the application of pressure.

pressure to an appliance

Gas welding A process of joining metals, using the heat of combustion of an oxygen/fuel gas mixture to melt and fuse together the edges of the parts to be welded, generally with the addition of a filler metal.

Gauze Perforated sheet metal often fitted below burner ports and used to 'even out' the internal gas pressure and reduce the danger of 'back lighting' in the burner port.

Governor A device which automatically controls the gas pressure in a pipeline.

Grease trap A chamber incorporated into a drainage pipeline used for preventing grease from passing into the system of drainage.

Ground water Water occurring naturally at or below the water table.

Gully A drainage fitting or assembly of fittings used to receive surface water and/or the liquid discharge from waste pipes. The top may have a grating or sealed access cover.

Haunching Additional concrete support at the sides of a drain pipe above the foundation bedding.

Hydraulic gradient The 'loss of head' in liquid flowing in a pipe or channel expressed per unit length in the pipe or channel.

Hydraulic mean depth A factor used in calculating the rate of flow of a liquid in a pipe or channel. It is obtained by dividing the cross-sectional area of the liquid by the length of the wetted perimeter of the pipe or channel.

Infiltration The unintended ingress of ground water into a drain or sewer.

Inspection chamber A covered chamber constructed on a drain or sewer so as to provide access to the drainage pipeline.

Interceptor A trap fixed on a drain to prevent the passage of sewer gases or vermin into the drain. It is normally fixed on the outlet side of the inspection chamber.

Interceptor (reverse action) A trap designed to be fitted on the inlet side of an inspection chamber with a reverse clearing arm giving access to the drain against the direction of water flow.

Invert The lowest point of the internal surface of a drain, sewer or channel.

Iron A grey, magnetic metal which forms the basis of a wide range of different types of steel.

Joule A unit of work. It is named after J. P. Joule who conducted research on the mechanical equivalence of heat.

Junction A fitting on a drainage pipeline designed to receive discharges from a branch drain.

Kinetic Due to movement or motion.

Lever A rigid bar pivoted about a fixed point of support called the fulcrum.

Lint A substance which may choke up pre-aerated gas burners, and is derived from dust and fibres in the room of a dwelling.

Manhole A term which is often used to describe an inspection chamber, i.e. a chamber constructed on a drain or sewer to provide access for inspection, testing or the clearance of an obstruction. The usual interpretation is that a shallow chamber is termed an inspection chamber, and chambers of such depth that an operative cannot work from ground level are referred to as manholes.

Manometer An instrument used to measure differences in pressure. The usual form consists of a U-shaped tube mounted vertically and filled with a liquid to a predetermined level.

Molecule The smallest part of a substance which can exist independently and still retain the properties of that substance.

Monel metal A copper–nickel alloy containing approximately 67% nickel and 33% copper.

Nominal size A numerical designation of the size of a pipe, fitting, or other component which is a convenient round number approximately equal to a manufactured dimension.

Parent metal A metal or component to be welded.

Physical change A change not involving any chemical change in a body or substance. Freezing, expansion and magnetisation are examples of physical changes.

Pipe hanger A support for a suspended pipe such as a drainage pipeline run beneath a ceiling. The hanger usually consists of a metal tube or bar with provision for adjusting the length, a flange at the upper end to provide fixing and a pipe ring or purpose-made metal strap at the lower end to carry the pipe.

Pitting A defect in welding, consisting of little hollows, brought about by the use of an incorrectly adjusted flame. These hollows are also known as blowholes.

Plasticisers Substances added to plastics to modify their elastic properties without altering their chemical properties.

Propane An inflammable gas.

Raising piece A fitting for extending the height of a gully or of a rainwater shoe. A gully raising piece may have branch inlets.

Refractory A substance which is not damaged by high temperature.

Reinforcement bead The built-up part of a weld above the parent metal.

Rest bend A bend with a foot or web formed integrally on its base. It is used to support a vertical pipe or line of pipes and is also known as a duckfoot bend.

Rodding A method of clearing obstructions or blockages from drains or sewers by the use of flexible rods which can be connected together and pushed into the pipeline. Various attachments are available which fit onto the feed end of the flexible rods to assist with

Rusting The corrosion of iron by the combined action of oxygen, carbonic acid and water.

Saddle junction A short spigot and socket pipe fitting with a flange moulded on near the spigot end. The flange is curved to fit the outside of a larger pipe into the barrel to which the spigot is connected. This type of junction is used to connect a branch pipe to a drain or sewer.

Sealing plate A cover and frame which fits into the socket of a drain pipe, drain fitting or gully top and which finishes level with the ground or floor surface.

Self-cleansing velocity The velocity of a flowing liquid in a pipe or channel necessary to prevent the deposition of solids in suspension.

Separate system A drainage system in which foul water and surface water are conveyed in separate pipes.

Sewer connection The length of pipe between the last inspection chamber on a drain or private sewer and the public sewer.

Soakaway A pit dug into permeable ground and lined or filled with hard-core to form a covered perforated chamber to which surface water is conveyed and from which it may soak away into the ground.

Socket (a) The end of a pipe, or pipe fitting, with an enlarged bore for the reception of the plain or spigot end of another pipe, or pipe fitting, for the formation of a spigot and socket joint;

(b) A pipe fitting in the form of a short cylindrical pipe, threaded on its inner surface, used for joining together two pipes with externally threaded ends.

Spun lead Lead prepared in long strands and twisted together like yarn and used for cold caulking (also known as lead wool).

Step iron A step, usually of maleable iron, which may be either straight, for building into corners, or U-shaped, for building into the walls of manholes or inspection chambers to facilitate access to the chamber.

Stopper An inflatable bag used to seal a drainage pipeline when testing is being carried out.

Subsoil water Water occurring naturally in the subsoil.

Substitute natural gas (SNG) A gas manufactured either as a direct substitute for natural gas or as a means of providing additional gas to meet peak demands.

Surcharge Excess flow in a drain or sewer when the normal flow capacity is exceeded.

Surface water sewer A sewer intended to convey surface water only.

Surround The concrete completely encasing a pipe.

System of drainage An arrangement of drains and sewers.

Combined system A system of drainage or sewers in which foul water and surface water are conveyed in the same pipes.

Separate system A system of drainage or sewers in which foul water and surface water are conveyed in separate pipes.

Partially separate system A modification of the separate system in which some of the surface water is admitted to foul water drains and sewers.

Taper pipe   A pipe fitting with a uniform reduction in diameter over its effective length; used for connecting two pipes of different diameters.

Tariff   A scale of charges.

Temperature   The degree of hotness or coldness of a body.

Tests for drainage systems

Air test   A test for soundness, carried out by applying air pressure internally.

Ball test   A test for obstruction in a drain, in which a steel ball, less in diameter than the bore of the drain, is rolled through the drain.

Colour test   A test for tracing the flow in a drain or sewer by introducing colouring matter (fluorescein).

Mirror test   A method of inspecting the interior of a pipeline by means of light reflected by a mirror.

Smoke test   A test for soundness, in which smoke is introduced under pressure to locate leaks in the pipeline.

Water test   A test for soundness, applied by filling the pipeline with water.

Test piece   A portion of a weld joint removed from a welded structure or component that has been welded together according to a specified welding procedure.

Test specimen   A portion of a test piece that has been removed and prepared for testing.

Thermometer   Any device which measures temperature.

Undercut   The term used to indicate the thinning of the metal adjacent to a weld bead.

Venturi   A tube which tapers to a narrow 'throat' and gradually widens out again to its original diameter.

Viscosity   The internal friction or drag in a fluid which tends to prevent its easy movement.

Water seal   The water in a trap which acts as a barrier to the passage of air through the trap.

Water table   The level of water in the sub-soil.

Answers to self-
~~ment questions~~

2	(b)	**7**	(a)
3	(c)	**8**	(c)
4	(a)	**9**	(c)
5	(c)	**10**	(b)

Chapter 2   Drainage

1	(c)	**6**	(d)
2	(d)	**7**	(a)
3	(d)	**8**	(c)
4	(b)	**9**	(c)
5	(b)	**10**	(b)

Chapter 3   Welding

1	(a)	**6**	(d)
2	(a)	**7**	(c)
3	(b)	**8**	(a)
4	(c)	**9**	(d)
5	(d)	**10**	(a)

Chapter 4   Science

1	(c)	**6**	(d)
2	(a)	**7**	(c)
3	(b)	**8**	(c)
4	(a)	**9**	(c)
5	(b)	**10**	(b)

Index